SHIPS OF CHINA

第二卷
VOLUME II

《中国船谱·第二卷》编委会
Compilation Committee of Ships of China - Volume II

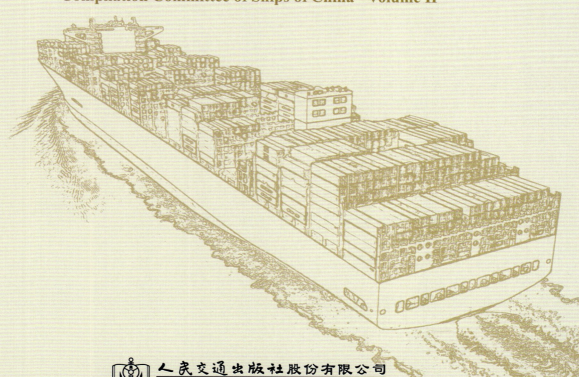

人民交通出版社股份有限公司
China Communications Press Co.,Ltd.

图书在版编目(CIP)数据

中国船谱.第二卷/《中国船谱·第二卷》编委会编著.—北京：人民交通出版社股份有限公司, 2021.6
ISBN 978-7-114-17360-8

Ⅰ.①中… Ⅱ.①中… Ⅲ.①船舶–史料–中国 Ⅳ.①U674-092

中国版本图书馆CIP数据核字(2021)第102259号

Zhongguo Chuanpu Di-er Juan

书　　名：	中国船谱·第二卷
著 作 者：	《中国船谱·第二卷》编委会
责任编辑：	崔　建　齐黄柏盈　杨　明
责任校对：	刘　芹
责任印制：	张　凯
出版发行：	人民交通出版社股份有限公司
地　　址：	(100011)北京市朝阳区安定门外外馆斜街3号
网　　址：	http://www.ccpress.com.cn
销售电话：	(010)59757973
总 经 销：	人民交通出版社股份有限公司发行部
经　　销：	各地新华书店
印　　刷：	北京印匠彩色印刷有限公司
开　　本：	880×1230　1/16
印　　张：	36.25
字　　数：	1127千
版　　次：	2021年7月　第1版
印　　次：	2021年7月　第1次印刷
书　　号：	ISBN 978-7-114-17360-8
定　　价：	580.00元

(有印刷、装订质量问题的图书由本公司负责调换)

《中国船谱·第二卷》编纂机构

编审委员会

主　　任：杨传堂　李小鹏
副 主 任：刘小明　赵冲久　王志清　汪　洋
委　　员：李天碧　徐成光　刘鹏飞　吴春耕　曹德胜　王　雷
　　　　　莫鉴辉　刘新中　张守国　张宝晨　朱伽林

专家委员会

主　　任：黄镇东　李盛霖
副 主 任：何建中
委　　员：朱英富　严新平　刘功臣　赵登平　李青平　信德利　刘正江
　　　　　孔凡邨　苏文金　孙家康　苏新刚　金晓剑　张鸿文　朱　恺

编纂工作委员会

主　　任：刘鹏飞　吴春耕　莫鉴辉
副 主 任：孙文剑　易继勇　李宏印　唐金龙　袁晓初　钟小金　谭　鸿
委　　员：佟　峰　马国栋　郭青松　谢　辉　郑松传　郑云亮　郭　睿　徐秋敏
　　　　　闫晓波　李彦庆　金　鹏　王俊利　白培军　李增忠　黄　函　景奉韬

编写工作组

组　　长：刘凤全　周立伟
副 组 长：曹　迪　杨　丽　孟　方
成　　员：（以姓氏笔画为序）
　　　　　王　亮　刘　巍　池英员　杜勇刚　杨清峡　吴昊洲　吴德藏　何天浪　张　宇　张　岩
　　　　　陈振业　林正锦　赵庆丰　赵新颖　顾晔昕　徐　剑　程远忠　蔡小华　蔡振雄　蔡梅江
美术设计：王永滔　许　刚　王　蕾　陈　昱

百年征程　扬帆远航

习近平总书记高度重视交通运输及水运事业发展，近年来先后作出"经济强国必定是海洋强国、航运强国""经济要发展，国家要强大，交通特别是海运首先要强起来"等一系列重要指示，为新时代水运业高质量发展指明了方向。

党的十八大以来，在以习近平同志为核心的党中央坚强领导下，我国造船、航运取得举世瞩目的成就。作为造船和航运事业主要载体的各类船舶，是这伟大成就的具体体现。目前我国水上运输船舶已达12.68万艘，水路年货运量达76.16亿吨，船舶大型化、专业化和标准化发展水平快速提升，形成了沟通全球、通江达海、干支衔接、支撑有力的现代航运体系，我国已成为名副其实的航运大国。

"十四五"时期是我国开启全面建设社会主义现代化国家新征程的第一个五年，也是加快建设交通强国的第一个五年，造船和航运发展面临高质量发展等重大机遇。要始终坚持把创新摆在核心位置，牢牢把握专业化、智能化、绿色化发展趋势，加快推进水上物流运输便利化、出行服务便捷化、运输装备自主化，全力服务共建"一带一路"和国家重大区域发展战略，维护国际海运重要通道安全与畅通，以一件又一件挺进深蓝的"大国重器"托举起实现中华民族伟大复兴的中国梦。

从"海运百年无我份"的深重磨难，到世界前列的历史跨越，我国航运事业由弱到强的历史巨变，是党领导我国交通事业发展壮大的一个缩影。作为庆祝建党100周年的交通文化成果《中国船谱·第二卷》续接《中国船谱》，收集整理了1986年至2020年期间中国船东拥有的重要船舶图谱，并视情补录了1986年之前有代表性但未编入《中国船谱》的船舶。这既是一部船舶"图志"，也是一部船舶"简明辞典"，对于总结回顾交通运输特别是水运发展历史，讲好新时代交通故事，弘扬新时代交通精神，激励广大交通人加快建设交通强国具有重要意义。

今天，处在"两个一百年"奋斗目标历史交汇点的中国巨轮再次扬帆，我们向着深蓝色的海洋起航，也正向着实现中华民族伟大复兴的中国梦进发。让我们更加紧密地团结在以习近平同志为核心的党中央周围，不忘初心、牢记使命，立足新发展阶段、贯彻新发展理念、服务构建新发展格局，奋力谱写加快建设交通强国新篇章，为全面建设社会主义现代化国家当好先行！

杨传堂

2021年6月

The irresistible tide: Charting China's centenary voyage to the future

China's President Xi Jinping places a high priority on the development of transportation, in particular, water transportation. In recent years, he has successively made a host of important instructions such as "An economic power is surely a maritime and shipping power", and "A country and its economy can only be strong when its transportation network, especially marine transport, is well developed". These instructions have shaped the high-quality development of water transportation in the new era.

Since the 18th National Congress of the Communist Party of China, with the strong leadership of the Central Committee of the Communist Party of China with comrade Xi Jinping at its core, China has made world-renowned achievements in shipbuilding and shipping. As the main carriers of shipbuilding and shipping, ships embody those remarkable achievements. Currently, there are 126,800 ships serving water transportation in China, and the annual volume of freight transport by water stands at 7.616 billion tons. The rapid development of larger, specialised and standardised ships has led to the establishment of a modern shipping system that brings the world together, connects the rivers with the seas and the trunks with tributaries. China has become a great maritime nation in the true sense.

The "14th Five-Year Plan" period will see China embark on a new journey to fully build a modern socialist country, and step up efforts to create a strong transportation network. It is critical that China's shipbuilding and shipping sector takes advantage of key opportunities to develop and grow during this period. Innovation, specialisation, intelligence and green development must always remain at the core of our approach. We must work faster to facilitate waterway logistics and transport, provide convenient transport services, realise transportation equipment independence and fully serve the Belt and Road Initiative as well as the national major strategies for regional development. We must also strive to safeguard the security and smooth passage of the important international shipping routes, and uphold the Chinese Dream of national rejuvenation through the "Pillars of a Great Power" that make it possible for China to move towards the oceans.

The astonishing transformation of China's shipping industry to being one of the biggest and most powerful in the world is refective of the efforts made to strengthen transportation led by the Communist Party of China. To celebrate the 100th anniversary of the founding of the Communist Party of China, the book *Ships of China - Volume II* build on the *Ships of China*, and presents a collection of important ship photographs owned by Chinese shipowners from 1986 to 2020. It further adds representative ships before 1986 that were not contained in the *Ships of China*. The book is not only an "atlas" but also a "concise dictionary" of ships. It is of great significance to review China's transportation history, especially water transport development, promote the stories and the spirit of transportation in the new era, and inspire millions of transportation workers to step up efforts to build national strength in transportation.

Standing at the historical intersection of the Two Centenary Goals, we, the Chinese giant ship, will set sail again, moving towards the blue oceans, realising the Chinese Dream of national rejuvenation. We will rally closer around the Party Central Committee with comrade Xi Jinping at its core, remaining true to our original aspiration and keeping our mission firmly in mind. We will base our work on the new development stage, applying the new development philosophy, striving to make China an even stronger maritime nation and driving the building of a modern socialist China.

YANG Chuantang   LI Xiaopeng

June 2021

前言

大潮激荡，沧海航程。船，是水上的交通运输工具，更是社会经济技术发展的缩影；船，是历史长河中的文明载体，更是诗词歌赋中的华美篇章；船，是海上丝绸之路的桥梁纽带，更是中外文明交流互鉴的友好使者。

运载梦想，传递文明。船，承载的不仅是人和物，更是时代的沧桑巨变。船，运载的不仅是商品和财富，更是民生的牵挂和家国的繁荣。船，驶过风云岁月，穿越沧海征程，铭刻时代记忆，见证大国崛起。

以船为证，以史为鉴。我国是船舶大国、航海大国，船舶历史源远流长，船舶在服务国计民生和国家战略中发挥着重要作用。展示船舶的发展，对于建设海洋强国、交通强国、航运强国具有十分重要的意义。一艘船舶，就是一部技术档案，更是一段重要历史。编写船谱，为船舶立传，记载船舶谱系，既有助于研究船舶、发展船舶事业，也能够反映航海历程，折射交通历史，总结以往经验、启迪光辉未来。

为了记录我国航海事业发展的悠久历史，积累学术文献、凝聚文化力量，1988年中国航海学会组织编辑出版了《中国船谱》，搜集了从远古到1986年前的1000多幅船舶图片，包括筏、独木舟、木船、帆船、蒸汽机船和现代船舶等。该书通过不同时期各种船舶图片的展现，彰显了我国船舶发展的光辉历程和伟大创造。

岁月光辉，航程壮丽。从《中国船谱》出版至今已三十余载。三十多年来，改革开放春风神州浩荡，海洋强国、交通强国建设催人奋进，"一带一路"倡议书写壮美华章，我国航运、造船、海上资源开发行业经历了千载难逢的"黄金时代"，伴随着中华民族迎来从站起来、富起来到强起来的伟大历史飞跃，我国航运、造船事业在国际舞台上奋力实现从追赶、跟跑到引领的历史跨越，加快推进从航运、造船大国向强国迈进的历史性转变。我国的船舶建造数量和质量创历史之最，船队规模世界瞩目，行进在凯歌高奏的如歌岁月，驶向辉煌灿烂的壮丽航程。

续编船谱，续写华章。站在"两个一百年"奋斗目标历史交汇点，中华民族正在实现伟大复兴中国梦的新征程上阔步前行。为了展现改革开放以来特别是党的十八大以来，我国各类船舶的发展演变历程，展现我国在航运、造船等领域取得的辉煌成就，展现交通强国建设风采，加强交通文化建设，交通运输部决定在中国航海学会编辑出版《中国船谱》的基础上，编写《中国船谱·第二卷》，成立编审委员会、专家委员会、编纂工作委员会和编写工作组。2020年3月编纂工作正式启动，由中国船级社具体承办《中国船谱·第二卷》的编纂工作。在交通运输部的直接领导、农业农村部的协助和专家委员会的悉心指导下，在相关企事业单位和社会同行的支持和帮助下，经过一年多的努力，数易其稿，完成了本书编纂工作，众多的参与者为之付出了智慧和汗水。

《中国船谱·第二卷》收录了1986年至2020年期间中国机构和船东（含港澳台）拥有的重点船舶，视情补录1986年之前有代表性的船舶。全书重点选取了不同船型、不同水域、不同时期有时代特征的"故事船舶"、先进船舶和代表性船舶，以展现现代船舶为主，配以精美的船舶照片和简要船舶参数，力求全面展示这一时期船舶的发展演变和技术特征，展示我国船舶事业发展进步的清晰脉络和造船大国的风貌风采。

　　《中国船谱·第二卷》共分为五篇，收录船舶1363艘。第一篇为海洋运输船舶篇，收录船舶423艘。共分两章，其中第一章货船306艘，第二章客船117艘。海上货物运输是实现国际贸易的主要物流方式，占国际贸易总运量中的三分之二以上，我国外贸物资90%以上通过海运完成运输。改革开放以来，我国海运船队发生了巨大变化，船队规模快速增长，目前已跃居世界第二位，平均船龄低于世界水平。我国海上客运以特定航线的短程国际和沿海客货运为主，随着人们生活水平的提高，客船单一交通功能逐步向海上体验、游览和观光休闲的方向转型。目前，我国海上运输船队已基本实现了向现代化、大型化和专业化的结构性转型的目标，成为名副其实的航运大国。本篇收录了海运船队发展过程中具有特殊意义的船舶、各年代船型发展的首制船舶、先进技术的高性能船舶、绿色智能船舶，以及有代表性的海上客运船舶等。

　　第二篇为内河运输船舶篇，收录船舶420艘。共分两章，其中第一章货船238艘，第二章客船182艘。我国是世界上河流最多的国家之一。1985年以来，经过内河航道整治、干线航道升级、三峡工程和高等级航道网的建设等，内河航行条件得到了极大改善。通过加快淘汰落后船型，全面推进内河船舶标准化，内河船队结构不断优化，实现了升级换代。2020年，内河运输船舶11.5万艘、净载重量13673.02万吨，载客量60.07万客位，内河通航里程达12.77万公里。全年内河运输完成货运量39.13亿吨，占我国水路运输货运量的52.4%。本篇重点收录了代表内河船舶特点和长江、珠江、京杭运河、黑龙江等主要水系的典型船舶，有20世纪80—90年代内河优选船型、曾经是内河货运主力的推／拖船队、京杭运河和三峡库区标准船型、万吨级长江货船、适应现代物流的江海直达船舶，以及具有特色的长江旅游船和地方游览船等。

　　第三篇为渔业船舶篇，收录船舶143艘。共分两章，其中第一章捕捞渔船109艘，第二章其他渔船34艘。渔船作为捕捞生产最重要的工具，是丰富人民群众菜篮子，增加优质动物蛋白质供给的重要支撑。中国是渔业大国和渔船大国，渔船数量长期稳居世界首位。1985年初我国第一支远洋渔船船队开赴大西洋西非海域渔场进行作业，揭开了中国远洋渔业发展的序幕。目前我国远洋渔业船队规模居世界前列，渔船装备水平有了长足进步，远洋渔船向着大型化、专业化、捕捞装备和保鲜加工储运技术现代化方向发展。此外，我国养殖渔船从过去为养殖生产服务的小船逐步向具有海上养殖生产工厂特征的大型船舶转变。渔获冷藏运输船和渔业调查船等渔业辅助船的主要功能和技术指标显著提升，为渔业生产提供了有利保障。作为新型渔业形态而逐步兴起的休闲渔船，促进了产业之间的融合。本篇收录了具有代表性的拖网、刺网、围网和钓鱼船等典型捕捞渔船、部分养殖船、渔业辅助和休闲渔船。

　　第四篇为工程和服务船舶篇，收录船舶212艘。分为三章，其中第一章工程船108艘，第二章海洋平台

38艘，第三章作业服务船66艘。近十几年来，我国工程船舶发展取得跨越式进步，一批性能优良、国际先进或领先的工程船舶和海洋平台成为大国重器，为我国经济发展和国防发挥着重要作用。工程船主要收录了用于码头修筑、航道疏浚、桥梁隧道建设、吹填造陆、管缆铺设等代表船舶。海洋平台主要收录海上移动式钻井平台和风电安装平台等，这些装备为海洋油气资源和绿色能源的开发发挥了重要作用。我国作业服务船舶发展快、船型多，并逐渐从单一功能船发展成多功能服务船，技术装备和支持服务能力显著提升，是海上工程作业的重要保障力量。

第五篇为特种和特殊船舶篇，收录船舶165艘。分为三章，其中第一章特种用途船舶52艘，第二章特殊船舶94艘，第三章游艇19艘。收录的特种用途船包括具有代表性的极地科考船、远望系列航天测量船、万米载人深潜器、深海多功能勘探船和教学实习船等，这些船舶是探索海洋、探知海洋，建设海洋强国的探路者和培养航海人才的"海上移动校园"。收录的特种船舶包括具有代表性的海巡船、海监船、渔政船、海警船、缉私船、公安船等执行特殊任务的公务船舶。这些船舶在水上维稳、执法方面发挥着重要作用。近二十几年来，我国游艇事业快速发展，或将成为未来海上消费拉动的重要行业。由于游艇的特殊用途和属性，故列为特殊船舶，收录的游艇包括了我国制造和引进的游艇代表船型。

领航时代，继往开来。2021年是中国共产党的百年华诞，南湖红船载梦想，巍巍巨轮谱华章。这一百年，是中国人民在中国共产党的领导下砥砺奋进的一百年。新中国成立以来我国航运、造船事业蓬勃发展，一代代交通人以梦想引领，以信念为帆，以奋斗为桨，怀赤子之心，在时代的洪流中扬帆远航，凝聚成新时代交通人伟大的精神谱系。浪奔浪涌，拾英撷萃，在这值得铭记的时刻，谨以此书献礼中国共产党成立100周年！并向百年来奋战在航运、造船、渔业、海工、船检战线上的千千万万劳动者致敬！

本卷的编纂，力求选取代表性强、历史感足、图片精美、顺序明晰的重要船舶，但由于编者水平有限，资料搜集困难和局限，难免存在不足之处，恳请读者批评指正。

本书编纂工作委员会
2021年6月

PREFACE

Tides roll, ships sail. Ships are a means of transportation on water, an epitome of social economy and technology; they are a carrier of civilization in the long river of history, the gorgeous melody of the poems; they are the bridge of the Maritime Silk Road, a friendly messenger of exchanges and mutual learning between China and the world.

As a dream carrier and civilization transmitter, ships carry not only people and more than 90 percent of various goods, but also the vicissitudes of the times. They bear not only the commodities and wealth, but also the concern of the people's livelihood and the prosperity of a country. Ships sailed through the stormy years, kept the memories of the times, and now, are witnessing the rise of a great nation.

The history is a mirror and the ship is a witness. China is now one of the biggest maritime nations on earth, a centre of shipbuilding, owning and finance. Ships are essential for our national economy and national strategy. Demonstrating the development of ships is of great significance for building a strong maritime, transportation and shipping country. A ship is a technical archive, and also an important piece of history. Thus, the *Ships of China* is compiled to create a profile of China's ships and to record their genealogy, which will be helpful for study of ships, development of ship course, reflection of navigation progress and transportation history. More importantly, the past experience can be summed up to enlighten our exciting future.

In order to record the long history of China's shipping industry, accumulate the academic literature and condense the cultural power, the China Institute of Navigation organized the compilation and publication of the *Ships of China* in 1988, which collected more than 1,000 ship pictures from the ancient times till 1986, including rafts, dugout canoes, wooden boats, sailboats, steam ships and modern ships. The book curates China's illustrious seafaring and shipping heritage spanning different eras.

It has been more than 30 years since the publication of the *Ships of China*. Over the past 30 years, the policy of reform and opening up has been implemented across China, and the mission of building a strong maritime country has driven huge economic change, evidenced by the vast Belt and Road Initiative which has maritime at its heart. This is a "Golden Era" for China's shipping, shipbuilding and offshore resources exploration. As China ushers in a giant leap from standing up, getting rich to becoming strong, China's maritime industry is striving to support our nation's growth. We are speeding up the transition from being a large shipping and shipbuilding country into a strong one. The quantity and quality of ships built in China have created a record high with the size of the fleet attracting worldwide attention.

Standing at the historical intersection of the Two Centenary Goals, the Chinese nation is striding forward on the new journey of realizing the Chinese Dream of great rejuvenation. In order to showcase the development and evolution of various types of ships in China since the reform and opening up, especially since the 18th National Congress of the

Communist Party of China, the Ministry of Transport decided to compile the *Ships of China - Volume II* on the basis of the *Ships of China* compiled and published by the China Institute of Navigation. For this purpose, an editorial board, an expert panel, a compilation working committee and a compilation working group were established. The compilation work of the *Ships of China - Volume II*, undertaken by China Classification Society (CCS), was officially launched in March 2020. Under the direct leadership of the Ministry of Transport, with the assistance of the Ministry of Agriculture and Rural Affairs and the guidance of the Expert Panel, as well as the support and help of the relevant enterprises, public institutions and social peers, this book is finally completed after more than one year of hard work, with the draft revised repeatedly and improved based on numerous contributions.

The *Ships of China - Volume II* documents the typical ships owned by various Chinese institutions and shipowners (including Hong Kong, Macao and Taiwan) from 1986 to 2020, and, where appropriate, adds ships that were representative before 1986. Through careful selection, the book includes "story-teller ships", advanced ships and representative ships of different types in different periods for the presentation. Mainly to present modern ships, with striking photography the book aims to showcase the evolution of ships during the period, demonstrating the progress of China's shipbuilding industry, and China's transformation into a great shipping and shipbuilding nation.

The *Ships of China - Volume II* is divided into five parts and includes 1,363 ships in total. The first part introduces marine transportation ships, 423 in total, including 306 ocean-going cargo ships in Chapter I and 117 passenger ships in Chapter II. Marine transportation is the lifeblood of international trade, and accounts for more than 90 per cent goods for China's foreign trade. Since the reform and opening up, China's fleet has undergone great changes, with the size expanding quickly to rank No.2 in the world at present and the average age lower than the world average. China's marine passenger transport is mainly short-range international as well as coastal passenger and freight mixed transport along specific routes. With the improvement of people's living standards, seafaring is evolving beyond cargo transportation to leisure sailing for pleasure on cruise ships and ferries. To date, the marine transportation fleet has achieved the goal of structural transformation to modernization, upsizing and specialization, helping China become a major shipping power. This part illustrates ships with special significance in the development of marine transportation fleet, the first ships representing the development of ship types in each era, the high-performance ships and the green and intelligent ships representing advanced technologies, as well as the representative marine passenger ships.

The second part documents the inland waterway transport ships, 420 in total. This part is divided into two chapters, with 238 cargo ships included in Chapter I and 182 passenger ships in Chapter II. China is one of the countries with the most rivers in the world. Since 1985, the navigation conditions of inland waterways have been greatly improved through the upgrading of trunk waterways, the construction of the Three Gorges Project and the high-grade waterway network. By retiring older ships and promoting the standardization of inland ships, the structure of inland fleets has been massively upgraded. By 2020, there were 115,000 inland waterway transport ships, with a net carrying capacity of 136.7302 million tons, 600,700 passengers, and an inland navigation mileage of 127,700 kilometers. The annual inland waterway cargo transport reached 3.913 billion tons, accounting for 52.4 per cent of China's waterway freight transport volume. This part mainly illustrates inland waterway ships and the typical ships on the main waterways, such as the

Yangtze River, the Pearl River, the Beijing-Hangzhou Canal and the Heilongjiang River. This includes the preferred types of inland waterway ships in the 1980s and 1990s, the pusher/tug combination which used to be the main force of inland waterway freight transport, the standard ships for Beijing-Hangzhou Grand Canal and Three Gorges Reservoir, the 10,000 CDW Yangtze River cargo ships, the river-sea ships adapted to modern logistics, and the Yangtze River tourist ships and local sightseeing ships.

The third part documents fishery vessels, 143 in total. This part is divided into two chapters, with 109 fishing vessels covered in Chapter I and 34 other fishing vessels in Chapter II. Fishing vessels provide an important means to improve diet and increase the supply of high-quality animal protein. China is a big country of fishery and fishing vessels, with the total number of fishing vessels ranking first in the world. In early 1985, China's first fleet of ocean-going fishing vessels went to the fishing ground in West Africa waters of Atlantic Ocean for operations, unveiling the prelude to the development of China's ocean-going fisheries. China's ocean-going fishing fleet is the biggest in the world. It also is evolving and modernizing in the use of fishing equipment, processing, storage and transportation technologies. In addition, China's culturing vessels have been gradually innovating from the small boats serving the fish farming in the past to the large-sized vessels featuring marine aquaculture production factory. The main functions and technical indicators of the fishery auxiliary vessels, such as the refrigerated fish carriers and the fishery survey vessels have been significantly improved, providing a favorable guarantee for fishery production. As a new form of fishery, the recreational fishing vessels are rising gradually, which promotes the integration of industries. This part illustrates typical fishing vessels such as trawlers, drift netters, seiners and angling boats, as well as some fish farming vessels, fishery auxiliary vessels and recreational fishing vessels.

The fourth part documents engineering and service ships, 212 in total. It is divided into three chapters, with 108 engineering ships in Chapter I, 38 offshore units in Chapter II and 66 service ships in Chapter III. In recent decades, China has made massive progress in maritime engineering, and has owned a number of engineering ships and offshore units with excellent performance at advanced international level, which have played an important role in China's economic development and national defense capacity. The ships illustrated in the first chapter include the ones used for wharf construction, channel dredging, bridge and tunnel construction, land reclamation, pipe and cable laying. The offshore units in the second chapter cover mobile offshore drilling units and wind power installation units. All these vessels have played an important role in the development of offshore oil and gas as well as green energy. Moreover, the service ships of China have developed rapidly into many types, gradually replacing the single function ships with multi-functional service ships, with the technical equipment and support service capacity significantly improved, becoming an important support force for offshore engineering.

The fifth part documents special purpose and special type ships, 165 in total. It is divided into three chapters with 52 special purpose ships in Chapter I, 94 special type ships in Chapter II and 19 yachts in Chapter III. The special purpose ships documented include the representative polar research ships, space survey ships of the YUAN WANG series, the 10,000 m deep-sea submersibles, the deep-sea multi-functional exploration ships and the training vessels, which are the pathfinders to explore the ocean, as well as the "Mobile Maritime Campus" to support greater education.

The special type ships documented cover the public service ships performing special tasks, including sea patrol ships, marine surveillance ships, fishery administration ships, coast guard ships, revenue cutters and public security ships that play an important role in water stability maintenance and law enforcement. Over the past two decades, China has witnessed a rapid development of yachts, which may become an important industry stimulating maritime consumption in future. Due to their special purpose and properties, yachts are listed as special type ships, and the ones documented here are the representative types built in or introduced to China.

2021 sees the centenary of the Communist Party of China. In the past 100 years, the Chinese people have forged ahead under the leadership of the Communist Party of China. Since the founding of the People's Republic of China, China's shipping and shipbuilding industry has developed vigorously driven by generations of maritime industry professionals. As a result, we would like to dedicate this book to the 100th anniversary of the founding of the Party and pay tribute to the millions of workers who have worked and continue to work tirelessly across our maritime industry over the past century.

In compilation of this volume, every effort was made to select the most representative ships with a strong sense of history, striking pictures and clear sequence. However, there may be some shortcomings due to limitations in data collection, for which we welcome comments for further improvement.

Compilation Working Committee
June 2021

目录
CONTENTS

第一篇　海洋运输船舶 1
PART Ⅰ　MARINE TRANSPORTATION SHIPS

第一章　海洋货船 2
CHAPTER Ⅰ　MARINE CARGO SHIPS

第一节　散货船 4
SECTION 1　BULK CARRIER

第二节　集装箱船 32
SECTION 2　CONTAINER SHIP

第三节　油船和化学品船 48
SECTION 3　OIL TANKER AND CHEMICAL TANKER

第四节　液化气体运输船 76
SECTION 4　LIQUEFIED GAS CARRIER

第五节　普通货船 85
SECTION 5　GENERAL CARGO SHIP

第六节　滚装货船 97
SECTION 6　RO-RO CARGO SHIP

第七节　甲板货船 106
SECTION 7　DECK CARGO SHIP

第八节　非机动货船 115
SECTION 8　NON-SELF-PROPELLED CARGO SHIPS

第二章　海洋客船 120
CHAPTER Ⅱ　MARINE PASSENGER SHIPS

第一节　客船 122
SECTION 1　PASSENGER SHIP

第二节　客滚船 139
SECTION 2　RO-RO PASSENGER SHIP

第三节　高速客船 155
SECTION 3　HIGH-SPEED PASSENGER SHIP

第二篇　内河运输船舶 ... 169
PART II　INLAND WATERWAY TRANSPORT SHIPS

第一章　内河货船 ... 170
CHAPTER I　INLAND WATERWAY CARGO SHIPS

第一节　干散货船 ... 172
SECTION 1　DRY BULK CARRIER

第二节　集装箱船和多用途船 ... 193
SECTION 2　CONTAINER SHIP AND MULTI-PURPOSE SHIP

第三节　液货船 ... 211
SECTION 3　LIQUID CARGO SHIP

第四节　滚装货船 ... 229
SECTION 4　RO-RO CARGO SHIP

第五节　推/拖船队 ... 235
SECTION 5　PUSHER/TUG/BARGE COMBINATION

第六节　江海直达船 ... 247
SECTION 6　RIVER-SEA SHIP

第二章　内河客船 ... 254
CHAPTER II　INLAND WATERWAY PASSENGER SHIPS

第一节　客船 ... 256
SECTION 1　PASSENGER SHIP

第二节　客滚船 ... 300
SECTION 2　RO-RO PASSENGER SHIP

第三节　客渡船 ... 304
SECTION 3　PASSENGER FERRY

第四节　高速客船 ... 316
SECTION 4　HIGH-SPEED PASSENGER SHIP

第三篇　渔业船舶 ... 323
PART III　FISHERY VESSELS

第一章　捕捞渔船 ... 324
CHAPTER I　FISHING VESSELS

第一节　海洋拖网渔船... 325
SECTION 1　MARINE TRAWLER

第二节　海洋围网渔船... 340
SECTION 2　MARINE SEINER

第三节　海洋刺网渔船... 343
SECTION 3　MARINE GILL NETTER

第四节　海洋钓具渔船... 350
SECTION 4　MARINE FISHING TACKLE VESSEL

第五节　其他海洋捕捞渔船... 358
SECTION 5　OTHER MARINE FISHING VESSELS

第六节　内河捕捞渔船... 363
SECTION 6　INLAND WATERWAY FISHING VESSEL

第二章　其他渔船.. 365
CHAPTER II　OTHER FISHING VESSELS

第一节　养殖渔船... 367
SECTION 1　CULTURING VESSEL

第二节　渔业辅助船.. 371
SECTION 2　FISHERY AUXILIARY VESSELS

第三节　休闲渔船... 376
SECTION 3　RECREATIONAL FISHING VESSEL

第四篇　工程和服务船舶... 379
PART IV　ENGINEERING AND SERVICE SHIPS

第一章　工程船... 380
CHAPTER I　ENGINEERING SHIPS

第一节　挖泥船... 380
SECTION 1　DREDGER

第二节　起重船... 397
SECTION 2　CRANE SHIP

第三节　其他工程作业船.. 405
SECTION 3　OTHER ENGINEERING SHIPS

第二章　海洋平台 421
CHAPTER Ⅱ　OFFSHORE UNITS

　第一节　海洋钻井平台 421
　SECTION 1　OFFSHORE DRILLING UNITS

　第二节　风电安装平台 432
　SECTION 2　WIND POWER INSTALLATION UNITS

　第三节　其他海洋平台 438
　SECTION 3　OTHER OFFSHORE UNITS

第三章　服务船 439
CHAPTER Ⅲ　SERVICE SHIPS

　第一节　拖船/供应船 440
　SECTION 1　TUG/SUPPLY VESSELS

　第二节　其他服务船 452
　SECTION 2　OTHER SERVICE SHIPS

第五篇　特种和特殊船舶 461
PART V　SPECIAL PURPOSE AND SPECIAL TYPE SHIPS

第一章　特种用途船 462
CHAPTER Ⅰ　SPECIAL PURPOSE SHIPS

　第一节　科考/调查船 463
　SECTION 1　RESEARCH/SURVEY SHIPS

　第二节　地质勘探/测量船 474
　SECTION 2　GEOLOGICAL EXPLORATION/SURVEY SHIPS

　第三节　教学实习船 482
　SECTION 3　TRAINING VESSEL

第二章　特殊船 484
CHAPTER Ⅱ　SPECIAL SHIPS

　第一节　海巡/救助船 484
　SECTION 1　SEA PATROL/RESCUE SHIPS

第二节　海警/海监/渔政船 497
SECTION 2　COAST GUARD / MARINE SURVEILLANCE / FISHERY ADMINISTRATION SHIPS

第三节　缉私/公安船 509
SECTION 3　REVENUE CUTTER/PUBLIC SECURITY SHIPS

第四节　其他特殊船 513
SECTION 4　OTHER SPECIAL TYPE SHIPS

第三章　游艇 522
CHAPTER Ⅲ　YACHTS

索引 528
INDEXES

后记 556
POSTSCRIPT

第一篇
海洋运输船舶

PART I
MARINE TRANSPORTATION
SHIPS

第一章　海洋货船

海上运输船舶按照运输货物类别可分为普通货船、散货船、集装箱船、液货船、滚装货船和甲板货船等。在世界船队中，散货船、油船、集装箱船三大船型的保有量占87%左右，是海洋运输船舶的主力船队。

在20世纪80年代改革开放初期，我国外贸运输处在初期阶段，1985年以后外贸运输开始加快增长。沿海货物运输保持传统的"南粮北调、北煤南运"的格局，以散杂货船为主。进入20世纪90年代，我国国民经济快速发展，出口货物量增加，同时铁矿石、石油等进口需求量也快速增长，海上运输迎来发展的春天。同时，集装箱船兴起，部分杂货运输逐步被集装箱运输取代。2001年中国加入世界贸易组织，推进了我国步入全球化的进程。此时，全球航运开始进入一个黄金时期，集装箱船迭代式发展，散货船和油船数量及吨位继续扩大。直到2010年，航运进入了调整期，降低航运成本，提高经济性的迫切需求，促进了船舶大型化的进程。集装箱船开启了万箱时代，大型散货船、矿砂船、集装箱、油船数量增加，逐步成为远洋船队的主要船型。

在船舶安全技术方面，20世纪80年代以来，国际海运经历了几十起海难和原油泄漏等重大事故，国际海事组织（IMO）及国际船级社协会（IACS）在技术安全标准方面做出了重大调整，增加了新的安全技术要求。对船舶影响较大的有：加强散货船结构，加强安全措施及提高检验要求；强制大型油船货油舱范围采用双壳双底结构，提前淘汰单壳油轮；采用全球海上遇险与安全系统（GMDSS），通过卫星和数字通信技术实现自动遇险报警；国际船级社协会制定了散货船、油船共同结构规范（CSR），在设计寿命、环境条件、结构强度、腐蚀和检验质量等方面提高了船舶结构安全标准；在环保方面，国际海事组织推出了EEDI能效设计指数减少温室气体排放、提高硫氧化物（SO_x）和氮氧化物（NO_x）限制排放要求。

当今，绿色船舶和智能船舶成为船舶技术发展的主题，我国在船舶节能减排和智能化等方面的研究与实践已经取得显著成效，处于世界先进水平。借助新一代信息技术和新能源技术的发展，未来船舶将向更加安全、经济、高效、环保的方向发展。

CHAPTER I MARINE CARGO SHIPS

Marine transportation ships can be divided into general cargo ships, bulk carriers, container ships, liquid cargo ships, Ro-Ro cargo ships and deck cargo ships depending on what they transport. The three major ship types (bulk carriers, oil tankers and container ships) account for around 87 per cent of the global fleet, and constitute the backbone of marine transport.

China's foreign trade and transportation took shape in the early stage of reform and opening up in the 1980s and its growth pick up pace after 1985. At that time, coastal transport maintained the traditional pattern of transferring grains from south to north and coal from north to south and the main ship types were general cargo ships and bulk carriers. In the 1990s, the rapid development of China's national economy brought about increased export volume, as well as sharply rising demand for iron ore and oil imports, and drove the boom in marine transportation. Concurrently, container ships emerged, which gradually replaced some of the general cargo ships. China's accession to the World Trade Organisation (WTO) in 2001, which kickstarted its globalization, coincided with a flourishing period for the global shipping industry, during which several generations of container ships were developed, and the number and tonnage of bulk carriers and oil tankers continued to grow. The trend continued until 2010, when the shipping industry began to adjust to an urgent need to reduce shipping costs, which led to the introduction of larger-size ships. The 10,000 TEU container ships began to appear, and the number of large bulk carriers, ore carriers, container ships and oil tankers increased and gradually became the mainstay of ocean-going fleet.

In terms of ship safety technology, international shipping has experienced dozens of major accidents since the 1980s, such as marine casualties and crude oil spills. The International Maritime Organization (IMO) and International Association of Classification Societies (IACS) made major adjustments in technical safety standards and added new safety technical requirements. The requirements that had a major impact on ships included: strengthening the structure of bulk carriers and enhancing safety measures as well as survey requirements, mandatory double-hull and double-bottom requirement for large oil tankers in the cargo oil tank and early phase-out of single-hulled tankers, adopting the Global Maritime Distress and Safety System (GMDSS) to realize automatic distress alarm through satellite and digital communication technology, the Common Structural Rules (CSR) for bulk carriers and oil tankers developed by IACS to improve the structural safety standards for ships in terms of design life, environmental conditions, structural strength, corrosion and survey quality, and in terms of environmental protection, the Energy Efficiency Design Index (EEDI) introduced by the IMO to reduce greenhouse gas emissions and set lower limits to the sulfur oxide (SO_x) and nitrogen oxide (NO_x) emissions.

Today, green ships and intelligent ships have become key themes in ship technology development. China is at the forefront of this vanguard driving research and practice in energy saving, emission reduction and intelligence of ships. Our work is achieving remarkable results and delivering some of the most advanced innovations in the world. Relying on the development of new generation information technology and new energy technology, ships are becoming safer, more economical, more efficient and environmentally friendly now and in the future.

第一节 散货船

散货船是指主要用于散装运输如谷物、煤、矿砂、盐、水泥等散装干货的船舶，包括矿砂船、兼装船等船型。散货船一般具有底边舱、顶边舱和双层底，便于装卸和压载航行。专用装运大比重矿砂的散货船亦称为矿砂船，矿砂船一般为单甲板、大舱口、双倾斜纵舱壁、高双层底结构。散货船根据其航线和载重吨大小通常可分为：灵便型、巴拿马型、好望角型、超大型矿砂船。灵便型散货船是指在巴拿马型吨位以下的散货船，根据其吨位又分为灵便型和大灵便型，载重吨一般在2万～6万吨；巴拿马型散货船是指老巴拿马运河通过能力尺度限制设计的船舶，载重吨一般在6万～8万吨。巴拿马新运河开通后大大提升了运河通过能力，通行船舶载重吨可达12万～17万吨。好望角型散货船是指在远洋航行中可以绕行好望角或者南美洲海角，载重吨在11万～30万吨左右，20万吨以上超大型散货船主要装运矿砂。我国近二十多年来陆续建造了2万吨至23万吨系列散货船和25万吨、40万吨矿砂船，目前中国船东拥有的散货船队规模已居世界第一。我国散货船队发展的规模和船舶大型化发展的过程，反映出我国经济水平和经济规模的提升，而散货船舶的大型化，为保障我国大宗货物的进出口和服务经济社会发展作出了重要贡献。

SECTION 1 BULK CARRIER

Bulk carrier refers to as ship mainly used for bulk transportation of dry goods such as grain, coal, ore, salt and cement, including ore carriers and multipurpose ships. Bulk carriers generally feature a hopper tank, a top side tank and double bottom, which is convenient for loading, unloading and ballast navigation. Bulk carriers specializing in carrying high specific gravity ore is also called ore carriers, which generally have a single deck, large hatch, double inclined longitudinal bulkheads and high double bottom structure. Bulk carriers can usually be divided into Handysize, Panamax, Capesize, and VLOC (Very Large Ore Carrier) according to their routes and deadweight tonnage. Handysize bulk carriers refer to bulk carriers with tonnage below Panamax, and are further divided into Handysize and Handymax types with deadweight tonnage generally between 20,000-60,000 DWT; Panamax bulk carriers refer to ships designed with the scale limitation of passing capacity of the old Panama Canal, with deadweight tonnage generally between 60,000-80,000 DWT. After the opening of the new Panama Canal, the passing capacity of the canal has been greatly improved, and the deadweight tonnage of the passing ships can reach 120,000-170,000 DWT. Capesize bulk carrier refers to the ocean voyage that can go around the Cape of Good Hope or Cape Horn, which has a deadweight tonnage of about 110,000-300,000 DWT, and very large bulk carriers of more than 200,000 DWT are mainly for ore transportation. China has built a series of 20,000-230,000 DWT bulk carriers and 250,000-400,000 DWT ore carriers in the past two decades, making the size of the bulk carrier fleet owned by Chinese shipowners rank first in the world. China's bulk carrier fleet development and the emergence of larger ships reflects Chinese economic growth, and larger bulk carriers made an important contribution to guarantee the import and export of bulk cargoes serving the economic and social development of China.

华铜海　64000 吨远洋散货船　1980 年
"海上中华名牌"管理模范船
主尺度 $L×B×D$（m×m×m）：224×31.6×18.4

HUA TONG HAI　64,000DWT Bulk Carrier, Ocean-going　1980
"Marine China Brand" ship for exemplary management

长城　27000 吨远洋散货船　1981 年
20 世纪 80 年代初我国设计建造的大型远洋散货船
主尺度 $L×B×D$（m×m×m）：197.2×23×14.3

REGENT TAMPOPO　27,000DWT Bulk Carrier, Ocean-going　1981
Large ocean-going bulk carrier designed and built by China in the early 1980s

振奋 2　21000 吨近海散货船　1984 年
20 世纪 80 年代我国沿海煤炭运输主力船
主尺度 $L \times B \times D$ (m×m×m)：164.9×22.9×13.5

ZHEN FEN 2　21,000DWT Bulk Carrier, Greater Coastal　1984
China's workhorse for coastal coal transportation in the 1980s

北极星　28000 吨远洋煤炭自卸船　1986 年购进
我国第一艘购进的煤炭自卸船
BEI JI XING　28,000DWT Self-unloading Coal Carrier, Ocean-going
Purchased in 1986
First self-unloading coal carrier purchased by China
主尺度 $L \times B \times D$ (m×m×m)：175×27.8×16

畅明 6 号　53000 吨近海散货船　1986 年
CHANG MING 6 HAO　53,000DWT Bulk Carrier, Greater Coastal　1986
主尺度 $L \times B \times D$ (m×m×m)：200.1×32.2×17.1

祥瑞　65000 吨远洋散货船　1987 年
CSK FORTUNE　65,000DWT Bulk Carrier, Ocean-going　1987
主尺度　$L \times B \times D$（m×m×m）：226×32×18

新盛海　180000 吨远洋散货船　1989 年
XIN SHENG HAI　180,000DWT Bulk Carrier, Ocean-going　1989
主尺度　$L \times B \times D$（m×m×m）：290×46×24.8

SHIPS OF CHINA

振奋13 20000吨近海散货船 1991年
ZHEN FEN 13 20,000DWT Bulk Carrier, Greater Coastal 1991
主尺度 $L \times B \times D$ (m×m×m)：164×22×13.4

宁安1 38000吨近海散货船 1991年
当年沿海煤炭运输的重点船舶，为浅吃水肥大船型
主尺度 $L \times B \times D$ (m×m×m)：185×32×15.4

NING AN 1 38,000DWT Bulk Carrier, Greater Coastal 1991
The then workhorse for coastal coal transportation, with smaller draft and greater block coefficent

冬青海　66000 吨远洋散货船 1991 年
DONG QING HAI　66,000DWT Bulk Carrier, Ocean-going 1991
主尺度　$L×B×D$ （m×m×m）：225×32.2×17.8

天盛 15　98000 吨远洋散货船 1991 年
TIAN SHENG 15　98,000DWT Bulk Carrier, Ocean-going 1991
主尺度　$L×B×D$ （m×m×m）：244.8×41.2×21.6

明锋　42000 吨远洋散货船 1992 年
系列船中的首制船
主尺度　$L×B×D$ （m×m×m）：180×30.5×15.8

PACIFIC PIONEER　42,000DWT Bulk Carrier, Ocean-going 1992
First ship in series

SHIPS OF CHINA

畅明胜　69000 吨远洋散货船　1993 年
CHANG MING SHENG　69,000DWT Bulk Carrier, Ocean-going　1993
主尺度　$L×B×D$（m×m×m）：225×32.2×18.3

明兴　73000 吨远洋散货船　1993 年
系列船中的首制船
主尺度　$L×B×D$（m×m×m）：225×32.3×19

PACIFIC PROSPECT　73,000DWT Bulk Carrier, Ocean-going　1993
First ship in series

满江海 17220 吨近海散货船 1995 年
20 世纪 90 年代沿海散货运输代表船
主尺度 $L×B×D$（m×m×m）：153×23×11

MAN JIANG HAI 17,220DWT Bulk Carrier, Greater Coastal 1995
A representative ship for coastal bulk cargo transportation in the 1990s

海象 30000 吨近海散货船 1995 年
HAI XIANG 30,000DWT Bulk Carrier, Greater Coastal 1995
主尺度 $L×B×D$（m×m×m）：178×30×13.8

天龙星　37500 吨远洋散货船　1995 年
TIAN LONG XING　37,500DWT Bulk Carrier, Ocean-going　1995
主尺度　$L×B×D$ (m×m×m)：186.6×29×15.2

华润电力 1　46000 吨近海散货船　1995 年
HUA RUN DIAN LI 1　46,000DWT Bulk Carrier, Greater Coastal　1995
主尺度　$L×B×D$ (m×m×m)：185.7×30.4×16.5

桃花山　39800 吨远洋散货船　1996 年
PEACH MOUNTAIN　39,800DWT Bulk Carrier, Ocean-going　1996
主尺度　$L×B×D$ (m×m×m)：195×32×15.2

大建　27000 吨远洋散货船　1998 年
GREAT CREATION　27,000DWT Bulk Carrier, Ocean-going　1998
主尺度 $L×B×D$ (m×m×m)：175×26×13.9

天丽海　149000 吨远洋散货船　1998 年
TIAN LI HAI　149,000DWT Bulk Carrier, Ocean-going　1998
主尺度 $L×B×D$ (m×m×m)：270×44×24

恒通海　74000 吨近海散货船　1999 年
HENG TONG HAI　74,000DWT Bulk Carrier, Greater Coastal　1999
主尺度 $L×B×D$ (m×m×m)：225×32.2×19.2

SHIPS OF CHINA

东方海泰　78000 吨远洋散货船　2001 年
DONG FANG HAI TAI　78,000DWT Bulk Carrier, Ocean-going　2001
主尺度　$L \times B \times D$ (m×m×m)：229×36.5×18.5

新旺海　175000 吨远洋散货船　2003 年
XIN WANG HAI　175,000DWT Bulk Carrier, Ocean-going　2003
主尺度　$L \times B \times D$ (m×m×m)：289×45×24.5

中华和平　175000 吨远洋散货船　2005 年
CHINA PEACE　175,000DWT Bulk Carrier, Ocean-going　2005
主尺度　$L \times B \times D$ (m×m×m)：289×45×24.5

长发海　48000 吨近海散货船　2006 年购进
CHANG FA HAI　48,000DWT Bulk Carrier, Greater Coastal
Purchased in 2006
主尺度　$L \times B \times D$ (m×m×m)：192×32×16.7

NEW EMPEROR 40000 吨远洋散货船 2006 年
NEW EMPEROR 40,000DWT Bulk Carrier, Ocean-going 2006
主尺度 L×B×D（m×m×m）：218×32.3×19.5

金泰 7　11000 吨近海散货船 2008 年改建
JIN TAI 7　11,000DWT Bulk Carrier, Greater Coastal Converted in 2008
主尺度 L×B×D（m×m×m）：135.9×19×10

浙海 521　54000 吨远洋散货船 2008 年
第一艘满足 IACS 共同结构规范（CSR）的散货船
主尺度 L×B×D（m×m×m）：189.9×32.3×17.6

ZHE HAI 521　54,000DWT Bulk Carrier, Ocean-going 2008
First bulk carrier in compliance with the IACS Common Structure Rules (CSR)

德新海　76000 吨远洋散货船　2008 年
DE XIN HAI　76,000DWT Bulk Carrier, Ocean-going　2008
主尺度 $L×B×D$（m×m×m）：225×32.3×19.6

盛发海　56000 吨近海散货船　2009 年
SHENG FA HAI　56,000DWT Bulk Carrier, Greater Coastal　2009
主尺度 $L×B×D$（m×m×m）：200×32.3×18

新世纪 128　58000 吨近海散货船　2009 年
XIN SHI JI 128　58,000DWT Bulk Carrier, Greater Coastal　2009
主尺度 $L×B×D$（m×m×m）：200×32.3×18

大欣　93000 吨远洋散货船　2009 年
GREAT CHEER　93,000DWT Bulk Carrier, Ocean-going 2009
主尺度　$L×B×D$（m×m×m）：229.2×38×20.7

畅明洋　100000 吨近海散货船　2009 年改建
CHANG MING YANG　100,000DWT Bulk Carrier, Greater Coastal Converted in 2009
主尺度　$L×B×D$（m×m×m）：246.5×41.5×22.9

河北领先　182000 吨远洋散货船　2009 年
我国自主设计建造好望角型散货船的代表船型
主尺度　$L×B×D$（m×m×m）：295×46×24.8

HEBEI NO.1　182,000DWT Bulk Carrier, Ocean-going 2009
Representative Capesize bulk carrier designed and built by China

SHIPS OF CHINA

长航和海　46000 吨近海散货船　2010 年
新型浅吃水肥大型
CHANG HANG HE HAI　46,000DWT Bulk Carrier, Greater Coastal　2010
New ship type with smaller draft and greater block coefficent
主尺度 $L \times B \times D$ (m×m×m)：190×32.3×15.8

工银 1　53000 吨远洋散货船　2010 年
系列船中的首制船
主尺度 $L \times B \times D$ (m×m×m)：190×32.3×17.5

GONG YIN 1　53,000DWT Bulk Carrier, Ocean-going　2010
First ship in series

银平 53000 吨远洋散货船 2010 年
我国第一艘满足涂层新标准（PSPC）的散货船
主尺度 $L×B×D$ (m×m×m)：190×32.3×17.5

YIN PING 53,000DWT Bulk Carrier, Ocean-going 2010
China's first bulk carrier meeting the new coating standard (PSPC)

粤电 55 57000 吨远洋散货船 2010 年
当年我国沿海煤炭运输的主力船型
主尺度 $L×B×D$ (m×m×m)：185×32.3×18

YUE DIAN 55 57,000DWT Bulk Carrier, Ocean-going 2010
The then main ship type for China's coastal coal transportation

山东鹏程　82000 吨远洋散货船　2010 年
SHANDONG PENG CHENG　82,000DWT Bulk Carrier, Ocean-going　2010
主尺度 $L \times B \times D$（m×m×m）：229×32.3×20.1

河北张家口　95000 吨远洋散货船　2011 年
HEBEI ZHANGJIAKOU　95,000DWT Bulk Carrier, Ocean-going　2011
主尺度 $L \times B \times D$（m×m×m）：235×38×20.7

玉霄峰　75400 吨远洋散货船　2012 年
YU XIAO FENG　75,400DWT Bulk Carrier, Ocean-going　2012
主尺度 $L×B×D$（m×m×m）：225×32.3×19.6

清平山　63000 吨远洋散货船　2015 年
QING PING SHAN　63,000DWT Bulk Carrier, Ocean-going　2015
主尺度 $L×B×D$（m×m×m）：199.9×32.3×18.5

明勇　64000 吨远洋散货船　2015 年
系列船中的首制船
主尺度 $L×B×D$（m×m×m）：199.9×32.3×18.5

PACIFIC VALOR　64,000DWT Bulk Carrier, Ocean-going　2015
First ship in series

大智 39000 吨远洋散货船 2017 年
我国第一艘具有智能标志的船舶
主尺度 $L×B×D$ (m×m×m)：180×32×15

GREAT INTELLIGENCE 39,000DWT Bulk Carrier, Ocean-going 2017
China's first ship with intelligent ship notation

Bright Venture 82000 吨远洋散货船 2020 年
Bright Venture 82,000DWT Bulk Carrier, Ocean-going 2020
主尺度 $L×B×D$ (m×m×m)：229×32.3×14.5

山东德祥　180000 吨远洋散货船 2020 年
具有绿色船舶标志
主尺度 $L×B×D$ (m×m×m)：292×45×24.9

SHANDONG DE XIANG　180,000DWT Bulk Carrier, Ocean-going 2020
With green ship notation

惠智海　210000 吨远洋散货船 2020 年
系列船中的首制船，具有智能船舶和绿色船舶标志
主尺度 $L×B×D$ (m×m×m)：299.95×50×25

HUI ZHI HAI　210,000DWT Bulk Carrier, Ocean-going 2020
First ship in series, with intelligent ship and green ship notations

SHIPS OF CHINA

日立勇士　270000 吨远洋矿砂船 1982 年
HITACHI VENTURE　270,000DWT Ore Carrier, Ocean-going 1982
主尺度 $L \times B \times D$ (m×m×m)：324.1×55×26.4

河北创新　237000 吨远洋矿砂船 2005 年改建
我国第一艘由单壳油轮改建的大型矿砂船
主尺度 $L \times B \times D$ (m×m×m)：319×54.5×25.6

HEBEI INNOVATOR　237,000DWT Ore Carrier, Ocean-going Converted in 2005
China's first large ore carrier converted from a single-hull tanker

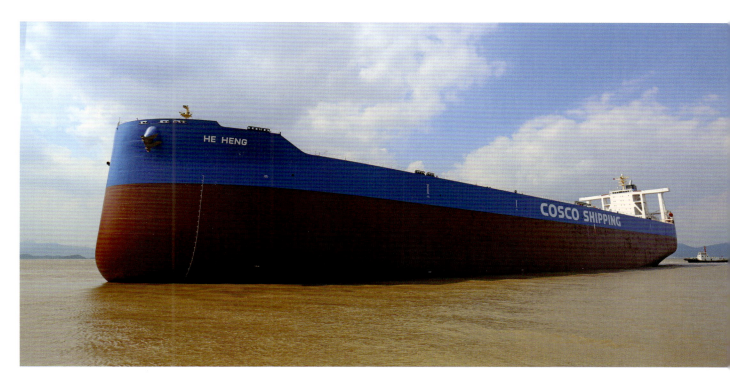

合恒　298000 吨远洋矿砂船（VLOC）2008 年
我国建造的第一艘 30 万吨级矿砂船
主尺度　$L×B×D$ （m×m×m）：327×55×29

HE HENG　298,000DWT Ore carrier (VLOC), Ocean-going　2008
First 300,000DWT ore carrier built by China

中海兴旺　230000 吨远洋矿砂船　2010 年
我国第一艘自主设计建造的 23 万吨级矿砂船
主尺度　$L×B×D$ （m×m×m）：325×52.5×24.3

CSB FORTUNE　230,000DWT Ore Carrier, Ocean-going　2010
First 230,000DWT ore carrier designed and built by China

中海荣华　315000 吨远洋矿砂船　2011 年
CSB GLORY　315,000DWT Ore Carrier, Ocean-going　2011
主尺度 $L×B×D$ (m×m×m)：330×57×28.6

明志　400000 吨远洋矿砂船　2012 年
我国第一艘 40 万吨级超大型矿砂船
主尺度 $L×B×D$ (m×m×m)：360×65×30.4

PACIFIC WARRIOR　400,000DWT Ore Carrier, Ocean-going　2012
First 400,000DWT VLOC in China

远真海　400000 吨远洋矿砂船　2013 年
YUAN ZHEN HAI　400,000DWT Ore Carrier, Ocean-going　2013
主尺度 $L×B×D$ (m×m×m)：360×65×30.4

山东政通　262000 吨远洋矿砂船　2015 年　　　　　　　**SHANDONG ZHENG TONG**　262,000DWT Ore Carrier, Ocean-going　2015
具有绿色船舶标志　　　　　　　　　　　　　　　　　　With green ship notation
主尺度 $L×B×D$ (m×m×m)：317.7×57×25

明远　398000 吨远洋矿砂船　2018 年
我国自主设计建造的超大型矿砂船，具有智能船舶和绿色船舶标志
主尺度　$L×B×D$（m×m×m）：362×65×30.4

PACIFIC VISION　398,000DWT Ore Carrier, Ocean-going　2018
VLOC designed and built by China, with intelligent ship and green ship notations

ORE TIANJIN　400000 吨远洋矿砂船　2018 年
系列船中的首制船，并具有绿色标志
主尺度　$L×B×D$（m×m×m）：361.9×65×30.4

ORE TIANJIN　400,000DWT Ore Carrier, Ocean-going　2018
First ship in series, with green ship notation

远津海　400000 吨远洋矿砂船　2019 年
YUAN JIN HAI　400,000DWT Ore Carrier, Ocean-going　2019
主尺度　$L×B×D$ (m×m×m)：361.9×65×30.4

浙普 01868　520 吨沿海水泥运输船　1987 年
ZHE PU 01868　520DWT Cement Carrier, Coastal　1987
主尺度　$L×B×D$ (m×m×m)：53.5×8×4.5

浙普 01858　560 吨沿海水泥运输船　1993 年
ZHE PU 01858　560DWT Cement Carrier, Coastal　1993
主尺度　$L×B×D$ (m×m×m)：50.6×7.8×3.9

安强76 500吨沿海水泥运输船 1999年
AN QIANG 76 500DWT Cement Carrier, Coastal 1999
主尺度 $L×B×D$ (m×m×m)：47×8.2×4.1

巨鲸 850吨沿海水泥运输船 2001年
JU JING 850DWT Cement Carrier, Coastal 2001
主尺度 $L×B×D$ (m×m×m)：53×9.4×4.8

水平7 800吨沿海水泥运输船 2003年
SHUI PING 7 800DWT Cement Carrier, Coastal 2003
主尺度 $L×B×D$ (m×m×m)：50.9×8.5×4.3

鸿富 368　4930 吨沿海沙石运输船 2008 年
HONG FU 368　4,930DWT Sand Carrier, Coastal　2008
主尺度 $L×B×D$ (m×m×m)：91.3×18.6×6

万祥 799　16000 吨沿海沙石运输船 2012 年
WAN XIANG 799　16,000DWT Sand Carrier, Coastal　2012
主尺度 $L×B×D$ (m×m×m)：139.8×22×10.5

宏翔 518　8900 吨沿海沙石运输船 2016 年
HONG XIANG 518　8,900DWT Sand Carrier, Coastal　2016
主尺度 $L×B×D$ (m×m×m)：109.7×22.8×7.8

富顺 399　26000 吨沿海沙石运输船 2017 年
FU SHUN 399　26,000DWT Sand Carrier, Coastal　2017
主尺度 $L×B×D$ (m×m×m)：160.8×28.2×12.6

第二节 集装箱船

集装箱船是指专门运载集装箱的船舶，通常以装载20英尺标准箱（TEU）的数量来表示大小。集装箱运输可以实现火车、汽车和水路货物运输联运，为物流带来了革命性的变化，实现货物运输的门到门。由于集装箱船运输具有效率高、成本低、货物损坏小等优点，得到迅速发展。

集装箱船船型经历几代变化。第一代载箱数量约1000TEU，第二代约2000TEU，依此类推，到第七代时载箱数达到了约7000TEU以上。随着万箱船的出现，止步于按"代"划分，目前超大型集装箱船直接用载箱数量来标定船型。集装箱船设计上采用了大甲板面积和大开口布置以提高装箱量，装货区域设有集装箱积载与系固装置以保障集装箱的安全，采用双舷侧抗扭箱、双层底结构、使用大比例的高强度钢以满足大型船舶结构安全的要求。为提高快速性，采用消瘦首部和外飘甲板的船型，设计航速一般在20节左右。

在20世纪80年代，我国主要通过改装和新建两个途径实现集装箱船运力的增长。进入21世纪，我国加速集装箱新船型的开发工作，近年来先后设计建造了万箱系列超大型集装箱船，技术水平和船队规模已经进入国际先进行列。我国已成为世界贸易集装箱航线的主要始发港和目的港。

SECTION 2　　CONTAINER SHIP

A container ship specializes in carrying containers, and its size is usually expressed by the number of loaded Twenty-foot Equivalent Units (TEU). Container transport enables the intermodal transportation of goods by train, car and water, and has brought revolutionary changes to logistics realizing the door-to-door transportation of goods. Due to its high efficiency, low cost, low risk of goods damage and other advantages, container ship transportation has experienced rapid development.

Container ship types have undergone several generations of changes. The first generation container ship had a carrying capacity of about 1,000 TEU, the second generation had about 2,000 TEU, and so on, to the seventh generation which can carry around 7,000 TEU. The emergence of 10,000 TEU ships saw the division by "generation" stopped and the current ultra-large container ships are sized directly by the number of TEUs they carry. The design of a container ship adopts a large deck area and large opening arrangement to improve loading capacity, and the loading area is equipped with container stowage and fastening devices to ensure container security, adopting double side torsion box and double bottom structure, using large proportion of high strength steel to meet the requirements of structural safety of large ships. In order to improve the speed, a slim bow and outer floating deck is adopted, and the design speed is generally around 20 knots.

In the 1980s, China primarily realised the growth of its container ship capacity through conversion and new construction. Since 2000, China has accelerated the development of new container ships, and in recent years, China has designed and built a series of 10,000 TEU ultra-large container ships. China's technical level and fleet size has reached the international advanced level. Furthermore, China has become the main port of origin and destination of global container ship routes.

潍河　1150TEU 远洋集装箱船　1983 年
WEI HE　1,150TEU Container Ship, Ocean-going　1983
主尺度　$L \times B \times D$ (m×m×m)：169×25.4×51.5

向浦　1020TEU 远洋集装箱船　1984 年
XIANG PU　1,020TEU Container Ship, Ocean-going　1984
主尺度　$L \times B \times D$ (m×m×m)：164.9×22.9×13.5

向丹　416TEU 近海集装箱船　1986 年
XIANG DAN　416TEU Container Ship, Greater Coastal　1986
主尺度　$L \times B \times D$ (m×m×m)：122.3×17.6×9

民河　2070TEU 远洋集装箱船　1989 年
MIN HE　2,070TEU Container Ship, Ocean-going　1989
主尺度　$L \times B \times D$ (m×m×m)：236×32.2×18.8

向菊　180TEU 远洋集装箱船　1991 年
批量杂货船改装集装箱船的代表船型
主尺度　$L×B×D$（m×m×m）：101.5×16.4×8.6

XIANG JU　180TEU Container Ship, Ocean-going　1991
Representative type of container ships converted from general cargo ship

雅河　1900TEU 远洋集装箱船　1993 年
YA HE　1,900TEU Container Ship, Ocean-going　1993
主尺度　$L×B×D$（m×m×m）：187.6×28.4×15.6

珍河　3800TEU 远洋集装箱船　1993 年
我国第一艘 3800TEU 集装箱船
ZHEN HE　3,800TEU Container Ship, Ocean-going　1993
First 3,800TEU container ship in China
主尺度　$L×B×D$（m×m×m）：275×32.2×21.4

恒辉 2 5710TEU 远洋集装箱船 1993 年
HENG HUI 2 5,710TEU Container Ship, Ocean-going 1993
主尺度 $L×B×D$ (m×m×m)：242×32.2×20.2

华凯 330TEU 远洋集装箱船 1994 年
HUA KAI 330TEU Container Ship, Ocean-going 1994
主尺度 $L×B×D$ (m×m×m)：113×19×8.5

林园 614TEU 远洋集装箱船 1996 年
我国南北集装箱班轮航线开通首航船
主尺度 $L×B×D$ (m×m×m)：123.4×20.8×10.5

LIN YUAN 614TEU Container Ship, Ocean-going 1996
First ship after the opening of China's North-South container liner route

SHIPS OF CHINA

景颇河　3400TEU 远洋集装箱船　1997 年
JING PO HE　3,400TEU Container Ship, Ocean-going　1997
主尺度 *L×B×D*（m×m×m）：242.9×32.2×19

鲁河　5250TEU 远洋集装箱船　1997 年
我国第一艘第五代集装箱船
主尺度 *L×B×D*（m×m×m）：280×39.8×23.6

LU HE　5,250TEU Container Ship, Ocean-going　1997
China's first fifth-generation container ship

中远安特卫普 5450TEU 远洋集装箱船 2001 年
我国建造的第一艘第五代集装箱船
COSCO ANTWERP 5,450TEU Container Ship, Ocean-going 2001
First fifth-generation container ship built by China
主尺度 $L×B×D$ (m×m×m)：280×39.8×23.6

信风扬子江 3740TEU 近海集装箱船 2002 年
XIN FENG YANG ZI JIANG 3,740TEU Container Ship, Greater Coastal 2002
主尺度 $L×B×D$ (m×m×m)：257.4×32.2×15.6

新重庆　4050TEU 远洋集装箱船　2003 年
XIN CHONG QING　4,050TEU Container Ship, Ocean-going　2003
主尺度 $L×B×D$ (m×m×m)：263.2×32.2×19.3

新浦东　5688TEU 远洋集装箱船　2003 年　　　　**XIN PU DONG**　5,688TEU Container Ship, Ocean-going　2003
我国建造的第六代集装箱船　　　　　　　　　　　Sixth-generation container ship built by China
主尺度 $L×B×D$ (m×m×m)：279.9×40.3×24.1

中海亚洲　8500TEU 远洋集装箱船　2004 年
系列船中的首制船
主尺度 $L×B×D$（m×m×m）：334×42.8×25

CSCL ASIA　8,500TEU Container Ship, Ocean-going　2004
First ship in series

源明　5551TEU 远洋集装箱船　2004 年
YM FOUNTAIN　5,551TEU Container Ship, Ocean-going　2004
主尺度 $L×B×D$（m×m×m）：274.7×40×14.02（吃水）

新洛杉矶　9570TEU 远洋集装箱船　2006 年
XIN LOS ANGELES　9,570TEU Container Ship, Ocean-going　2006
主尺度 $L×B×D$（m×m×m）：336.7×45.6×27.2

长航洋山 1　400TEU 沿海集装箱船　2007 年
上海港中的"穿梭巴士"
CHANG HANG YANG SHAN 1　400TEU Container Ship, Coastal　2007
Shuttle Bus in Shanghai Port
主尺度 $L×B×D$（m×m×m）：122.8×18.8×8.6

新亚洲　8530TEU 远洋集装箱船　2007 年
我国第一艘自主设计建造的 8500 箱级集装箱船
主尺度 $L×B×D$（m×m×m）：335×42.8×24.8

XIN YA ZHOU　8,530TEU Container Ship, Ocean-going　2007
First 8,500TEU container ship designed and built by China

中远大洋洲　10000TEU 远洋集装箱船　2008 年
我国建造的第一艘万箱级集装箱船
主尺度 $L×B×D$（m×m×m）：348.5×45.6×27.2

COSCO OCEANIA　10,000TEU Container Ship, Ocean-going　2008
First 10,000TEU container ship built by China

天隆河　5090TEU 远洋集装箱船　2010 年
TIAN LONG HE　5,090TEU Container Ship, Ocean-going　2010
主尺度 $L×B×D$（m×m×m）：294×32.2×21.8

中海之星　14000TEU 远洋集装箱船　2011 年　　**CSCL STAR**　14,000TEU Container Ship, Ocean-going　2011
系列船中的首制船　　First ship in series
主尺度 $L×B×D$（m×m×m）：351.5×51.2×23

中外运青岛 1100TEU 远洋集装箱船 2013 年
系列船中的首制船
主尺度 L×B×D (m×m×m)：141×23.3×11.5

SINOTRANS QINGDAO 1,100TEU Container Ship, Ocean-going 2013
First ship in series

中海之春 10000TEU 远洋集装箱船 2014 年
我国第一艘自主设计建造的万箱级超大型集装箱船
主尺度 L×B×D (m×m×m)：335.3×48.6×27.2

CSCL SPRING 10,000TEU Container Ship, Ocean-going 2014
First very large 10,000TEU container ship designed and built by China

中海环球 19000TEU 超大型远洋集装箱船 2014 年系列船中的首制船
CSCL GLOBE 19,000TEU Ultra Large Container Ship, Ocean-going 2014
First ship in series
主尺度 $L×B×D$ (m×m×m)：399.7×58.6×30.5

海丰广西 1808TEU 远洋集装箱船 2015 年
SITC GUANGXI 1,808TEU Container Ship, Ocean-going 2015
主尺度 $L×B×D$ (m×m×m)：172×27.6×14

中谷上海　2540TEU 近海集装箱船 2015 年
ZHONG GU SHANG HAI　2,540TEU Container Ship, Greater Coastal 2015
主尺度　L×B×D（m×m×m）：179.9×32.2×16

伦明　14080TEU 远洋集装箱船 2015 年
YM WELLNESS　14,080TEU Container Ship, Ocean-going 2015
主尺度　L×B×D（m×m×m）：368.1×51×16（吃水）

视明　14080TEU 远洋集装箱船 2015 年
YM WITNESS　14,080TEU Container Ship, Ocean-going 2015
主尺度　L×B×D（m×m×m）：368.1×51×16（吃水）

群明　14080TEU 远洋集装箱船 2015 年
YM WHOLESOME　14,080TEU Container Ship, Ocean-going 2015
主尺度　L×B×D（m×m×m）：368.1×51×16（吃水）

集发南海　1200TEU 近海集装箱船 2016 年
JI FA NAN HAI　1,200TEU Container Ship, Greater Coastal 2016
主尺度　L×B×D（m×m×m）：151.8×25×13.8

中远海运多瑙河　9092TEU 远洋集装箱船 2016 年
具有绿色船舶标志
COSCO SHIPPING DANUBE　9,092TEU Container Ship, Ocean-going　2016
With green ship notation
主尺度 *L*×*B*×*D* (m×m×m)：299.9×48.2×24.8

中远海运巴拿马　9470TEU 远洋集装箱船 2016 年
全球第一艘通过新巴拿马运河的船舶
主尺度 *L*×*B*×*D* (m×m×m)：300×48.2×24.8

COSCO SHIPPING PANAMA　9,470TEU Container Ship, Ocean-going　2016
World's first ship passing through the new Panama Canal

中外运渤海　4020TEU 近海集装箱船 2017 年
ZHONG WAI YUN BO HAI　4,020TEU Container Ship, Greater Coastal　2017
主尺度 *L*×*B*×*D* (m×m×m)：210×37.3×18.9

长喜　2881TEU 远洋集装箱船 2017 年
EVER BLISS　2,881TEU Container Ship, Ocean-going　2017
主尺度 *L*×*B*×*D* (m×m×m)：211.9×32.8×16.8

SHIPS OF CHINA

中远海运白羊座 19273TEU 超大型远洋集装箱船 2018 年
具有绿色船舶标志
主尺度 $L×B×D$ (m×m×m): 400×58.6×30.7

COSCO SHIPPING ARIES 19,273TEU Ultra Large Container Ship, Ocean-going 2018
With green ship notation

中远海运金牛座 20120TEU 超大型远洋集装箱船 2018 年
我国第一艘自主设计建造的 2 万箱级超大型集装箱船,具有智能船舶和绿色船舶标志
主尺度 $L×B×D$ (m×m×m): 399.8×58.6×30.5

COSCO SHIPPING TAURUS 20,120TEU Ultra Large Container Ship, Ocean-going 2018
First 20,000TEU ultra large container ship designed and built by China, with intelligent ship and green ship notations

中远海运宇宙　21000TEU 超大型远洋集装箱船 2018 年
我国自主设计建造的 2.1 万箱超大型集装箱船，具有绿色船舶标志
主尺度 $L \times B \times D$ (m×m×m)：399.9×58.6×33.5

COSCO SHIPPING UNIVERSE　21,000TEU Ultra Large Container Ship, Ocean-going　2018
21,000TEU ultra large container ship designed and built by China, with green ship notation

华达 609　1910TEU 近海集装箱船 2019 年
HUA DA 609　1,910TEU Container Ship, Greater Coastal　2019
主尺度 $L \times B \times D$ (m×m×m)：188×27.6×14.1

长隆　20160TEU 远洋集装箱船 2019 年
EVER GLORY　20,160TEU Container Ship, Ocean-going　2019
主尺度 $L \times B \times D$ (m×m×m)：400×58.8×26.2

兰春　2038TEU 远洋集装箱船 2020 年
WAN HAI 283　2,038TEU Container Ship, Ocean-going　2020
主尺度 $L \times B \times D$ (m×m×m)：175×28.6×10.5

第三节 油船和化学品船

油船是指载运原油或成品油的液货船。原油船根据其航线和载重吨大小通常可分为：灵便型、巴拿马型、阿芙拉型、苏伊士型和超大型油轮。灵便型油轮载重吨一般在5.5万吨以下；巴拿马型油轮主尺度受老巴拿马运河尺度限制，载重吨一般在6万～8万吨之间；阿芙拉型油轮是指为符合平均运费指数（AFRA）的船型，载重吨在8万～12万吨之间；苏伊士型油轮是指以苏伊士运河通过能力为标准的船型，载重吨在12万～20万吨之间；超大型油轮是指载重吨在20万吨以上的油船。2002年国际防污染公约规定要求淘汰单壳油轮，促进了油轮的更新换代，成为油轮船型发展的重要节点，目前，30万吨级超大型油轮已成为主流船型。我国油轮船队历经了由小到大、绿色智能的发展阶段，2019年建造了全球首艘30.8万吨级具有智能附加标志的VLCC，实现了历史性的跨越。我国油轮船队拥有的油轮数量位居世界第一，为保障我国能源运输发挥了重要作用。

成品油船是运输石油产品（包括汽油、柴油、煤油）的船舶。成品油船的种类可根据其运输距离分为短程（SR）、中程（MR）和远程（LR）运输种类。化学品船是专门用于运输散装危险化学品或有毒化学品的液货船船型，国际海运危险品运输规则定义的散装运输危险化学品有约800种，分为"非常严重危险""相当严重危险""足够严重危险"三大类。由于化学品具有易燃、易爆、有毒、腐蚀和污染等特性，化学品船通常采用双壳形式，液货舱被分隔成很多独立舱，各舱设有独立的管系，而且液货舱周界往往为光滑平面并采用不锈钢材料或覆以涂层以提高抗腐蚀性能。我国自主设计建造的38000吨级双相不锈钢化学品船，技术性能指标达到世界先进水平。化学品船技术含量高、造价成本高和管理要求高，我国化学品船队规模居世界前列，为我国化工行业的发展作出了重要贡献。

SECTION 3　OIL TANKER AND CHEMICAL TANKER

An oil tanker refers to a liquid cargo ship carrying crude oil or product oil. Crude oil tankers are usually divided into Handysize, Panamax, Aframax, Suezmax and Very Large Crude Carrier (VLCC) according to their routes and deadweight tonnage. Handysize oil tankers are generally below 55,000 DWT, Panamax is limited by the passing capacity of the old Panama Canal, generally between 60,000 and 80,000 DWT, Aframax is a ship type conforming to the Average Freight Rate Assessment (AFRA), with a deadweight of 80,000-120,000 DWT, Suezmax refers to the ship type based on the passing capacity of Suez Canal, with a deadweight of 120,000-200,000 DWT and VLCC refers to oil tankers with a deadweight of over 200,000 DWT. In 2002, the International Convention for the Prevention of Pollution from Ships required the phase-out of single-hull tankers, which promoted the renewal of tankers and became a milestone in the development of tanker types. Nowadays, 300,000 DWT VLCC has become the mainstream ship type. China's oil tanker fleet has gone through the development stage from small to large, green and intelligent. In 2019, China built the world's first 308,000 DWT VLCC (with intelligent notation), a major historic milestone. China's tanker combination now ranks first in terms of ship number in the world and plays an important role in safeguarding China's energy transportation.

Product oil tankers are ships that transport petroleum products, including gasoline, diesel oil and kerosene. They can be divided into short-range (SR), medium-range (MR) and long-range (LR) transportation types according to their transportation distance.

A chemical ship is a type of liquid cargo ship specially used for transporting dangerous chemicals or toxic chemicals in bulk. There are about 800 kinds of dangerous chemicals in bulk transport as defined by the International Maritime Dangerous Goods Code (IMDG Code), divided into three groups "cargo which are extremely dangerous", "cargo with moderate danger" and "cargo with less danger". Since chemicals are flammable, explosive, toxic, corrosive, polluting, etc, chemical ships usually adopt double-hulled form, and the cargo tanks are separated into many independent tanks, each equipped with independent piping system. The perimeter of cargo tanks is often smooth and made of stainless steel or coated to improve corrosion resistance performance. The technical performance indicators of 38,000 DWT duplex stainless steel chemical ships designed and constructed by China have reached the most advanced level in the world. Chemical ships feature high technology, high cost and stringent management requirements. China's chemical fleet ranks among the best in the world, and plays a key role in the development of China's chemical industry.

海上巨人　565000 吨远洋原油船　1981 年
世界最大油船
主尺度 $L×B×D$ (m×m×m)：458.5×68.9×29.8

SEAWISE GIANT　565,000DWT Crude Oil Tanker, Ocean-going　1981
World's largest oil tanker

枫林湾　110000 吨远洋原油/成品油船　1988 年
FENG LIN WAN　110,000DWT Crude Oil/Product Oil Tanker, Ocean-going　1988
主尺度 $L×B×D$ (m×m×m)：243×42×20.6

玉池　39000 吨远洋原油船　1992 年
YU CHI　39,000DWT Crude Oil Tanker, Ocean-going　1992
主尺度 $L×B×D$ (m×m×m)：180×32.2×14.2

凯勇　285000 吨远洋原油船　1992 年
NEW VALOR　285,000DWT Crude Oil Tanker, Ocean-going　1992
主尺度 $L×B×D$ (m×m×m)：328×57×30.8

大庆 73　35000 吨近海原油船　1993 年
DA QING 73　35,000DWT Crude Oil Tanker, Greater Coastal　1993
主尺度 $L×B×D$ (m×m×m)：185.5×27.5×15

北海之星　70000 吨远洋原油船　1993 年
BEI HAI ZHI XING　70,000DWT Crude Oil Tanker, Ocean-going　1993
主尺度 $L×B×D$ (m×m×m)：235×36×18.3

雁水湖　44000 吨远洋原油船 1995 年
YAN SHUI HU　44,000DWT Crude Oil Tanker, Ocean-going 1995
主尺度　$L×B×D$ (m×m×m)：182×30×17.3

玄武湖　68000 吨远洋原油船 2000 年
XUAN WU HU　68,000DWT Crude Oil Tanker, Ocean-going 2000
主尺度　$L×B×D$ (m×m×m)：229×32.2×19.2

远大湖　300000 吨远洋原油船 2002 年
我国建造的第一艘 30 万吨超大型油船
主尺度　$L×B×D$ (m×m×m)：333×60×29.3

COSGREAT LAKE　300,000DWT Crude Oil Tanker, Ocean-going 2002
First 300,000DWT very large oil tanker built by China

SHIPS OF CHINA

大明湖　159000 吨远洋原油船　2003 年
系列船中的首制船
主尺度 $L \times B \times D$ (m×m×m)：274.7×48×24

DA MING HU　159,000DWT Crude Oil Tanker, Ocean-going　2003
First ship in series

新金洋　297000 吨远洋原油船　2004 年
我国第一艘自主设计建造的 30 万吨超大型油船
XIN JIN YANG　297,000DWT Crude Oil Tanker, Ocean-going　2004
First 300,000DWT very large oil tanker designed and built by China
主尺度 $L \times B \times D$ (m×m×m)：330×60×29.7

凯鸿　300000 吨远洋原油船　2004 年
系列船中的首制船
NEW CENTURY　300,000DWT Crude Oil Tanker, Ocean-going　2004
First ship in series
主尺度 $L \times B \times D$ (m×m×m)：330×60×29.7

大源湖　159000 吨远洋原油船 2004 年
DA YUAN HU　159,000DWT Crude Oil Tanker, Ocean-going 2004
主尺度　$L \times B \times D$（m×m×m）：274.7×48×24

连运湖　75000 吨远洋原油/成品油船 2006 年
LIAN YUN HU　75,000DWT Crude Oil/Product Oil Tanker, Ocean-going 2006
主尺度　$L \times B \times D$（m×m×m）：228.6×32.3×21.1

白鹭洲　111000 吨远洋原油/成品油船 2007 年
BAI LU ZHOU　111,000DWT Crude Oil/Product Oil Tanker, Ocean-going 2007
主尺度　$L \times B \times D$（m×m×m）：244.5×42×21.9

河北伟岸　307000 吨远洋超大型原油船 2007 年改建
HEBEI MOUNTAIN　307,000DWT Very Large Crude Carrier, Ocean-going　Converted in 2007
主尺度 $L×B×D$ (m×m×m)：328.1×57×30.8

长航珊瑚　50000 吨远洋原油船 2008 年
CSC CORAL　50,000DWT Crude Oil Tanker, Ocean-going　2008
主尺度 $L×B×D$ (m×m×m)：185×32.2×19.2

长江之珠 297000 吨远洋原油船 2008 年
我国自主设计建造的 30 万吨超大型油船
主尺度 $L×B×D$ (m×m×m)：330×60×29.7

YANGTZE PEARL 297,000DWT Crude Oil Tanker, Ocean-going 2008
300,000DWT very large oil tanker designed and built by China

凯浙 310000 吨远洋原油船 2008 年
系列船中的首制船
NEW ENTERPRISE 310,000DWT Crude Oil Tanker, Ocean-going 2008
First ship in series
主尺度 $L×B×D$ (m×m×m)：333×60×28.8

凯吉 296000 吨远洋原油船 2009 年
系列船中的首制船
NEW TALISMAN 296,000DWT Crude Oil Tanker, Ocean-going 2009
First ship in series
主尺度 $L×B×D$ (m×m×m)：330×60×29.7

新甬洋　309000 吨远洋原油船 2010 年
XIN YONG YANG　309,000DWT Crude Oil Tanker, Ocean-going 2010
主尺度 $L×B×D$（m×m×m）：332.9×60×29.8

大连勇士　298000 吨远洋原油船 2011 年
DALIAN VENTURE　298,000DWT Crude Oil Tanker, Ocean-going 2011
主尺度 $L×B×D$（m×m×m）：317.6×60×29.7

桃林湾　110000 吨远洋原油 / 成品油船　2012 年
TAO LIN WAN　110,000DWT Crude Oil/Product Oil Tanker, Ocean-going　2012
主尺度 $L×B×D$（m×m×m）：244.7×42×21.6

连松湖　72000 吨远洋原油船　2017 年
LIAN SONG HU　72,000DWT Crude Oil Tanker, Ocean-going　2017
主尺度 $L×B×D$（m×m×m）：220×36×20

凯力　307000 吨远洋原油船 2018 年
全球第一艘装有风帆节能装置的超大型原油船
主尺度　$L×B×D$（m×m×m）：332.7×60×30

NEW VITALITY　307,000DWT Crude Oil Tanker, Ocean-going 2018
World's first very large crude oil tanker equipped with sail energy-saving device

凯征　308000 吨远洋原油船 2019 年
具有智能船舶标志
主尺度　$L×B×D$（m×m×m）：332.7×60×30

NEW JOURNEY　308,000DWT Crude Oil Tanker, Ocean-going 2019
With intelligent ship notation

新海辽　307000 吨远洋原油船　2019 年
具有智能标志船舶
主尺度　$L \times B \times D$ (m×m×m)：332.7×60×30

NEW VISION　307,000DWT Crude Oil Tanker, Ocean-going　2019
With intelligent ship notation

瑞春　308000 吨远洋原油船　2019 年
LANDBRIDGE GLORY　308,000DWT Crude Oil Tanker, Ocean-going　2019
主尺度　$L \times B \times D$ (m×m×m)：333×60×30

北海凤凰　65000 吨远洋原油船　2019 年
BEI HAI FENG HUANG　65,000DWT Crude Oil Tanker, Ocean-going　2019
主尺度　$L \times B \times D$ (m×m×m)：224.9×38×18.4

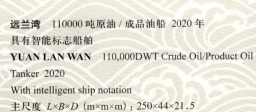

远兰湾　110000 吨原油 / 成品油船　2020 年
具有智能标志船舶
YUAN LAN WAN　110,000DWT Crude Oil/Product Oil Tanker　2020
With intelligent ship notation
主尺度　$L \times B \times D$ (m×m×m)：250×44×21.5

圣世　1700 吨沿海成品油船　1985 年
SHENG SHI　1,700DWT Product Oil Tanker, Coastal　1985
主尺度 $L \times B \times D$ (m×m×m)：77.4×11.2×5

滨海 606　4750 吨近海成品油船　1988 年
BIN HAI 606　4,750DWT Product Oil Tanker, Greater Coastal　1988
主尺度 $L \times B \times D$ (m×m×m)：107.4×15×7.5

青油 9　2000 吨近海供油船　1989 年
QING YOU 9　2,000DWT Bunkering tanker, Greater Coastal　1989
主尺度 $L \times B \times D$ (m×m×m)：87×12.5×6

金源 518　5700 吨近海成品油船　1992 年
JIN YUAN 518　5,700DWT Product Oil Tanker, Greater Coastal　1992
主尺度 $L×B×D$ (m×m×m)：106.7×17.6×7.1

埔油 10 号　5000 吨近海供油船　1993 年
PU YOU 10 HAO　5,000DWT Bunkering tanker, Greater Coastal　1993
主尺度 $L×B×D$ (m×m×m)：104.6×16.4×8.2

中港永和　19000 吨近海成品油船　1994 年
ZHONG GANG YONG HE　19,000DWT Product Oil Tanker, Greater Coastal　1994
主尺度 $L×B×D$ (m×m×m)：159.3×26×12

连油 10　1100 吨近海供油船　2001 年
LIAN YOU 10　1,100DWT Bunkering Tanker, Greater Coastal　2001
主尺度 $L×B×D$ (m×m×m)：69×10.7×4.9

东海 210　7700 吨近海成品油船　2005 年
DONG HAI 210　7,700DWT Product oil tanker, Greater Coastal　2005
主尺度 $L×B×D$ (m×m×m)：117.8×17.6×8.7

中燃 21　2400 吨近海供油船　2006 年
ZHONG RAN 21　2,400DWT Bunkering Tanker, Greater Coastal　2006
主尺度　$L×B×D$（m×m×m）：82×14.8×6

沪油 12　8800 吨沿海成品油船　2007 年
HU YOU 12　8,800DWT Product Oil Tanker, Coastal　2007
主尺度　$L×B×D$（m×m×m）：126.6×18.8×9.9

长航勇士　46000 吨远洋成品油船　2007 年
CSC BRAVE　46,000DWT Product Oil Tanker, Ocean-going　2007
主尺度　$L×B×D$（m×m×m）：185×32.2×18.2

航供油 501 579 吨近海成品油船 2007 年
HANG GONG YOU 501 579DWT Product Oil Tanker, Greater Coastal 2007
主尺度 $L×B×D$ (m×m×m)：49.3×9.8×4.1

福宁湾 6100 吨远洋成品油船 / 沥青船 2008 年
FU NING WAN 6,100DWT Product Oil Tanker/Asphalt Carrier, Ocean-going 2008
主尺度 $L×B×D$ (m×m×m)：107×18×10

昆仑油 106 13000 吨近海成品油船 2008 年
KUN LUN YOU 106 13,000DWT Product Oil Tanker, Greater Coastal 2008
主尺度 $L×B×D$ (m×m×m)：137.8×20.8×10.8

明祥　18000 吨远洋成品油船　2010 年
MING XIANG　18,000DWT Product Oil Tanker, Ocean-going 2010
主尺度　$L \times B \times D$（m×m×m）：150.6×22.6×12.5

海关山 126　970 吨近海成品油船　2010 年
HAI GUAN SHAN 126　970DWT Product Oil Tanker, Greater Coastal 2010
主尺度　$L \times B \times D$（m×m×m）：53.2×9.2×4.1

新润 18　4600 吨近海成品油船　2011 年
XIN RUN 18　4,600DWT Product Oil Tanker, Greater Coastal 2011
主尺度　$L \times B \times D$（m×m×m）：96.2×15.2×7

盛飞 601　6900 吨近海成品油船　2011 年
SHENG FEI 601　6,900DWT Product Oil Tanker, Greater Coastal　2011
主尺度 $L×B×D$ (m×m×m)：117.2×16.3×8.3

华辰 56　9600 吨近海成品油船　2011 年
HUA CHEN 56　9,600DWT Product Oil Tanker, Greater Coastal　2011
主尺度 $L×B×D$ (m×m×m)：121.9×18×9

昆仑油 201　30000 吨远洋原油 / 成品油船　2011 年
KUN LUN YOU 201　30,000DWT Crude Oil/Product Oil Tanker, Ocean-going　2011
主尺度 $L×B×D$ (m×m×m)：177.2×29×14.4

浙兴 169　20000 吨近海成品油船　2011 年
ZHE XING 169　20,000DWT Product Oil Tanker, Greater Coastal　2011
主尺度 $L×B×D$ (m×m×m)：157.1×23×13

博丰油供 16　498 吨沿海成品油船　2011 年
BO FENG YOU GONG 16　498DWT Product Oil Tanker, Coastal 2011
主尺度 $L \times B \times D$ (m×m×m)：53.2×9.2×4.1

中燃 33　3600 吨近海供油船　2012 年
ZHONG RAN 33　3,600DWT Bunkering Tanker, Coastal 2012
主尺度 $L \times B \times D$ (m×m×m)：87.7×15×7.1

中燃 37　3600 吨近海供油船　2012 年
ZHONG RAN 37　3,600DWT Bunkering Tanker, Greater Coastal 2012
主尺度 $L \times B \times D$ (m×m×m)：87.6×15×7.1

港联油 6　840 吨沿海成品油船 2013 年
GANG LIAN YOU 6　840DWT Product Oil Tanker, Coastal 2013
主尺度　$L×B×D$（m×m×m）：53.2×9.2×4.1

航供油驳 9　6500 吨近海成品油船 2017 年
HANG GONG YOU BO 9　6,500DWT Product Oil Tanker, Greater Coastal 2017
主尺度　$L×B×D$（m×m×m）：79×24×6

航供油 1003　2000 吨近海成品油船 2018 年改建　　**HANG GONG YOU 1003**　2,000DWT Product Oil Tanker, Greater Coastal Converted in 2018
单壳油船改双壳油船　　Double-hull oil tanker converted from a single-hull oil tanker
主尺度　$L×B×D$（m×m×m）：64.8×10.8×4.4

裕东　20000 吨远洋成品油船 2018 年
YU DONG　20,000DWT Product Oil Tanker, Ocean-going　2018
主尺度 $L×B×D$（m×m×m）：146.9×30×12.5

长航油 188　8600 吨近海成品油船 2019 年
CHANG HANG YOU 188　8,600DWT Product Oil Tanker, Greater Coastal　2019
主尺度 $L×B×D$（m×m×m）：115×19×9

海鑫油 619　16500 吨远洋成品油船 2019 年
HAI XIN YOU 619　16,500DWT Product Oil Tanker, Ocean-going　2019
主尺度 $L×B×D$（m×m×m）：149.1×23×12.6

恒晖 39　8000 吨远洋化学品船　1991 年
HENG HUI 39　8,000DWT Chemical Tanker, Ocean-going　1991
主尺度 $L \times B \times D$ (m×m×m)：111.3×18.2×9

WEALTHY BAY　12800 吨远洋化学品船　1998 年
WEALTHY BAY　12,800DWT Chemical Tanker, Ocean-going　1998
主尺度 $L \times B \times D$ (m×m×m)：124×20.2×11.2

SHIPS OF CHINA

天顺海 1 4000 吨近海化学品船 2004 年
TIAN SHUN HAI 1 4,000DWT Chemical Tanker, Greater Coastal 2004
主尺度 $L×B×D$ (m×m×m)：99.2×13.8×7.7

东茂 6 2150 吨近海化学品船 2006 年
DONG MAO 6 2,150DWT Chemical Tanker, Greater Coastal 2006
主尺度 $L×B×D$ (m×m×m)：81.7×12×5.6

鼎衡 1　4030 吨远洋化学品船　2006 年
DING HENG 1　4,030DWT Chemical Tanker, Ocean-going　2006
主尺度 $L×B×D$ (m×m×m)：96.6×15×7.4

嘉信 1 号　3500 吨近海硫黄运输船　2007 年
JIA XIN 1 HAO　3,500DWT Chemical Tanker, Greater Coastal　2007
主尺度 $L×B×D$ (m×m×m)：89.6×15×7.6

宁化 419　3560 吨远洋不锈钢化学船　2007 年
NING HUA 419　3,560DWT Chemical Tanker, Ocean-going　2007
主尺度 $L×B×D$ (m×m×m)：87×15×7.4

游神 1　8300 吨远洋化学品船　2007 年
YOU SHEN 1　8,300DWT Chemical Tanker, Ocean-going　2007
主尺度 $L×B×D$ (m×m×m)：115.2×18×8.9

鼎衡 5　4060 吨远洋化学品船　2008 年
DING HENG 5　4,060DWT Chemical Tanker, Ocean-going　2008
主尺度 $L×B×D$ (m×m×m)：96.6×15×7.4

恒信　14000 吨远洋化学品船 2010 年
HENG XIN　14,000DWT Chemical Tanker, Ocean-going 2010
主尺度 $L×B×D$（m×m×m）：142.2×20.8×11.2

南炼 5　5700 吨远洋化学品船 2012 年
NAN LIAN 5　5,700DWT Chemical Tanker, Ocean-going 2012
主尺度 $L×B×D$（m×m×m）：101.3×15.6×8.5

华威 8　28000 吨远洋化学品船 2012 年
HUA WEI 8　28,000DWT Chemical Tanker, Ocean-going 2012
主尺度 $L×B×D$（m×m×m）：180.1×26.8×14.1

水瓶座　38000 吨远洋化学品船 2016 年
我国自主设计建造的大型先进的不锈钢化学品船
主尺度 $L×B×D$（m×m×m）：182.8×32.01×15.7

SC AQUARIUS　38,000DWT Chemical Tanker, Ocean-going 2016
Advanced large stainless steel chemical tanker designed and built by China

东桂 16 5380 吨远洋化学品/成品油船 2017 年
DONG GUI 16 5,380DWT Chemical/Product Oil Tanker, Ocean-going 2017
主尺度 $L×B×D$ (m×m×m)：103.8×16.5×8.4

永荣 50000 吨远洋化学品/成品油船 2017 年
FOREVER GLORY 50,000DWT Chemical/Product Oil Tanker, Ocean-going 2017
主尺度 $L×B×D$ (m×m×m)：183.2×32.3×18.2

永和 50000 吨远洋化学品/成品油船 2018 年
FOREVER HARMONY 50,000DWT Chemical/Product Oil Tanker, Ocean-going 2018
主尺度 $L×B×D$ (m×m×m)：183.2×32.3×18.2

月亮湾　11000 吨远洋沥青船 1999 年
YUE LIANG WAN　11,000DWT Asphalt Carrier, Ocean-going　1999
主尺度 $L \times B \times D$ (m×m×m)：126.8×21.4×11.8

亚龙湾　6000 吨远洋沥青船 2007 年
YA LONG WAN　6,000DWT Asphalt Carrier, Ocean-going　2007
主尺度 $L \times B \times D$ (m×m×m)：106.8×17.6×10.1

大明山　12800 吨远洋沥青船 2016 年
DA MING SHAN　12,800DWT Asphalt Carrier, Ocean-going　2016
主尺度 $L \times B \times D$ (m×m×m)：139×22.8×11.8

广州湾 13000 吨远洋沥青船 2017 年
GUANG ZHOU WAN 13,000DWT Asphalt Carrier, Ocean-going 2017
主尺度 $L×B×D$ (m×m×m)：145.9×22.6×11.8

荣华湾 7900 吨远洋沥青船 2018 年
RONG HUA WAN 7,900DWT Asphalt Carrier, Ocean-going 2018
主尺度 $L×B×D$ (m×m×m)：114.9×19.5×11

第四节 液化气体运输船

液化气体运输船是指专门运载液化气体的液货船，需要满足IMO《国际散装运输液化气体船舶构造与设备规则》（简称IGC规则）规定。由于液化气体大多具有易燃、易爆、腐蚀性和毒性等特殊化学物理特性，液化气体运输船在总体布置、货舱维护系统和建造工艺等方面难度大，技术要求高，是国际上公认的高技术、高难度、高附加值的"三高"船舶。常见的液化气种类包括：液化天然气(LNG)、液化石油气(LPG)、液化乙烯(LEG)等。液化气体运输可以通过低温常压、常温高压或者半冷半压方式实现。LNG运输采用低温常压方式，LNG运输船一般设计成薄膜舱型，货物温度保持在-163℃；LPG运输采用常温高压方式，LPG运输船一般设计成独立罐舱，舱内压力1.75～2.00兆帕。

20世纪90年代初，我国自主设计建造的第一艘常温压力式3000立方米液化气体运输船，填补了我国液化气体运输船建造技术空白。2008年，我国自行建造了首艘14.7万立方米薄膜型液化气船，标志着我国在世界顶级船舶建造领域实现了突破。近年来，我国交付的大型液化气体运输船数量不断增加，积累了丰富的各类大型液化气体运输船设计建造检验经验，全面突破了各类船型关键技术，跻身于世界高端液化气体运输船建造的先进行列。

SECTION 4   LIQUEFIED GAS CARRIER

Liquefied gas carriers are liquid cargo ships specializing in carrying liquefied gases, and need to meet the requirements of *the International Code for the Construction and Equipment of Ships Carrying Liquefied Gases in Bulk* (IGC Code). Due to the special chemical and physical characteristics of liquefied gases, such as flammable, explosive, corrosive, toxic, etc, liquefied gas carriers are highly sophisticated and technically demanding in terms of general arrangement, cargo tank maintenance system and construction process. They are internationally known for their high technology, sophistication and high value. The common types of liquefied gas include: liquefied natural gas (LNG), liquefied petroleum gas (LPG) and liquefied ethylene (LEG). Liquefied gas transportation can be realised by low-temperature atmospheric pressure, ambient temperature high-pressure or semi-cold and semi-pressure methods. LNG transportation adopts low-temperature atmospheric pressure method, and LNG carriers are generally designed as membrane tank type, with cargo temperature kept at -163°C; LPG transportation adopts atmospheric temperature high-pressure method, and LPG carriers are generally designed as independent tanks with a pressure of 1.75-2.00MPa.

In the early 1990s, China independently designed and built the first ambient temperature and pressure type 3,000 m³ LPG carriers, which filled the technical gap in the construction of LPG carriers in China. In 2008, China built the first 147,000m³ membrane-type liquefied gas carrier on its own, marking a breakthrough in the world's top shipbuilding field. In recent years, the number of large liquefied gas carriers delivered in China has been increasing, and we have accumulated rich experience in the design and construction survey of various types of large liquefied gas carriers, broken through the key technologies of various types of vessels, and become one of the leading players in the construction of high-end liquefied gas carriers in the world.

大鹏昊 147736 立方米远洋液化天然气（LNG）运输船 2008 年
我国建造的第一艘大型 LNG 运输船
主尺度 $L×B×D$（m×m×m）：291.5×43.4×26.3

DAPENG SUN 147,736m³ LNG Carrier, Ocean-going 2008
First large LNG carrier built by China

海洋石油 301 30000 立方米远洋液化天然气（LNG）运输船 2015 年
我国第一艘自主设计建造的 C 型舱 LNG 运输船
具有绿色船舶标志
主尺度 $L×B×D$（m×m×m）：184.7×28.1×18.7

HAI YANG SHI YOU 301 30,000m³ LNG Carrier, Ocean-going 2015
First Type C LNG carrier designed and built by China
with green ship notation

华祥 8　14021 立方米远洋液化天然气（LNG）运输船　2016 年
HUA XIANG 8　14,021m³ LNG Carrier, Ocean-going　2016
主尺度 $L \times B \times D$ (m×m×m)：125.8×22.7×13.1

中能福石　174000 立方米远洋液化天然气（LNG）运输船　2016 年
CESI GLADSTONE　174,000m³ LNG Carrier, Ocean-going　2016
主尺度 $L \times B \times D$ (m×m×m)：290×45.6×26.5

泛亚号 174035 立方米远洋液化天然气（LNG）运输船 2017 年
我国自主设计建造的国内最大液化天然气运输船
主尺度 $L \times B \times D$ (m×m×m)：290×47×26.3

PAN ASIA 174,035m³ LNG Carrier, Ocean-going 2017
Largest LNG carrier designed and built by China

天璇星 174000 立方米远洋液化天然气（LNG）运输船 2020 年
采用双燃料动力系统
主尺度 $L \times B \times D$ (m×m×m)：295×45×26.25

LNG MERAK 174,000m³ LNG Carrier, Ocean-going 2020
With dual fuel power system

宁顺　1455 立方米远洋液化石油气（LPG）运输船　1985 年
NING SHUN　1,455m³ LPG Carrier, Ocean-going　1985
主尺度　$L \times B \times D$（m×m×m）：66.5×11×4.9

百合源　1600 立方米远洋液化石油气（LPG）运输船　1986 年
BAI HE YUAN　1,600m³ LPG Carrier, Ocean-going　1986
主尺度　$L \times B \times D$（m×m×m）：68×11×5

顺源 108　3000 立方米远洋液化石油气（LPG）运输船　1991 年
我国第一艘自主设计建造液化石油气运输船
SHUN YUAN 108　3,000m³ LPG Carrier, Ocean-going　1991
First liquefied petroleum gas carrier designed and built by China
主尺度　$L \times B \times D$（m×m×m）：97×14.6×6.6

竹源　3207 立方米远洋液化石油气（LPG）运输船　1991 年
ZHU YUAN　3,207m³ LPG Carrier, Ocean-going　1991
主尺度　$L \times B \times D$（m×m×m）：99.6×15.8×7.3

苏瑞 139　3514 立方米远洋液化石油气（LPG）运输船　1995 年
SU RUI 139　3,514m³ LPG Carrier, Ocean-going　1995
主尺度　$L \times B \times D$（m×m×m）：94.5×16.6×7.1

芙蓉源　4013 立方米远洋液化石油气（LPG）运输船　1996 年
FU RONG YUAN　4,013m³ LPG Carrier, Ocean-going　1996
主尺度 $L \times B \times D$ (m×m×m)：99.9×16.2×7.2

苏瑞 169　5016 立方米远洋液化石油气（LPG）运输船　1996 年
SU RUI 169　5,016m³ LPG Carrier, Ocean-going　1996
主尺度 $L \times B \times D$ (m×m×m)：99.9×19.6×7.7

安华勇士　38484立方米远洋液化石油气（LPG）运输船　1996年
ANTWERPEN VENTURE　38,484m³ LPG Carrier, Ocean-going　1996
主尺度 $L×B×D$ (m×m×m)：195.9×29.4×17

百花源　3500立方米远洋液化石油气（LPG）运输船　1997年
BAI HUA YUAN　3,500m³ LPG Carrier, Ocean-going　1997
主尺度 $L×B×D$ (m×m×m)：96.6×16×7.2

银珠号　3200立方米远洋液化石油气（LPG）运输船　2007年
YIN ZHU HAO　3,200m³ LPG Carrier, Ocean-going　2007
主尺度 $L×B×D$ (m×m×m)：96×14.4×7

同心源　3500立方米远洋液化石油气（LPG）运输船　2008年
TONG XIN YUAN　3,500m³ LPG Carrier, Ocean-going　2008
主尺度 $L×B×D$ (m×m×m)：99×16.4×7.2

鹏顺　8033立方米远洋液化石油气（LPG）运输船　2010年购进
PENG SHUN　8,033m³ LPG Carrier, Ocean-going　Purchased in 2010
主尺度 $L×B×D$ (m×m×m)：115×18.6×10.6

平安源　3700立方米远洋液化石油气（LPG）运输船　2011年
PING AN YUAN　3,700m³ LPG Carrier, Ocean-going　2011
主尺度 $L×B×D$ (m×m×m)：100×15×7

宝泽 6900立方米远洋液化石油气（LPG）运输船 2012年
BAO ZE 6,900m³ LPG Carrier, Ocean-going 2012
主尺度 $L×B×D$ (m×m×m)：119×18.8×8.4

雁顺 6500立方米远洋液态乙烯（LEG）运输船 2013年
我国第一艘自主设计建造的半冷半压液态乙烯（LEG）运输船
主尺度 $L×B×D$ (m×m×m)：112×19×10.6

YAN SHUN 6,500m³ LEG Carrier, Ocean-going 2013
First semi-cold and semi-pressure LEG carrier designed and built by China

白羊座　83088 立方米远洋超大型液化石油气运输船　2016 年
GAS ARIES　83,088m³ Very Large LPG Carrier, Ocean-going　2016
主尺度 $L×B×D$ (m×m×m)：226×36.6×22.2

PACIFIC RIZHAO　84160 立方米远洋超大型液化石油气运输船 2016 年
PACIFIC RIZHAO　84,160m³ Very Large LPG Carrier, Ocean-going　2016
主尺度 $L×B×D$ (m×m×m)：226.1×36.6×22.2

鲲顺　6640 立方米乙烯（LEG）运输船 2020 年　　**KUN SHUN**　6,640m³ LEG Carrier　2020
具有绿色船舶标志　　With green ship notation
主尺度 $L×B×D$ (m×m×m)：113×18×11.9

第五节　普通货船

普通货船一般包括杂货船、多用途船、重吊船和牲畜运输船等。

杂货船是最为传统的一种船型，装载一般包装、袋装、箱装和桶装的普通货物。杂货船通常在甲板上配有起货设备，在货物和港口适应性等方面具有优势，是支线货物运输的主力。为提高船舶对各种货物运输的适应性，现代杂货船往往设计成多用途船。

多用途船多为载运集装箱、散货和件杂货等的船舶。货舱通常设计成桶形，二层舱盖设计成可吊式，就位后可作为二甲板使用，对货物适应性较强。

重吊船是指自带重型吊机，专门载运重件货物并能依靠自身设备装卸的运输船舶。重吊船适用于装运发电设备、机车等过重过大货物，或受港口条件限制一般货船无法装运的货物。

牲畜运输船是指专门运输牛、羊、猪等活动物的船舶。该船型通常具有多层甲板结构，配有专门为运送牲畜服务的设施，包括通风系统、饲料和饮水供给系统、专用电源供应系统、水清洁系统和污水排放系统等。

普通货船的船型也在不断优化，载重吨从2万～3万吨，逐步发展到近年的6万多吨，为便于装卸货，在分舱布置、货舱结构、甲板机械等方面都有很大改进。

SECTION 5　GENERAL CARGO SHIP

General cargo ships include general dry cargo ships, multi-purpose ships, heavy lift ships, livestock carriers, etc.

A general cargo ship is the most traditional ship type, carrying general cargo in general packages, bags, boxes and barrels. Usually equipped with lifting equipment on deck, general cargo ships have advantages in cargo and port adaptability, and are the mainstay of feeder cargo transportation. In order to improve the adaptability of the ship to various types of cargo transportation, modern general cargo ships are often designed as multi-purpose ships.

Multi-purpose ships are mostly ships carrying containers, bulk cargo and break bulk cargo. The cargo hold is usually designed as a barrel shape, and the second deck hatch cover is designed as a lift-away type, which can be used as the second deck after being put in position and is more adaptable to cargo.

A heavy lift ship refers to a vessel with its own heavy lift capability, which specializes in carrying heavy cargo and can rely on its own equipment for loading and unloading. A heavy lift ship is suitable for loading and transporting overweight and oversized cargoes such as power generation equipment and locomotives, or cargoes that cannot be loaded by general cargo ships due to port conditions.

A livestock carrier is a ship specializing in transporting cattle, sheep, pigs and other living animals. This type of ship usually has a multi-layered deck structure and is equipped with facilities specially designed for transporting livestock, including ventilation system, feed and water supply system, special power supply system, water cleaning system, sewage discharge system, etc.

These types of general cargo ships are also being optimised, and the deadweight tonnage is being gradually developed from 20,000-30,000 DWT to more than 60,000 DWT in recent years. For the convenience of loading and unloading, there are great improvements in compartment arrangement, cargo hold structure type, deck machinery, etc.

肖邦　18000 吨远洋杂货船　1989 年
CHOPIN　18,000DWT General Cargo Ship, Ocean-going　1989
主尺度　$L \times B \times D$ （m×m×m）：159×23×13.6

良河　4000 吨远洋杂货船　2000 年
LIANG HE　4,000DWT General Cargo Ship, Ocean-going　2000
主尺度　$L \times B \times D$ （m×m×m）：93×16.2×7.2

建荣 966　5000 吨近海杂货船　2003 年
JIAN RONG 966　5,000DWT General Cargo Ship, Greater Coastal　2003
主尺度　$L \times B \times D$ （m×m×m）：98×15.8×7.4

新锦源　5500 吨近海杂货船　2004 年
XIN JIN YUAN　5,500DWT General Cargo Ship, Greater Coastal　2004
主尺度　$L \times B \times D$ （m×m×m）：102.8×15.8×7

永安城 23000 吨远洋多用途船 1992 年
YONG AN CHENG 23,000DWT Multi-purpose Ship, Ocean-going 1992
主尺度 $L×B×D$ (m×m×m)：174×25.6×14.2

崇明 22000 吨远洋多用途船 1993 年
CHONG MING 22,000DWT Multi-purpose Ship, Ocean-going 1993
主尺度 $L×B×D$ (m×m×m)：169.8×27.5×13.8

恒裕 8370 吨远洋多用途船 1998 年
HENG YU 8,370DWT Multi-purpose Ship, Ocean-going 1998
主尺度 $L×B×D$ (m×m×m)：127×20.4×10.4

新大中　17000 吨远洋重吊多用途船　1998 年
XIN DA ZHONG　17,000DWT Heavy Lift Multi-purpose Ship, Ocean-going　1998
主尺度　$L×B×D$ (m×m×m)：153×23×14.1

金吉源　36000 吨远洋多用途船　1998 年
JIN JI YUAN　36,000DWT Multi-purpose Ship, Ocean-going　1998
主尺度　$L×B×D$ (m×m×m)：189.7×27.7×15.5

信风福州　44570 吨远洋多用途船　1998 年
XIN FENG FU ZHOU　44,570DWT Multi-purpose Ship, Ocean-going　1998
主尺度　$L×B×D$ (m×m×m)：185×32.2×17

乐锦　22000 吨远洋多用途船　1999 年
LE JIN　22,000DWT Multi-purpose Ship, Ocean-going　1999
主尺度　$L \times B \times D$ (m×m×m)：169×26.2×14.1

乐同　22000 吨远洋多用途船　2000 年
LE TONG　22,000DWT Multi-purpose Ship, Ocean-going　2000
主尺度　$L \times B \times D$ (m×m×m)：169×25.2×14.1

乐从　29000 吨远洋多用途船　2000 年
LE CONG　29,000DWT Multi-purpose Ship, Ocean-going　2000
主尺度　$L \times B \times D$ (m×m×m)：182.7×26.2×14.7

永盛　19000 吨远洋多用途重吊船　2002 年
我国第一艘试航北极航线的商船
主尺度 $L×B×D$（m×m×m）：160×23.7×12

YONG SHENG　19,000DWT Heavy Lift Multi-purpose Ship, Ocean-going　2002
China's first merchant ship performing sea trial on the Arctic route

太阳　30000 吨远洋多用途重吊船　2004 年
CHIPOLBROK SUN　30,000DWT Heavy Lift Multi-purpose Ship, Ocean-going　2004
主尺度 $L×B×D$（m×m×m）：199.8×27.8×15.5

建荣 268　4800 吨近海多用途船　2005 年
JIAN RONG 268　4,800DWT Multi-purpose Ship, Greater Coastal　2005
主尺度 $L×B×D$（m×m×m）：95.9×13.8×7.4

尚航99　11000吨近海多用途船　2006年
SHANG HANG 99　11,000DWT Multi-purpose Ship, Greater Coastal　2006
主尺度 $L×B×D$ (m×m×m)：131.3×18×9.7

锦江之宇　14000吨远洋多用途船　2006年
JJ SKY　14,000DWT Multi-purpose Ship, Ocean-going　2006
主尺度 $L×B×D$ (m×m×m)：147.8×23.3×11.5

海王之星　9100吨远洋多用途船　2008年
HAI WANG ZHI XING　9,100DWT Multi-purpose Ship, Ocean-going　2008
主尺度 $L×B×D$ (m×m×m)：122.2×19.8×10.7

凤凰松　27000 吨远洋多用途船　2009 年
FENG HUANG SONG　27,000DWT Multi-purpose Ship, Ocean-going　2009
主尺度　$L \times B \times D$（m×m×m）：179.5×27.2×14.5

长和　8000 吨远洋重吊船　2009 年
SCSC FORTUNE　8,000DWT Heavy Lift Ship, Ocean-going　2009
主尺度　$L \times B \times D$（m×m×m）：117.8×18×10.4

SEIYO GODDESS　12000 吨远洋重吊船　2010 年
SEIYO GODDESS　12,000DWT Heavy Lift Ship, Ocean-going　2010
主尺度　$L \times B \times D$（m×m×m）：120×20.8×13

吉祥松　27000 吨远洋多用途船　2011 年
JI XIANG SONG　27,000DWT Multi-purpose Ship, Ocean-going　2011
主尺度 $L×B×D$ (m×m×m)：179.5×27.2×14.5

乾坤　30000 吨远洋多用途重吊船　2011 年
QIAN KUN　30,000DWT Heavy Lift Multi-purpose Ship, Ocean-going　2011
主尺度 $L×B×D$ (m×m×m)：199.8×27.8×15.5

长航鑫海　12500 吨远洋多用途重吊船　2012 年
CSC XIN HAI　12,500DWT Heavy Lift Multi-purpose Ship, Ocean-going　2012
主尺度 $L×B×D$ (m×m×m)：125×22×14.3

远望 21 9080 吨火箭运输船 2013 年
新型运载火箭船
主尺度 $L \times B \times D$ (m×m×m)：130×19×12

YUAN WANG 21 9,080DWT Rocket Carrier 2013
New type rocket carrier

大德 28000 吨远洋多用途重吊船 2014 年
DA DE 28,000DWT Heavy Lift Multi-purpose Ship, Ocean-going 2014
主尺度 $L \times B \times D$ (m×m×m)：179.6×28×14.8

天寿 38000 吨远洋多用途船 2015 年
TIAN SHOU 38,000DWT Multi-purpose Ship, Ocean-going 2015
主尺度 $L \times B \times D$ (m×m×m)：190×28.5×15.8

天福 38000 吨远洋多用途船 2015 年
TIAN FU 38,000DWT Multi-purpose Ship, Ocean-going 2015
主尺度 $L \times B \times D$ (m×m×m)：190×28.5×15.8

荣安城 38000 吨远洋多用途船 2015 年
RONG AN CHENG 38,000DWT Multi-purpose Ship, Ocean-going 2015
主尺度 $L \times B \times D$ (m×m×m)：180×32×15

中远海运开拓 62000 吨远洋多用途纸浆船 2018 年
具有绿色船舶标志
主尺度 L×B×D（m×m×m）：201.8×32.3×19.3

ZHONG YUAN HAI YUN KAI TUO 62,000DWT Multi-purpose Wood-pulp Carrier, Ocean-going 2018
With green ship notation

长和 4850 吨远洋牲畜运输船 2017 年改建
由集装箱船改装成牲畜运输船
YANGTZE HARMONY 4,850DWT Livestock Carrier, Ocean-going
Converted in 2017
Livestock carrier converted from container ship
主尺度 L×B×D（m×m×m）：132.6×19.2×9.2

长顺 4810 吨远洋牲畜运输船 2017 年改建
由集装箱船改装成牲畜运输船舶
YANGTZE FORTUNE 4,810DWT Livestock Carrier, Ocean-going
Converted in 2017
Livestock carrier converted from container ship
主尺度 L×B×D（m×m×m）：132.6×19.2×9.2

第六节　滚装货船

滚装货船是指适用于装运汽车或者采用汽车装载上船的货物，包括车辆、集卡、管状货物等。专门运输商品汽车的滚装船又称汽车运输船。滚装船在首尾或两舷设有跳板伸到码头上，装货处所设有多层甲板，各层甲板之间用斜坡道或升降平台连通，便于车辆通行。为了防止货物移动，滚装甲板上设有专门系固系统。滚装船的优点是装卸效率高，还可装运无法通过集装箱装载的大型货物。

我国汽车工业和汽车贸易的不断发展，带来了对汽车运输船的旺盛需求，汽车运输船已广泛用于国内和国际汽车运输。我国长江三角洲地区、东北三省、长江中上游地区、珠江三角洲地区、环渤海湾地区等是汽车生产企业聚集区，这种产业布局的特点形成商品汽车南北对流的基本平衡，南北航线基本无空载。近年来，我国汽车海外销量不断增长，服务于东南亚航线、南美航线的大型汽车运输船，可一次装载商品小轿车3800辆。

SECTION 6　　RO-RO CARGO SHIP

A roll-on-roll-off cargo ship refers to ships suitable for carrying automobiles or cargoes loaded onto the ship by automobiles, including vehicles, container trucks, and tubular cargo. Ro-Ro ships specializing in transporting commercial automobiles are also called vehicle carriers. The Ro-Ro ship is equipped with a springboard at the fore and aft ends or on both sides to reach the quay, and the cargo spaces are equipped with multi-story decks that are connected with a ramp or a lifting platform with one another to facilitate the traffic of vehicles. In order to prevent the cargo from moving, the Ro-Ro deck is equipped with a special securing system. The advantages of Ro-Ro ships include high loading and unloading efficiency, and the ability to carry large size cargo that the containers cannot handle.

The continuous development of China's automobile industry and automobile trade is driving a strong demand for vehicle carriers, which have been widely used in domestic and international transportation. China's Yangtze River Delta region, the three northeastern provinces, the middle and upper reaches of the Yangtze River, the Pearl River Delta region and the Bohai Bay region are the prime areas for automobile production. The characteristics of this industrial layout help maximise car flow between North and South China, so the north-south route is almost without empty vehicle carriers. In recent years, the overseas sales of China's automobiles have been growing, and the large car carriers serving the Southeast Asia route and South America route, which can load 3,800 cars at one time.

赤峰口　13000 吨远洋滚装货船　1980 年
CHI FENG KOU　13,000DWT Ro-Ro Cargo Ship, Ocean-going　1980
主尺度　$L×B×D$（m×m×m）：146.5×22.7×15

常发口　2950 车位远洋汽车运输船　1985 年
CHANG FA KOU　2,950CEU Car Carrier, Ocean-going 1985
主尺度　$L×B×D$（m×m×m）：158.9×27.8×26.2

长吉　250 车位近海汽车运输船　1992 年购进
我国购进第一艘专用汽车运输船舶
CHANG JI　250CEU Car Carrier, Greater Coastal Purchased in 1992
First special purpose car carrier purchased by China
主尺度　$L×B×D$（m×m×m）：71.5×14.5×4.5

潍营　6000 吨近海滚装货船　1997 年
WEI YING　6,000DWT Ro-Ro Cargo Ship, Greater Coastal　1997
主尺度　$L×B×D$（m×m×m）：167.7×24×9.3

恒运 1 640 吨沿海滚装货船 1998 年
HENG YUN 1 640DWT Ro-Ro Cargo Ship, Coastal 1998
主尺度 $L \times B \times D$ (m×m×m): 69.8×14.8×4

玉衡先锋 5380 车位远洋汽车运输船 1998 年
YU HENG XIAN FENG 5,380CEU Car Carrier, Ocean-going 1998
主尺度 $L \times B \times D$ (m×m×m): 180×32.3×15.3

大丰港和顺号 3800 车位沿海汽车运输船 1999 年
DA FENG GANG HE SHUN HAO 3,800CEU Car Carrier, Coastal 1999
主尺度 $L×B×D$（m×m×m）：164×28×29.3

常安口 4310 车位远洋汽车运输船 1999 年
CHANG AN KOU 4,310CEU Car Carrier, Ocean-going 1999
主尺度 $L×B×D$（m×m×m）：177×31×28

上汽安吉凤凰　4300 车位远洋汽车运输船 2000 年
SAIC ANJI PHOENIX　4,300CEU Car Carrier, Ocean-going　2000
主尺度 $L×B×D$（m×m×m）：176×31.1×28

长盛鸿　4310 车位远洋汽车运输船 2000 年
CHANG SHENG HONG　4,310CEU Car Carrier, Ocean-going　2000
主尺度 $L×B×D$（m×m×m）：176.7×31.1×28

安吉 2　265 车位近海汽车运输船 2006 年购进
AN JI 2　265CEU Car Carrier, Greater Coastal
Purchased in 2006
主尺度 $L×B×D$（m×m×m）：80.5×13.3×6.5

富瀚口　780车位远洋汽车运输船　2007年购进
FU HAN KOU　780CEU Car Carrier, Ocean-going　Purchased in 2007
主尺度 $L×B×D$（m×m×m）：160.5×20.8×18.8

长吉隆　2000车位远洋汽车运输船　2009年
我国第一艘自主设计建造的新型汽车运输船
CHANG JI LONG　2,000CEU Car Carrier, Ocean-going　2009
First new-type car carrier designed and built by China
主尺度 $L×B×D$（m×m×m）：140.5×24.4×10.4

长泰鸿　4900车位远洋汽车运输船　2010年购进
CHANG TAI HONG　4,900CEU Car Carrier, Ocean-going Purchased in 2010
主尺度 $L×B×D$（m×m×m）：176×31.1×30

中远腾飞　5276车位远洋汽车运输船　2011年
配有光伏太阳能装置
COSCO TENG FEI　5,276CEU Car Carrier, Ocean-going　2011
Equipped with photovoltaic solar devices
主尺度 $L×B×D$ (m×m×m)：182.8×32.2×15

中远盛世　5276车位远洋汽车运输船　2011年
COSCO SHENG SHI　5,276CEU Car Carrier, Ocean-going　2011
主尺度 $L×B×D$ (m×m×m)：182.8×32.2×15

世江　2100车位远洋汽车运输船　2016年
我国自主设计建造的新一代汽车运输船
主尺度 $L×B×D$ (m×m×m)：141.2×24.4×13.1

SHI JIANG　2,100CEU Car Carrier, Ocean-going　2016
New-generation car carrier designed and built by China

安吉26　2905车位远洋汽车运输船　2017年购进
AN JI 26　2,905CEU Car Carrier, Ocean-going Purchased in 2017
主尺度　$L×B×D$（m×m×m）：173×27.4×8.9

安吉23　3759车位远洋汽车运输船　2017年
我国设计建造的新型汽车运输船，具有绿色船舶标志
主尺度　$L×B×D$（m×m×m）：169.1×28×13

AN JI 23　3,759CEU Car Carrier, Ocean-going 2017
New type of car carrier designed and built by China, with green ship notation

安吉 27 2333 车位近海汽车运输船 2019 年
我国第一艘"江海直达"汽车运输船，具有绿色船舶标志
主尺度 $L \times B \times D$ (m×m×m)：141.9×24.4×13.1

AN JI 27 2,333CEU Car Carrier, Greater Coastal 2019
China's first river-sea car carrier, with green ship notation

渤海恒通 11370 吨滚装货船 2020 年
BO HAI HENG TONG 11,370DWT Ro-Ro Cargo Ship 2020
主尺度 $L \times B \times D$ (m×m×m)：189.9×26.4×9.2

第七节 甲板货船

甲板货船属于特种海运船舶。其特点是货物装载在甲板上，船舶不设货舱，运载货物的尺度不受船舶货舱的限制，一般用于装运大型结构物、钻井平台、中小型船舶等。

半潜船是一种特殊的甲板货船。它可以把装货甲板潜入水中一定深度，将浮在水面或者水面上的结构物拖拽到装货甲板上方，再通过排出压载水将货物托举到甲板上。反之将船体潜入水中将货物拖离达到卸货的目的。这种浮装浮卸方式可以不受码头起重设备的限制，在海上进行，具备动力定位功能的半潜船是目前从事大型海上设施运输和海上安装的主力。

我国从20世纪80年代开始从国外购进半潜船。2002年我国自主设计建造第一艘18000吨级大型多功能半潜船。目前我国设计建造的最大的半潜船，堪称海上"巨无霸"，下潜水深达到30.5米，可在海上轻松举起10万吨级重物，处于世界领先水平。

我国半潜船船队规模位居世界前列，随着我国装备制造业的大力发展，超长、超大、超重货逐年增长，海上模块化运输船队快速发展，为我国在海上石油平台运输与安装、海上风电运输与出口和海上特种运输提供了保障。

SECTION 7   DECK CARGO SHIP

A deck cargo ship falls into the category of special marine transportation ships. Its characteristics include having the cargo loaded on the deck, the ship does not have cargo hold, so the size of carried cargo is not limited by the ship's cargo hold. It is generally used for carrying large structures, drilling units and small to medium-size ships.

A semi-submersible ship is a special type of deck cargo ship. It can submerge the loading deck into the water to a certain depth, tow the structures floating on the surface or on the water to the top of the loading deck, and then lift the cargo to the deck by discharging ballast water. In reverse, the unloading is achieved by submerging the hull into the water to tow the cargo away. This kind of floating loading and unloading can be carried out at sea without the restriction of quay lifting equipment, and the semi-submersible ship with power positioning function is the main force engaged in transportation and installation of large offshore facilities at present.

China began to purchase semi-submersible ships from abroad in the 1980s. In 2002, China designed and built the first 18,000 DWT large multifunctional semi-submersible ships. At present, the largest semi-submersible ship designed and built in China, likened to a "mammoth" at sea, has a diving depth of 30.5 metres and can easily lift 100,000 tons of heavy objects, which is at the world's leading level.

China's semi-submersible fleet size ranks among the world's best. Moreover, with the rapid development of China's equipment manufacturing industry, super-long, super-large and super-heavy cargoes grow year by year. Meanwhile the massive growth in China's offshore modular transport fleet provides strong support for our offshore oil platform transportation and installation, offshore wind power installations transportation and export, and special goods transportation.

发展之路　50000 吨远洋半潜船　1983 年
DEVELOPMENT WAY　50,000DWT Semi-submersible Ship, Ocean-going　1983
主尺度 $L \times B \times D$（m×m×m）：215×34×12.7

泰安口　17550 吨远洋半潜船　2002 年
我国第一艘自主设计建造的大型多功能半潜船
TAI AN KOU　17,550DWT Semi-submersible Ship, Ocean-going　2002
First large multi-purpose semi-submersible ship designed and built by China
主尺度 $L \times B \times D$（m×m×m）：156×36.2×10

振华 28　47000 吨远洋半潜船　2009 年
ZHEN HUA 28　47,000DWT Semi-submersible Ship, Ocean-going　2009
主尺度 $L \times B \times D$（m×m×m）：232×42×13.5

希望之路　20000 吨远洋半潜船　2010 年
WISH WAY　20,000DWT Semi-submersible Ship, Ocean-going　2010
主尺度 $L×B×D$ (m×m×m)：156×36×10

振华 29　51500 吨远洋半潜船　2010 年改建
ZHEN HUA 29　51,500DWT Semi-submersible Ship, Ocean-going Converted in 2010
主尺度 $L×B×D$ (m×m×m)：245.4×42×13.5

祥云口　48000 吨远洋半潜船　2011 年
XIANG YUN KOU　48,000DWT Semi-submersible Ship, Ocean-going　2011
主尺度 $L×B×D$ (m×m×m)：216.7×43×13

华海龙　30000吨远洋半潜船　2012年
HUA HAI LONG　30,000DWT Semi-submersible Ship, Ocean-going　2012
主尺度　$L×B×D$（m×m×m）：181.9×43.6×11

致远口　38000吨远洋半潜船　2012年
ZHI YUAN KOU　38,000DWT Semi-submersible Ship, Ocean-going　2012
主尺度　$L×B×D$（m×m×m）：195.2×41.5×12

海洋石油 278　52800 吨远洋半潜船　2012 年
HAI YANG SHI YOU 278　52,800DWT Semi-submersible Ship, Ocean-going　2012
主尺度　$L \times B \times D$（m×m×m）：221.6×42×13.3

振华 7　48000 吨远洋半潜船　2015 年改建
ZHEN HUA 7　48,000DWT Semi-submersible Ship, Ocean-going Converted in 2015
主尺度　$L \times B \times D$（m×m×m）：244.5×42×13.5

华洋龙　52000 吨远洋半潜船　2015 年
HUA YANG LONG　52,000DWT Semi-submersible Ship, Ocean-going　2015
主尺度　$L \times B \times D$（m×m×m）：228.1×43×13.5

新光华 98000 吨远洋半潜船 2016 年
我国设计建造的大型半潜船
主尺度 $L×B×D$ (m×m×m)：255×68×14.5

XIN GUANG HUA　98,000DWT Semi-submersible Ship, Ocean-going　2016
Large semi-submersible ship designed and built by China

振华 34 49800 吨远洋半潜船 2017 年
ZHEN HUA 34　49,800DWT Semi-submersible Ship, Ocean-going　2017
主尺度 $L×B×D$ (m×m×m)：244.5×42×13.5

创新之路　65000 吨远洋半潜船　2017 年改建
INNOVATION WAY　65,000DWT Semi-submersible Ship, Ocean-going Converted in 2017
主尺度 $L×B×D$（m×m×m）：248.4×48.8×13.5

华兴龙　26000 吨远洋半潜救助船　2018 年
HUA XING LONG　26,000DWT Semi-submersible Ship, Ocean-going 2018
主尺度 $L×B×D$（m×m×m）：166.6×39.8×10.9

泛洲 10　62000 吨远洋半潜船　2019 年
FAN ZHOU 10　62,000DWT Semi-submersible Ship, Ocean-going 2019
主尺度 $L×B×D$（m×m×m）：239.6×48×13.5

振华 4　17000 吨远洋甲板货船 1998 年改建
ZHEN HUA 4　17,000DWT Deck Cargo Ship, Ocean-going Converted in 1998
主尺度 $L \times B \times D$ (m×m×m)：219×32.3×12.3

远鉴　6500 吨远洋甲板货船 2006 年
YUAN JIAN　6,500DWT Deck Cargo Ship, Ocean-going　2006
主尺度 $L \times B \times D$ (m×m×m)：130×23×6.8

远景　13000 吨远洋甲板货船 2009 年
YUAN JING　13,000DWT Deck Cargo Ship, Ocean-going　2009
主尺度 $L \times B \times D$ (m×m×m)：142.8×32.2×8

恒通鑫运　9900 吨沿海甲板货船 2011 年
HENG TONG XIN YUN　9,900DWT Deck Cargo Ship, Coastal　2011
主尺度 $L \times B \times D$ (m×m×m)：118.9×29×6.5

德渤　11400 吨远洋甲板货船 2012 年
DE BO　11,400DWT Deck Cargo Ship, Ocean-going　2012
主尺度 $L×B×D$（m×m×m）：128.4×33×7.8

德渤 2　20000 吨远洋甲板货船 2016 年
DE BO 2　20,000DWT Deck Cargo Ship, Ocean-going　2016
主尺度 $L×B×D$（m×m×m）：159.6×38.8×10.9

振华 35　52000 吨远洋甲板货船 2019 年
ZHEN HUA 35　52,000DWT Deck Cargo Ship, Ocean-going　2019
主尺度 $L×B×D$（m×m×m）：244×42×13.5

第八节 非机动货船
SECTION 8　NON-SELF-PROPELLED CARGO SHIPS

南天顺　2700吨甲板驳　1983年
参与"南澳一号"打捞工程项目
主尺度 L×B×D（m×m×m）：61.5×21.8×5

NAN TIAN SHUN　2,700DWT Deck Barge　1983
Involved in the *NAN AO YI HAO* salvage work

航工半潜驳2号　4400吨半潜驳　1989年
HANG GONG BAN QIAN BO 2 HAO　4,400DWT Semi-submersible Barge　1989
主尺度 L×B×D（m×m×m）：53.8×35×4.8

重任1500 13000 吨半潜驳 1994 年
ZHONG REN 1500   13,000DWT Semi-submersible Barge 1994
主尺度 $L×B×D$（m×m×m）：110×32×7.5

重任 3 50000 吨大型半潜驳 2002 年改建
当年我国先进的半潜驳
主尺度 $L×B×D$（m×m×m）：196×46×12.7

ZHONG REN 3   50,000DWT Large Semi-submersible Barge Converted in 2002
The then advanced semi-submersible barge in China

半潜驳 9 号　4000 吨半潜驳　2006 年
BAN QIAN BO 9 HAO　4,000DWT Semi-submersible Barge　2006
主尺度　$L×B×D$（m×m×m）：58×34×4.5

海港特 001　11000 吨干货驳　2006 年
HAI GANG TE 001　11,000DWT Dry Cargo Barge　2006
主尺度　$L×B×D$（m×m×m）：118×28×7.8

德浮 2 号　25000 吨半潜驳　2008 年
DE FU ER HAO　25,000DWT Semi-submersible Barge　2008
主尺度　$L×B×D$（m×m×m）：111×67×8

招商重工1号　33000吨半潜驳　2009年
ZHAO SHANG ZHONG GONG 1 HAO　33,000DWT Semi-submersible Barge　2009
主尺度 $L×B×D$ (m×m×m)：140×56×8.8

德浮15001　15000吨甲板驳　2011年
DE FU 15001　15,000DWT Deck Barge　2011
主尺度 $L×B×D$ (m×m×m)：125×35×7.5

铁建潜 01 32000 吨半潜驳 2015 年
TIE JIAN QIAN 01 32,000DWT Semi-submersible Barge 2015
主尺度 $L×B×D$（m×m×m）：82.8×40×6

招商重工 3 50000 吨大型半潜驳 2015 年
ZHAO SHANG ZHONG GONG 3 50,000DWT Large Semi-submersible Barge 2015
主尺度 $L×B×D$（m）：152.5×60×11.5

汉拿山 20000 吨半潜驳 2016 年
HAN NA SHAN 20,000DWT Semi-submersible Barge 2016
主尺度 $L×B×D$（m×m×m）：189.6×47×6.8

航工半潜驳 3 号 9000 吨半潜驳 2018 年
HANG GONG BAN QIAN BO 3 HAO 9,000DWT Semi-submersible Barge 2018
主尺度 $L×B×D$（m×m×m）：76.8×42×6

第二章　海洋客船

客船是指载运乘客超过12人的船舶（乘客不包括船舶船员和船上服务人员），通常在指定港口之间定期航班营运。根据用途不同，客船主要包括客船、客滚船、高速客船。

自20世纪60年代中期开始至80年代末，海上客运是交通运输的重要组成部分。当时我国设计建造了一批优秀的沿海客货船，如：长字号系列沿海客货船，主要在上海、大连、青岛、厦门、广州航线营运；新字号系列沿海客货船，主要在上海至宁波、温州和福州航线运营。这些客货船的运营，对有效缓解当时沿海水上客运紧张局面发挥了关键作用。进入20世纪90年代，我国民航、高速公路和高速铁路快速发展，海上客运逐步退出长途客运市场。取而代之的是水上旅游观光产业的快速发展，但是陆岛之间的客运运输仍然是不可缺少的。近年来，海上邮轮旅游成为一种中高端的旅游方式，以休闲旅游为目的的近海游览观光客船和远洋航行的大型豪华邮轮正在成为当今以及未来国家产业发展的方向。我国国际邮轮尚处在起步阶段，随着需求的不断增长，在引进豪华邮轮的同时，也开始建造大型豪华邮轮。

客滚船主要用于海峡和岛屿之间，成为水陆联运网络的重要组成部分。我国沿海客滚船主要经营航线包括烟台到大连、琼州海峡、舟山群岛等。客滚船中的火车轮渡使列车跨越海峡成为现实，粤海铁路的开通，结束了海南岛与大陆之间无法通行火车的历史。

高速客船在20世纪80年代末兴起，连接内河和出海口城市，一度十分繁荣。但随着高速公路网的建成，高速客船到21世纪逐渐萎缩，但目前仍作为珠江口和长江口、港澳间重要的交通工具。

客船安全性至关重要。大型客船上层建筑发达，受风面积大，重心高，稳性和消防安全是重中之重。"泰坦尼克号"海难催生了国际海事组织（IMO）的海上人命安全公约（SOLAS）的诞生。21世纪以来，随着大型客船的发展和多起客船海难事故的发生，国际海事组织（IMO）基于"船舶本身是最好的救生艇"的理念，在SOLAS公约中引入了安全返港（SRtP）的要求。即在火灾或进水的事故界限内可以依靠自身动力，返回最近的港口，且船上安全区域能够满足乘客和船员的基本生活，提高船舶的生存能力。基于此，客船的稳性、消防、救生、抗沉性和撤离系统等安全指标得到了大幅提高，客船安全水准提升到新的台阶。

CHAPTER II   MARINE PASSENGER SHIPS

Passenger ships are vessels carrying more than 12 passengers, excluding the ship's crew and service personnel on board, usually operating in regular trips between designated ports. According to different purposes, they mainly include passenger ships, Ro-Ro passenger ships, high-speed passenger ships.

From the mid-1960s to the end of 1980s, sea passenger transportation was an important part of transportation, and at that time, China designed and built a number of high class coastal passenger and cargo ships, such as the series of coastal passenger and cargo ships with names containing "CHANG", mainly operating in Shanghai, Dalian, Qingdao, Xiamen and Guangzhou routes as well as the series of coastal passenger and cargo ships with names containing "XIN", mainly operating in the route from Shanghai to Ningbo, Wenzhou and Fuzhou. The operation of these passenger and cargo ships played a key role in effectively relieving the tense situation of coastal water passenger transportation at that time. In the 1990s, with China's rapid development of aviation, highways and high-speed railway, sea passenger transportation diminished from the long-distance passenger transportation market. In its place is the rapid development of water tourism industry, while passenger ships have evolved to focus more on the critical role of transporting people between the mainland and islands. In recent years, sea cruise tourism has grown and the offshore excursion and sightseeing passenger ships and large cruise ships for leisure tourism purposes are becoming big industries. China's international cruise is still in its infancy, and with the growing demand, China has also started to import and build large cruise ships.

Ro-Ro passenger ships are mainly used between straits and islands as an important part of the water to land intermodal transport network. The main routes operated by China's coastal Ro-Ro passenger ships include Yantai to Dalian, Qiongzhou Strait, Zhoushan Islands, etc. The train ferry makes it possible for trains to cross the strait. The opening of the Guangdong-Hainan Railway saw the first train connection between Hainan and the mainland.

High-speed passenger ships emerged in the late 1980s, connecting inland waterways and sea port cities, and initially flourished. However, with the completion of the highway network, high-speed passenger ships have been gradually shrinking in the last two decades, even though they remain an important means of transport between the estuaries of the Pearl River and the Yangtze River, and between Hong Kong and Macao.

Safety is essential for passenger ships. Stability and fire safety are of paramount importance for large passenger ships with developed superstructure, large wind area, and high center of gravity. The *TITANIC* disaster resulted in the formulation of the IMO's *International Convention* for the *Safety of Life at Sea* (SOLAS). In the 21st century, with the development of large passenger ships and following a number of passenger ship disasters, the IMO introduced the requirement of Safe Return to Port (SRtP) in SOLAS based on the concept that *the ship itself is the best lifeboat*. Essentially this means, within the limits of fire or water inflow accidents, the ship can rely on its own power to return to the nearest port, and the safe area on board can provide basic living services for passengers and crew, and improve the survivability of ships. Based on this, the safety indexes of passenger ships such as stability, firefighting, life-saving, anti-sinking and evacuation system have been greatly improved.

第一节 客船

客船具有多层甲板的上层建筑，用于布置旅客舱室；设有较完善的餐厅卫生娱乐设施；具有较好的稳性和抗沉性，可以保证多舱破损下的船舶安全；船舶消防分隔为不同的区域，限制火灾的蔓延；配备足够的救生设备，足以承载所有乘客和船员安全撤离；配有减摇、避震、隔声系统，提升船上舒适性。客货船是以载客为主，载货为辅，船上设有货舱，可装载旅客携带的货物，其共同特点为吃水浅，载客多，操纵灵便，航速快，功率储备较大。旅游观光船舶设计追求美观舒适，受到人们的欢迎，船上还设有娱乐设施。

邮轮设有餐饮、娱乐、游艺、影剧院、休闲、健身、美容、购物等种种设施，被誉为"海上移动度假村"，目前世界最大邮轮已超过20万总吨。由于邮轮甲板层数多、上层建筑跨度长且大面积使用玻璃材料和其他轻质材料，以及娱乐处所空间大等结构的特殊性，为满足国际公约的严格要求，在邮轮设计中常采用基于定量风险分析的、以满足公约规则为目标的等效设计替代方法。2014年我国购进了第一艘自主经营管理的远洋豪华邮轮，拉开了我国邮轮产业发展的新篇章。

2019年我国开始建造第一艘远洋豪华邮轮，开启了我国建造大型邮轮的新时代。

SECTION 1   PASSENGER SHIP

Passenger ships have a multi-deck superstructure for arranging passenger cabins and a complete set of dining rooms, guest rooms and bathrooms. The ship has good stability and subdivision, which can ensure the safety of the ship under the damage of multiple cabins. The ship is separated into different areas to limit the spread of fire; and is equipped with enough life-saving equipment to carry passengers and crew members for safe evacuation; it is further equipped with vibration reduction, shock absorption and sound insulation systems to enhance the comfort on board. Passenger and cargo ships, for carrying passengers mainly and cargo partly, are equipped with cargo compartments to carry passenger luggage, and their common features are shallow draft, many passengers, convenient maneuvering, fast speed and large power reserve. The design of sightseeing ships focuses on comfortable interior design with a wide range of entertainment facilities on board.

Known as "mobile resorts at sea", cruise ships are equipped with various facilities such as catering, entertainment, amusement, theater, leisure, fitness, cosmetic, shopping, etc. The world's largest cruise ship at present has surpassed 200,000 GT. Due to the structural requirements of cruise ships such as multiple decks, long superstructure spans and the extensive use of glass materials and other lightweight materials, as well as large spaces for entertainment, an alternative method of equivalent design based on quantitative risk analysis is often used. This is in order to meet the stringent requirements of international convention. In 2014, China purchased the first ocean-going cruise ship for independent operation and management, international convention which opened a new chapter in the development of China's cruise industry.

In 2019, China began a new era by starting to build the first ocean-going cruise ship.

中华泰山 930客位远洋豪华邮轮 2014年购进
我国第一艘自主经营管理的远洋豪华邮轮
主尺度 $L×B×D$ (m×m×m)：180.5×25.5×12.7

CHINESE TAISHAN 930P Cruise Ship, Ocean-going Purchased in 2014
China's first self-operated and managed ocean-going cruise ship

鼓浪屿 1880客位远洋豪华邮轮 2016年购进
我国自主经营管理的远洋豪华邮轮
主尺度 $L×B×D$ (m×m×m)：260.7×32.2×14.3

PIANO LAND 1,880P Cruise Ship, Ocean-going Purchased in 2016
China's self-operated and managed ocean-going cruise ship

假日　394 客位沿海普通客船　1986 年
JIA RI　394P General Passenger Ship, Coastal 1986
主尺度 $L×B×D$ (m×m×m)：120×18.8×7.1

椰香公主　317 客位琼州海峡客货船　1986 年
YE XIANG GONG ZHU　317P Passenger-cargo Ship, Qiongzhou Strait 1986
主尺度 $L×B×D$ (m×m×m)：140×20.4×8

东极　280 客位沿海普通客船　1988 年
DONG JI　280P General Passenger Ship, Coastal 1988
主尺度 $L×B×D$ (m×m×m)：42×7.5×3.5

华东明珠 VI　1000 客位远洋客货船　1988 年
HUADONG PEARL VI　1,000P Passenger-cargo Ship, Ocean-going 1988
主尺度 $L×B×D$ (m×m×m)：174.5×26.8×14.3

燕京 442客位远洋客船 1989年
YAN JING 442P Passenger Ship, Ocean-going 1989
主尺度 $L \times B \times D$ (m×m×m)：135×20.6×13.7

新金桥Ⅱ 630客位近海客船 1990年
大陆直航台湾客船的代表船
主尺度 $L \times B \times D$ (m×m×m)：186.5×24.8×14.7

NEW GOLDEN BRIDGE II 630P Passenger Ship, Greater Coastal 1990
Representative cross-Taiwan Strait ship

普陀山　728 客位沿海客船　1990 年
PU TUO SHAN　728P Passenger Ship, Coastal　1990
主尺度　$L×B×D$（m×m×m）：78×14×4.7

东远 3　500 客位近海客船　1991 年
DONG YUAN 3　500P Passenger Ship, Greater Coastal　1991
主尺度　$L×B×D$（m×m×m）：71.7×13×4.6

海虹一号　588 客位琼州海峡客船 1994 年
HAI HONG YI HAO　588P Passenger Ship, Qiongzhou Strait 1994
主尺度 $L \times B \times D$ (m×m×m)：51×13.4×4

新郁金香　376 客位中韩航线客箱船 1995 年
XIN YU JIN XIANG　376P Passenger-container Ship, China-South Korea Service 1995
主尺度 $L \times B \times D$ (m×m×m)：148.7×22.7×10.2

紫玉兰　392 客位远洋客箱船　1995 年
ZI YU LAN　392P Passenger-container Ship, Ocean-going　1995
主尺度 $L \times B \times D$ (m×m×m)：150.1×24×13.2

玖龙王子　98 客位沿海客船　2004 年
JIU LONG WANG ZI　98P Passenger Ship, Coastal　2004
主尺度 $L \times B \times D$ (m×m×m)：41.8×6.6×3

琼沙 3 号　200 客位远洋客货船　2007 年
QIONG SHA 3 HAO　200P Passenger-cargo Ship, Ocean-going　2007
主尺度 $L \times B \times D$ (m×m×m)：84×13.8×7.5

舟山群岛东极 498 客位沿海客货船 2009 年
ZHOU SHAN QUN DAO DONG JI 498P Passenger-cargo Ship, Coastal 2009
主尺度 $L×B×D$ (m×m×m)：49.9×8.8×3.5

东方华晨 2 82 客位远洋客船 2015 年
DONG FANG HUA CHEN 2 82P Passenger Ship, Ocean-going 2015
主尺度 $L×B×D$ (m×m×m)：64.8×13×6

嵊翔9　498客位沿海客船　2015年
SHENG XIANG 9　498P Passenger Ship, Coastal　2015
主尺度　$L×B×D$ (m×m×m)：58.9×9×3.7

深港游轮1　149客位沿海客船　2016年
SHEN GANG YOU LUN 1　149P Passenger Ship, Coastal　2016
主尺度　$L×B×D$ (m×m×m)：35.2×9.8×3.4

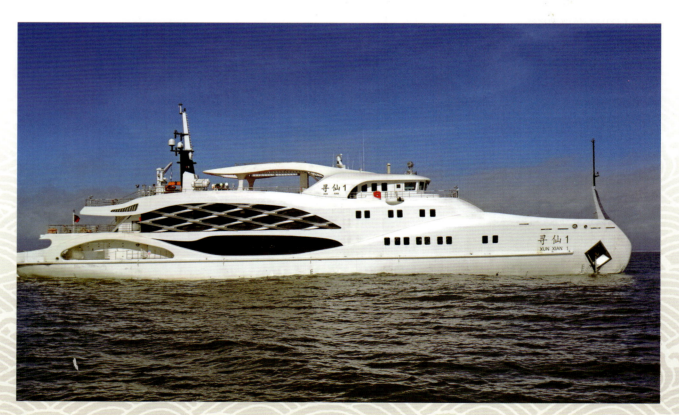

寻仙1　192客位沿海客船　2017年
XUN XIAN 1　192P Passenger Ship, Coastal　2017
主尺度　$L×B×D$ (m)：66.9×12×4.5

海蓝鲸 932客位远洋客箱船 2017年
我国自主设计建造的新型客箱船
主尺度 $L×B×D$（m×m×m）：182.7×25.2×12.1

OCEAN BLUE WHALE 932P Passenger-container Ship, Ocean-going 2017
New type of passenger-container ship designed and built by China

天成2号 196客位沿海客船 2019年
TIAN CHENG 2 HAO 196P Passenger Ship, Coastal 2019
主尺度 $L×B×D$（m×m×m）：41.2×9.8×3.2

新天恒　82客位沿海客渡船　1996年
XIN TIAN HENG　82P Passenger Ferry, Coastal　1996
主尺度　$L \times B \times D$ (m×m×m)：33.5×6.3×2.5

石南6　130客位沿海客渡船　2001年
SHI NAN 6　130P Passenger Ferry, Coastal　2001
主尺度　$L \times B \times D$ (m×m×m)：34.5×6.4×2.8

威游108　200客位特定航线客渡船　2001年
WEI YOU 108　200P Passenger Ferry, Specific Route Service　2001
主尺度　$L \times B \times D$ (m×m×m)：35.3×6.6×2.8

建民2　300客位沿海客渡船　2012年
JIAN MIN 2　300P Passenger Ferry, Coastal　2012
主尺度　$L \times B \times D$ (m×m×m)：48.8×9.5×2.8

海神6号 450客位沿海客渡船 2014年
HAI SHEN 6 HAO 450P Passenger Ferry, Coastal 2014
主尺度 $L \times B \times D$ (m×m×m)：36.2×8.4×3.2

舟桥3 498客位沿海客渡船 2016年
ZHOU QIAO 3 498P Passenger Ferry, Coastal 2016
主尺度 $L \times B \times D$ (m×m×m)：82.1×15.5×5.5

皖神舟 89 250 客位沿海车客渡船 2017 年
WAN SHEN ZHOU 89 250P Vehicle-passenger Ferry, Coastal 2017
主尺度 $L×B×D$ (m×m×m)：76×16×3.5

海顺安 9 478 客位沿海客渡船 2019 年
HAI SHUN AN 9 478P Passenger Ferry, Coastal 2019
主尺度 $L×B×D$ (m×m×m)：31.1×9×2.8

神游 94客位沿海旅游客船 1994年
SHEN YOU 94P Tourist Ship, Coastal 1994
主尺度 $L×B×D$ (m×m×m)：31.8×6.3×2.8

海鸥7号 99客位沿海旅游客船 1999年
HAI OU 7 HAO 99P Tourist Ship, Coastal 1999
主尺度 $L×B×D$ (m×m×m)：29.8×5×2.6

海神17 113客位沿海旅游客船 2006年
HAI SHEN 17 113P Tourist Ship, Coastal 2006
主尺度 $L×B×D$ (m×m×m)：29.3×5.6×2.4

海娃 2　99 客位沿海旅游客船　2009 年
HAI WA 2　99P Tourist Ship, Coastal 2009
主尺度　$L×B×D$（m×m×m）：25×5.3×1.9

不肯去观音　98 客位沿海仿古旅游客船　2010 年
BU KEN QU GUAN YIN　98P Antique Tourist Ship, Coastal 2010
主尺度　$L×B×D$（m×m×m）：43.8×10.5×3.8

侨乡号　478 客位沿海旅游客船　2013 年
QIAO XIANG HAO　478P Tourist Ship, Coastal 2013
主尺度　$L×B×D$（m×m×m）：95.8×15.8×5.4

永乐 01 310 客位沿海旅游客船 2014 年
YONG LE 01 310P Tourist Ship, Coastal 2014
主尺度 $L \times B \times D$ (m×m×m)：50×10.6×4

北游 15 636 客位沿海旅游客船 2015 年
BEI YOU 15 636P Tourist Ship, Coastal 2015
主尺度 $L \times B \times D$ (m×m×m)：78.4×14.2×5.2

正丰之星　11客位交通船　1989年
ZHENG FENG ZHI XING　11P Crew Boat 1989
主尺度 $L×B×D$ （m×m×m）：28.8×5.6×2.4

新世纪一号　49客位小水线面近海双体油田交通船　2004年
XIN SHI JI NO.1　49P Small Waterplane Area Catamaran for Oilfield Transportation, Greater Coastal 2004
主尺度 $L×B×D$ （m×m×m）：39.8×15×6.6

江南长兴号　83客位沿海交通船　2008年
JIANG NAN CHANG XING HAO　83P Crew Boat, Coastal 2008
主尺度 $L×B×D$ （m×m×m）：33×5.7×2.9

第二节 客滚船

客滚船是指载客超过12人，同时也装载各种客运和货运车辆或其他轮式托盘的运输船舶，多用于中近程海运，作为定点航班，在指定港口之间往返运输。由于客滚船各甲板间设有斜坡道或升降平台互相连通，车辆通过船上的首门、尾门或舷门的跳板与岸搭接开进开出，装卸效率很高，是"海上高速路"不可或缺的重要船型。我国渤海湾和琼州海峡航线运营的客滚船已经逐步更新为更安全、舒适的新型客滚船。目前我国最大的渤海湾客滚船，按照无限航区国际航行标准并参照了邮轮设计理念设计和建造，乘客定额达到2000余人，可载大小车辆300余辆，而且在装载超长、超高、超宽的特种车辆方面具有明显优势。

SECTION 2　RO-RO PASSENGER SHIP

Ro-Ro passenger ships are capable of carrying more than 12 passengers, and are able to accommodate various passenger vehicles, freight vehicles or wheeled pallets, mostly used for medium- and short-haul sea transportation on fixed schedules to and from designated ports. As ramps or lifting platforms are arranged between the decks of the Ro-Ro passenger ship to connect each other, the vehicles roll onto and off the ship through the connection between the shore and the springboard of the bow door, tailgate or gangway on the ship. This makes the loading and unloading of the Ro-Ro passenger ship very efficient. It is an indispensable ship type comprising the "offshore expressway". Ro-Ro passenger ships operating on China's Bohai Bay and Qiongzhou Strait routes have been gradually updated to new types of safer and more comfortable Ro-Ro passenger ships. At present, China's largest Bohai Bay Ro-Ro passenger ship, designed and built in accordance with the international navigation standards for unlimited navigation area and with reference to the design concept of cruise ships, has a carrying capacity of more than 2,000 passengers and more than 300 vehicles of various sizes. It has obvious advantages in loading extra-long, extra-high and extra-wide special vehicles.

天鹅　1500客位渤海湾滚装客船　1985年购进
TIAN E　1,500P Ro-Ro Passenger Ship, Bohai Bay Purchased in 1985
主尺度　$L \times B \times D$ (m×m×m)：126.1×19.3×7.2

天鹏　1050 客位渤海湾滚装客船　1987 年购进
TIAN PENG　1,050P Ro-Ro Passenger Ship, Bohai Bay　Purchased in 1987
主尺度 $L \times B \times D$ (m×m×m)：110.2×17.6×6.7

紫荆一号　320 米/300 客位琼州海峡客滚船　1991 年
ZI JING YI HAO　320Lane meter (Lm)/300P Ro-Ro Passenger Ship, Qiongzhou Strait　1991
主尺度 $L \times B \times D$ (m×m×m)：76.8×15×4.5

苏州号　316 客位中日航线客滚船　1992 年购进
SU ZHOU HAO　316P Ro-Ro Passenger Ship, China-Japan Service　Purchased in 1992
主尺度 $L \times B \times D$ (m×m×m)：154.7×22×9.9

新鉴真 345 客位远洋客滚船 1994 年购进
中日航线，接替"鉴真"轮
主尺度 $L×B×D$ (m×m×m)：156.7×23×8.5

XIN JIAN ZHEN 345P Ro-Ro Passenger Ship, Ocean-going Purchased in 1994
Replacing the ship *JIAN ZHEN* on China-Japan route

紫荆八号 260 米/475 客位沿海客滚船 1994 年
ZI JING BA HAO 260Lm/475P Ro-Ro Passenger Ship, Coastal 1994
主尺度 $L×B×D$ (m×m×m)：85.1×15.4×5.5

棒棰岛 835米/1200客位渤海湾客滚船 1995年
BANG CHUI DAO 835Lm/1200P Ro-Ro Passenger Ship, Bohai Bay 1995
主尺度 $L \times B \times D$ (m×m×m)：134.8×23.4×8.6

大华 363客位渤海湾客滚船 1999年购进
DA HUA 363P Ro-Ro Passenger Ship, Bohai Bay Purchased in 1999
主尺度 $L \times B \times D$ (m×m×m)：129.9×20×5.8

宝华 720客位渤海湾客滚船 1999年购进
BAO HUA 720P Ro-Ro Passenger Ship, Bohai Bay Purchased in 1999
主尺度 $L \times B \times D$ (m×m×m)：141.8×20×6.4

银河王子 600米/768客位渤海湾客滚船 1999年购进
YIN HE WANG ZI 600Lm/768P Ro-Ro Passenger Ship, Bohai Bay Purchased in 1999
主尺度 $L×B×D$ (m×m×m)：142.5×23.5×7.3

信海6号 244米/380客位琼州海峡客滚船 2002年改建
XIN HAI 6 HAO 244Lm/380P Ro-Ro Passenger Ship, Qiongzhou Strait Converted in 2002
主尺度 $L×B×D$ (m×m×m)：69.8×14.8×4

信海12号 540米/790客位琼州海峡客滚船 2004年
XIN HAI 12 HAO 540Lm/790P Ro-Ro Passenger Ship, Qiongzhou Strait 2004
主尺度 $L×B×D$ (m×m×m)：98×19.8×6.5

金紫荆 392米/650客位沿海客滚船 2004年
JIN ZI JING 392Lm/650P Ro-Ro Passenger Ship, Coastal 2004
主尺度 $L×B×D$ (m×m×m)：92.8×19×5.9

普陀岛　835米/1428客位渤海湾客滚船　2005年
我国自主设计建造的先进客滚船
主尺度　$L×B×D$（m×m×m）：137.3×23.4×8.6

PU TUO DAO　835Lm/1,428P Ro-Ro Passenger Ship, Bohai Bay　2005
Advanced Ro-Ro passenger ship designed and built by China

生生1　615米/1026客位近海客滚船　2006年
SHENG SHENG 1　615Lm/1,026P Ro-Ro Passenger Ship, Greater Coastal　2006
主尺度　$L×B×D$（m×m×m）：120×20.4×6.8

渤海金珠 1800 米 /1128 客位渤海湾客滚船 2006 年
我国自主设计建造的先进客滚船
主尺度 $L×B×D$ (m×m×m)：161.2×24.8×7.9

BO HAI JIN ZHU 1,800Lm/1,128P Ro-Ro Passenger Ship, Bohai Bay 2006
Advanced Ro-Ro passenger ship designed and built by China

岱山 9 392 客位沿海客滚船 2009 年
DAI SHAN 9 392P Ro-Ro Passenger Ship, Coastal 2009
主尺度 $L×B×D$ (m×m×m)：57×14.5×4.5

中远之星　683客位沿海客滚船 2009年购进
COSCO STAR　683P Ro-Ro Passenger Ship, Coastal Purchased in 2009
主尺度 $L×B×D$ (m×m×m)：186×25.5×9.7

银紫荆　510米/900客位沿海客滚船 2010年
YIN ZI JING　510Lm/900P Ro-Ro Passenger Ship, Coastal 2010
主尺度 $L×B×D$ (m×m×m)：106×20.2×6

渤海宝珠　1993米/1571客位渤海湾客滚船 2010年
BO HAI BAO ZHU　1,993Lm/1,571P Ro-Ro Passenger Ship, Bohai Bay 2010
主尺度 $L×B×D$ (m×m×m)：164×25×7.9

海峡号 760 客位平潭至台中双体高速客滚船 2011 年购进
HAI XIA HAO 760P High-speed Ro-Ro Passenger Catamaran, Pingtan-Taizhong Service Purchased in 2011
主尺度 $L \times B \times D$ (m×m×m)：97.2×26.2×4.6

南海之梦 1288 米/721 客位沿海滚装客船 2011 年
NAN HAI ZHI MENG 1,288Lm/721P Ro-Ro Passenger Ship, Coastal 2011
主尺度 $L \times B \times D$ (m×m×m)：169.5×25.2×7.9

双泰 16　570 米 /499 客位装运危险品的客滚船　2012 年
SHUANG TAI 16　570Lm/499P Ro-Ro Passenger Ship Carrying Dangerous Goods　2012
主尺度 *L*×*B*×*D*（m×m×m）：112×20.5×6.1

长山岛　2000 米 /1400 客位渤海湾客滚船　2012 年
CHANG SHAN DAO　2,000Lm/1,400P Ro-Ro Passenger Ship, Bohai Bay　2012
主尺度 *L*×*B*×*D*（m×m×m）：167.5×25.2×7.9

渤海翠珠　2500 米 /2038 客位渤海湾客滚船　2012 年
BO HAI CUI ZHU　2,500Lm/2,038P Ro-Ro Passenger Ship, Bohai Bay　2012
主尺度 *L*×*B*×*D*（m×m×m）：178.8×28×9

生生 2　1100 米 /2160 客位渤海湾客滚船　2013 年
SHENG SHENG 2　1,100Lm/2,160P Ro-Ro Passenger Ship, Bohai Bay　2013
主尺度 *L*×*B*×*D*（m×m×m）：164×24×7.9

五指山 1650 米 /999 客位琼州海峡客滚船 2013 年
WU ZHI SHAN 1,650Lm/999P Ro-Ro Passenger Ship, Qiongzhou Strait 2013
主尺度 $L \times B \times D$ (m×m×m)：123.9×20.5×6.3

凤凰岭 925 米 /999 客位琼州海峡客滚船 2014 年
FENG HUANG LING 925Lm/999P Ro-Ro Passenger Ship, Qiongzhou Strait 2014
主尺度 $L \times B \times D$ (m×m×m)：127×20.5×6.5

渤海钻珠 2452 米 /1804 客位渤海湾客滚船 2015 年
BO HAI ZUAN ZHU 2,452Lm/1,804P Ro-Ro Passenger Ship, Bohai Bay 2015
主尺度 $L \times B \times D$ (m×m×m)：179.5×28×9

海口九号　654米/986客位沿海客滚船　2015年
HAI KOU JIU HAO　654Lm/986P Ro-Ro Passenger Ship, Coastal　2015
主尺度 $L \times B \times D$ (m×m×m)：128.6×20.3×6.3

日照东方　2506米/420客位沿海客滚船　2015年
RI ZHAO ORIENT　2,506Lm/420P Ro-Ro Passenger Ship, Coastal　2015
主尺度 $L \times B \times D$ (m×m×m)：199×26.6×9.6

和谐云港　1080客位沿海客滚船　2017年
HARMONY YUNGANG　1,080P Ro-Ro Passenger Ship, Coastal　2017
主尺度 $L \times B \times D$ (m×m×m)：196.3×28.6×9

新永安 2160 米 /880 客位远洋客滚船 2018 年
NEW GRAND PEACE 2,160Lm/880P Ro-Ro Passenger Ship, Ocean-going 2018
主尺度 $L \times B \times D$ (m×m×m)：188.9×28.6×9.3

中华复兴 3000 米 /1689 客位渤海湾客滚船 2019 年
ZHONG HUA FU XING 3,000Lm/1,689P Ro-Ro Passenger Ship, Bohai Bay 2019
主尺度 $L \times B \times D$ (m×m×m)：212×28.6×9.2

双泰 37　1136 米 /999 客位沿海客滚船 2019 年
SHUANG TAI 37　1,136Lm/999P Ro-Ro Passenger Ship, Coastal 2019
主尺度 $L×B×D$ (m×m×m)：127.5×20.9×6.5

新香雪兰　700 客位远洋客滚船 2020 年
中韩航线新型客滚船，具有智能船舶标志
主尺度 $L×B×D$ (m×m×m)：189.5×26.5×9.1

XIN XIANG XUE LAN　700P Ro-Ro Passenger Ship, Ocean-going 2020
New type of Ro-Ro passenger ship on the China-South Korea route, with intelligent ship notation

第一篇 海洋运输船舶
PART I MARINE TRANSPORTATION SHIPS

粤海铁1号 1108客位琼州海峡铁路车辆渡船 2002年
我国第一艘跨海铁路车辆渡船
主尺度 $L×B×D$ (m×m×m)：165.4×22.6×9

YUE HAI TIE 1 HAO 1,108P Train/Car Ferry, Qiongzhou Strait 2002
China's first cross-sea train/car ferry

中铁渤海1号 580客位渤海湾铁路车辆渡船 2006年
我国第一艘全电力推进铁路车辆渡船
主尺度 $L×B×D$ (m×m×m)：182.6×24.8×9

ZHONG TIE BO HAI 1 HAO 580P Train/Car Ferry, Bohai Bay 2006
China's first all-electric propulsion train/car ferry

中铁渤海 3 号　716 客位渤海湾铁路车辆渡船　2008 年
ZHONG TIE BO HAI 3 HAO　716P Train/Car Ferry, Bohai Bay　2008
主尺度 $L \times B \times D$（m×m×m）：182×24.8×9

粤海铁 3 号　1398 客位琼州海峡铁路车辆渡船　2011 年
YUE HAI TIE 3 HAO　1,398P Train/Car Ferry, Qiongzhou Strait　2011
主尺度 $L \times B \times D$（m×m×m）：188×23×9.3

第三节　高速客船

高速客船系指最大航速达到 ≥ 3.7 ▽ $^{0.1667}$ 米/秒(▽是指对应的设计水线下的排水体积)或设计静水时速沿海水域 ≥ 25 海里的客船，高速客船要求船体质量轻功率大，多数采用铝合金或者玻璃钢作为船体材料。高速船种类主要有常规高速单体船、高速双体船、气垫船、水翼船和地效翼船等。

气垫船利用气垫的原理，将船体托起，减少了船体与水面的直接接触，使船的航行能适应各种多变的航道情况，如浅水、沼泽和沙滩等。

水翼船在其底部前后各装有一对水翼，水翼产生的升力将船体托出水面，因而能减少水对船的阻力，达到高速航行的目的。

地效翼船是一种介于船舶与飞机之间的航速极快的"飞行器"，它在距离水面 1～6 米的高度低空高速掠海飞行，速度为每小时 120～550 公里，是常规船舶的数倍至数十倍，可谓当今最快船舶。

SECTION 3　HIGH-SPEED PASSENGER SHIP

High-speed passenger ships refer to passenger ships of which the maximum speed reaches $\geq 3.7 \triangledown^{0.1667}$ m/s ($\triangledown$ indicates the drainage volume under the design waterline) or the designed speed is ≥ 25 nautical miles in calm coastal waters. High-speed passenger ships require light weight and high power, and most of them use aluminum alloy or glass fiber reinforced plastic as hull materials. The types of high-speed ships mainly include conventional high-speed monohull, high-speed catamaran, hovercraft, hydrofoil, wing-in ground craft, etc.

The hovercraft uses the principle of an air cushion to lift the hull, which reduces the direct contact between the hull and the water surface, so that the navigation of the boat can adapt to various variable channel conditions, such as shallow water, swamp, beach, etc.

A hydrofoil ship is equipped with a pair of hydrofoils at the front and rear of its bottom, and the lifting force generated by the hydrofoils lifts the hull out of the water, thus reducing the resistance of water to the ship and achieving the purpose of high-speed navigation.

Wing-in ground craft is an extremely fast "aircraft" with a speed between a ship and an aircraft. It flies across the sea at a low altitude of 1-6m above the water surface, and has a speed of 120-550 km/h, which is several or dozens of times that of conventional ships. It is the fastest ship today.

飞鸽 250客位沿海高速单体船 1989年
FEI GE 250P High-speed Monohull Craft, Coastal 1989
主尺度 $L×B×D$ (m×m×m)：28.9×9×3.5

东方春 150客位港澳高速双体船 1991年
DONG FANG CHUN 150P High-speed Catamaran, Hong Kong-Macao Service 1991
主尺度 $L×B×D$ (m×m×m)：23.6×8.7×2.3

海鸥 400 客位渤海湾双体高速客船 1993 年购进
HAI OU 400P High-speed Catamaran, Bohai Bay Purchased in 1993
主尺度 $L\times B\times D$ (m×m×m): 40×10.1×4

飞逸 1 号 303 客位沿海高速单体船 1993 年
FEI YI 1 HAO 303P High-speed Monohull Craft, Coastal 1993
主尺度 $L\times B\times D$ (m×m×m): 40×10.1×4

北游 19 439 客位沿海高速单体船 1994 年
BEI YOU 19 439P High-speed Monohull Craft, Coastal 1994
主尺度 $L\times B\times D$ (m×m×m): 40.1×11.5×3.8

顺德 355 客位高速双体船 1995 年
SHUN DE 355P High-speed Catamaran 1995
主尺度 $L\times B\times D$ (m×m×m): 40.1×11.5×3.8

迅隆壹号 312 客位珠江港澳航线高速单体船 1995 年
XUN LONG YI HAO 312P High-speed Monohull Craft,
Pearl River-Hong Kong-Macao Service 1995
主尺度 $L \times B \times D$ (m×m×m)：35×9.6×3.7

和平之星 422 客位沿海高速双体船 1996 年
HE PING ZHI XING 422P High-speed Catamaran, Coastal 1996
主尺度 $L \times B \times D$ (m×m×m)：49.9×12.4×3.8

南沙叁拾捌号　382 客位沿海高速双体船 1996 年
NANSHA NO.38　382P High-speed Catamaran, Coastal 1996
主尺度　$L×B×D$（m×m×m）：42×12×3.7

海琨　349 客位沿海高速双体船 1997 年
HAI KUN　349P High-speed Catamaran, Coastal 1997
主尺度　$L×B×D$（m×m×m）：40.1×11.5×3.7

北游18　372 客位沿海高速双体船 2002 年
BEI YOU 18　372P High-speed Catamaran, Coastal 2002
主尺度　$L×B×D$（m×m×m）：38.2×10.2×3.5

茂盛 2　286 客位沿海高速单体船　2003 年
MAO SHENG 2　286P High-speed Monohull Craft, Coastal　2003
主尺度 $L \times B \times D$ (m×m×m)：48×6.2×3.3

飞舟 9　130 客位沿海高速单体船　2004 年
FEI ZHOU 9　130P High-speed Monohull Craft, Coastal　2004
主尺度 $L \times B \times D$ (m×m×m)：38×4.4×2.3

恒星　199 客位港澳高速双体船　2007 年
HENG XING　199P High-speed Catamaran, Hong Kong-Macao Service　2007
主尺度 $L \times B \times D$ (m×m×m)：24.4×8.5×3

北游 16 1146 客位沿海高速双体船 2008 年
BEI YOU 16 1,146P High-speed Catamaran, Coastal 2008
主尺度 $L \times B \times D$ (m×m×m)：64.9×16×4.7

THE PLAZA 港澳高速客船 2008 年
THE PLAZA High-speed Passenger Ship,
Hong Kong-Macao Service 2008
主尺度 $L \times B \times D$ (m×m×m)：47.5×11.8×1.6（吃水）

瑞星 196 客位沿海高速双体船 2009 年
RUI XING 196P High-speed Catamaran, Coastal 2009
主尺度 $L \times B \times D$ (m×m×m)：26×8.5×3

顺逸 01 320 客位沿海高速单体船 2009 年
SHUN YI 01 320P High-speed Monohull Craft, Coastal 2009
主尺度 $L \times B \times D$ (m×m×m)：44.9×9.2×3.2

扬帆之星 1 288 客位沿海高速双体船 2011 年
YANG FAN ZHI XING 1 288P High-speed Catamaran, Coastal 2011
主尺度 $L \times B \times D$ (m×m×m)：42×10×3.5

新武夷 303 客位沿海高速单体船 2011 年
XIN WU YI 303P High-speed Monohull Craft, Coastal 2011
主尺度 $L \times B \times D$ (m×m×m)：49.7×9×3.7

寰岛019　94客位沿海高速单体船 2013年
HUAN DAO 019　94P High-speed Monohull Craft, Coastal 2013
主尺度 $L×B×D$ (m×m×m)：26.8×5.2×2

寻仙70　360客位沿海高速单体船 2014年
XUN XIAN 70　360P High-speed Monohull Craft, Coastal 2014
主尺度 $L×B×D$ (m×m×m)：50×10×3.4

金珠湖　270客位珠三角至港澳碳纤维高速双体客船 2016年购进
JIN ZHU HU　270P High-speed Carbon Fiber Catamaran, Pearl River Delta-Hong Kong-Macao Service Purchased in 2016
主尺度 $L×B×D$ (m×m×m)：40.8×10.8×3.7

新五缘　322客位近海高速双体船 2016年
XIN WU YUAN　322P High-speed Catamaran, Greater Coastal 2016
主尺度 $L×B×D$ (m×m×m)：42×10×3

新海威　288客位近海高速双体船 2017年
XIN HAI WEI　288P High-speed Catamaran, Greater Coastal 2017
主尺度 $L×B×D$ (m×m×m)：42.1×10.6×3.7

海棠之星 1 号　298 客位沿海高速双体船　2017 年
HAI TANG ZHI XING 1 HAO　298P High-speed Catamaran, Coastal　2017
主尺度 $L×B×D$ (m×m×m): 40.5×10×3.4

机场 19　280 客位近海高速双体船　2019 年
JI CHANG 19　280P High-speed Catamaran, Greater Coastal　2019
主尺度 $L×B×D$ (m×m×m): 42.4×10.5×3.5

铭珠湖　300 客位近海高速双体船　2019 年
MING ZHU HU　300P High-speed Catamaran, Greater Coastal　2019
主尺度 $L×B×D$ (m×m×m): 42.8×10.8×3.7

新海天 356 客位沿海高速双体船 2019 年
XIN HAI TIAN 356P High-speed Catamaran, Coastal 2019
主尺度 $L×B×D$ (m×m×m): 40.2×11.3×3.5

西岛 288 399 客位沿海高速双体船 2019 年
XI DAO 288 399P High-speed Catamaran, Coastal 2019
主尺度 $L×B×D$ (m×m×m): 42.5×10.3×3.4

西岛 088 399 客位沿海高速双体船 2019 年
XI DAO 088 399P High-speed Catamaran, Coastal 2019
主尺度 $L×B×D$ (m×m×m): 42.5×10.3×3.4

北游 26 1200 客位大型铝合金高速客船 2020 年
BEI YOU 26 1,200P High-speed Aluminum Alloy Passenger Ship 2020
主尺度 $L×B×D$ (m×m×m): 71.26×17×5.7

鸿翔 258 客位沿海双体气垫船 1988 年
当年大型的全钢质船体气垫船
主尺度 $L×B×D$ (m×m×m)：40×8×3.3

HONG XIANG 258P Hovercraft Catamaran, Coastal 1988
The then large-size all-steel hull hovercraft

南星 300 客位港澳水翼高速船 1996 年
NAN XING 300P High-speed Hydrofoil, Hong Kong-Macao Service 1996
主尺度 $L×B×D$ (m×m×m)：30.1×9.2×2.6

翔州 1　地效翼船　2014 年
我国第一艘商用地效翼船
主尺度 $L \times B \times D$ (m×m×m)：12.7×11×4

XIANG ZHOU 1　Wing-in Ground Craft　2014
China's first commercial wing-in ground craft

三沙气垫船 01　28 客位近海位气垫船　2017 年
SAN SHA QI DIAN CHUAN 01　28P Hovercraft, Greater Coastal　2017
主尺度 $L \times B \times D$ (m×m×m)：16.2×3.2×0.8

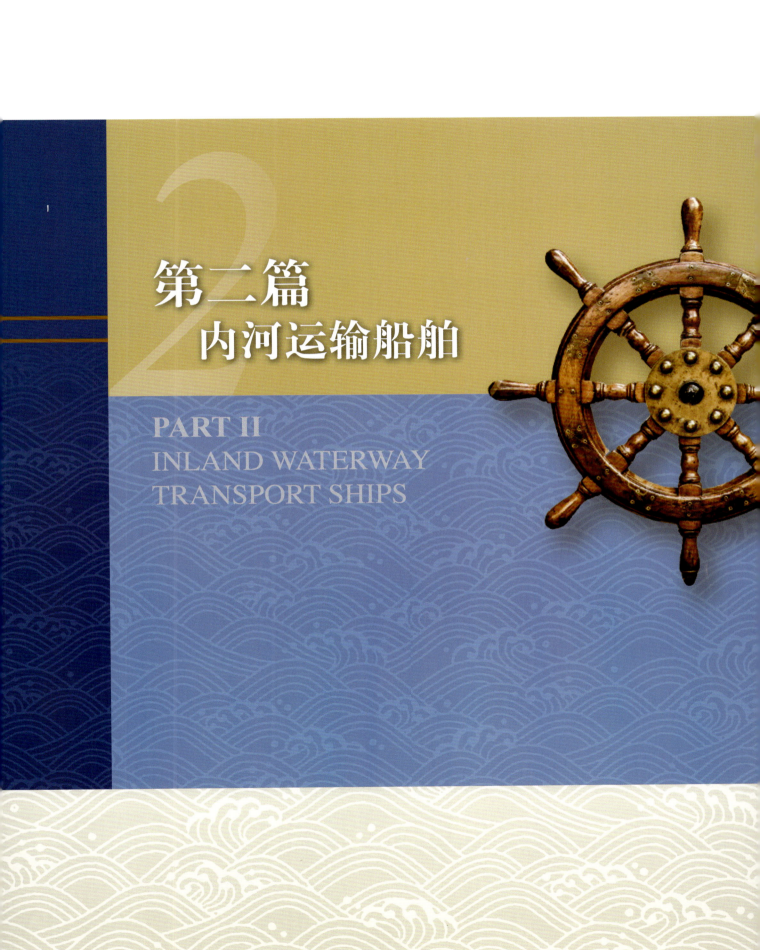

第二篇
内河运输船舶

PART II
INLAND WATERWAY TRANSPORT SHIPS

第一章　内河货船

我国内河货船主要有：干散货船（包括散货船、杂货船、散装水泥船、自卸砂船等）、集装箱船、集散两用多用途船、液货船（包括油船、化学品船、液化气体船等）、滚装货船、推/拖船与驳船组成的船队和江海直达船等。

散货船、杂货船、油船和船队是我国内河传统的货运船舶，在20世纪80年代初期，散货船、杂货船和油船等自航船舶的吨位较小，内河货运主要采用船队运输。在20世纪80年代后期及90年代，我国大力发展内河自航船舶，加快了船型的更新换代步伐，集装箱船、化学品船、液化气体船、滚装货船等一批专业化船舶得到了快速发展。到了20世纪90年代后期，随着物流环境变化、航道条件改善和船型推陈出新，驳船组成的船队逐步被大吨位自航船取代，江海直达船也逐渐发展起来。进入21世纪后，为提高内河航运效率和优化运力结构，以京杭运河和三峡库区船型标准化示范工程为引领，推进了内河船型标准化发展，淘汰了水泥船、挂桨机船等落后的船型，实现了内河船舶的专业化、系列化和标准化。与此同时，为适应内河船舶大型化和绿色环保的要求，我国完善了船舶结构、分舱与稳性、消防、防污染和绿色技术等方面的船舶技术规范标准，提升了内河船舶技术性能。

我国内河货船主要分布在长江、珠江、京杭运河等水系，随着内河船型标准化的实施，内河船舶总艘数减少，船舶平均载货量增加，船龄结构优化，船舶技术状态改善，节能减排效果明显，并且提升了船闸通航效率。借助绿色智能等新技术发展，内河船舶将更加安全、环保、经济、智能、高效。

CHAPTER I   INLAND WATERWAY CARGO SHIPS

China's inland waterway cargo ships mainly include dry bulk carriers (including bulk carriers, general cargo ships, bulk cement carriers, self-unloading sand carriers), container ships, conbulkers, liquid cargo ships(including oil tankers, chemical tankers, liquefied gas carriers as well as Ro-Ro cargo ships, pusher tug-barge combinations and river-sea ships.

Bulk carriers, general cargo ships, oil tankers and pusher/tug/barge combinations are the traditional freight ships in China's inland waterways. In the early 1980s, the tonnage of self-propelled ships such as bulk carriers, general cargo ships and oil tankers was small, and inland waterways freight was mainly transported by pusher/tug/barge combinations. In the late 1980s and 1990s, China vigorously developed inland waterway self-navigating ships, accelerated the pace of upgrading ship types, and a number of specialized ships such as container ships, chemical tankers, liquefied gas carriers and Ro-Ro cargo ships were developed rapidly. In the late 1990s, with the change of logistics environment, the improvement of channel conditions and the introduction of new ship types, the pusher/tug/barge combination was gradually replaced by large-tonnage self-propelled ships, and river-sea ships were gradually developed. From the year 2000, to improve the efficiency of inland waterway shipping and optimize the capacity structure, China promoted the standardization of inland waterway ship types. This eliminated the obsolete ship types such as cement carriers and hanging oar-engine ships and realised the specialisation, serialisation and standardization of inland waterway ships. This was led by the standardization demonstration projects in Beijing-Hangzhou Canal and Three Gorges reservoir. At the same time, in order to meet the need of larger ships and environmental protection in inland waterways, China has improved technical rules and standards for ship structure, subdivision and stability, fire-fighting, pollution prevention and green technology and enhanced the technical performance of inland waterway ships.

China's inland waterway cargo ships are mainly operating on the Yangtze River, Pearl River and Beijing-Hangzhou Canal. With the standardization of inland waterway ship types, the total number of inland waterway ships has reduced, while the average cargo capacity of ships has increased and the age structure of ships is optimised and the technical condition of ships is improved. This has led to energy saving and emission reductions, and an improvement in the navigation efficiency of ship locks. As a result of the development of innovative green and intelligent technologies, inland waterway ships will be safer, more environmentally friendly, economical, intelligent, efficient, etc.

第一节　干散货船

内河干散货船是指在舱内或甲板上主要载运干散货（包括桶装液体货物）的船舶。内河干散货运输以载运煤、黄沙、矿石、粮食等为主。干散货船每次装载的货种通常比较单一，由于内河风浪较小，一般为敞口式；由于航道水浅和通航环境复杂，为改善船舶的推进和操纵性能，一般采用双机双桨；为了便于装卸并保证结构安全，货舱一般采取长大开口、双底、双舷、单甲板形式。

在20世纪80—90年代，长江干散货船的载货量在1000～2000吨级，西江干散货船的载货量在200～1000吨级，京杭运河干散货船的载货量在80～300吨级。进入21世纪后，船舶大型化趋势较为明显。长江及三峡库区以5000～8000吨级标准船型为主力船型，西江干线以3000～5000吨级标准船型为主力船型，京杭运河以1000～2000吨级标准船型为主力船型。另外，我国长江和西江沿岸地区，拥有丰富的石灰岩、砂石资源，有大量水泥、砂石运输需求。20世纪90年代后，长江水系和珠江水系出现大量的自卸砂船和散装水泥船等专业运输船型。

SECTION 1　DRY BULK CARRIER

An inland waterway dry bulk carrier refers to a ship that mainly carries dry bulk cargo, including liquid cargo in barrels, in the cargo hold or on the deck. Inland waterway dry bulk cargo transportation mainly covers coal, yellow sand, ore and grain. Due to the shallow water channel and complicated navigation environment, double engines and double propellers are used to improve the propulsion and maneuvering of the ship. In order to facilitate loading and unloading and ensure structural safety, the cargo hold generally takes the form of long opening, double bottom, double side and single deck.

In the 1980s and 1990s, the cargo capacity of dry bulk carriers operating on the Yangtze River was 1,000-2,000 cargo deadweight (CDW), that of dry bulk carrier operating on the Xijiang River was 200-1,000 CDW, and that of dry bulk carrier operating on Beijing-Hangzhou Canal was 80-300 CDW. After entering the 21st century, the size of ships increased. The main ship type in the Yangtze River and the Three Gorges Reservoir is of 5,000-8,000 CDW, the Xijiang River trunk line of 3,000-5,000 CDW and the Beijing-Hangzhou Canal of 1000-2000 CDW standard. In addition, the areas along the Yangtze River and the Xijiang River are rich in limestone and sandstone resources, and there is a large demand for transportation of cement and sandstone. After the 1990s, a large number of specialised transport ships such as self-unloading sand carriers and bulk cement carriers appeared on the Yangtze River and Pearl River waterway systems.

浙嘉善货 03199 京杭运河 128 吨散货船 1989 年
ZHE JIA SHAN HUO 03199 128CDW Bulk Carrier, Beijing-Hangzhou Canal 1989
主尺度 $L×B×D$ (m×m×m)：26.6×5.3×1.9

南宽 501 号 澜沧江 150 吨半舱货船 1992 年
NAN KUAN 501 HAO 150CDW Well-deck Cargo Ship, Lantsang River 1992
主尺度 $L×B×D$ (m×m×m)：35.3×7×2

坦机 16 珠江 200 吨运泥船 1993 年
TAN JI 16 200CDW Mud Carrier, Pearl River 1993
主尺度 $L×B×D$ (m×m×m)：38×8×2.2

粤德庆货 3868　珠江 520 吨杂货船 1993 年
YUE DE QING HUO 3868　520CDW General Cargo Ship, Pearl River　1993
主尺度 $L×B×D$ (m×m×m)：41.7×9×2.7

沪振华货 11　长江 230 吨杂货船 1994 年
HU ZHEN HUA HUO 11　230CDW General Cargo Ship, Yangtze River　1994
主尺度 $L×B×D$ (m×m×m)：38.8×6.9×2.6

志航 803　珠江 960 吨散货船 1995 年
ZHI HANG 803　960CDW Bulk Carrier, Pearl River　1995
主尺度 $L×B×D$ (m×m×m)：49.8×10.8×4.4

坦机 119　珠江 600 吨杂货船 1996 年改建
TAN JI 119　600CDW General Cargo Ship, Pearl River　Converted in 1996
主尺度 $L×B×D$ (m×m×m)：49.8×10×3

江淮货 9　京杭运河 410 吨杂货船 1999 年
JIANG HUAI HUO 9　410CDW General Cargo Ship, Beijing-Hangzhou Canal 1999
主尺度 $L \times B \times D$ (m×m×m)：39.9×7.5×2.8

鲁泰安货 0089　京杭运河 430 吨杂货船 1999 年
LU TAI AN HUO 0089　430CDW General Cargo Ship, Beijing-Hangzhou Canal 1999
主尺度 $L \times B \times D$ (m×m×m)：39.8×7.5×2.8

恒顺 8　京杭运河 480 吨散货船 2000 年
HENG SHUN 8　480CDW Bulk Carrier, Beijing-Hangzhou Canal 2000
主尺度 $L \times B \times D$ (m×m×m)：41.8×7.9×2.8

闽南平货 4599　闽江 260 吨散货船 2001 年
MIN NAN PING HUO 4599　260CDW Bulk Carrier, Minjiang River 2001
主尺度 $L \times B \times D$ (m×m×m)：43.1×8×2.4

东电号　长江 800 吨大件运输船 2001 年
DONG DIAN HAO　800CDW Heavy-cargo Carrier, Yangtze River 2001
主尺度 $L \times B \times D$ (m×m×m)：67.4×12.8×3.2

肇港发 0102　珠江 300 吨杂货船　2004 年改建
ZHAO GANG FA 0102　300CDW General Cargo Ship, Pearl River　Converted in 2004
主尺度 $L×B×D$（m×m×m）：39.6×7.5×2.4

长运大件　长江 450 吨大件运输船　2004 年
CHANG YUN DA JIAN　450CDW Heavy-cargo Carrier, Yangtze River　2004
主尺度 $L×B×D$（m×m×m）：68×12.8×3.2

石宝1002　长江3100吨散货船　2004年
SHI BAO 1002　3,100CDW Bulk Carrier, Yangtze River　2004
主尺度 $L×B×D$ (m×m×m)：91.2×14.2×4.5

粤新会货1033　珠江320吨杂货船　2005年改建
YUE XIN HUI HUO 1033　320CDW General Cargo Ship, Pearl River Converted in 2005
主尺度 $L×B×D$ (m×m×m)：37.3×7.2×2.6

粤广宁货2828　珠江330吨杂货船　2005年改建
YUE GUANG NING HUO 2828　330CDW General Cargo Ship, Pearl River Converted in 2005
主尺度 $L×B×D$ (m×m×m)：39.5×7.8×2.4

鑫河369　京杭运河1040吨散货船　2005年
XIN HE 369　1,040CDW Bulk Carrier, Beijing-Hangzhou Canal　2005
主尺度 $L×B×D$ (m×m×m)：56.3×10×3.5

粤蓝海633　珠江1800吨甲板货船　2006年
YUE LAN HAI 633　1,800CDW Deck Cargo Ship, Pearl River　2006
主尺度 $L×B×D$ (m×m×m)：80×18×4

经纬 7188　长江 900 吨甲板货船 2009 年改建
JING WEI 7188　900CDW Deck Cargo Ship, Yangtze River　Converted in 2009
主尺度 $L×B×D$（m×m×m）：64×11×3

鑫盛 6 号　长江及三峡库区 2600 吨半舱货船 2009 年改建
XIN SHENG 6 HAO　2,600CDW Well-deck Cargo Ship,
Yangtze River and Three Gorges Reservoir　Converted in 2009
主尺度 $L×B×D$（m×m×m）：82.3×14×4.3

万港 820　长江及三峡库区 2600 吨杂货船 2009 年改建
WAN GANG 820　2,600CDW General Cargo Ship, Yangtze River and
Three Gorges Reservoir　Converted in 2009
主尺度 $L×B×D$（m×m×m）：90×15×5

平南永佳 889　珠江 1700 吨杂货船 2010 年
PING NAN YONG JIA 889　1,700CDW General Cargo Ship, Pearl River　2010
主尺度 $L×B×D$（m×m×m）：50×12.5×4.3

三港6号 长江及三峡库区 7600 吨散货船 2010 年
SAN GANG 6 HAO 7,600CDW Bulk Carrier, Yangtze River and Three Gorges Reservoir 2010
主尺度 $L×B×D$ (m×m×m)：110×19×6

华航长运 长江 10200 吨散货船 2010 年
HUA HANG CHANG YUN 10,200CDW Bulk Carrier,
Yangtze River 2010
主尺度 $L×B×D$ (m×m×m)：109.1×19.2×7.6

新长江 25010 长江及三峡库区 5100 吨散货船 2011 年
XIN CHANG JIANG 25010 5,100CDW Bulk Carrier,
Yangtze River and Three Gorges Reservoir 2011
主尺度 $L×B×D$ (m×m×m)：92×14.8×5.8

SHIPS OF CHINA

重轮货 5008　长江及三峡库区 7500 吨散货船 2011 年
CHONG LUN HUO 5008　7,500CDW Bulk Carrier, Yangtze River and Three Gorges Reservoir 2011
主尺度 $L×B×D$ (m×m×m)：110×19.2×5.6

润通 518　长江 9560 吨散货船 2011 年
RUN TONG 518　9,560CDW Bulk Carrier, Yangtze River 2011
主尺度 $L×B×D$ (m×m×m)：110.6×19×8.2

乐辉 88　长江及三峡库区 5740 吨散货船 2012 年
LE HUI 88　5,740CDW Bulk Carrier, Yangtze River and Three Gorges Reservoir 2012
主尺度 $L×B×D$ (m×m×m)：105×16×6

新长江 06010　长江及三峡库区 7000 吨散货船 2013 年
XIN CHANG JIANG 06010　7,000CDW Bulk Carrier, Yangtze River and Three Gorges Reservoir 2013
主尺度 $L×B×D$ (m×m×m)：110×19.2×5.6

润航 8999 长江 12660 吨散货船 2014 年
RUN HANG 8999 12,660CDW Bulk Carrier, Yangtze River 2014
主尺度 $L \times B \times D$ (m×m×m): 118.8×20×8.2

绿动 6005 长江 630 吨天然气动力散货船 2015 年
采用 LNG 动力系统
LV DONG 6005 630CDW LNG-powered Bulk Carrier,
Yangtze River 2015
With LNG power system
主尺度 $L \times B \times D$ (m×m×m): 44.4×8.8×3.2

浙上虞货 0529 京杭运河 500 吨散货船 2015 年
ZHE SHANG YU HUO 0529 500CDW Bulk Carrier, Beijing-Hangzhou Canal 2015
主尺度 $L \times B \times D$ (m×m×m): 44.8×7.8×2.9

万里阳光　澜沧江 420 吨杂货船 2015 年
WAN LI YANG GUANG　420CDW General Cargo Ship, Lantsang River 2015
主尺度 *L×B×D*（m×m×m）：56×8.7×2.8

沪振华货 20　京杭运河 1500 吨散货船 2015 年
HU ZHEN HUA HUO 20　1,500CDW Bulk Carrier, Beijing-Hangzhou Canal 2015
主尺度 *L×B×D*（m×m×m）：56×11.6×4

赣恒顺 2 号　长江 1500 吨散货船 2015 年改建
GAN HENG SHUN 2 HAO　1,500CDW Bulk Carrier, Yangtze River Converted in 2015
主尺度 *L×B×D*（m×m×m）：68.7×11.6×3.8

河牛 58 长江及三峡库区 7390 吨散货船 2015 年
HE NIU 58 7,390CDW Bulk Carrier, Yangtze River and Three Gorges Reservoir 2015
主尺度 $L×B×D$ (m×m×m)：129.9×16.2×6

海牛 1003 长江及三峡库区 7430 吨散货船 2015 年
HAI NIU 1003 7,430CDW Bulk Carrier, Yangtze River and Three Gorges Reservoir 2015
主尺度 $L×B×D$ (m×m×m)：129.9×16.2×6

旺顺 65　长江 20180 吨散货船　2015 年
WANG SHUN 65　20,180CDW Bulk Carrier, Yangtze River　2015
主尺度 $L \times B \times D$ (m×m×m)：142.5×25.3×9.2

航电 2 号　贵州 500 吨散货船　2016 年
HANG DIAN 2 HAO　500CDW Bulk Carrier, Guizhou　2016
主尺度 $L \times B \times D$ (m×m×m)：55×10.5×3

天统 28　京杭运河 660 吨散货船　2016 年
TIAN TONG 28　660CDW Bulk Carrier, Beijing-Hangzhou Canal 2016
主尺度 $L \times B \times D$ (m×m×m)：44.7×9.8×3

江和 89　长江 20000 吨散货船　2016 年
JIANG HE 89　20,000CDW Bulk Carrier, Yangtze River　2016
主尺度 $L \times B \times D$ (m×m×m)：140.4×24×9

浙萧山货 25177　京杭运河 800 吨散货船　2017 年
ZHE XIAO SHAN HUO 25177　800CDW Bulk Carrier, Beijing-Hangzhou Canal　2017
主尺度 $L \times B \times D$ (m×m×m)：49.6×10.6×3

桂平滨海 2288　珠江 3740 吨散货船　2019 年
GUI PING BIN HAI 2288　3,740CDW Bulk Carrier, Pearl River　2019
主尺度 $L \times B \times D$ (m×m×m)：71.6×13.7×5.6

航万 933　长江及三峡库区 5740 吨散货船　2019 年
HANG WAN 933　5,740CDW Bulk Carrier, Yangtze River and Three Gorges Reservoir　2019
主尺度 $L \times B \times D$ (m×m×m)：105×16.2×5.6

羊城 8 号　珠江 780 吨散装水泥运输船　1991 年
YANG CHENG 8 HAO　780CDW Bulk Cement Carrier, Pearl River 1991
主尺度　$L×B×D$ (m×m×m)：48.7×12×3.2

鄂黄石华新散 2 号　长江 220 吨散装水泥运输船　1998 年改建
E HUANG SHI HUA XIN SAN 2 HAO　220CDW Bulk Cement Carrier, Yangtze River Converted in 1998
主尺度　$L×B×D$ (m×m×m)：39.2×7.8×2.2

志航 688　珠江 1300 吨散装水泥运输船　1998 年
ZHI HANG 688　1,300CDW Bulk Cement Carrier, Pearl River 1998
主尺度　$L×B×D$ (m×m×m)：50×13×5

穗联和 318　珠江 1000 吨散装水泥运输船　2000 年
SUI LIAN HE 318　1,000CDW Bulk Cement Carrier, Pearl River　2000
主尺度 *L*×*B*×*D*（m×m×m）：50×13×4

长亚一号　长江 7400 吨散装水泥运输船　2003 年
CHANG YA YI HAO　7,400CDW Bulk Cement Carrier, Yangtze River　2003
主尺度 *L*×*B*×*D*（m×m×m）：106×20×7

赣九江货 1139　长江 930 吨散装水泥运输船　2009 年
GAN JIU JIANG HUO 1139　930CDW Bulk Cement Carrier, Yangtze River　2009
主尺度 *L*×*B*×*D*（m×m×m）：52.6×10×3.5

华航机 6168　长江 780 吨散装水泥运输船　2010 年
HUA HANG JI 6168　780CDW Bulk Cement Carrier, Yangtze River　2010
主尺度 *L*×*B*×*D*（m×m×m）：50.5×9.3×3.7

Ships of China

安信货 9 号　长江 1720 吨散装水泥运输船　2014 年
AN XIN HUO 9 HAO　1,720CDW Bulk Cement Carrier, Yangtze River　2014
主尺度　$L×B×D$（m×m×m）：64.8×13×4.3

西宝 313　珠江 2000 吨散装水泥运输船　2016 年
XI BAO 313　2,000CDW Bulk Cement Carrier, Pearl River　2016
主尺度　$L×B×D$（m×m×m）：69×14×5

顺行 268　珠江 2600 吨散装水泥运输船　2017 年
SHUN XING 268　2,600CDW Bulk Cement Carrier, Pearl River　2017
主尺度　$L×B×D$（m×m×m）：72×16×5

浙桐乡槽 01818 京杭运河 930 吨散装水泥运输船 2019 年
ZHE TONG XIANG CAO 01818 930CDW Bulk Cement Carrier, Beijing-Hangzhou Canal 2019
主尺度 $L×B×D$ (m×m×m)：49.6×9.7×3.8

粤英德货 8901 珠江 340 吨自卸砂船 1993 年
YUE YING DE HUO 8901 340CDW Self-unloading Sand Carrier, Pearl River 1993
主尺度 $L×B×D$ (m×m×m)：41.4×9.1×2.5

梧州三水司 188 珠江 240 吨自卸砂船 1995 年改建
WU ZHOU SAN SHUI SI 188 240CDW Self-unloading Sand Carrier, Pearl River Converted in 1995
主尺度 $L×B×D$ (m×m×m)：36.8×7.2×2.5

顺宏海 83　珠江 1400 吨自卸砂船　2000 年
SHUN HONG HAI 83　1,400CDW Self-unloading Sand Carrier, Pearl River 2000
主尺度 $L×B×D$ (m×m×m)：59.7×13×3.8

粤惠州货 9306　珠江 922 吨自卸砂船　2002 年
YUE HUI ZHOU HUO 9306　922CDW Self-unloading Sand Carrier, Pearl River 2002
主尺度 $L×B×D$ (m×m×m)：53.8×11.8×3.2

粤惠州货 9226　珠江 2500 吨自卸砂船　2005 年
YUE HUI ZHOU HUO 9226　2,500CDW Self-unloading Sand Carrier, Pearl River 2005
主尺度 $L×B×D$ (m×m×m)：75×15.3×4.5

天力 288　珠江 5100 吨自卸砂船　2008 年
TIAN LI 288　5,100CDW Self-unloading Sand Carrier, Pearl River 2008
主尺度 $L×B×D$ (m×m×m)：89.4×19.5×5.3

粤鼎湖货 0878　珠江 4600 吨自卸砂船　2009 年
YUE DING HU HUO 0878　4,600CDW Self-unloading Sand Carrier, Pearl River 2009
主尺度 $L×B×D$ (m×m×m)：90.3×18.5×4.8

湘汉寿货 1918　长江 4000 吨自卸砂船　2010 年
XIANG HAN SHOU HUO 1918　4,000CDW Self-unloading Sand Carrier, Yangtze River　2010
主尺度 $L \times B \times D$（m×m×m）：101×15.8×5

昇航 027　珠江 6400 吨自卸砂船　2010 年
SHENG HANG 027　6,400CDW Self-unloading Sand Carrier, Pearl River　2010
主尺度 $L \times B \times D$（m×m×m）：98.5×19.8×5.7

云宏 787　长江 5000 吨自卸砂船　2013 年
YUN HONG 787　5,000CDW Self-unloading Sand Carrier, Yangtze River　2013
主尺度 $L \times B \times D$（m×m×m）：105×17.2×5.3

粤广州货 2888　珠江 5000 吨自卸砂船　2014 年
YUE GUANG ZHOU HUO 2888　5,000CDW Self-unloading Sand Carrier, Pearl River　2014
主尺度 $L \times B \times D$（m×m×m）：89.6×18.8×5

长兴 1009　长江及三峡库区 6000 吨运砂船　2014 年
CHANG XING 1009　6,000CDW Sand Carrier, Yangtze River and Three Gorges Reservoir　2014
主尺度 $L×B×D$ (m×m×m)：105×17.2×5.6

泰华航 368　珠江 6000 吨自卸砂船　2015 年
TAI HUA HANG 368　6,000CDW Self-unloading Sand Carrier, Pearl River　2015
主尺度 $L×B×D$ (m×m×m)：91.7×20.8×5.2

乔泰 15 号　长江及三峡库区 4300 吨自卸砂船　2015 年改建
QIAO TAI 15 HAO　4,300CDW Self-unloading Sand Carrier, Yangtze River and Three Gorges Reservoir　Converted in 2015
主尺度 $L×B×D$ (m×m×m)：99.8×16.2×4.8

远舟 8　长江 1500 吨自卸砂船　2016 年
YUAN ZHOU 8　1,500CDW Self-unloading Sand Carrier, Yangtze River　2016
主尺度 $L×B×D$ (m×m×m)：80×13.8×3.4

赣丰城货 8199　长江 1950 吨自卸砂船　2016 年
GAN FENG CHENG HUO 8199　1,950CDW Self-unloading Sand Carrier, Yangtze River　2016
主尺度 $L×B×D$ (m×m×m)：66×15.2×3.4

第二节　集装箱船和多用途船

内河集装箱船系指其构造适合于在货舱内或在甲板上专门装载集装箱的船舶。多用途船是以载运集装箱和载运散货为主的船舶。20世纪90年代以来，内河集装箱运输得以迅猛发展。依靠独特的地理环境，珠江水系集装箱运输发展最早，集装箱船和多用途船在珠江三角洲地区至港澳航线转运上发挥了重要的作用，系列船型从36～72TEU发展到198～256TEU。随着《西江航运干线过闸运输船舶标准船型主尺度系列》的实施，新建造多艘较大的1000～3000吨多用途集装箱船。长江集装箱船在21世纪快速发展，长江流域沿线大部分外贸集装箱都是通过上海港进行中转，逐步形成了以沿江上海、南京、武汉、重庆四大中心城市为核心的对长江集装箱物流的较强需求，长江中上游集装箱船以80～300TEU为主，中下游以500～1100TEU为主；京杭运河水网地区的集装箱船也在同步发展，系列船型以36～72TEU为主。

SECTION 2　CONTAINER SHIP AND MULTI-PURPOSE SHIP

An inland waterway container ship refers to a vessel whose structure is suitable for loading containers in the cargo hold or on the deck. The multi-purpose ship mainly carries containers and bulk cargo. Since the 1990s, inland waterway container transport has developed rapidly. Relying on the unique geographical advantages, the Pearl River waterway system saw the earliest development of container transport. Container ships and multi-purpose ships played an important role in transshipment from the Pearl River Delta region to Hong Kong-Macao route. The series of ship type have been developed from 36-72 TEU to 198-256 TEU. With the implementation of *Main dimensions of standard types of transportation ships passing through locks in the Xijiang River Trunk Line*, a number of larger multi-purpose container ships of 1,000-3,000 CDW were built. Container ships operating on Yangtze River have developed rapidly in the 21st century, and most of the foreign trade containers along the Yangtze River are transshipped through Shanghai port, gradually forming a stronger demand for Yangtze River container logistics with four major cities along the river, Shanghai, Nanjing, Wuhan and Chongqing as the core. Container ships in the middle and upper reaches of Yangtze River are mainly 80-300 TEU, and 500-1,100 TEU in the middle and lower reaches. The container ships in the waterway network of Beijing-Hangzhou Canal are developing at the same time, and the series of ships are mainly 36-72 TEU.

沪航货1　长江1000吨多用途船　1986年
HU HANG HUO 1　1,000CDW Multi-purpose Ship, Yangtze River　1986
主尺度 $L×B×D$ (m×m×m)：69.4×11×4.9

粤海328　珠江320吨多用途船　1991年
YUE HAI 328　320CDW Multi-purpose Ship, Pearl River　1991
主尺度 $L×B×D$ (m×m×m)：49.2×8.4×3.4

粤海518　珠江500吨多用途船　1992年
YUE HAI 518　500CDW Multi-purpose Ship, Pearl River　1992
主尺度 $L×B×D$ (m×m×m)：49.4×9.8×3.5

鹤山星航311　珠江40TEU集装箱船　1996年
HE SHAN XING HANG 311　40TEU Container Ship, Pearl River　1996
主尺度 $L×B×D$ (m×m×m)：49.9×14.8×4

润隆928　珠江960吨多用途船　1997年
RUN LONG 928　960CDW Multi-purpose Ship, Pearl River　1997
主尺度 $L×B×D$ (m×m×m)：49.8×13×4.8

中航903　珠江60TEU集装箱船　1998年
ZHONG HANG 903　60TEU Container Ship, Pearl River　1998
主尺度 $L×B×D$ (m×m×m)：49.8×13×4.2

佳航 88 珠江 720 吨多用途船 1998 年
JIA HANG 88 720CDW Multi-purpose Ship, Pearl River 1998
主尺度 $L \times B \times D$ (m×m×m)：49.8×10.3×3.3

勤力 331 珠江 16TEU 集装箱船 1999 年
QIN LI 331 16TEU Container Ship, Pearl River 1999
主尺度 $L \times B \times D$ (m×m×m)：46×9.6×3

粤洋 18 珠江 1200 吨多用途船 1999 年
YUE YANG 18 1,200CDW Multi-purpose Ship, Pearl River 1999
主尺度 $L \times B \times D$ (m×m×m)：50×13×4

远江城　长江 106TEU 集装箱船 1999 年
YUAN JIANG CHENG　106TEU Container Ship, Yangtze River 1999
主尺度 $L×B×D$（m×m×m）：70×14.2×4.8

志航 638　珠江 1700 吨多用途船 2000 年
ZHI HANG 638　1,700CDW Multi-purpose Ship, Pearl River 2000
主尺度 $L×B×D$（m×m×m）：50×13×6

鄂鸿运 818　长江 2000 吨多用途船 2005 年
E HONG YUN 818　2,000CDW Multi-purpose Ship, Yangtze River 2005
主尺度 $L×B×D$（m×m×m）：66.2×13×3.8

浦海 215　长江 200TEU 集装箱船 2005 年
PU HAI 215　200TEU Container Ship, Yangtze River 2005
主尺度 $L×B×D$（m×m×m）：88.2×15.6×5.6

民治　长江及三峡库区 200TEU 集装箱船　2005 年
MIN ZHI　200TEU Container Ship, Yangtze River and Three Gorges Reservoir　2005
主尺度 $L×B×D$ (m×m×m)：90.1×14.6×4.8

赣吉安货 3169　长江 1850 吨多用途船　2007 年
GAN JI AN HUO 3169　1,850CDW Multi-purpose Ship, Yangtze River　2007
主尺度 $L×B×D$ (m×m×m)：64.8×13.2×4.2

锦海 86　长江 1940 吨多用途船　2007 年
JIN HAI 86　1,940CDW Multi-purpose Ship, Yangtze River　2007
主尺度 $L×B×D$ (m×m×m)：65.8×13.4×4.2

集海昌 3 号　长江 2000 吨多用途船　2008 年
JI HAI CHANG 3 HAO　2,000CDW Multi-purpose Ship, Yangtze River 2008
主尺度　$L×B×D$（m×m×m）：65.8×13.4×4.2

港盛 1000　长江及三峡库区 150TEU 集装箱船　2008 年
GANG SHENG 1000　150TEU Container Ship, Yangtze River and Three Gorges Reservoir 2008
主尺度　$L×B×D$（m×m×m）：92×16.2×4.8

重轮 J3001　长江及三峡库区 4440 吨多用途船　2008 年
CHONG LUN J3001　4,440CDW Multi-purpose Ship, Yangtze River and Three Gorges Reservoir 2008
主尺度　$L×B×D$（m×m×m）：105×16.2×6

民楷 长江及三峡库区 330TEU 集装箱船 2008 年
MIN KAI 330TEU Container Ship, Yangtze River and Three Gorges Reservoir 2008
主尺度 $L \times B \times D$ (m×m×m): 112×17×6

港盛 1003 长江及三峡库区 237TEU 多用途船 2009 年
GANG SHENG 1003 237TEU Multi-purpose Ship, Yangtze River and Three Gorges Reservoir 2009
主尺度 $L \times B \times D$ (m×m×m): 92×16.2×4.8

SHIPS OF CHINA

天海 1 号　长江 5600 吨多用途船　2009 年
TIAN HAI 1 HAO　5,600CDW Multi-purpose Ship, Yangtze River　2009
主尺度 $L \times B \times D$ (m×m×m)：105×16.2×5.2

重轮 J3007　长江及三峡库区 306TEU 集装箱船　2009 年
CHONG LUN J3007　306TEU Container Ship, Yangtze River and Three Gorges Reservoir　2009
主尺度 $L \times B \times D$ (m×m×m)：105×16.2×5.8

河牛 136 长江及三峡库区 5000 吨多用途船 2009 年
HE NIU 136 5,000CDW Multi-purpose Ship, Yangtze River and Three Gorges Reservoir 2009
主尺度 $L×B×D$ (m×m×m)：110×19.2×5.6

富安 283 珠江 1900 吨多用途船 2010 年
FU AN 283 1,900CDW Multi-purpose Ship, Pearl River 2010
主尺度 $L×B×D$ (m×m×m)：50×13×4.6

翔富 1 珠江 150TEU 集装箱船 2010 年
XIANG FU 1 150TEU Container Ship, Pearl River 2010
主尺度 $L×B×D$ (m×m×m)：50×16×6

新谷 301　珠江 140TEU 重箱集装箱船　2010 年改建
XIN GU 301　140TEU Heavy-container Ship, Pearl River Converted in 2010
主尺度 $L \times B \times D$ (m×m×m)：59.8×15.3×4.8

石宝 997　长江 7800 吨多用途船　2010 年
SHI BAO 997　7,800CDW Multi-purpose Ship, Yangtze River 2010
主尺度 $L \times B \times D$ (m×m×m)：110×19.2×5.6

长航集运 0325　长江及三峡库区 325TEU 集装箱船　2011 年
CHANG HANG JI YUN 0325　325TEU Container Ship, Yangtze River and Three Gorges Reservoir 2011
主尺度 $L \times B \times D$ (m×m×m)：107×17.2×5.2

重轮集 3012 长江及三峡库区 5140 吨多用途船 2011 年
CHONG LUN JI 3012 5,140CDW Multi-purpose Ship, Yangtze River and Three Gorges Reservoir 2011
主尺度 $L \times B \times D$ (m×m×m)：110×17.2×6

民觉 长江及三峡库区 325TEU 集装箱船 2012 年
MIN JUE 325TEU Container Ship, Yangtze River and Three Gorges Reservoir 2012
主尺度 $L \times B \times D$ (m×m×m)：107×17.2×5.2

南港 18　珠江 288TEU 集装箱船　2013 年
NAN GANG 18　288TEU Container Ship, Pearl River　2013
主尺度　$L \times B \times D$ (m×m×m)：66×18×6

志航 128　珠江 210TEU 集装箱船　2014 年
ZHI HANG 128　210TEU Container Ship, Pearl River　2014
主尺度　$L \times B \times D$ (m×m×m)：60×18×6

浦海 211　长江 197TEU 集装箱船　2014 年改建
采用双燃料动力系统
PU HAI 211　197TEU Container Ship, Yangtze River　Converted in 2014
With dual fuel power system
主尺度 $L×B×D$（m×m×m）：88.2×15.6×5.6

穗港 4001　珠江 4200 吨多用途船　2014 年
SUI GANG 4001　4,200CDW Multi-purpose Ship, Pearl River　2014
主尺度 $L×B×D$（m×m×m）：93×16×6

邕航 988　珠江 1560 吨多用途船　2015 年
YONG HANG 988　1,560CDW Multi-purpose Ship, Pearl River　2015
主尺度 $L×B×D$（m×m×m）：56.8×10.8×4.1

志航118 珠江3750吨多用途船 2015年
ZHI HANG 118　3,750CDW Multi-purpose Ship, Pearl River 2015
主尺度 $L×B×D$ (m×m×m)：60×18×6

国粤06 珠江2400吨多用途船 2016年
GUO YUE 06　2,400CDW Multi-purpose Ship, Pearl River 2016
主尺度 $L×B×D$ (m×m×m)：70×15.5×4.5

翔宇98 京杭运河2400吨多用途船 2016年
XIANG YU 98　2,400CDW Multi-purpose Ship, Beijing-Hangzhou Canal 2016
主尺度 $L×B×D$ (m×m×m)：67.7×13.6×4.8

绿动 8008　长江 800 吨多用途船　2017 年
采用 LNG 动力系统
主尺度 $L×B×D$（m×m×m）：49.8×10×3.2

LV DONG 8008　800CDW Multi-purpose Ship, Yangtze River　2017
With LNG power system

鼎达集 96　京杭运河 36TEU/900 吨多用途船　2017 年
DING DA JI 96　36TEU/900CDW Multi-purpose Ship, Beijing-Hangzhou Canal　2017
主尺度 $L×B×D$（m×m×m）：54.4×10.2×3.2

兴桂 1062　珠江 1400 吨 LNG 动力多用途船　2017 年
XING GUI 1062　1,400CDW LNG-powered Multi-purpose Ship, Pearl River　2017
主尺度 $L×B×D$（m×m×m）：56.78×10.8×4.2

鼎达集 86 京杭运河 36TEU 集装箱船 2018 年
DING DA JI 86 36TEU Container Ship, Beijing-Hangzhou Canal 2018
主尺度 $L \times B \times D$ (m×m×m)：54.5×10.2×3.2

河牛 81 长江及三峡库区 7360 吨多用途船 2018 年
HE NIU 81 7,360CDW Multi-purpose Ship, Yangtze River and Three Gorges Reservoir 2018
主尺度 $L \times B \times D$ (m×m×m)：129.9×16.2×5.7

海盛集 002 京杭运河 690 吨多用途船 2019 年
HAI SHENG JI 002 690CDW Multi-purpose Ship, Beijing-Hangzhou Canal 2019
主尺度 $L×B×D$ (m×m×m)：44.8×10.6×3.1

顺通集 001 京杭运河 1100 吨多用途船 2019 年
SHUN TONG JI 001 1,100CDW Multi-purpose Ship, Beijing-Hangzhou Canal 2019
主尺度 $L×B×D$ (m×m×m)：54.6×10.6×3.5

新鸿基 8868 珠江 3500 吨多用途船 2019 年
XIN HONG JI 8868 3,500CDW Multi-purpose Ship, Pearl River 2019
主尺度 $L×B×D$ (m×m×m)：74×15.7×5.5

南宁和顺 238　珠江 4000 吨多用途船 2019 年
NAN NING HE SHUN 238　4,000CDW Multi-purpose Ship, Pearl River 2019
主尺度　$L×B×D$（m×m×m）：73.6×15.5×5.3

南宁和顺 078　珠江 5800 吨多用途船　2019 年
NAN NING HE SHUN 078　5,800CDW Multi-purpose Ship, Pearl River 2019
主尺度　$L×B×D$（m×m×m）：89.5×15.5×6

重轮集 3021　长江及三峡库区 7900 吨多用途船　2019 年
CHONG LUN JI 3021　7,900CDW Multi-purpose Ship, Yangtze River and Three Gorges Reservoir 2019
主尺度　$L×B×D$（m×m×m）：130×16.2×6.2

盛源 8 号　长江 494TEU 集装箱船 2020 年
SHENG YUAN 8 HAO　494TEU Container Ship, Yangtze River 2020
主尺度　$L×B×D$（m×m×m）：109.8×18.7×7.2

第三节　液货船

内河液货船是指其构造主要适用于载运散装液态货物的内河船舶，包括油船、化学品船、液化气体船、沥青船等。20世纪80—90年代，内河油船的载货量在500～1000吨，其货油区域一般为单壳结构形式（单底单舷或双底单舷）；到了21世纪后，随着内河船型标准化的实施，油船主力船型提升到2000～5000吨级。为防止油船因碰撞和触礁等事故对内河水域造成污染，提升船舶防污染能力，减小了货油舱单舱的长度，货油区域采用了双壳结构形式（双底双舷）。为了降低失火风险，根据货油闪点的高低，船舶实行了分级安全要求，提升了船舶消防安全能力。

从20世纪90年代开始，内河液体化工产品和液化气体的运输需求增加，使得化学品船和液化气体船迅速发展。为了防控货物泄露对船员、船舶和周围环境造成的危害，内河化学品船和液化气体船的布置与结构形式均按照国际通行的方法设计建造，一般采用带凸形甲板的整体液货舱型，且由于化学品货物的品种多，运量多少不一，液货舱一般分隔为多个货舱。目前，内河化学品船主力船型在3000～5000吨级。内河液化气体船一般采用独立液货舱型，主力船型在1000～2000吨级。

SECTION 3　LIQUID CARGO SHIP

An inland waterway liquid cargo ship refers to the inland waterway ship whose structure is mainly suitable to carry bulk liquid cargo, including oil tankers, chemical tankers, liquefied gas carriers and asphalt carriers. In the 1980s and 1990s, the cargo capacity of inland waterway oil tankers was between 500-1,000 CDW, and their cargo oil areas were generally of single-hull structure, single bottom and single side or double bottom and single side. After the 21st century, with the standardization of inland river ship types, the main type of tankers was upgraded to 2,000-5,000 CDW class. In order to prevent oil tankers from polluting inland waters due to accidents such as a collision or striking rocks and to improve the anti-pollution ability of ships, the length of single tank of cargo oil tanks was reduced and double-hull structure, double bottom and double side, was adopted in the cargo oil area. In order to reduce the risk of fire, the graded safety requirements have been implemented according to the flash points of cargo oil, and the fire safety capability of ships has been improved.

Since the 1990s, the demand for transportation of liquid chemical products and liquefied gas by inland waterway has increased, leading to the rapid development of chemical tankers and liquefied gas carriers. In order to prevent and control the hazards caused by the leakage of cargo to the crew, the ship and the surrounding environment, the arrangement and structure of inland waterway chemical tankers and liquefied gas carriers have been designed and built according to the internationally accepted methods, and generally adopt the overall liquid cargo tank type with convex deck. Due to the variety and quantity of chemical cargoes carried, the cargo tank is generally divided into several compartments. At present, the main ship type of inland waterway chemical tankers is 3,000-5,000 CDW. Inland waterway liquefied gas carriers generally adopt independent liquid cargo tank type, and the main ship type is 1,000-2,000 CDW.

海供油 9　长江 358 吨供油船 1987 年
HAI GONG YOU 9　358CDW Bunkering Tanker, Yangtze River　1987
主尺度 $L×B×D$（m×m×m）：46.6×8.6×3.9

永顺 23　珠江 200 吨油船 1991 年
YONG SHUN 23　200CDW Oil Tanker, Pearl River　1991
主尺度 $L×B×D$（m×m×m）：36.3×7.4×2.2

宁化 403　长江 3600 吨化学品船 1993 年
NING HUA 403　3,600CDW Chemical Tanker, Yangtze River　1993
主尺度 $L×B×D$（m×m×m）：106.8×17.4×5.1

粤惠州油 168　珠江 300 吨油船 1995 年
YUE HUI ZHOU YOU 168　300CDW Oil Tanker, Pearl River　1995
主尺度 $L×B×D$（m×m×m）：39.6×7.5×2.5

湘君 长江 1000 吨化学品 / 油液货船 1998 年改建
XIANG JUN 1,000CDW Chemical/Oil Liquid Cargo Ship, Yangtze River Converted in 1998
主尺度 $L×B×D$ (m×m×m)：59.3×10.8×4.5

兴运 1 号 长江 450 吨化学品船 1999 年改建
XING YUN 1 HAO 450CDW Chemical Tanker, Yangtze River Converted in 1999
主尺度 $L×B×D$ (m×m×m)：39.7×8×3.4

鹤油 03 珠江 515 吨供油船 2001 年改建
HE YOU 03 515CDW Bunkering Tanker, Pearl River Converted in 2001
主尺度 $L×B×D$ (m×m×m)：50.7×8.5×3.1

铜庆 3 珠江 500 吨油船 2002 年改建
TONG QING 3 500CDW Oil Tanker, Pearl River Converted in 2002
主尺度 $L×B×D$ (m×m×m)：52.2×8.5×3.2

石油 601 珠江 1300 吨油船 2002 年
SHI YOU 601 1,300CDW Oil Tanker, Pearl River 2002
主尺度 $L×B×D$ (m×m×m)：66×12×4

远洋 3 号　长江 2300 吨油船　2002 年
YUAN YANG 3 HAO　2,300CDW Oil Tanker, Yangtze River　2002
主尺度　$L×B×D$（m×m×m）：88×13.8×4.2

粤肇庆槽 333　珠江 487 吨化学品船　2003 年
YUE ZHAO QING CAO 333　487CDW Chemical Tanker, Pearl River　2003
主尺度　$L×B×D$（m×m×m）：43×8.8×2.8

大洋　长江 1640 吨沥青船　2003 年改建
DA YANG　1,640CDW Asphalt Carrier, Yangtze River　Converted in 2003
主尺度　$L×B×D$（m×m×m）：80×12×4

长燃 41 号　长江 210 吨供油船　2004 年改建
CHANG RAN 41 HAO　210CDW Bunkering Tanker, Yangtze River Converted in 2004
主尺度　$L×B×D$ (m×m×m)：40×6×2

润通油 8　珠江 1760 吨油船　2004 年
RUN TONG YOU 8　1,760CDW Oil Tanker, Pearl River 2004
主尺度　$L×B×D$ (m×m×m)：73×12×4

新平江 1013　长江及三峡库区 2150 吨油船　2004 年
XIN PING JIANG 1013　1,260CDW Oil Tanker, Yangtze River and Three Gorges Reservoir　2004
主尺度 $L \times B \times D$ (m×m×m)：87×13.6×4.4

长燃 51　长江 1530 吨供油船　2005 年改建
CHANG RAN 51　1,530CDW Bunkering Tanker, Yangtze River Converted in 2004
主尺度 $L \times B \times D$ (m×m×m)：77×13×3

南南燃油 33　珠江 3000 吨油船　2005 年
NAN NAN RAN YOU 33　3,000CDW Oil Tanker, Pearl River　2005
主尺度 $L \times B \times D$ (m×m×m)：85×15×5

赣恒顺 1 号 长江 2000 吨化学品船 2006 年
GAN HENG SHUN 1 HAO 2,000CDW Chemical Tanker, Yangtze River 2006
主尺度 $L \times B \times D$ (m×m×m)：77.8×11.8×4.2

南运油 363 珠江 2400 吨油船 2006 年
NAN YUN YOU 363 2,400CDW Oil Tanker, Pearl River 2006
主尺度 $L \times B \times D$ (m×m×m)：77×14×4

乾峰 826　长江及三峡库区 2250 吨化学品船 2007 年
QIAN FENG 826　2,250CDW Chemical Tanker, Yangtze River and Three Gorges Reservoir 2007
主尺度 $L\times B\times D$ （m×m×m）：75×12.8×4.5

远洋 1007　长江及三峡库区 5330 吨化学品船 2007 年
YUAN YANG 1007　5,330CDW Chemical Tanker, Yangtze River and Three Gorges Reservoir 2007
主尺度 $L\times B\times D$ （m×m×m）：99.8×17.2×5.5

鑫辉 66　长江 2100 吨化学品船 2008 年
XIN HUI 66　2,100CDW Chemical Tanker, Yangtze River 2008
主尺度 $L\times B\times D$ （m×m×m）：75×14×4

锦龙 100 长江 3200 吨油船 2010 年
JIN LONG 100 3,200CDW Oil Tanker, Yangtze River 2010
主尺度 *L×B×D*（m×m×m）：87×15×5

久鑫 011 长江 3300 吨化学品船 2011 年
JIU XIN 011 3,300CDW Chemical Tanker, Yangtze River 2011
主尺度 *L×B×D*（m×m×m）：87×14.8×5.1

远洋 7606 长江及三峡库区 4400 吨化学品船 2011 年
YUAN YANG 7606 4,400CDW Chemical Tanker, Yangtze River and Three Gorges Reservoir 2011
主尺度 *L×B×D*（m×m×m）：100×17×5

宁化 501 长江及三峡库区 5700 吨化学品船 2011 年
NING HUA 501 5,700CDW Chemical Tanker, Yangtze River and Three Gorges Reservoir 2011
主尺度 *L×B×D*（m×m×m）：100×17×6

皖通达 588 长江 1000 吨油船 2012 年改建
WAN TONG DA 588 1,000CDW Oil Tanker, Yangtze River Converted in 2012
主尺度 *L×B×D*（m×m×m）：57.9×9.8×4

海供油 31　长江 940 吨供油船　2012 年
HAI GONG YOU 31　940CDW Bunkering Tanker, Yangtze River　2012
主尺度 $L×B×D$（m×m×m）：52.7×9.2×4.1

桂运 3568　珠江 1020 吨化学品船　2012 年
GUI YUN 3568　1,020CDW Chemical Tanker, Pearl River　2012
主尺度 $L×B×D$（m×m×m）：50×10.8×3.5

恒达沥青 005　长江及三峡库区 2500 吨油船　2012 年
HENG DA LI QING 005　2,500CDW Oil Tanker, Yangtze River and Three Gorges Reservoir　2012
主尺度 $L×B×D$（m×m×m）：89×16×4

新平江 3003　长江及三峡库区 3000 吨油船　2012 年
XIN PING JIANG 3003　3,000CDW Oil Tanker, Yangtze River and Three Gorges Reservoir　2012
主尺度 $L×B×D$（m×m×m）：87×14.8×5.1

三通 801　长江及三峡库区 4300 吨油船 2013 年改建
SAN TONG 801　4,300CDW Oil Tanker, Yangtze River and Three Gorges Reservoir Converted in 2013
主尺度 $L×B×D$（m×m×m）：100×17×5

东桂 11　珠江 3220 吨化学品船 2013 年
DONG GUI 11　3,220CDW Chemical Tanker, Pearl River 2013
主尺度 $L×B×D$（m×m×m）：83.4×15.8×5.6

清江号　长江3400吨油船　2013年
QING JIANG HAO　3,400CDW Oil Tanker, Yangtze River　2013
主尺度 *L×B×D*（m×m×m）：94.8×16.2×4.8

东琪　长江及三峡库区4800吨油船　2013年
DONG QI　4,800CDW Oil Tanker, Yangtze River and Three Gorges Reservoir　2013
主尺度 *L×B×D*（m×m×m）：100×17×5

神州3501　长江及三峡库区5340吨化学品船　2013年
SHEN ZHOU 3501　5,340CDW Chemical Tanker, Yangtze River and Three Gorges Reservoir　2013
主尺度 *L×B×D*（m×m×m）：100×17×6

恒达沥青058　长江4620吨沥青船　2014年
HENG DA LI QING 058　4,620CDW Asphalt Carrier, Yangtze River　2014
主尺度 *L×B×D*（m×m×m）：105×16×6

腾龙1号　长江4000吨油船　2015年
TENG LONG 1 HAO　4,000CDW Oil Tanker, Yangtze River　2015
主尺度 *L×B×D*（m×m×m）：86.8×14.8×4.8

华通油 78　长江 4400 吨油船　2015 年
HUA TONG YOU 78　4,400CDW Oil Tanker, Yangtze River　2015
主尺度 $L×B×D$ （m×m×m）：94.8×16.2×5.5

三通 5003　长江及三峡库区 5500 吨沥青船　2017 年
SAN TONG 5003　5,500CDW Asphalt Carrier, Yangtze River and Three Gorges Reservoir　2017
主尺度 $L×B×D$ （m×m×m）：100×17×6

远达 301　珠江 2820 吨化学品船　2018 年
YUAN DA 301　2,820CDW Chemical Tanker, Pearl River　2018
主尺度 $L×B×D$ （m×m×m）：81.8×18×5.6

江隆 9001　长江及三峡库区 5240 吨化学品船 2018 年
JIANG LONG 9001　5,240CDW Chemical Tanker, Yangtze River and Three Gorges Reservoir 2018
主尺度 $L×B×D$（m×m×m）：105×16.2×5.8

龙川 9　长江 5600 吨油船 2018 年
LONG CHUAN 9　5,600CDW Oil Tanker, Yangtze River 2018
主尺度 $L×B×D$（m×m×m）：109.8×18×5.8

南和油 26　珠江 1900 吨油船 2019 年
NAN HE YOU 26　1,900CDW Oil Tanker, Pearl River 2019
主尺度 $L×B×D$（m×m×m）：67×14×5

大洋 98 长江及三峡库区 4610 吨沥青船 2019 年
DA YANG 98 4,610CDW Asphalt Carrier, Yangtze River and Three Gorges Reservoir 2019
主尺度 $L×B×D$ (m×m×m): 105×16.2×6

苏鑫海 1 长江 4980 吨化学品船 2019 年
SU XIN HAI 1 4,980CDW Chemical Tanker, Yangtze River 2019
主尺度 $L×B×D$ (m×m×m): 104.9×16.2×5.5

长茂 1 长江 1000 立方米液化气体运输船 1997 年
CHANG MAO YI 1,000m³ Liquefied Gas Tanker, Yangtze River 1997
主尺度 $L \times B \times D$ (m×m×m)：71×13×3

天恩 1001 长江 2000 立方米液化气体运输船 1999 年
TIAN EN 1001 2,000m³ Liquefied Gas Tanker, Yangtze River 1999
主尺度 $L \times B \times D$ (m×m×m)：87×14×4

民发 长江 2027 立方米液化气体运输船 2011 年改建
MIN FA 2,027m³ Liquefied Gas Tanker, Yangtze River Converted in 2011
主尺度 $L \times B \times D$ (m×m×m)：78.2×14×4.6

岳化一号 长江1900立方米液化气体运输船 2000年
YUE HUA YI HAO 1,900m³ Liquefied Gas Tanker, Yangtze River 2000
主尺度 $L \times B \times D$（m×m×m）：85×14×4

宁化运2号 长江2298立方米液化气体运输船 2002年
NING HUA YUN 2 HAO 2,298m³ Liquefied Gas Tanker, Yangtze River 2002
主尺度 $L \times B \times D$（m×m×m）：80×16×4.7

海港星01 长江500立方米天然气燃料加注船 2013年
HAI GANG XING 01 500m³ LNG Bunkering Tanker, Yangtze River 2013
主尺度 $L \times B \times D$（m×m×m）：100×18×3.8

海港星 02 长江 500 立方米天然气燃料加注船 2016 年
HAI GANG XING 02 500m³ LNG Bunkering Tanker, Yangtze River 2016
主尺度 $L×B×D$ (m×m×m)：136.5×18×5.2

珠港西江能源 01 珠江 200 立方米天然气燃料加注船 2019 年
ZHU GANG XI JIANG NENG YUAN 01 200m³ LNG Bunkering Tanker, Pearl River 2019
主尺度 $L×B×D$ (m×m×m)：78×16×3.1

第四节 滚装货船

内河滚装货船主要为商品汽车滚装船，主要航行于长江干线。20世纪80—90年代，内河早期的商品汽车水上运输以驳船零散方式为主。21世纪初，汽车工业迅猛发展，长江沿线汽车制造走廊形成，给长江水运整车物流运输带来了前所未有的发展机遇。在经历了由旧船改造到新建专业商品汽车滚装船的历程后，目前长江基本上形成了重庆、武汉、芜湖、南京、上海等城市之间的多条商品汽车运输航线，商品汽车滚装船的主力船型为800～1000车位的标准船型。

SECTION 4　RO-RO CARGO SHIP

The inland waterway Ro-Ro cargo ships are mainly used for carrying commercial automobiles and primarily sail on the trunk line of the Yangtze River. In the 1980s and 1990s, the early transportation of commercial vehicles on inland waterway was in the form of barges in a piecemeal manner. At the beginning of the 21st century, the rapid development of the automobile industry and the formation of automobile manufacturing corridors along the Yangtze River brought unprecedented development opportunities for the whole-vehicle logistics and transportation. After experiencing the transformation from modification of old ships to construction of new specialized Ro-Ro vehicle carriers, the Yangtze River has formed multiple commercial car transportation routes between Chongqing, Wuhan, Wuhu, Nanjing, Shanghai, etc, and the main type of Ro-Ro commercial vehicle carriers has a carrying capacity of 800-1,000 CEU.

长航江浩　长江及三峡库区 350 车位汽车运输船　2006 年改建　由客船改装的汽车运输船
主尺度 $L×B×D$ (m×m×m)：84.5×14×3.5

CHANG HANG JIANG HAO　350CEU Car Carrier, Yangtze River and Three Gorges Reservoir　Converted in 2006
Car carrier converted from passenger ship

长航江平 长江及三峡库区 450 车位汽车运输船 2008 年改建
由客船改装的汽车运输船
CHANG HANG JIANG PING 450CEU Car Carrier, Yangtze River and Three Gorges Reservoir Converted in 2008
Car carrier converted from passenger ship
主尺度 $L \times B \times D$（m×m×m）：84×14×4

长航江兴 长江及三峡库区 550 车位汽车运输船 2009 年改建
由客船改装的汽车运输船
CHANG HANG JIANG XING 550CEU Car Carrier, Yangtze River and Three Gorges Reservoir Converted in 2009
Car carrier converted from passenger ship
主尺度 $L \times B \times D$（m×m×m）：90×14×4

民生 长江及三峡库区 176 车位汽车运输船 2000 年
MIN SHENG 176CEU Car Carrier, Yangtze River and Three Gorges Reservoir 2000
主尺度 $L \times B \times D$（m×m×m）：77×11×3

民苏 长江及三峡库区 300 车位汽车运输船 2001 年
MIN SU 300CEU Car Carrier, Yangtze River and Three Gorges Reservoir 2001
主尺度 $L×B×D$ (m×m×m)：85.5×14.8×3.7

民宪 长江及三峡库区 500 车位汽车运输船 2006 年
MIN XIAN 500CEU Car Carrier, Yangtze River and Three Gorges Reservoir 2006
主尺度 $L×B×D$ (m×m×m)：99×16×4

SHIPS OF CHINA

长航江旺　长江 800 车位汽车运输船　2010 年
CHANG HANG JIANG WANG　800CEU Car Carrier, Yangtze River　2010
主尺度 $L×B×D$ （m×m×m）：107×17.8×4.1

民福　长江及三峡库区 1300 车位汽车运输船　2011 年
MIN FU　1,300CEU Car Carrier, Yangtze River and Three Gorges Reservoir　2011
主尺度 $L×B×D$ （m×m×m）：120×22×5

安吉 201　长江 800 车位汽车运输船　2012 年
系列船中的首制船
主尺度 $L×B×D$ （m×m×m）：110×19×5

AN JI 201　800CEU Car Carrier, Yangtze River　2012
First ship in series

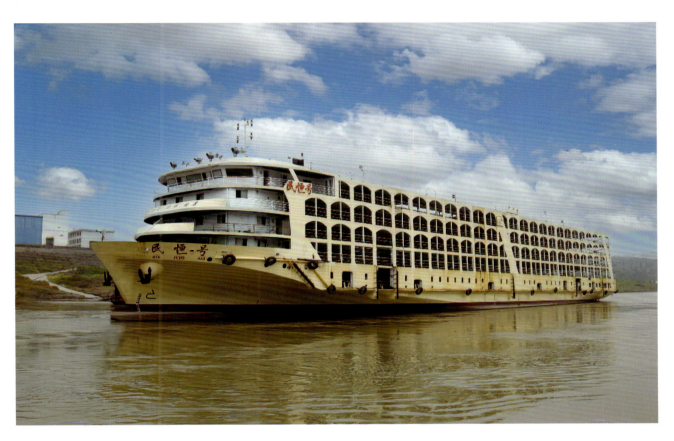

民恒号　长江 922 车位汽车运输船　2014 年
MIN HENG HAO　922CEU Car Carrier, Yangtze River　2014
主尺度 $L×B×D$ (m×m×m)：110×18×5

安吉204　长江 924 车位汽车运输船　2015 年
具有光伏太阳能装置和绿色船舶标志
AN JI 204　924CEU Car Carrier, Yangtze River　2015
With photovoltaic solar devices and green ship notation
主尺度 $L×B×D$ (m×m×m)：110×18.8×5.2

长航江泰　长江及三峡库区 1000 车位汽车运输船　2016 年
具有绿色船舶标志
CHANG HANG JIANG TAI　1,000CEU Car Carrier, Yangtze River and Three Gorges Reservoir　2016
With green ship notation
主尺度 $L×B×D$ (m×m×m)：110×19×4.5

民快 长江及三峡库区 860 车位汽车运输船 2017 年
MIN KUAI 860CEU Car Carrier, Yangtze River and Three Gorges Reservoir 2017
主尺度 $L \times B \times D$ (m×m×m)：110×17×5

长航江荣 长江及三峡库区 800 车位汽车运输船 2019 年
CHANG HANG JIANG RONG 800CEU Car Carrier, Yangtze River and Three Gorges Reservoir 2019
主尺度 $L \times B \times D$ (m×m×m)：110×17×5

第五节 推／拖船队

船队是指由推/拖船和驳船组成的货物运输船队。船队运输具有运量大、投资少、成本低、效益好等优点，在内河运输中发挥了重要作用。我国内河早期的货物运输船队采用的是拖带船队，一般由1艘拖船和若干艘被拖带的驳船组成，20世纪80年代后期，我国大力发展顶推船队，特别是出现分节驳顶推运输后，顶推船队成为内河货运的主要运输方式。其中，长江干线的典型顶推船队有1.4万吨油船船队、2万吨油船船队、1.8万吨散货船队、3.2万吨散货船队和4万吨散货船队，4万吨散货船队由1艘4512千瓦推船和20艘2000吨级分节槽型驳组成，船队总长291米、总宽54米，是我国内河最大的顶推船队。同时，珠江水系和黑龙江水系的船队运输也得到了发展。

在技术方面，为减小船队阻力，提出了内河分节驳阻力计算编队系数法；为提高推轮的推进性能，开发了大浸深比＋导管技术；为提高船队的操纵性能，针对短缆系结进行操纵系结力试验，并在推轮上配置了倒车舵系统。

2000年以后，内河大宗散货运输持续增长，受到内河散货运输货源结构变化、航道港口码头变化（深水航道建设、浮式码头变为专业化岸臂式码头、货主码头大型化）以及自航货船的发展，船队及驳船运输逐步退出市场，被自航货船所取代。

SECTION 5 PUSHER/TUG/BARGE COMBINATION

The pusher/tug/barge combination has the advantages of large capacity, low investment, low cost, good efficiency, etc., and plays an important role in inland waterway transportation. China's early combination for inland waterway cargo transportation was a towing combination, generally consisting of a tug and a number of towed barges. In the late 1980s, China strived to develop the pusher combination, especially after the emergence of the integrated barge push transportation, the pusher combination has become the main mode of freight transport in inland waterway. Among them, the typical pusher combination on the Yangtze River Trunk Line includes 14,000 CDW oil tanker combination, 20,000 CDW oil tanker combination, 18,000 CDW bulker combination, 32,000 CDW bulker combination and 40,000 CDW bulker combination. In particular, the 40,000 CDW bulker combination consists of one 4,512 kW pusher and twenty 2,000 CDW integrated flute profile barges, with a total length of 291 meters and total width of 54 meters, which is the largest pusher combination in China's inland waterways. Meanwhile, the combination transportation on the Pearl River waterway system and Heilongjiang River waterway system has also been developed.

For technical improvement, the method of calculating coefficient of inland waterway sectional barge resistance was proposed in order to reduce the combination resistance. The technology of large immersion depth ratio plus conduit was developed in order to improve the propulsion performance of the push tug. The maneuvering tying force test was conducted for the short cable tying and the reverse rudder system was installed on the push tug in order to improve the maneuvering performance of the combination.

After 2000, bulk cargo transportation continued to grow on inland waterways. Barge transportation was gradually withdrawn from the market and replaced by self-propelled cargo ships. This was due to the changes in the structure of inland waterway bulk cargo transportation as well as changes in the channel, port and wharf such as deep water channel construction, the changing of floating docks into specialised bulkhead wharfs and large-scale cargo owners' terminals as well as the development of self-propelled cargo ships.

"长江26004" 船队　长江40000吨散货顶推船队（4413千瓦推船+5×4分节槽型驳）1980年
CHANG JIANG 26004 COMBINATION　40,000CDW Bulk Carrier Pusher Combination (4,413kW pusher + 5×4 integrated flute profile barges), Yangtze River　1980
主尺度 $L×B×D$ (m×m×m)：推 45.7×12.8×3.5　驳 61×10.7×4.3

"龙推603" 船队　黑龙江4000吨木材顶推船队（440千瓦推船+2×2分节甲板驳）1984年
LONG TUI 603 COMBINATION　4,000CDW Timber Carrier Pusher Combination (440kW pusher + 2×2 integrated flute profile deck barges), Heilongjiang River　1984
主尺度 $L×B×D$ (m×m×m)：推 34.4×9×2.6　驳 65.9×13×2.6

"长江24001"船队 长江32000吨散货顶推船队（3530千瓦推船+4×4分节槽型驳）1985年
CHANG JIANG 24001 COMBINATION 32,000CDW Bulk Carrier Pusher Combination (3,530kW pusher + 4×4 integrated flute profile barges), Yangtze River 1985
主尺度 $L×B×D$ (m×m×m)：推 46.4×12.8×3.5　驳 61×10.7×4.3

"龙推317"船队 黑龙江4000吨砂石顶推船队（272千瓦推船+2×2分节甲板驳）1985年
LONG TUI 317 COMBINATION 4,000CDW Sand Carrier Pusher Combination (272kW pusher + 2×2 integrated flute profile deck barges), Heilongjiang River 1985
主尺度 $L×B×D$ (m×m×m)：推 23×7.6×2　驳 65.9×13×2.6

"长江2809"船队 长江液化气体运输顶推船队（596千瓦推船+2298立方米液化气体驳）1985年
CHANG JIANG 2809 COMBINATION Liquefied Gas Carrier Pusher Combination (596kW pusher + 2,298m³ liquefied gas barges), Yangtze River 1985
主尺度 $L×B×D$ (m×m×m)：推 34×9.4×3.8　驳 75×13×3

"长江22040"船队　长江18000吨散货顶推船队（1944千瓦推船+3×3分节槽型驳）1987年
CHANG JIANG 22040 COMBINATION　18,000CDW Bulk Carrier Pusher Combination (1,944kW pusher + 3×3 integrated flute profile barges), Yangtze River 1987
主尺度 $L×B×D$ (m×m×m)：推 45×13×4.4　驳 61×10.7×4.3

"长江2048"船队　长江18000吨散货顶推船队（1500千瓦推船+3×3分节槽型驳）1993年
CHANG JIANG 2048 COMBINATION　18,000CDW Bulk Carrier Pusher Combination (1,500kW pusher + 3×3 integrated flute profile barges), Yangtze River 1993
主尺度 $L×B×D$ (m×m×m)：推 42×9.6×4.8　驳 61×10.7×4.3

"长江63003"船队　长江17000吨油运顶推船队（2640千瓦推船+2×2分节油驳）1994年
CHANG JIANG 63003 COMBINATION　17,000CDW Oil Carrier Pusher Combination (2,640kW pusher + 2×2 integrated oil barges), Yangtze River 1994
主尺度 $L×B×D$ (m×m×m)：推 45.1×12.4×4.2　驳 85.2×20.8×4.8

"长江63002"船队
长江20000吨油运顶推船队（2640千瓦推船+2×2分节油驳）1994年
CHANG JIANG 63002 COMBINATION　20,000CDW Oil Carrier Pusher Combination (2,640kW pusher + 2×2 integrated oil barges), Yangtze River 1994
主尺度 $L×B×D$ (m×m×m)：推 45.1×12.4×4.2　驳 85.2×20.8×4.8

"生峡"船队　长江2460吨汽车运输顶推船队（2426千瓦推船+3甲板驳）1998年
SHENG XIA COMBINATION　2,460CDW Car Carrier Pusher Combination (2,426kW pusher + 3 deck barges), Yangtze River 1998
主尺度 $L×B×D$ (m×m×m)：推 46.9×10.5×3.6　驳 64×11×2.8

"长江62034"船队　长江14000吨油运顶推船队
（2640千瓦推船+2×2分节油驳）1998年
YANGTZE 62034 COMBINATION　14,000CDW Oil Carrier Pusher Combination (2,640kW pusher + 2×2 integrated oil barges), Yangtze River 1998
主尺度 $L×B×D$ (m×m×m)：推 45.1×12.4×4.2　驳 66.8×20.8×4.5

"徐联航拖666"船队　京杭运河9000吨散货吊拖船队
（397千瓦拖船+9分节槽型驳）2016年
XU LIAN HANG TUO 666 COMBINATION　9,000CDW Bulk Carrier Trailer Combination (397kW tug + 9 integrated flute profile barges), Beijing-Hangzhou Grand Canal 2016
主尺度 $L×B×D$ (m×m×m)：推 32×7×2.8　驳 44.8×9.8×3.6

"徐兴航推669"船队　京杭运河9000吨散货顶推船队
（764千瓦推船+3×3分节槽型驳）2017年
XU XING HANG TUI 669 COMBINATION　9,000CDW Bulk carrier Pusher Combination (764kW pusher + 3×3 integrated flute profile barges), Beijing-Hangzhou Grand Canal 2017
主尺度 $L×B×D$ (m×m×m)：推 27.5×10.6×3.1　驳 65×15.8×4.6

生振　长江 596 千瓦拖船　1984 年
SHENG ZHEN　596kW Tug, Yangtze River 1984
主尺度　$L \times B \times D$ (m×m×m)：36.5×7.6×2.7

龙推 611　黑龙江 485 千瓦推船　1987 年
LONG TUI 611　485kW Pusher, Heilongjiang River 1987
主尺度　$L \times B \times D$ (m×m×m)：35×9×2.6

长江 63001　长江 2320 千瓦推船　1989 年
CHANG JIANG 63001　2,320kW Pusher, Yangtze River 1989
主尺度　$L \times B \times D$ (m×m×m)：45.1×12.4×4.2

先行607 广东441千瓦拖船 1990年
XIAN XING 607 441kW Tug, Pearl River 1990
主尺度 $L \times B \times D$ (m×m×m)：28.6×7×3.3

长江02034 长江1656千瓦推船 1991年
CHANG JIANG 02034 1,656kW Pusher, Yangtze River 1991
主尺度 $L \times B \times D$ (m×m×m)：45.8×10.5×3.6

万港拖 818　长江 588 千瓦油拖船　1995 年
WAN GANG TUO 818　588kW Oil tug, Yangtze River　1995
主尺度 $L×B×D$（m×m×m）：37×8×2.8

龙工拖 8002　黑龙江 588 千瓦推船　1998 年
LONG GONG TUO 8002　588kW Pusher, Heilongjiang River　1998
主尺度 $L×B×D$（m×m×m）：37.5×10.4×2.6

九石化 1902 长江 1658 千瓦油推船 2000 年
JIU SHI HUA 1902 1,658kW Oil pusher, Yangtze River 2000
主尺度 $L \times B \times D$ (m×m×m)：43×10×4.2

长江 82017 长江 1500 千瓦推船 2008 年改建
CHANG JIANG 82017 1,500kW Pusher, Yangtze River Converted in 2008
主尺度 $L \times B \times D$ (m×m×m)：42×9.6×4.8

长江 64001 长江 2940 千瓦推船 2018 年
CHANG JIANG 64001 2,940kW Pusher, Yangtze River 2018
主尺度 $L \times B \times D$ (m×m×m)：45.5×13.2×4.3

龙捞驳 601　黑龙江 600 吨分节甲板驳　1987 年
LONG LAO BO 601　600CDW Integrated Deck Barge, Heilongjiang River　1987
主尺度　$L×B×D$（m×m×m）：58×11×2.3

分节油 63001　长江 3500 吨半分节油驳　1989 年
FEN JIE YOU 63001　3,500CDW Integrated Oil Barge, Yangtze River　1989
主尺度　$L×B×D$（m×m×m）：66.8×20.8×4.5

民货 853　长江 40TEU 集装箱驳　1993 年
MIN HUO 853　40TEU Container Barge, Yangtze River　1993
主尺度 $L \times B \times D$ (m×m×m)：64×11×3

分节油 65011　长江 5000 吨半分节油驳　1994 年
FEN JIE YOU 65011　5,000CDW Integrated Oil Barge, Yangtze River　1994
主尺度 $L \times B \times D$ (m×m×m)：85.2×20.8×4.8

天恩 102　长江 1017 吨液化气体驳　1998 年
TIAN EN 102　1,017CDW Liquefied Gas Barge, Yangtze River　1998
主尺度 $L \times B \times D$ (m×m×m)：60×10.8×3.5

润泽驳 1004　京杭运河 72TEU 集装箱驳　2006 年
RUN ZE BO 1004　72TEU Container Barge, Beijing-Hangzhou Canal　2006
主尺度 $L×B×D$（m×m×m）：56.6×13.6×3.8

长燃油 2001　长江 2230 吨油驳　2012 年
CHANG RAN YOU 2001　2,230CDW Oil Barge, Yangtze River　2012
主尺度 $L×B×D$（m×m×m）：80×16×3.8

海供油 303　长江 3100 吨油驳　2013 年
HAI GONG YOU 303　3,100CDW Oil Barge, Yangtze River　2013
主尺度 $L×B×D$（m×m×m）：85×18.2×4.2

第六节　江海直达船

江海直达船通常指航行于内河水域与其出海口附近海港的船舶。从20世纪80年代开始，随着内河港口对外开放，长江、珠江、黑龙江开始江海联运，以"海船进江"模式的江海直达船（以符合海船规范为主，同时满足特定内河航线规范要求）得以发展，主要包括散货船、集装箱船、集散两用船和推驳组合船组等。近年来，随着我国经济的高质量发展，物流运输需求增加，发展江海直达船舶对于提高货物水路运输效率优势明显。2017年我国出台了特定航线江海通航船舶法规和规范，助推了以"江船出海"模式的江海直达船（符合特定航线技术要求）的发展，率先在长江至上海洋山港、宁波—舟山港航线实施，首艘2万载重吨的特定航线江海航行船"江海直达1"于2018年3月投入营运，开启了江海直达运输的新模式。

SECTION 6　RIVER-SEA SHIP

River-sea ships usually refer to ships sailing in inland waterways and seaports near their estuaries. Since the 1980s, with the opening of inland ports to the outside world, the Yangtze River, Pearl River and Heilongjiang River started river-sea combined transportation. The river-sea ships in the mode of "sea to river" (mainly conforming to the rules for sea-going vessels and meeting the rules for specific inland waterway routes), were developed, primarily bulk carriers, container ships, conbulkers and pusher-barge combination. In recent years, with the high quality development of China's economy, the demand for logistics and transportation has increased, and the development of river-sea ships has obvious advantages in improving the efficiency of cargo waterway transportation. In 2017, China introduced regulations and rules for river-sea ships navigating on specific routes, which were first implemented on the Yangtze River-Shanghai Yangshan Port and Ningbo-Zhoushan Port routes, boosting the development of river-sea ships in the mode of "river to sea" while meeting the technical requirements for specific routes. The first 20,000 DWT river-sea ship "JIANG HAI ZHI DA 1" for specific routes entered operation in March 2018, which opened a new mode of river-sea transportation.

木兰　黑龙江1500吨江海直达多用途船　1992年
MU LAN　1,500DWT Multi-purpose Ship, Heilongjiang River-sea　1992
主尺度　$L×B×D$ (m×m×m)：85.9×13.8×5.5

SHIPS OF CHINA

宁化 401　6240 吨江海直达化学品船　1992 年
NING HUA 401　6,240DWT Chemical Tanker, River-sea　1992
主尺度　$L×B×D$ (m×m×m)：114.8×17×8

集远　5000 吨江海直达多用途船　1994 年
JI YUAN　5,000DWT Multi-purpose Ship, River-sea　1994
主尺度　$L×B×D$ (m×m×m)：98.5×16.8×7.8

春江海　15980 吨江海直达散货船 1994 年
CHUN JIANG HAI　15,980DWT Bulk Carrier, River-sea 1994
主尺度　$L×B×D$ (m×m×m)：153×23×11

长通海　7000 吨江海直达多用途船 2003 年
系列船中的首制船
CHANG TONG HAI　7,000DWT Multi-purpose Ship, River-sea 2003
First ship in series
主尺度　$L×B×D$ (m×m×m)：112.1×17.5×7.6

"长航洋山 3001" 船组　360TEU 江海直达船组（2206 千瓦推船）2005 年
上海洋山港区开展江海联运的代表船舶
CHANG HANG YANG SHAN 3001 COMBINATION　360TEU Integrated Pusher Combination (2,206kW pusher), River-sea 2005
Representative ship carrying out river-sea combined transport in Yangshan Port Area, Shanghai
主尺度　$L×B×D$ (m×m×m)：推 30.5×10×4.5　驳 96.8×18×7.2

长跃海　10000 吨江海直达多用途船 2005 年
CHANG YUE HAI　10,000DWT Multi-purpose Ship, River-sea 2005
主尺度　$L×B×D$ (m×m×m)：121×20×9

江夏文　12000 吨江海直达散货船 2007 年
JIANG XIA WEN　12,000DWT Bulk Carrier, River-sea　2007
主尺度 $L×B×D$ (m×m×m)：128×21.6×9.4

"国裕海拖 1 号" 船组　44000 吨江海直达船组（3824 千瓦推船）2007 年
GUO YU HAI TUO 1 HAO COMBINATION　44,000DWT Integrated Pusher Combination (3,824kW pusher), River-sea　2007
主尺度 $L×B×D$ (m×m×m)：推 45×19×7.8　驳 181.5×33.6×15.2

江夏鸿　9800 吨江海直达散货船 2010 年
JIANG XIA HONG　9,800DWT Bulk Carrier, River-sea　2010
主尺度 $L×B×D$ (m×m×m)：125×19.4×9

第二篇　内河运输船舶
PART II　INLAND WATERWAY TRANSPORT SHIPS

宝航 11　24000 吨江海直达散货船　2011 年
BAO HANG 11　24,000DWT Bulk Carrier, River-sea　2011
主尺度 $L×B×D$ (m×m×m)：159.6×24.4×14

汉唐上海　124TEU 江海直达集装箱船　2017 年　　HAN TANG SHANG HAI　124TEU Container Ship, River-sea　2017
长江—洋山港特定航线代表船　　Representative ship for specific route from Yangtze River to Yangshan Port
主尺度 $L×B×D$ (m×m×m)：85×13×5

251

汉唐苏州　124TEU 江海直达集装箱船　2018 年
长江—洋山港特定航线代表船
主尺度 $L×B×D$（m×m×m）：84.9×12.6×4.7

HAN TANG SU ZHOU　124TEU Container Ship, River-sea　2018
Representative ship for specific route from Yangtze River to Yangshan Port

汉海1号　1086TEU 江海直达集装箱船　2018 年
HAN HAI YI HAO　1,086TEU Container Ship, River-sea　2018
主尺度 $L×B×D$（m×m×m）：129.8×23.9×11

江海直达 1　20000 吨江海直达散货船　2018 年
长江—舟山港特定航线代表船
主尺度 $L×B×D$（m×m×m）：154×24×11.8

JIANG HAI ZHI DA 1　20,000DWT Bulk Carrier, River-sea　2018
Representative ship for specific route from Yangtze River to Zhoushan Port

湘水运 26　653TEU 江海直达集装箱船　2020 年
长江—洋山港特定航线双燃料集装箱船
主尺度 $L×B×D$（m×m×m）：118.9×21.6×9.2

XIANG SHUI YUN 26　653TEU Container Ship, River-sea　2020
Dual-fuel container ship for specific route from Yangtze River to Yangshan Port

第二章　内河客船

客船是指载运乘客超过12人的船舶，我国内河客船主要有普通客船、旅游船、游览船、客滚船（Ⅰ型客滚船、Ⅱ型客滚船）、客渡船、车客渡船和高速客船。

普通客船是我国内河传统的客运船舶，20世纪80年代改革开放初期，人们出行需求增加，普通客船得以快速发展，长江、珠江、黑龙江等水域相继开通了短途班轮和长途班轮。长江代表性航线有汉申、汉渝等班轮，载客人数在800人以上；珠江代表性航线有广州至梧州、梧州至南宁等班轮，载客人数在400人左右，内河客运达到鼎盛时期。20世纪90年代开始，受公路、铁路和民用航空快速发展的影响，内河客运出现结构化调整，普通客船的客运量逐渐减少，客运航线也逐步萎缩。但此时以水上旅游观光为目的的旅游船日益兴盛，旅游船的代表船型有国宾1号、蓝鲸、长江天使等。三峡大坝建成后，促进了川江及三峡库区的旅游船发展，我国开始建造豪华型旅游船，如世纪游轮系列、维多利亚系列、黄金系列等。旅游船向大型化、舒适性和绿色智能方向发展，功能定位也逐步从游览观光型向休闲体验型转变。游览船主要航行于城区、水库、公园、风景区等水域。游览船营运水域分布很广，有漓江、千岛湖、洱海、青海湖等水域观光航线，以及上海、武汉、重庆、广州、桂林等城市滨江水域观光等。游览船的船型往往都带有地方文化特色。

内河客滚船、客渡船、车客渡船是国家水陆联运网络的重要组成部分。客滚船满足货物国内水陆联运的需求，满足乘客自驾游与游轮游无缝对接。客渡船和车客渡船作为"桥梁"，在我国内河各个水系承担着服务民生、解决群众基本交通需求的作用。进入21世纪后，由于桥梁、隧道和城市地铁的建设，渡运需求减少，客渡船和车客渡船的数量逐年减少，但仍然在我国内河运输中发挥着重要的渡运作用。

随着内河客船向大型化和舒适性方向发展，船舶技术性能也在提升，目前内河客船已经在客船结构、抗沉性及稳性衡准、消防救生、振动噪声、绿色环保等方面全面提高了客船的安全技术标准。

CHAPTER II
INLAND WATERWAY PASSENGER SHIPS

Passenger ships refer to ships carrying more than 12 passengers. Inland waterway passenger ships in China mainly include ordinary passenger ships, tourist ships, sightseeing ships, Ro-Ro passenger ships (Type I and Type II), passenger ferries, car and passenger ferries and high-speed passenger ships.

Ordinary passenger ships are traditional vessels navigating in China's inland waterways. At the beginning of reform and opening up in the 1980s, the increasing demand for travel led to the rapid development of ordinary passenger ships, and short and long-distance liners were opened on the Yangtze River, Pearl River and Heilongjiang River, the river passenger transportation reached its heyday. The representative routes of the Yangtze River included Wuhan-Shanghai liner and Wuhan-Chongqing liner, with a capacity of more than 800 passengers, the representative routes of the Pearl River included Guangzhou-Wuzhou liner and Wuzhou-Nanning liner, with a capacity of about 400 passengers. Since the 1990s, influenced by the rapid development of highway, railway and civil aviation, the structure of river passenger transport changed, with the passenger volume of ordinary passenger ships and the number of passenger routes gradually reduced. Meanwhile, tourist ships for the purpose of water travel and sightseeing were increasingly flourishing, and the representative types of tourist ships included GUOBIN 1 HAO, LAN JING, CHANG JIANG TIAN SHI, etc. The completion of the Three Gorges Dam promoted the development of tourist ships in Chuanjiang River and the Three Gorges Reservoir, and China began to build luxury tourist ships, such as Century Cruise Series, Victoria Series and Gold Series. With the development of large-size, comfortable, green and intelligent tourist ships, the functional orientation has gradually changed from sightseeing to leisure experience. Tourist ships mainly sail in urban areas, reservoirs, parks, scenic spots and other waters. Tourist ships operate in a wide range of waters. There are sightseeing routes along Li River, Qiandao Lake, Erhai Lake and Qinghai Lake, as well as waterfront sightseeing spots in Shanghai, Wuhan, Chongqing, Guangzhou, Guilin and other cities. Different types of tourist ships are often with local cultural characteristics.

Inland waterway Ro-Ro passenger ships, passenger ferries, and vehicle and passenger ferries play an important role in country's water and land transport network. Ro-Ro passenger ships meet the demand for domestic water and land transportation of cargo and seamlessly connect passengers' self-drive tours with cruise ship tours. Considered equivalent to "bridges", passenger ferries and vehicle and passenger ferries assume the role of serving people's livelihood and solving the basic transportation needs of the masses in various inland waterway systems in China. After entering the 21st century, due to the construction of bridges, tunnels and urban subways, the demand for ferry transportation has decreased, and the number of passenger ferries and vehicle and passenger ferries has decreased year by year, but they still play an important role in China's inland waterway transportation.

As the comfort of inland waterway passenger ships has evolved, the technical performance of ships is also being improved. The technical standards for safety of passenger ships have been comprehensively strengthened in areas ship structure, subdivision and stability criteria, fire-fighting as well as life-saving, vibration and noise, green, environmental protection, etc.

第一节　客船

普通客船包括长途客船和短途客船，其中，长途客船有多层甲板，设有卧席、坐席或散席客舱，以及餐厅、阅览室等服务处所；短途客船一般仅有一层或两层甲板，设有坐席或散席的客舱。旅游船是由长途客船发展而来的，尺度较大，除设有卧席客舱、餐厅和阅览等服务处所外，还设有观景、休闲等功能区。20世纪80—90年代，长江长途客船和旅游船的船长为80～90m，21世纪以后，主流船型的船长为100～150m。旅游船的功能也向多元化拓展，以满足开展各种水上主题旅游活动的需求。游览船是由短途客船发展而来，设有坐席客舱或餐饮、休闲娱乐和观光处所，游览船的造型多样化、风格各异，为体现当地文化特色，派生出仿古、现代、山水融合等类船型。

较大型内河客船主船体采用双底双舷结构形式，主船体和上层建筑按主竖区进行分隔，以提高船舶抗沉和消防能力，配备有足够的消防救生设备。部分游览船为降低重心高度，第一层客舱设计为下沉式。内河客船多采用柴油动力或柴电混合动力，也有部分船舶应用了新能源技术。

SECTION 1　PASSENGER SHIP

Ordinary passenger ships include long-distance and short-distance passenger ships. Long-distance passenger ships have multi-layer deck structure, equipped with sleeping berths, seats or casual passenger cabins, as well as restaurants, reading rooms and other service spaces; short-distance passenger ships are generally of one- or two-deck structure, equipped with seats or casual passenger cabins. Tourist ships are developed from long-distance passenger ships, with large sizes. Besides the service spaces such as sleeping cabin, dining room and reading room, there are also functional areas such as viewing and leisure. In the 1980s and 1990s, the length of Yangtze River long-distance passenger ships and tourist ships was between 80-90 m, and after entering the 21st century, the length of mainstream ships is between 100-150 m. The function of tourist ships also diversified to meet the demand of carrying out various water-themed tourism activities. Sightseeing ships are developed from short-distance passenger ships, with seating cabins or catering, leisure and entertainment and sightseeing spaces, and the shape of sightseeing ships is diversified and of different styles. Antique, modern, landscape fusion and other types of ships are designed in order to reflect local cultural characteristics.

The main hull of larger inland river passenger ships adopts double bottom and double side structure, with the main hull and superstructure separated into main vertical areas to improve the ship's anti-sinking and fire-fighting ability. The ships are further equipped with extensive fire-fighting and life-saving equipment. In order to reduce the height and centre of gravity, the bottom cabin of some tourist ships is designed as sinking type. Inland waterway passenger ships mostly adopt diesel power or diesel-electric hybrid power, and some ships also apply new energy technology.

长航江渝 112　长江汉渝线 690 客位客船　1983 年
CHANG HANG JIANG YU 112　690P Passenger Ship, Yangtze River Wuhan-Chongqing　1983
主尺度　$L×B×D$（m×m×m）：74×12.4×3.5

江汉 18　长江汉申线 1922 客位客船　1984 年
20 世纪 80 年代长江客船代表船型
JIANG HAN 18　1,922P Passenger Ship, Yangtze River Wuhan-Shanghai　1984
Representative type of Yangtze River passenger ships in 1980s
主尺度　$L×B×D$（m×m×m）：113×16.4×4.7

龙客 108　黑龙江 366 客位双体客船　1985 年
LONG KE 108　366P Passenger Catamaran, Heilongjiang River　1985
主尺度　$L×B×D$（m×m×m）：39.4×11.4×2.5

SHIPS OF CHINA

龙客 208　黑龙江 200 客位双体客船　1986 年
LONG KE 208　200P Passenger Catamaran, Heilongjiang River　1986
主尺度 $L×B×D$ (m×m×m)：32.5×9.6×2

江汉 59 号　长江申渝线 820 客位客船　1988 年
20 世纪 80 年代长江客船代表船型
JIANG HAN 59 HAO　820P Passenger Ship, Yangtze River Shanghai-Chongqing　1988
Representative type of Yangtze River passenger ships in 1980s
主尺度 $L×B×D$ (m×m×m)：84.5×14×3.5

新浏　"八一浏" 航线 920 客位双体客船　1988 年
XIN LIU　920P Passenger Catamaran, Yangtze River　1988
主尺度 $L×B×D$ (m×m×m)：50×12.6×3.3

江申 115　长江申高线 1600 客位客船　1988 年
20 世纪 80 年代长江客船代表船型
JIANG SHEN 115　1,600P Passenger Ship, Yangtze River Shanghai-Gaoyou　1988
Representative type of Yangtze River passenger ships in 1980s
主尺度 $L×B×D$ (m×m×m)：90.3×14.2×4

天龙轮 长江汉宜线170客位客船 1992年
TIAN LONG LUN 170P Passenger Ship, Yangtze River Wuhan-Yichang 1992
主尺度 $L \times B \times D$ （m×m×m）：60×9.6×3

华山号 清江200客位双体客船 1993年
HUA SHAN HAO 200P Passenger Catamaran, Qingjiang River 1993
主尺度 $L \times B \times D$ （m×m×m）：38.5×6.8×1.8

云锦 长江渝宜线730客位客船 1993年
YUN JIN 730P Passenger Ship, Yangtze River Chongqing-Yichang 1993
主尺度 $L \times B \times D$ （m×m×m）：67.3×10×3.1

抚远长城1701 黑龙江80客位客船 1994年
FU YUAN CHANG CHENG 1701 80P Passenger Ship, Heilongjiang River 1994
主尺度 $L \times B \times D$ （m×m×m）：37×7×2

江汉 21 号轮　长江渝申线 764 客位客船　1994 年
JIANG HAN 21 HAO LUN　764P Passenger Ship, Yangtze River Chongqing-Shanghai　1994
主尺度 $L×B×D$（m×m×m）：89.5×16.8×3.9

上海号　长江 80 客位交通船　1995 年
SHANG HAI HAO　80P Crew Boat, Yangtze River　1995
主尺度 $L×B×D$（m×m×m）：46×9×4

湘常德客贰号　洞庭湖 100 客位客船　1995 年
XIANG CHANG DE KE ER HAO　100P Passenger Ship, Dongting Lake　1995
主尺度 $L×B×D$（m×m×m）：22×4.4×1.2

江渝 118 号　长江渝万线 652 客位客船　1996 年
JIANG YU 118 HAO　652P Passenger Ship, Yangtze River Chongqing-Wanzhou　1996
主尺度 $L×B×D$（m×m×m）：77×13.2×3.5

金龙江　黑龙江 50 客位交通船 1999 年
JIN LONG JIANG　50P Crew Boat, Heilongjiang River 1999
主尺度 $L \times B \times D$ (m×m×m)：44×7.2×2.2

粤清远客 6372　北江 100 客位客船 2003 年改建
YUE QING YUAN KE 6372　100P Passenger Ship, Pearl River Converted in 2003
主尺度 $L \times B \times D$ (m×m×m)：31.1×6×1.4

长神 2 号　长江宜万线 300 客位客船　2004 年改建
CHANG SHEN 2 HAO　300P Passenger Ship, Yangtze River Yichang-Wanzhou　Converted in 2004
主尺度　$L \times B \times D$（m×m×m）：37.3×8×2

永安号 1　闽江 300 客位客船　2007 年
YONG AN HAO 1　300P Passenger Ship, Minjiang River　2007
主尺度　$L \times B \times D$（m×m×m）：36×8×1.8

云长号　三峡库区 324 客位客船　2007 年
YUN CHANG HAO　324P Passenger Ship, Three Gorges Reservoir　2007
主尺度　$L \times B \times D$（m×m×m）：36×7.6×2.2

神龙 999 三峡库区 180 客位客船 2012 年
SHEN LONG 999 180P Passenger Ship, Three Gorges Reservoir 2012
主尺度 $L×B×D$ (m×m×m)：33×6.6×1.8

黔蕴号 乌江 30 客位交通船 2012 年
QIAN YUN HAO 30P Crew Boat, Wujiang River 2012
主尺度 $L×B×D$ (m×m×m)：28.8×5.3×1.6

任达8号 澜沧江 150 客位客船 2015 年改建
REN DA 8 HAO 150P Passenger Ship, Lantsang River Converted in 2015
主尺度 $L×B×D$ (m×m×m)：42.4×6.8×2.1

孖洲交1 珠江 845 客位交通船 2016 年
MA ZHOU JIAO 1 845P Crew Boat, Pearl River 2016
主尺度 $L×B×D$ (m×m×m)：33.8×11×3

新三峡号　93 客位交通船　2016 年
具有绿色船舶标志
主尺度 $L×B×D$ (m×m×m)：91.8×16×3.8

XIN SAN XIA HAO　93P Crew Boat, Yangtze River　2016
With green ship notation

蒙工 010029　呼伦湖 20 客位交通船　2018 年
MENG GONG 010029　20P Crew Boat, Hulun Lake　2018
主尺度 $L×B×D$ (m×m×m)：28×6.7×2.6

扬子江二号　长江 128 客位旅游船　1988 年
YANGTZE NO.2　128P Tourist Ship, Yangtze River　1988
主尺度 $L \times B \times D$ (m×m×m)：86.8×14×3.5

长江之星　长江 140 客位旅游船　1988 年
20 世纪 80 年代长江旅游船代表船型
主尺度 $L \times B \times D$ (m×m×m)：79×14×3.5

CHANG JIANG ZHI XING　140P Tourist Ship, Yangtze River　1988
Representative type of Yangtze River tourist ships in 1980s

长江明珠　长江 158 客位旅游船　1992 年
CHANG JIANG MING ZHU　158P Tourist Ship, Yangtze River　1992
主尺度 $L \times B \times D$ (m×m×m)：87.2×14.8×4.2

维多利亚 1 号　长江 160 客位旅游船　1992 年
20 世纪 90 年代初长江旅游船代表船型
主尺度 $L \times B \times D$ (m×m×m)：87.5×14.4×3.6

WEI DUO LI YA 1 HAO　160P Tourist Ship, Yangtze River　1992
Representative type of Yangtze River tourist ships in early 1990s

长江公主　长江 160 客位旅游船　1993 年
CHANG JIANG GONG ZHU　160P Tourist Ship, Yangtze River　1993
主尺度 $L \times B \times D$ (m×m×m)：87.2×14.8×4

锦绣中华　长江 168 客位旅游船　1994 年
SPLENDID CHINA　168P Tourist Ship, Yangtze River　1994
主尺度 $L \times B \times D$ (m×m×m)：92×15×4

SHIPS OF CHINA

美维凯娅　长江 216 客位旅游船 1994 年
MVPRINCE　216P Tourist Ship, Yangtze River 1994
主尺度 $L×B×D$（m×m×m）：91.6×14.8×4.2

蓝鲸　长江 202 客位旅游船 1995 年
20 世纪 90 年代初长江旅游船代表船型
BLUE WHALE　202P Tourist Ship, Yangtze River 1995
Representative type of Yangtze River tourist ships in early 1990s
主尺度 $L×B×D$（m×m×m）：91.5×14.8×3.7

长江探索　长江 136 客位旅游船 1995 年
CHANG JIANG TAN SUO　136P Tourist Ship, Yangtze River 1995
主尺度 $L×B×D$（m×m×m）：91.5×16.4×3.7

神州号　长江 136 客位旅游船 1995 年
20 世纪 90 年代长江旅游船代表船型
主尺度 $L×B×D$（m×m×m）：87.2×14.8×4.2

SHEN ZHOU HAO　136P Tourist Ship, Yangtze River 1995
Representative type of Yangtze River tourist ships in 1990s

三国　长江 178 客位旅游船 1995 年
SAN GUO　178P Tourist Ship, Yangtze River 1995
主尺度　$L×B×D$ (m×m×m)：92.1×14.8×3.7

总统一号　长江 186 客位旅游船 1995 年
ZONG TONG YI HAO　186P Tourist Ship, Yangtze River 1995
主尺度　$L×B×D$ (m×m×m)：90×15.2×3.8

长江天使　长江 146 客位旅游船　1998 年
CHANG JIANG TIAN SHI　146P Tourist Ship, Yangtze River 1998
主尺度　$L×B×D$ (m×m×m)：91.5×16.5×3.7

维多利亚 7 号　长江 154 客位旅游船 2002 年
WEI DUO LI YA 7 HAO　154P Tourist Ship,
Yangtze River 2002
主尺度　$L×B×D$ (m×m×m)：87.5×14.4×3.6

龙腾星光　长江 201 客位旅游船　2003 年
LONG TENG XING GUANG　201P Tourist Ship, Yangtze River　2003
主尺度 $L×B×D$（m×m×m）：90.5×14.8×3.7

世纪天子　长江及三峡库区 320 客位旅游船　2005 年
SHI JI TIAN ZI　320P Tourist Ship, Yangtze River and Three Gorges Reservoir　2005
主尺度 $L×B×D$（m×m×m）：126.8×17.2×4.2

长江壹号 长江及三峡库区 222 客位旅游船 2006 年
长江旅游船代表船型
主尺度 $L \times B \times D$ (m×m×m)：103.8×16×3.6

CHANG JIANG YI HAO 222P Tourist Ship, Yangtze River and Three Gorges Reservoir 2006
Representative type of Yangtze River tourist ships

美维凯珍 三峡库区 410 客位旅游船 2008 年
MEI WEI KAI ZHEN 410P Tourist Ship, Three Gorges Reservoir 2008
主尺度 $L \times B \times D$ (m×m×m)：133.8×18.8×4

SHIPS OF CHINA

长江黄金1号　三峡库区350客位旅游船　2011年
YANGTZE GOLD 1　350P Tourist Ship, Three Gorges Reservoir　2011
主尺度　$L×B×D$（m×m×m）：136×19.6×4.2

长江黄金2号　三峡库区570客位旅游船　2012年
YANGTZE GOLD 2　570P Tourist Ship, Three Gorges Reservoir　2012
主尺度　$L×B×D$（m×m×m）：150×24×4.4

世纪神话　三峡库区400客位旅游船　2013年
我国第一艘电力推进长江旅游船
主尺度　$L×B×D$（m×m×m）：141×19.1×4.2

SHI JI SHEN HUA　400P Tourist Ship, Three Gorges Reservoir　2013
China's first electric propulsion Yangtze River tourist ship

总统七号 三峡库区 565 客位旅游船 2013 年
ZONG TONG QI HAO 565P Tourist Ship, Three Gorges Reservoir 2013
主尺度 $L \times B \times D$ (m×m×m): 146.5×20.2×4.3

华夏神女 2 长江及三峡库区 400 客位旅游船 2014 年
HUA XIA SHEN NV 2 400P Tourist Ship, Yangtze River and Three Gorges Reservoir 2014
主尺度 $L \times B \times D$ (m×m×m): 120×19×4

世纪荣耀 三峡库区 650 客位旅游船 2017 年
具有智能船舶和绿色船舶标志
主尺度 $L \times B \times D$ (m×m×m): 150×21.2×4.6

SHI JI RONG YAO 650P Tourist Ship, Three Gorges Reservoir 2017
With intelligent ship and green ship notations

春秋 太湖 62 客位仿古游览船 1986 年
CHUN QIU 62P Antique Sightseeing Ship, Taihu Lake 1986
主尺度 $L×B×D$（m×m×m）：39×6.6×1.5

特步 珠江 392 客位游览船 1990 年
TE BU 392P Sightseeing Ship, Pearl River 1990
主尺度 $L×B×D$（m×m×m）：47×10×2

太和号 颐和园昆明湖 200 客位游览船 1992 年
TAI HE HAO 200P Sightseeing Ship, Summer Palace Kunming Lake 1992
主尺度 $L×B×D$（m×m×m）：37.2×8.4×1.8

蒙游 010026　额尔古纳河 70 客位游览船　1993 年
MENG YOU 010026　70P Sightseeing Ship, Ergun River　1993
主尺度　$L×B×D$ (m×m×m)：24×4.8×1.7

公主　澜沧江 150 客位游览船　1996 年改建
GONG ZHU　150P Sightseeing Ship, Lantsang River　Converted in 1996
主尺度　$L×B×D$ (m×m×m)：37×6.8×1.6

鸿运 21　漓江 60 客位游览船　1994 年
HONG YUN 21　60P Sightseeing Ship, Lijiang River　1994
主尺度　$L×B×D$ (m×m×m)：23.7×4.1×0.9

濠江明珠　312 客位澳门环岛游览船　1995 年
HAO JIANG MING ZHU　312P Sightseeing Ship, Macao Island Tour　1995
主尺度　$L×B×D$（m×m×m）：37×10×3

杜鹃号　洱海 960 客位双体游览船　1999 年
DU JUAN HAO　960P Sightseeing Catamaran, Erhai Lake　1999
主尺度　$L×B×D$（m×m×m）：56.8×15×2.6

黄河一代天骄 黄河 120 客位游览船 2001 年
HUANG HE YI DAI TIAN JIAO 120P Sightseeing Ship, Yellow River 2001
主尺度 $L×B×D$ (m×m×m)：36×6.8×2

黄山 12 千岛湖 120 客位游览船 2003 年
HUANG SHAN 12 120P Sightseeing Ship, Thousand-island Lake 2003
主尺度 $L×B×D$ (m×m×m)：28×6×1.6

乌江画廊 1 乌江 120 客位游览船 2003 年
WU JIANG HUA LANG 1 120P Sightseeing Ship, Wujiang River 2003
主尺度 $L×B×D$ (m×m×m)：33×6.4×1.8

小三峡 6　大宁江 136 客位游览船　2003 年
XIAO SAN XIA 6　136P Sightseeing Ship, Daning River 2003
主尺度　$L×B×D$ (m×m×m)：33×6.4×1.8

神农溪 1 号　神农溪 200 客位双体游览船　2003 年
SHEN NONG XI 1 HAO　200P Sightseeing Catamaran, Shennongxi River 2003
主尺度　$L×B×D$ (m×m×m)：25.8×7×2.3

工行牡丹号 长江 400 客位游览船 2004 年
GONG HANG MU DAN HAO 400P Sightseeing Ship, Yangtze River 2004
主尺度 $L×B×D$ (m×m×m): 54.5×15×3

北琴海 兴凯湖 50 客位游览船 2004 年
BEI QIN HAI 50P Sightseeing Ship, Xingkai Lake 2004
主尺度 $L×B×D$ (m×m×m): 39.2×7.4×2

SHIPS OF CHINA

洱海一号　洱海 1000 客位双体游览船 2005 年
ER HAI YI HAO　1,000P Sightseeing Catamaran, Erhai Lake　2005
主尺度 $L×B×D$ (m×m×m)：68.8×18×2.7

南海神广州日报　珠江 268 客位仿古游览船 2006 年
NAN HAI SHEN GUANG ZHOU RI BAO　268P Antique Sightseeing Ship, Pearl River　2006
主尺度 $L×B×D$ (m×m×m)：48×13×4

金城一号 黄河 80 客位游览船 2008 年
JIN CHENG YI HAO 80P Sightseeing Ship, Yellow River 2008
主尺度 $L \times B \times D$ (m×m×m)：31.2×6.8×1.5

镜客游 4010 镜泊湖 180 客位游览船 2008 年
JING KE YOU 4010 180P Sightseeing Ship, Jingpo Lake 2008
主尺度 $L \times B \times D$ (m×m×m)：34×8.2×2.6

船长 3　黄浦江 620 客位双体游览船　2008 年
特色游览船
主尺度　$L×B×D$（m×m×m）：47.4×17.6×4

CHUAN ZHANG 3　620P Sightseeing Catamaran, Huangpu River　2008
Special sightseeing ship

抚远东方一号　黑龙江 100 客位游览船　2009 年
FU YUAN DONG FANG YI HAO　100P Sightseeing Ship,
Heilongjiang River　2009
主尺度　$L×B×D$（m×m×m）：58×9.2×2.5

滇游 1 号　滇池 200 客位游览船　2009 年
DIAN YOU 1 HAO　200P Sightseeing Ship, Dianchi Lake　2009
主尺度　$L×B×D$（m×m×m）：35.8×8.6×1.9

船长 8 黄浦江 300 客位游览船 2009 年
CHUAN ZHANG 8 300P Sightseeing Ship, Huangpu River 2009
主尺度 $L \times B \times D$ (m×m×m)：59.2×12.8×3.6

尚德国盛 黄浦江 134 客位太阳能电力混合动力游览船 2010 年
具有光伏系统和燃油混合动力船舶
主尺度 $L \times B \times D$ (m×m×m)：32.6×9.2×2.5

SHANG DE GUO SHENG 134P Solar-electric Hybrid Power Sightseeing Ship, Huangpu River 2010
Ship with photovoltaic system and fuel oil hybrid power

林都号　黑龙江 150 客位游览船　2010 年
LIN DU HAO　150P Sightseeing Ship, Heilongjiang River　2010
主尺度　$L×B×D$ (m×m×m)：40.2×9×2.8

海河观光 9　海河 190 客位游览船　2010 年
HAI HE GUAN GUANG 9　190P Sightseeing Ship, Haihe River　2010
主尺度　$L×B×D$ (m×m×m)：42×7.5×1.7

穗水巴 08　珠江 199 客位游览船　2010 年
SUI SHUI BA 08　199P Sightseeing Ship, Pearl River 2010
主尺度 $L×B×D$ (m×m×m)：32×8×2

汉水女神号　汉江 318 客位玻璃钢游览船　2010 年
HAN SHUI NV SHEN HAO　318P FRP Sightseeing Ship, Hanjiang River 2010
主尺度 $L×B×D$ (m×m×m)：40×10×2.8

青海湖 11　青海湖 94 客位高速游览船　2011 年
QING HAI HU 11　94P High-speed Sightseeing Ship, Qinghai Lake 2011
主尺度 $L×B×D$ (m×m×m)：26.8×5.2×2

开元　大运河 100 客位游览船　2011 年
北京运河游览船
主尺度　$L×B×D$ (m×m×m)：28×6×1.3

KAI YUAN　　100P Sightseeing Ship, the Grand Canal　2011
Beijing Canal sightseeing ship

太阳岛　松花江 118 客位游览船　2011 年
TAI YANG DAO　　118P Sightseeing Ship, Songhua River　2011
主尺度　$L×B×D$ (m×m×m)：37×10×1.8

镜泊湖 430　镜泊湖 120 客位游览船　2011 年
JING PO HU 430　　120P Sightseeing Ship, Jingpo Lake　2011
主尺度　$L×B×D$ (m×m×m)：26.4×5.6×1.7

黄鹤楼号　长江 300 客位游览船 2011 年
HUANG HE LOU HAO　300P Sightseeing Ship, Yangtze River　2011
主尺度 $L×B×D$（m×m×m）：60×11×3

长航朝天门　三峡库区 800 客位双体游览船 2011 年
CHANG HANG CHAO TIAN MEN　800P Sightseeing Catamaran, Three Gorges Reservoir　2011
主尺度 $L×B×D$（m×m×m）：65.9×15.8×3

长江三峡 6　三峡库区 399 客位游览船 2012 年
CHANG JIANG SAN XIA 6　399P Sightseeing Ship, Three Gorges Reservoir 2012
主尺度 $L×B×D$（m×m×m）：69.8×11.2×3.4

东湖号　长江 500 客位双体游览船 2012 年
DONG HU HAO　500P Sightseeing Catamaran, Yangtze River 2012
主尺度 $L×B×D$（m×m×m）：57×16×4

昭君号　黄河 80 客位双体游览船 2013 年
ZHAO JUN HAO　80P Sightseeing Catamaran, Yellow River 2013
主尺度 $L×B×D$（m×m×m）：27×8.1×1.1

滕王阁号 赣江 230 客位游览船 2013 年
TENG WANG GE HAO 230P Sightseeing Ship, Ganjiang River 2013
主尺度 $L×B×D$ (m×m×m)：36.1×10×3.2

和谐号 青海湖 248 客位双体游览船 2013 年
HE XIE HAO 248P Sightseeing Catamaran , Qinghai Lake 2013
主尺度 $L×B×D$ (m×m×m)：42.4×12.6×3.8

龙客 203　黑龙江 240 客位游览船　2013 年
LONG KE 203　240P Sightseeing Ship, Heilongjiang River　2013
主尺度　$L×B×D$（m×m×m）：44×8×2.4

清江画廊 15 号　清江 490 客位游览船　2013 年　　**QING JIANG HUA LANG SHI WU HAO**　490P Sightseeing Ship, Qingjiang River　2013
特色游览船　　　　　　　　　　　　　　　　　　　Special sightseeing ship
主尺度　$L×B×D$（m×m×m）：46.4×8.5×2

印象澜沧江1号　澜沧江636客位双体游览船　2013年
特色游览船
YIN XIANG LAN CANG JIANG 1 HAO　636P Sightseeing Catamaran,
Lantsang River　2013
Special sightseeing ship
主尺度 $L \times B \times D$ (m×m×m)：48×12.6×2.3

广东工行　珠江628客位双体游览船　2014年
GUANG DONG GONG HANG　628P Sightseeing Catamaran,
Pearl River　2014
主尺度 $L \times B \times D$ (m×m×m)：50×16×3.2

于家堡1　海河59客位游览船　2015年
YU JIA PU 1　59P Sightseeing Ship, Haihe River　2015
主尺度 $L \times B \times D$ (m×m×m)：32×8.5×3.2

灵秀2号　大金湖150客位游览船　2015年
LING XIU 2 HAO　150P Sightseeing Ship, Dajin Lake　2015
主尺度 $L \times B \times D$ (m×m×m)：39×7×2

珠江水晶　珠江350客位游览船　2015年
特色游览船
主尺度 $L \times B \times D$ (m×m×m)：54.5×10.8×2.8

ZHU JIANG SHUI JING　350P Sightseeing Ship, Pearl River　2015
Special sightseeing ship

巴都　三峡库区 294 客位游览船 2015 年
特色游览船
主尺度　$L×B×D$（m×m×m）：62×13×3

BA DU　294P Sightseeing Ship, Three Gorges Reservoir 2015
Special sightseeing ship

月亮河 16 号　赤水 60 客位游览船 2016 年
YUE LIANG HE 16 HAO　60P Sightseeing Ship, Chishui River 2016
主尺度　$L×B×D$（m×m×m）：30.7×5.8×1.7

西海游0168　庐山西海196客位游览船　2016年
XI HAI YOU 0168　196P Sightseeing Ship, Lushan Xihai Lake 2016
主尺度 $L \times B \times D$ (m×m×m)：32.1×7.3×2.1

珠江红船　珠江280客位游览船　2016年
ZHU JIANG HONG CHUAN　280P Sightseeing Ship, Pearl River 2016
主尺度 $L \times B \times D$ (m×m×m)：50×15×3

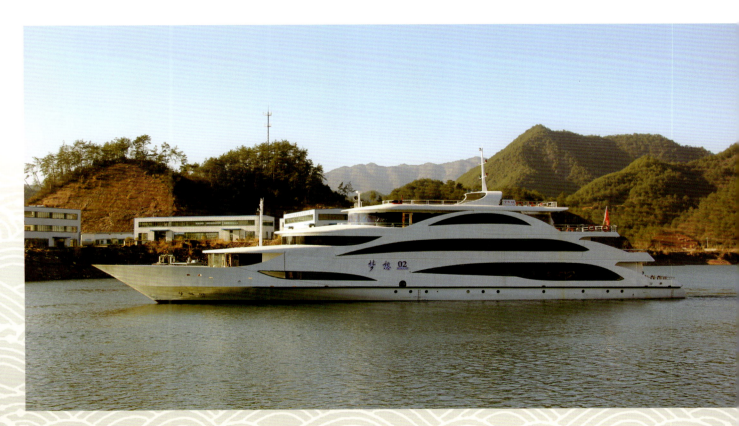

梦想02　千岛湖320客位游览船　2016年
MENG XIANG 02　320P Sightseeing Ship, Thousand-island Lake 2016
主尺度 $L \times B \times D$ (m×m×m)：57.4×10.9×3.2

武汉知音号　长江 1200 客位游览船　2016 年
特色游览船
主尺度 $L×B×D$（m×m×m）：120×22×5

WU HAN ZHI YIN HAO　1,200P Sightseeing Ship, Yangtze River　2016
Special sightseeing ship

阳航 30　漓江 100 客位游览船　2017 年
YANG HANG 30　100P Sightseeing Ship, Lijiang River　2017
主尺度 $L×B×D$（m×m×m）：32.5×5.8×1.1

新安 7 号　千岛湖 200 客位游览船　2017 年
XIN AN 7 HAO　200P Sightseeing Ship, Thousand-island Lake　2017
主尺度 $L×B×D$（m×m×m）：42×9×2.3

海星 洱海 400 客位游览船 2017 年
HAI XING 400P Sightseeing Ship, Erhai Lake 2017
主尺度 $L×B×D$ （m×m×m）：54×14×3

武汉东湖号 武汉东湖 60 客位游览船 2018 年
特色游览船
WU HAN DONG HU HAO 60P Sightseeing Ship, Wuhan Donghu Lake 2018
Special sightseeing ship
主尺度 $L×B×D$ （m×m×m）：22.8×5.2×1.4

城中湖 07 千岛湖 60 客位铝合金游览船 2018 年
特色游览船
CHENG ZHONG HU 07 60P Aluminum alloy Sightseeing Ship, Thousand-island Lake 2018
Special sightseeing ship
主尺度 $L×B×D$ （m×m×m）：23.8×6.6×1.8

凤山烟雨　京杭运河 114 客位游览船　2018 年
FENG SHAN YAN YU　114P Sightseeing Ship, Beijing-Hangzhou Canal 2018
主尺度　$L×B×D$（m×m×m）：28.8×7.3×1.9

观光 26 号　广西漓江 120 客位游览船　2018 年
GUAN GUANG 26 HAO　120P Sightseeing Ship, Guangxi Lijiang River 2018
主尺度　$L×B×D$（m×m×m）：32.2×5.8×1.1

鑫灿 9　滇池 112 客位电动双体游览船　2018 年
XIN CAN 9　112P Electric Sightseeing Catamaran, Dianchi Lake 2018
主尺度　$L×B×D$（m×m×m）：32×8×2.2

永明号　大运河 80 客位游览船　2019 年
YONG MING HAO　80P Sightseeing Ship, the Grand Canal 2019
主尺度　$L×B×D$（m×m×m）：20.5×4.5×1.2

万寿舫　颐和园昆明湖 98 客位游览船　2019 年
特色游览船
主尺度　$L×B×D$（m×m×m）：21.8×4.4×1.2

WAN SHOU FANG　98P Sightseeing Ship, Summer Palace Kunming Lake 2019
Special sightseeing ship

逸舟玉桂 杭州西湖 150 客位游览船 2019 年
YI ZHOU YU GUI 150P Sightseeing Ship, Hangzhou West Lake 2019
主尺度 $L×B×D$ (m×m×m)：22.6×5.6×1.5

紫阳商舫 汉江 60 客位画舫游览船 2019 年
ZI YANG SHANG FANG 60P Gaily-painted Sightseeing Ship, Hanjiang River 2019
主尺度 $L×B×D$ (m×m×m)：25.8×6×1.4

越州舫 杭甬运河 124 客位游览船 2019 年
特色游览船
YUE ZHOU FANG 124P Sightseeing Ship, Hangyong (Hangzhou-Ningbo) Canal 2019
Special sightseeing ship
主尺度 $L×B×D$ (m×m×m)：30×8×1.9

日月山　青海湖182客位高速游览船　2019年
RI YUE SHAN　182P High-speed Sightseeing Ship, Qinghai Lake 2019
主尺度 $L×B×D$（m×m×m）：32.1×7.2×2.5

睡美人6号　滇池78客位游览船　2019年
SHUI MEI REN 6 HAO　78P Sightseeing Ship, Dianchi Lake 2019
主尺度 $L×B×D$（m×m×m）：40.1×9.3×2

君旅号　长江300客位游览船　2019年
电池动力系统并具有绿色船舶标志
JUN LV HAO　300P Sightseeing Ship, Yangtze River 2019
With battery power system and green ship notation
主尺度 $L×B×D$（m×m×m）：53.2×10.8×2.7

长航朝天皓月　三峡库区 500 客位双体游览船 2019 年
CHANG HANG CHAO TIAN HAO YUE　500P Sightseeing Catamaran, Three Gorges Reservoir 2019
主尺度 $L \times B \times D$ (m×m×m)：68.9×18×4

长江三峡 10　三峡库区 1000 客位游览船 2019 年
CHANG JIANG SAN XIA 10　1,000P Sightseeing Ship, Three Gorges Reservoir 2019
主尺度 $L \times B \times D$ (m×m×m)：87×14.4×3.6

第二节　客滚船

内河客滚船系指设有滚装处所的客船（车客渡船除外），包括Ⅰ型客滚船和Ⅱ型客滚船。Ⅱ型客滚船主要载运柴油汽车、载货汽车驾驶员和随车工作人员，原称川江载货汽车滚装船，始于1998年。最早的客滚船一般由货船改建而成，三峡成库后新建的客滚船大多为60车位标准船型。Ⅰ型客滚船是在Ⅱ型客滚船的基础上，为满足"乘船＋自驾"的旅游方式发展起来的新船型，Ⅰ型客滚船除了载运柴油汽车、载货汽车驾驶员和随车工作人员外，还能载运汽油汽车和一般乘客。

SECTION 2　RO-RO PASSENGER SHIP

The inland waterway Ro-Ro passenger ship refers to the passenger ship with Ro-Ro spaces excluding vehicle and passenger ferries, including Type Ⅰ and Type Ⅱ Ro-Ro passenger ships. Type Ⅱ Ro-Ro passenger ships mainly carry diesel cars, cargo car drivers and accompanying staff, originally called Chuanjiang River Ro-Ro cargo truck ships, first appearing in 1998. The earliest Ro-Ro passenger ships are generally converted from cargo ships, and the new Ro-Ro passenger ships built after the completion of Three Gorges Reservoir are mostly standard 60 CEU carrier. Type Ⅰ Ro-Ro passenger ship is a new type of ship developed on the basis of Type Ⅱ Ro-Ro passenger ship to meet the travel mode of "ship + self-driving". Type Ⅰ Ro-Ro passenger ship can carry gasoline cars and general passengers in addition to diesel cars, truck drivers and accompanying staff.

串通918　三峡库区51车位Ⅱ型客滚船　2002年
CHUAN TONG 918　　Type Ⅱ 51Truck Ro-Ro Passenger Ship, Three Gorges Reservoir　2002
主尺度 $L×B×D$ (m×m×m)：99.1×16.2×3.6

庆宜 210　三峡库区 30 车位 II 型客滚船　2003 年
QING YI 210　Type II 30Truck Ro-Ro Passenger Ship, Three Gorges Reservoir 2003
主尺度 $L×B×D$ (m×m×m)：99×16.2×3.6

吉祥 698　三峡库区 60 车位 II 型客滚船　2003 年
JI XIANG 698　Type II 60Truck Ro-Ro Passenger Ship, Three Gorges Reservoir 2003
主尺度 $L×B×D$ (m×m×m)：102.8×17.8×4

峨嵋山　三峡库区 50 车位 II 型客滚船　2003 年
E MEI SHAN　Type II 50Truck Ro-Ro Passenger Ship, Three Gorges Reservoir 2003
主尺度 $L×B×D$ (m×m×m)：103×19×4

天门山　三峡库区 60 车位 II 型客滚船　2005 年
TIAN MEN SHAN　Type II 60Truck Ro-Ro Passenger Ship, Three Gorges Reservoir　2005
主尺度　$L×B×D$（m×m×m）：112×23.1×4.4

河牛 796　三峡库区 60 车位 II 型客滚船　2005 年
HE NIU 796　Type II 60Truck Ro-Ro Passenger Ship, Three Gorges Reservoir　2005
主尺度　$L×B×D$（m×m×m）：114×23×4

强舟 88　三峡库区 60 车位 II 型客滚船 2006 年
QIANG ZHOU 88　Type II 60Truck Ro-Ro Passenger Ship, Three Gorges Reservoir 2006
主尺度 $L×B×D$ （m×m×m）：114×23×4

新高湖　三峡库区 80 车位 I 型客滚船 2013 年
XIN GAO HU　Type I 80Truck Ro-Ro Passenger Ship, Three Gorges Reservoir 2013
主尺度 $L×B×D$ （m×m×m）：110×19×4.5

第三节 客渡船

内河渡船是指往返于内河渡口之间，按照核定的航线渡运乘客、车辆和货物的船舶，包括客渡船和车客渡船。客渡船是一种短程客运船舶，历史悠久，我国内河的各个水系都有客渡船存在。在20世纪80—90年代，上海、武汉等城市为了满足人们出行需要，开辟了多条轮渡航线，部分客渡船的载客人数达到1000人左右。车客渡船是连接两岸公路供人和机动车渡运的交通工具，20世纪80年代开始，长江、珠江、黄河、黑龙江等水域大力发展车客渡船。长江中下游车客渡船的主力船型一般设计为对称、双头、中机型、舯桥楼式，黄河、黑龙江等水域大多为双体的车客渡船。

SECTION 3 PASSENGER FERRY

Inland waterway ferries refer to ships that ferry passengers, vehicles and goods between inland ferry terminals according to the approved routes, including passenger ferries and vehicle and passenger ferries. A passenger ferry is a type of short-range passenger ship with a long history and exists in all systems of inland waterways in China. In the 1980s and 1990s, Shanghai, Wuhan and other cities opened up many ferry routes to meet people's travel needs, and some passenger ferries carried about 1,000 passengers. Vehicle and passenger ferry is a means of transportation connecting highways along the river for people, and motor vehicles. Since the 1980s, it has been vigorously developed in the waters of Yangtze River, Pearl River, Yellow River, Heilongjiang River, etc. The main type of vehicle and passenger ferry in the middle and lower reaches of Yangtze River is generally designed as symmetrical, double-headed, medium-sized and midship bridge type and those in the waters of Yellow River and Heilongjiang River mostly have double-hull structure.

沪航客22　黄浦江700客位客渡船　1984年
HU HANG KE 22　700P Passenger Ferry, Huangpu River 1984
主尺度 $L×B×D$ （m×m×m）：21.5×9×2.2

沪航客74　黄浦江1000客位客渡船　1985年
HU HANG KE 74　1,000P Passenger Ferry, Huangpu River 1985
主尺度 $L×B×D$ （m×m×m）：26.8×11.6×2.2

沪航 3　黄浦江 500 客位客渡船　1987 年
HU HANG 3　500P Passenger Ferry, Huangpu River　1987
主尺度 $L×B×D$（m×m×m）：42×12×4.3

沪航客 88　黄浦江 400 客位客渡船　1988 年
HU HANG KE 88　400P Passenger Ferry, Huangpu River　1988
主尺度 $L×B×D$（m×m×m）：25.9×11.6×2.2

SHIPS OF CHINA

哈渡客 439　松花江 150 客位客渡船　1988 年
HA DU KE 439　150P Passenger Ferry, Songhua River　1988
主尺度 $L\times B\times D$（m×m×m）：25×5×1.6

粤番禺渡 8501　珠江 100 客位客渡船　1991 年
YUE PAN YU DU 8501　100P Passenger Ferry, Pearl River　1991
主尺度 $L\times B\times D$（m×m×m）：29×5×1

江华 6 号　三峡库区 120 客位客渡船　2004 年
JIANG HUA 6 HAO　120P Passenger Ferry, Three Gorges Reservoir　2004
主尺度 $L\times B\times D$（m×m×m）：28×5.4×1.5

运发号　三峡库区 256 客位客渡船　2005 年
YUN FA HAO　256P Passenger Ferry, Three Gorges Reservoir　2005
主尺度 $L\times B\times D$（m×m×m）：27×5.4×1.5

安达 1 号 长江 80 客位客渡船 2007 年
AN DA 1 HAO 80P Passenger Ferry, Yangtze River 2007
主尺度 $L×B×D$ (m×m×m)：55×11×2

哈客渡 008 松花江 200 客位客渡船 2008 年
HA KE DU 008 200P Passenger Ferry, Songhua River 2008
主尺度 $L×B×D$ (m×m×m)：26×6×1.5

世博志愿者号　黄浦江 500 客位客渡船 2009 年
2010 年上海世界博览会接待船舶
主尺度 $L×B×D$ (m×m×m)：26.8×9.6×2.4

SHI BO ZHI YUAN ZHE HAO　500P Passenger Ferry, Huangpu River 2009
Ship for the Expo 2010 Shanghai China

龙客 201　黑龙江 239 客位客渡船 2010 年
LONG KE 201　239P Passenger Ferry, Heilongjiang River 2010
主尺度 $L×B×D$ (m×m×m)：41×7×2

江城 1 号　长江 800 客位客渡船 2010
JIANG CHENG 1 HAO　800P Passenger Ferry, Yangtze River 2010
主尺度 $L×B×D$ (m×m×m)：46.6×9.0×2.9

晴川阁　长江 800 客位客渡船 2010 年
QING CHUAN GE　800P Passenger Ferry, Yangtze River 2010
主尺度 $L \times B \times D$ (m×m×m)：46.6×9×2.9

江城 5 号　长江 800 客位客渡船 2010 年
JIANG CHENG 5 HAO　800P Passenger Ferry, Yangtze River 2010
主尺度 $L \times B \times D$ (m×m×m)：46.6×9×2.9

渝丰 21 号　三峡库区 120 客位客渡船 2012 年
YU FENG 21 HAO　120P Passenger Ferry, Three Gorges Reservoir 2012
主尺度 $L \times B \times D$ (m×m×m)：26×5.4×1.5

沪航客 92　黄浦江 400 客位客渡船 2014 年改建
HU HANG KE 92　400P Passenger Ferry, Huangpu River Converted in 2014
主尺度 $L \times B \times D$ (m×m×m)：25.9×11.6×2.2

上海轮渡 3　黄浦江 300 客位客渡船 2018 年
SHANG HAI LUN DU 3　300P Passenger Ferry, Huangpu River 2018
主尺度 $L \times B \times D$ (m×m×m)：26.2×10.6×2.4

"龙推312" 船组　黑龙江汽车渡船组　1985 年
LONG TUI 312 COMBINATION　Vehicle Passenger Ferry Combination, Heilongjiang River 1985
主尺度 $L×B×D$ （m×m×m）：推 23×7.6×2　驳 67.2×16×2.3

江苏路渡 2007　长江 73 米车客渡船　1987 年
JIANG SU LU DU 2007　73m Vehicle Passenger Ferry, Yangtze River 1987
主尺度 $L×B×D$ （m×m×m）：73×13.8×3.4

江苏渡 7 号　长江 44 米车客渡船　1988 年
JIANG SU DU 7 HAO　44m Vehicle Passenger Ferry, Yangtze River 1988
主尺度 $L×B×D$ （m×m×m）：44.5×13.5×3

穗港渡车 2　珠江 38 米车客渡船　1989 年
SUI GANG DU CHE 2　38m Vehicle Passenger Ferry, Pearl River　1989
主尺度　$L×B×D$（m×m×m）：37.8×8.4×2

北京号　长江 135 米火车渡船　1990 年
BEI JING HAO　135m Train Passenger Ferry, Yangtze River　1990
主尺度　$L×B×D$（m×m×m）：134.6×17.2×6.5

黄船 023　珠江 38 米车客渡船　1991 年
HUANG CHUAN 023　38m Vehicle Passenger Ferry, Pearl River　1991
主尺度　$L×B×D$（m×m×m）：37.8×8.4×2

马当江洲渡 2　长江 59 米车客渡船　1992 年
MA DANG JIANG ZHOU DU 2　59m Vehicle Passenger Ferry, Yangtze River　1992
主尺度　$L×B×D$（m×m×m）：59×13.2×3

崇明 1　长江 57 米车客渡船　1997 年
CHONG MING 1　57m Vehicle Passenger Ferry, Yangtze River　1997
主尺度 $L×B×D$ (m×m×m)：57.1×11.9×3.2

龙渡 004　黑龙江 74 米车客渡船　2004 年
中俄界江第一艘车客渡船
LONG DU 004　74m Vehicle Passenger Ferry, Heilongjiang River　2004
First vehicle passenger ferry on the China-Russia border river
主尺度 $L×B×D$ (m×m×m)：74×13.6×2.7

闽三明渡 3005　闽江 33 米车客渡船　2006 年
MIN SAN MING DU 3005　33m Vehicle Passenger Ferry, Minjiang River　2006
主尺度 $L×B×D$ (m×m×m)：33.3×6.1×1.6

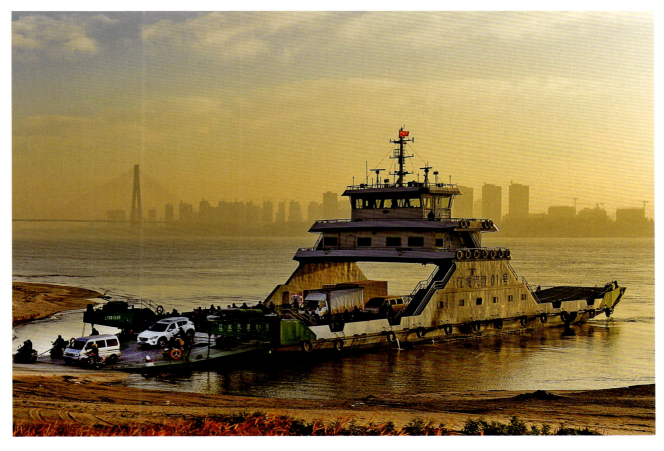

江城汽渡 01 号　长江 77 米车客渡船　2011 年
JIANG CHENG QI DU 01 HAO　77m Vehicle Passenger Ferry, Yangtze River　2011
主尺度　$L \times B \times D$ (m×m×m)：76.6×14.4×3.3

新长号　长江 135 米火车渡船　2011 年
XIN CHANG HAO　135m Train Passenger Ferry, Yangtze River　2011
主尺度　$L \times B \times D$ (m×m×m)：135.3×17.2×6.5

穗港渡车 6　珠江 48 米车客渡船　2012 年
SUI GANG DU CHE 6　48m Vehicle Passenger Ferry, Pearl River　2012
主尺度　$L \times B \times D$ (m×m×m)：48×10.5×2.5

江苏路渡 3011　长江 90 米全回转车客渡船　2017 年
JIANG SU LU DU 3011　90m Z-propulsion Vehicle Passenger Ferry, Yangtze River　2017
主尺度　$L×B×D$（m×m×m）：89.5×15.4×3.5

生态岛 2　长江 70 米快速车客渡船　2018 年
SHENG TAI DAO 2　70m High-speed Vehicle Passenger Ferry, Yangtze River　2018
主尺度　$L×B×D$（m×m×m）：70.3×12.8×3.8

板新贰号　长江 80 米全回转车客渡船 2018 年
BAN XIN ER HAO　80m Z-propulsion Vehicle Passenger Ferry, Yangtze River 2018
主尺度 $L×B×D$ (m×m×m)：80.5×14.4×3.3

江苏渡 26 号　长江 90 米车客渡船 2019 年
JIANG SU DU 26 HAO　90m Vehicle Passenger Ferry, Yangtze River 2019
主尺度 $L×B×D$ (m×m×m)：89.6×15.4×3.5

第四节 高速客船

内河高速客船是指航行于内河水域、航速达到高速船界定的船舶。20世纪80年代，珠江三角洲通过进口或新建双体高速客船，率先开始了高速客船的营运。20世纪80年代后期，长江、黑龙江相继开通高速客船的航线，主要船型有单体高速船、双体高速船、水翼船和气垫船等类型。其中，水翼船时速最快可达90公里，被称为"水上高速"，成为当时长江三峡水上客运的标志之一。当时的高速客船以满足人们的交通出行需求为主，进入21世纪后，由于高速公路、高速铁路的建设，高速客船已向旅游观光转型。

SECTION 4　HIGH-SPEED PASSENGER SHIP

An inland high-speed passenger ship refers to a vessel sailing in inland waters, the speed of which reaches the definition of high-speed ship. In the 1980s, the Pearl River Delta took the lead in the operation of high-speed passenger ships by importing or building new catamaran high-speed passenger ships. In the late 1980s, the Yangtze River and Heilongjiang River successively opened the routes of high-speed passenger ships. The main ship types were high-speed monohull craft, high-speed catamaran, hydrofoil and hovercraft. Among them, the speed of the fastest hydrofoil, which is called "water expressway", could reach 90km/h, becoming one of the symbols of passenger transportation on the Yangtze River Three Gorges at that time. In this period, high-speed passenger ships mainly aimed to meet people's travel needs. After entering the 21st century, however, they have evolved into tourism ships as the road and railways network has massively expanded.

北湖　长江250客位高速客船　2005年
BEI HU　250P High-speed Passenger Ship, Yangtze River　2005
主尺度 $L \times B \times D$ (m×m×m)：33×8.8×2.7

东海绿洲　长江 365 客位高速双体客船　2008 年
DONG HAI LV ZHOU　365P High-speed catamaran, Yangtze River　2008
主尺度 $L×B×D$ (m×m×m)：41.3×11.5×3.9

东屿岛 5 号　海南 80 客位高速客船　2009 年
DONG YU DAO 5 HAO　80P High-speed Passenger Ship, Hainan　2009
主尺度 $L×B×D$ (m×m×m)：25×4.5×1.6

瀛洲 2　长江 150 客位高速客船　2012 年
YING ZHOU 2　150P High-speed Passenger Ship, Yangtze River　2012
主尺度 $L×B×D$ (m×m×m)：33.3×6×2.4

建业 002 号　澜沧江 114 客位高速客船　2013 年
JIAN YE 002 HAO　114P High-speed Passenger Ship, Lantsang River 2013
主尺度　$L×B×D$（m×m×m）：27.6×5.2×1.8

牛山宿雁　东江湖 123 客位高速客船　2014 年
NIU SHAN SU YAN　123P High-speed Passenger Ship, Dongjiang Lake 2014
主尺度　$L×B×D$（m×m×m）：27×5.1×2.1

瀛洲 7　长江 150 客位高速客船　2015 年
YING ZHOU 7　150P High-speed Passenger Ship, Yangtze River 2015
主尺度　$L×B×D$（m×m×m）：35.5×6×2.4

澜湄 1 号　澜沧江 92 客位高速客船　2016 年
LAN MEI 1 HAO　92P High-speed Passenger Ship, Lantsang River 2016
主尺度　$L×B×D$（m×m×m）：26×4.8×2

东江湖 1 号　东江湖 118 客位高速客船　2016 年
DONG JIANG HU 1 HAO　118P High-speed Passenger Ship, Dongjiang Lake 2016
主尺度　$L \times B \times D$ (m×m×m)：27×5.6×2.3

飞翼 11　长江 120 客位高速客船　2016 年
FEI YI 11　120P High-speed Passenger Ship, Yangtze River 2016
主尺度　$L \times B \times D$ (m×m×m)：32.8×6×2.3

易水湖 12 号　易水湖 94 客位高速客船　2017 年
YI SHUI HU 12 HAO　94P High-speed Passenger Ship, Yishui Lake 2017
主尺度　$L \times B \times D$ (m×m×m)：26×4.8×1.9

长航飞翔 4　长江 128 客位水翼客船　1988 年
CHANG HANG FEI XIANG 4　128P Hydrofoil Passenger Ship, Yangtze River　1988
主尺度　$L×B×D$（m×m×m）：34.6×5.6×1.6

飞鱼 01　镜泊湖 53 客位水翼客船　1989 年
FEI YU 01　53P Hydrofoil Passenger Ship, Jingpo Lake　1989
主尺度　$L×B×D$（m×m×m）：21×4×1

海巡 13202　黑龙江 51 客位侧壁式气垫客船　1992 年
HAI XUN 13202　51P Side-wall Passenger Hovercraft, Heilongjiang River　1992
主尺度　$L×B×D$（m×m×m）：23×4×1

长江 1 号　长江 139 客位水翼客船　1992 年
CHANG JIANG 1 HAO　139P Hydrofoil Passenger Ship, Yangtze River　1992
主尺度　$L×B×D$（m×m×m）：34.6×5.6×1.6

龙腾 20　黑龙江 45 客位水翼客船　1995 年
LONG TENG 20　45P Hydrofoil Passenger Ship, Heilongjiang River　1995
主尺度 $L \times B \times D$ (m×m×m)：21.3×3.6×1.2

长江 9 号　长江 140 客位水翼客船　1998 年
CHANG JIANG 9 HAO　140P Hydrofoil Passenger Ship, Yangtze River　1998
主尺度 $L \times B \times D$ (m×m×m)：34.6×5.6×1.6

启航舰旗　黄河 80 客位全垫升气垫客船　2002 年
QI HANG JIAN QI　80P Fully Cushioned Passenger Hovercraft, Yellow River　2002
主尺度 $L \times B \times D$ (m×m×m)：22.1×4.8×1.2

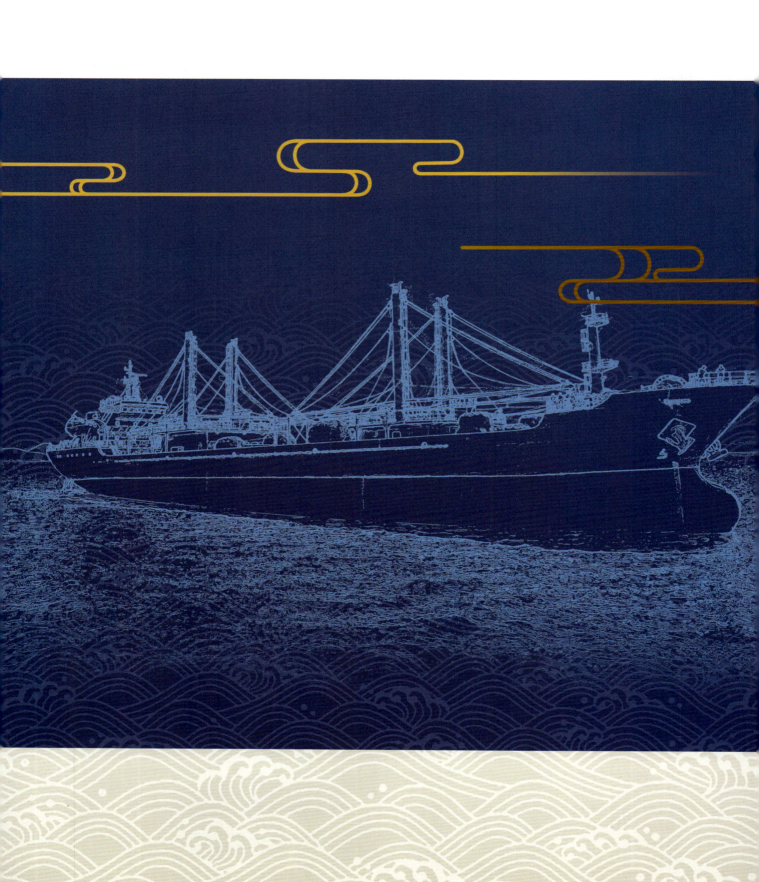

第一章 捕捞渔船

捕捞渔船是指捕捞鱼类或其他经济水生动植物的专用船舶。主要类型有拖网渔船、围网渔船、钓具渔船、刺网渔船、张网渔船、耙刺渔船、笼壶渔船等。

捕捞渔船按作业水域分为海洋捕捞渔船和内河（淡水）捕捞渔船。海洋捕捞渔船又分沿岸、近海和远洋捕捞渔船。远洋渔船有大洋性和过洋性两种，大洋性渔业是指主要在公海海域进行捕捞作业的远洋渔业活动，过洋性渔业是指主要在外国专属经济区海域进行捕捞作业的远洋渔业活动。大型远洋渔船的作业半径可达上万海里。

捕捞渔船按船体材料分为木质、钢质、玻璃钢、铝合金、钢丝网水泥渔船及各种混合结构渔船。钢丝网水泥渔船已基本淘汰，木质渔船仍较普遍但已落后，沿岸玻璃钢渔船发展迅速，远洋渔船则主要为钢质渔船。为高效捕捞和抵御风浪，海洋捕捞渔船要求具有良好的适航性，在鱼舱和燃油舱布置、稳性、推进装置配置和结构强度等方面有较高的要求。渔船作业期间捕捞作业会产生额外的力矩，因此控制渔船稳性和浮态至关重要。捕捞渔船除配置一般船用设备外，还需配备渔船专用捕捞机械、保鲜设备、助渔导航设备。鱼舱要求具有良好的隔热性，大型渔船还配有加工设备以便在海上直接加工渔获物。渔船常采用带冰保鲜、制冷装置冷冻冷藏保鲜、冷海水保鲜等方式来保持渔获物的鲜度。大型捕捞加工渔船装备有清洗、分级、原料处理、切片、鱼糜制品和鱼粉等加工设备。

20世纪80年代，我国开始引进大型拖网加工船。进入21世纪，我国开始自行设计建造金枪鱼围网船，并实现了高纬度金枪鱼延绳钓船技术的突破。

CHAPTER I   FISHING VESSELS

A fishing vessel refers to special ships for catching fish or other economic aquatic animals and plants. The main types are trawler, seiner, liner, gill netter, stow netter, rakes and pricks, baskets and pots fishing vessels, etc.

Fishing vessels are divided into marine fishing vessels and inland waterway (freshwater) fishing vessels depending on the operating waters. Marine fishing vessels are further divided into three types: coastal, offshore and ocean-going fishing vessels. Ocean-going fishing vessels have two types: oceanic and transoceanic. Oceanic fishery refers to fishing activities mainly in the high seas, while transoceanic fishery refers to fishing activities mainly in the waters of foreign exclusive economic zones. The operating radius of large ocean-going fishing vessels can reach tens of thousands of nautical miles.

According to the hull materials, fishing vessels are divided into wooden, steel, fiberglass reinforced plastic, aluminum alloy, Ferrocement fishing vessels and various mixed structure fishing vessels. Wire mesh cement fishing vessels have been eliminated while wooden fishing vessels are still common but functionally lag behind while coastal fiberglass fishing vessels are developing rapidly. Ocean-going fishing vessels mainly comprise steel fishing vessels. In order to improve fishing efficiency and resist wind and waves, marine fishing vessels are required to have good seaworthiness and have high requirements for fish and fuel tank arrangement, stability, propulsion device configuration and structural strength. The fishing operation will generate additional torque, so it is crucial to control the stability of the vessel. In addition to the general marine equipment, fishing vessels need to be equipped with special fishing machinery, preservation equipment and navigation equipment to aid fishing. The fish tank is required to have good heat insulation, and large fishing vessels are equipped with processing equipment to process the catch at sea directly. Fishing vessels often use ice preservation, refrigeration, freezing, cold seawater preservation and other methods to maintain catch freshness. Large fishing and processing ships are equipped with equipment for cleaning, grading, raw material handling, filleting mincing, etc.

In the 1980s, China began to introduce large factory trawlers. Entering the 21st century, China started to design and build its own tuna purse seiners, and achieved a technical breakthrough in high-latitude tuna longliners.

第一节　海洋拖网渔船

SECTION 1　MARINE TRAWLER

开创　远洋大型拖网加工渔船 1986 年
我国第一艘远洋拖网加工渔船
主尺度 $L×B×D$ (m×m×m)：92×15×9.6

KAI CHUANG　Large Factory-trawler, Ocean-going　1986
China's first ocean-going factory trawler

粤霞渔 90023　海洋单拖渔船　1988 年
YUE XIA YU 90023　Otter Trawler, Marine　1988
主尺度　$L×B×D$（m×m×m）：30.4×5.8×2.7

闽霞渔 02287　海洋双拖渔船　1991 年
MIN XIA YU 02287　Bull Trawler, Marine　1991
主尺度　$L×B×D$（m×m×m）：29.9×5.7×2.5

辽大高渔 25358　海洋单拖渔船　1995 年
LIAO DA GAO YU 25358　Otter Trawler, Marine　1995
主尺度　$L×B×D$（m×m×m）：30.4×5.8×2.7

浙椒渔 76045　海洋桁拖渔船　1995 年
ZHE JIAO YU 76045　Beam Trawler, Marine　1995
主尺度　$L×B×D$（m×m×m）：34.5×6.2×2.9

浙普渔 68318　海洋单拖渔船 1996 年
ZHE PU YU 68318　Otter Trawler, Marine　1996
主尺度 $L \times B \times D$ (m×m×m)：35.1×6.5×2.9

浙椒渔 72016　海洋桁拖渔船 1999 年
ZHE JIAO YU 72016　Beam Trawler, Marine　1999
主尺度 $L \times B \times D$ (m×m×m)：34×6×2.7

浙临渔 21696　海洋桁拖渔船 1999 年
ZHE LIN YU 21696　Beam Trawler, Marine　1999
主尺度 $L \times B \times D$ (m×m×m)：36.5×6.2×2.9

粤廉渔 28288　海洋双拖渔船 2008 年
YUE LIAN YU 28288　Bull Trawler, Marine　2008
主尺度 $L \times B \times D$ (m×m×m)：34.8×6.4×3.5

鲁海渔 1482 海洋拖网渔船 2009 年
LU HAI YU 1482 Trawler, Marine 2009
主尺度 $L×B×D$ (m×m×m)：19×4×1.5

鲁文渔 67558 海洋双拖渔船 2009 年
LU WEN YU 67558 Bull Trawler, Marine 2009
主尺度 $L×B×D$ (m×m×m)：22×4.5×1.7

鲁威渔 0137 海洋拖网渔船 2009 年
LU WEI YU 0137 Trawler, Marine 2009
主尺度 $L×B×D$ (m×m×m)：33×5.6×2.7

远渔 908 远洋双甲板深水拖网渔船 2009 年
YUAN YU 908 Double Decked Deep-water Trawler, Ocean-going 2009
主尺度 $L×B×D$ (m×m×m)：36.8×8.6×6

沪崇渔1256　海洋拖网渔船　2009年
HU CHONG YU 1256　Trawler, Marine　2009
主尺度　$L×B×D$（m×m×m）：36×6.3×3

海润3　海洋双拖渔船　2010年
HAI RUN 3　Bull Trawler, Marine　2010
主尺度　$L×B×D$（m×m×m）：39.6×7.9×4.5

龙发 远洋大型拖网加工渔船 2010 年
LONG FA Large Factory-trawler, Ocean-going 2010
主尺度 $L×B×D$ (m×m×m)：120.7×19×9.3

福荣海 远洋大型拖网加工渔船 2012 年
FU RONG HAI Large Factory-trawler, Ocean-going 2012
主尺度 $L×B×D$ (m×m×m)：110.8×17.8×11

浙岱渔 10279　海洋桁拖渔船 2013 年
ZHE DAI YU 10279　Beam Trawler, Marine 2013
主尺度　$L×B×D$（m×m×m）：47.6×7×3.7

辽东渔 537　远洋单拖渔船 2013 年
LIAO DONG YU 537　Otter Trawler, Ocean-going 2013
主尺度　$L×B×D$（m×m×m）：49.8×9.8×6.3

鲁荣远渔 989　远洋单拖渔船 2013 年
LU RONG YUAN YU 989　Otter Trawler, Ocean-going　2013
主尺度 $L×B×D$ (m×m×m)：51.7×8.8×4.6

沪渔 1205　远洋双甲板拖网渔船 2014 年
HU YU 1205　Double Decked Trawler, Ocean-going　2014
主尺度 $L×B×D$ (m×m×m)：33.2×9×5.9

鲁青远渔 209　远洋单拖渔船 2014 年
LU QING YUAN YU 209　Otter Trawler, Ocean-going　2014
主尺度 $L×B×D$ (m×m×m)：65×13.2×5.6

鲁荣渔 69689　海洋拖网渔船　2015 年
LU RONG YU 69689　Trawler, Marine　2015
主尺度 $L×B×D$ (m×m×m)：27.2×5×2.2

龙达 8801　远洋双甲板拖网渔船　2015 年
LONG DA 8801　Double Decked Trawler, Ocean-going　2015
主尺度 $L×B×D$ (m×m×m)：49.8×9.8×6.3

鲁烟开远渔 977　远洋拖网渔船　2015 年
LU YAN KAI YUAN YU 977　Trawler, Ocean-going　2015
主尺度 $L×B×D$ (m×m×m)：57×9.6×4.6

鲁文渔 53797　海洋拖网渔船　2016 年
LU WEN YU 53797　Trawler, Marine　2016
主尺度 $L×B×D$ (m×m×m)：32×5.4×2.5

红宝石壹号　海洋双拖渔船　2016 年
HONG BAO SHI YI HAO　Bull Trawler, Marine　2016
主尺度 $L×B×D$ (m×m×m)：42.8×8.5×4.6

鲁青远渔 338　远洋拖网渔船　2017 年
LU QING YUAN YU 338　Trawler, Ocean-going　2017
主尺度 $L×B×D$ (m×m×m)：46.7×7.6×4

闽狮渔 03989　海洋拖网渔船 2017 年
MIN SHI YU 03989　Trawler, Marine 2017
主尺度 $L×B×D$ (m×m×m)：48.9×8.4×4.2

福远渔 9801　远洋尾滑道拖网渔船 2018 年
FU YUAN YU 9801　Stern Ramp Trawler, Ocean-going 2018
主尺度 $L×B×D$ (m×m×m)：45×7.8×4.1

辽庄渔 85161　海洋拖网渔船 2018 年
LIAO ZHUANG YU 85161　Trawler, Marine 2018
主尺度 $L×B×D$ (m×m×m)：48×7.6×4

鲁乳渔 64919 海洋拖网渔船 2019 年
LU RU YU 64919 Trawler, Marine 2019
主尺度 $L×B×D$ (m×m×m)：21.3×4×1.8

国际 839 远洋尾滑道拖网渔船 2019 年
GUO JI 839 Stern Ramp Trawler, Ocean-going 2019
主尺度 $L×B×D$ (m×m×m)：40.9×7.3×3.6

粤汕城渔 16118　海洋 LNG 动力拖网渔船　2019 年
YUE SHAN CHENG YU 16118　Trawler, LNG as fuel, Marine　2019
主尺度　$L×B×D$（m×m×m）：53.5×8.5×4.4

大洲 1006　远洋尾滑道拖网渔船　2019 年
DA ZHOU 1006　Stern Ramp Trawler, Ocean-going　2019
主尺度　$L×B×D$（m×m×m）：59×9.6×6.6

鲁青远渔 228　远洋尾滑道拖网渔船　2019 年
LU QING YUAN YU 228　Stern Ramp Trawler, Ocean-going　2019
主尺度　$L×B×D$（m×m×m）：70×13.6×8.4

深蓝 远洋大型捕捞加工船 2019 年
SHEN LAN Large Fishing Factory Vessel, Ocean-going 2019
主尺度 $L \times B \times D$ (m×m×m)：120.3×21.6×12.5

海义伍 海洋双拖渔船
HAI YI WU Bull Trawler, Marine
主尺度 $L \times B \times D$ (m×m×m)：44.8×8.5×4.6

第二节　海洋围网渔船
SECTION 2　MARINE SEINER

泰隆1　远洋大型金枪鱼围网船 2012年购进
TAI LONG 1　Large Tuna Seiner, Ocean-going Purchased in 2012
主尺度 $L×B×D$ (m×m×m)：64.7×12.2×7.2

金汇8　远洋大型金枪鱼围网船 2012年
我国设计建造的第一艘大型金枪鱼围网船
JIN HUI 8　Large Tuna Seiner, Ocean-going 2012
First large tuna seiner designed and built by China
主尺度 $L×B×D$ (m×m×m)：75.5×12.8×7.8

鲁荣远渔118　远洋围网渔船 2013年
LU RONG YUAN YU 118　Seiner, Ocean-going 2013
主尺度 $L×B×D$ (m×m×m)：56×9.2×4.2

乐亭 05 远洋欧式围网渔船 2015 年
LAO TING 05 European Seiner, Ocean-going 2015
主尺度 $L \times B \times D$ (m×m×m)：24.2×8.2×4.5

新世纪 112 远洋大型金枪鱼围网船 2015 年
XIN SHI JI 112 Large Tuna Seiner, Ocean-going 2015
主尺度 $L \times B \times D$ (m×m×m)：75.3×13.6×7.7

金汇 58 远洋大型金枪鱼围网船 2016 年
JIN HUI 58 Large Tuna Seiner, Ocean-going 2016
主尺度 $L×B×D$ (m×m×m)：75.9×13.5×7.7

台沙 2138（顺景） 海洋单船围网渔船 2019 年
TAI SHA 2138 (SHUN JING) Single-Vessel Seiner, Marine 2019
主尺度 $L×B×D$ (m×m×m)：55.3×9.8×5

第三节 海洋刺网渔船
SECTION 3　　MARINE GILL NETTER

粤湛渔 01261　海洋定置刺网渔船　1989 年
YUE ZHAN YU 01261　Set Gill Netter, Marine　1989
主尺度 $L×B×D$（m×m×m）：21×4.9×2

粤湛渔 07138　海洋木质流刺网渔船　1990 年
YUE ZHAN YU 07138　Wooden Drift Gillnetter, Marine　1990
主尺度 $L×B×D$（m×m×m）：21×4.6×2.1

粤雷渔 11071　海洋木质围刺网渔船　1993 年
YUE LEI YU 11071　Wooden Circle Gill Netter, Marine　1993
主尺度 $L×B×D$（m×m×m）：20×4.8×2.2

辽庄渔 65066　海洋流刺网渔船　1997 年
LIAO ZHUANG YU 65066　Drift Gillnetter, Marine　1997
主尺度　$L×B×D$ (m×m×m)：29.5×5.8×2.2

浙临渔 12809　海洋流刺网渔船　2002 年
ZHE LIN YU 12809　Drift Gillnetter, Marine　2002
主尺度　$L×B×D$ (m×m×m)：37.2×6.4×3.2

闽闽渔 61108　海洋流刺网渔船　2007 年
MIN MIN YU 61108　Drift Gillnetter, Marine　2007
主尺度　$L×B×D$ (m×m×m)：29.2×5.3×2.4

浙临渔 12698　海洋流刺网渔船　2010 年
ZHE LIN YU 12698　Drift Gillnetter, Marine　2010
主尺度 $L×B×D$ (m×m×m)：23.8×4.3×1.8

闽东渔 61226　海洋流刺网渔船　2011 年
MIN DONG YU 61226　Drift Gillnetter, Marine　2011
主尺度 $L×B×D$ (m×m×m)：36.5×6.3×3

福远渔 961　远洋流刺网渔船　2011 年
FU YUAN YU 961　Drift Gillnetter, Ocean-going　2011
主尺度 $L×B×D$ (m×m×m)：45×7.3×3.8

苏赣渔 03369　海洋流刺网渔船 2012 年
SU GAN YU 03369　Drift Gillnetter, Marine 2012
主尺度　$L×B×D$（m×m×m）：35×6.2×2.9

福远渔 098　远洋流刺网渔船 2012 年
FU YUAN YU 098　Drift Gillnetter, Ocean-going 2012
主尺度　$L×B×D$（m×m×m）：50×8.6×4

琼临渔 12242　海洋木质流刺网渔船 2013 年
QIONG LIN YU 12242　Wooden Drift Gillnetter, Marine 2013
主尺度　$L×B×D$（m×m×m）：29.4×5.8×2.7

福远渔 9613　远洋流刺网渔船　2014 年
FU YUAN YU 9613　Drift Gillnetter, Ocean-going　2014
主尺度　$L \times B \times D$（m×m×m）：36.8×7×3.4

闽福鼎渔 02333　海洋流刺网渔船　2014 年
MIN FU DING YU 02333　Drift Gillnetter, Marine　2014
主尺度　$L \times B \times D$（m×m×m）：45×6.8×3.6

闽狮渔 07607　海洋流刺网渔船　2015 年
MIN SHI YU 07607　Drift Gillnetter, Marine　2015
主尺度 $L×B×D$（m×m×m）：25.3×5.7×2.8

鲁威高渔 65007　海洋玻璃钢流刺网渔船　2016 年
LU WEI GAO YU 65007　FRP Drift Gillnetter, Marine　2016
主尺度　$L×B×D$（m×m×m）：21.3×4×1.8

闽霞渔 01110　海洋流刺网渔船　2016 年
MIN XIA YU 01110　Drift Gillnetter, Marine　2016
主尺度　$L×B×D$（m×m×m）：46.2×7×3.6

鲁东渔 60003　海洋流刺网渔船　2018 年
LU DONG YU 60003　Drift Gillnetter, Marine　2018
主尺度 $L \times B \times D$ (m×m×m)：29.8×5.3×2.3

粤廉渔 21133　海洋流刺网渔船　2019 年
YUE LIAN YU 21133　Drift Gillnetter, Marine　2019
主尺度 $L \times B \times D$ (m×m×m)：47.7×7.3×4.2

第四节 海洋钓具渔船

SECTION 4   MARINE FISHING TACKLE VESSEL

辽长渔 55112　海洋木质刺钓渔船　1994 年
LIAO CHANG YU 55112　Wooden Gillnet Fishing Vessel, Marine　1994
主尺度 $L×B×D$ (m×m×m)：14.4×3.5×0.9

新世纪三十七号　远洋金枪鱼延绳钓渔船　2001 年　　　**XIN SHI JI NO. 37**　Tuna Longliner, Ocean-going　2001
我国第一艘大型超低温金枪鱼延绳钓渔船　　　　　　　　China's first large ultra-low temperature tuna longliner
主尺度 $L×B×D$ (m×m×m)：56.4×8.7×3.8

昌荣1号　远洋金枪鱼延绳钓渔船　2003年
我国第一艘高纬度金枪鱼延绳钓渔船
主尺度　L×B×D（m×m×m）：58.2×9×4

CHANG RONG NO. 1　Tuna Longliner, Ocean-going　2003
China's first high-latitude tuna longliner

京远906　远洋金枪鱼延绳钓渔船　2004年
JING YUAN 906　Tuna Longliner, Ocean-going　2004
主尺度　L×B×D（m×m×m）：55.8×8.7×3.8

SHIPS OF CHINA

中水 706　远洋金枪鱼延绳钓渔船 2008 年
ZHONG SHUI 706　Tuna Longliner, Ocean-going 2008
主尺度　$L×B×D$ (m×m×m)：36.6×6.6×3.3

普远 801　远洋鱿鱼钓渔船 2009 年
PU YUAN 801　Squid Jigger, Ocean-going 2009
主尺度　$L×B×D$ (m×m×m)：48.3×8×3.8

平太荣 19　远洋金枪鱼延绳钓渔船 2011 年
PING TAI RONG NO. 19　Tuna Longliner, Ocean-going 2011
主尺度　$L×B×D$ (m×m×m)：44.8×7×3.8

宁泰 16　远洋鱿鱼钓渔船　2011 年
NING TAI 16　Squid Jigger, Ocean-going　2011
主尺度 $L×B×D$ （m×m×m）：60×8.6×6

国际 902　远洋鱿鱼钓渔船　2011 年
GUO JI 902　Squid Jigger, Ocean-going　2011
主尺度 $L×B×D$ （m×m×m）：60.9×9.5×6.4

东渔 1518　远洋金枪鱼延绳钓渔船 2012 年
DONG YU 1518　Tuna Longliner, Ocean-going　2012
主尺度　$L×B×D$（m×m×m）：45.8×7.2×3.7

鲁威远渔 388　远洋金枪鱼延绳钓渔船 2013 年
LU WEI YUAN YU 388　Tuna Longliner, Ocean-going　2013
主尺度　$L×B×D$（m×m×m）：50×7.8×3.8

鲁蓬远渔 017　远洋鱿鱼钓渔船 2013 年
LU PENG YUAN YU 017　Squid Jigger, Ocean-going　2013
主尺度　$L×B×D$（m×m×m）：76.7×11.3×7.4

鲁青远渔 026　远洋金枪鱼延绳钓渔船 2014 年
LU QING YUAN YU 026　Tuna Longliner, Ocean-going　2014
主尺度　$L×B×D$（m×m×m）：59.6×9.1×4

舟渔 9　远洋鱿鱼钓渔船　2014 年
ZHOU YU NO.9　Squid Jigger, Ocean-going　2014
主尺度 $L \times B \times D$ (m×m×m)：66×10×6.5

鲁黄远渔 118　远洋鱿鱼钓渔船　2014 年
LU HUANG YUAN YU 118　Squid Jigger, Ocean-going　2014
主尺度 $L \times B \times D$ (m×m×m)：77.8×11.6×7.3

闽漳渔 60256　海洋曳绳钓渔船　2015 年
MIN ZHANG YU 60256　Trolling Vessel, Marine　2015
主尺度 $L \times B \times D$ (m×m×m)：26.3×5.4×2.4

中巨 18　远洋鱿鱼钓渔船　2015 年
ZHONG JU 18　Squid Jigger, Ocean-going　2015
主尺度　L×B×D (m×m×m)：58×8.2×4.2

京远 626　远洋鱿鱼钓渔船　2015 年
JING YUAN 626　Squid Jigger, Ocean-going　2015
主尺度　L×B×D (m×m×m)：73.6×11.3×6.9

隆兴 801　远洋玻璃钢金枪鱼延绳钓渔船　2017 年
LONG XING 801　FRP Tuna Longliner, Ocean-going　2017
主尺度　L×B×D (m×m×m)：39×7×3

鲁青远渔 117　远洋金枪鱼延绳钓渔船　2018 年
LU QING YUAN YU 117　Tuna Longliner, Ocean-going　2018
主尺度　L×B×D (m×m×m)：47×7.6×3.8

福远渔 7869　远洋鱿鱼钓渔船　2018 年
FU YUAN YU 7869　Squid Jigger, Ocean-going　2018
主尺度　L×B×D (m×m×m)：66×10.4×6.2

鲁荣渔 58930　海洋竿钓渔船　2019 年
LU RONG YU 58930　Pole Fishing Vessel, Marine　2019
主尺度 $L×B×D$ (m×m×m)：34.2×6×2.5

鲁荣远渔 938　远洋金枪鱼延绳钓渔船　2019 年
LU RONG YUAN YU 938　Tuna Longliner, Ocean-going　2019
主尺度 $L×B×D$ (m×m×m)：43.6×7.2×3.8

琼儋渔 19327　海洋金枪鱼延绳钓渔船　2019 年
采用电力推进系统
QIONG DAN YU 19327　Tuna Longliner, Marine　2019
With electric propulsion system
主尺度 $L×B×D$ (m×m×m)：49.5×8.2×3.6

第五节　其他海洋捕捞渔船
SECTION 5　OTHER MARINE FISHING VESSELS

浙鄞渔 81266　海洋张网渔船　1995 年
ZHE YIN YU 81266　Stow Netter, Marine　1995
主尺度　$L×B×D$ (m×m×m)：34.4×6.4×2.9

闽福鼎渔 01918　海洋张网渔船　2007 年
MIN FU DING YU 01918　Stow Netter, Marine　2007
主尺度　$L×B×D$ (m×m×m)：47.8×7.1×3.6

辽丹渔 7716　远洋灯光罩网渔船 2009 年
LIAO DAN YU 7716　Light Falling-net Fishing Vessel, Ocean-going　2009
主尺度 $L×B×D$ (m×m×m)：45×7.6×3.8

桂北渔 80208　海洋灯光罩网渔船 2010 年
GUI BEI YU 80208　Light Falling-net Fishing Vessel, Marine　2010
主尺度 $L×B×D$ (m×m×m)：43.6×7.6×4.1

琼陵水 12222　海洋灯光罩网渔船 2011 年
QIONG LING SHUI 12222　Light Falling-net Fishing Vessel, Marine　2011
主尺度 $L×B×D$ (m×m×m)：37.8×6.3×3.4

福远渔 976　远洋笼壶渔船　2012 年
FU YUAN YU 976　Baskets and Pots Fishing Vessel, Ocean-going　2012
主尺度　$L \times B \times D$（m×m×m）：26×5.3×2.4

苏启渔 03109　海洋张网渔船　2013 年
SU QI YU 03109　Stow Netter, Marine　2013
主尺度　$L \times B \times D$（m×m×m）：39.2×7.3×3.2

桂北渔 65828　海洋灯光罩网渔船　2013 年
GUI BEI YU 65828　Light Falling-net Fishing Vessel, Marine　2013
主尺度　$L \times B \times D$（m×m×m）：58.6×8.2×4.5

福远渔163　远洋灯光罩网渔船　2014年
FU YUAN YU 163　Light Falling-net Fishing Vessel, Ocean-going　2014
主尺度 $L×B×D$（m×m×m）：56.7×10.8×5.3

苏启渔03444　海洋张网渔船　2015年
SU QI YU 03444　Stow Netter, Marine　2015
主尺度 $L×B×D$（m×m×m）：55×8.2×4

鲁岚渔65767　海洋耙刺作业渔船　2019年
LU LAN YU 65767　Rakes and Pricks Fishing Vessel, Marine　2019
主尺度 $L×B×D$（m×m×m）：19.2×4.8×1.8

闽狮渔 06868　海洋灯光罩网渔船　2019 年
MIN SHI YU 06868　Light Falling-net Fishing Vessel, Marine　2019
主尺度 $L×B×D$（m×m×m）：53.9×9.8×4.6

粤汕尾渔 16117　海洋灯光罩网渔船　2019 年
采用电力推进系统
YUE SHAN WEI YU 16117　Light Falling-net Fishing Vessel, Marine　2019
With electric propulsion system
主尺度 $L×B×D$（m×m×m）：60×9.8×5

福远渔 8679　远洋灯光罩网渔船　2019 年
FU YUAN YU 8679　Light Falling-net Fishing Vessel, Ocean-going　2019
主尺度 $L×B×D$（m×m×m）：66×10.5×5.7

第六节 内河捕捞渔船
SECTION 6　　INLAND WATERWAY FISHING VESSEL

皖明渔 80536　内河捕捞渔船　2000 年
WAN MING YU 80536　Fishing Vessel, Inland Waterway　2000
主尺度 $L×B×D$ (m×m×m)：39.5×7×2.3

湘岳阳渔 00031　内河捕捞渔船　2006 年
XIANG YUE YANG YU 00031　Fishing Vessel, Inland Waterway　2006
主尺度 $L×B×D$ (m×m×m)：26×5.2×1.3

湘岳阳渔 00026　内河捕捞渔船　2006 年
XIANG YUE YANG YU 00026　Fishing Vessel, Inland Waterway　2006
主尺度 $L×B×D$ (m×m×m)：26×5.2×1.3

皖天渔 80646　内河捕捞渔船 2012 年
WAN TIAN YU 80646　Fishing Vessel, Inland Waterway 2012
主尺度　$L×B×D$（m×m×m）：23.6×4×1.2

皖宣渔 80622　内河钢丝网水泥捕捞渔船 2013 年
WAN XUAN YU 80622　Ferrocement Fishing Vessel, Inland Waterway 2013
主尺度　$L×B×D$（m×m×m）：20.5×3.9×1.5

粤东源渔 10302　内河捕捞渔船 2016 年
YUE DONG YUAN YU 10302　Fishing Vessel, Inland Waterway 2016
主尺度　$L×B×D$（m×m×m）：21.4×2.8×0.9

皖宣渔 82071　内河捕捞渔船 2018 年
WAN XUAN YU 82071　Fishing Vessel, Inland Waterway 2018
主尺度　$L×B×D$（m×m×m）：20.1×3.9×1.2

第二章　其他渔船

养殖渔船伴随着水产养殖业的发展而出现，初期作为养殖生产的辅助工具，主要用于运送养殖苗种、物资、饲料和人员。养殖渔船基本上为小型船和艇，长度多在20米以下，且以12米左右居多。随着海上养殖业的发展，海上养殖工船日益受到重视并被陆续推出。此类养殖渔船，其功能为海上生产工厂，设备和工艺复杂，管理和操作严格，相当于渔业基地船，有些为大型船舶改装而成。目前我国首艘大型养殖工船即将投入使用。

渔业辅助船系指为渔业生产、科研、教学等服务的船舶，如冷藏运输船、渔业加工船、渔业补给船、渔业调查船等。渔业运输船是用于运输渔获物、半成品及成品鱼的生产性渔业辅助船。大多数渔业运输船兼具补给功能，可为捕捞渔船补给淡水、燃油和必要的生产生活物资。运输船一般多带冷藏功能，大型的还具备海上加工能力，小型的具有冰鲜储运能力。渔业运输船以快速性、装载量、稳性、过鲜能力、保鲜质量等为主要技术指标。目前，国内自主研发的最大吨位超低温冷藏运输船船长百米以上，冷藏舱容积7000多立方米，最低设计温度为零下55℃。

渔业资源调查船主要用于调查研究潜在的可开发渔场，如渔汛期的发生和持续时间，鱼类资源的种类、分布密度和变化动态，以及试验渔具、渔法和渔获物保鲜的加工方法等。船上一般设有鱼类实验室、海洋实验室、化学实验室、浮游生物及底栖生物实验室、捕捞实验室、保鲜加工实验室等多种可满足渔业科学研究用途的实验室。我国远洋渔业资源调查船已实现海洋渔业资源、水文、物理、化学、声学、遥感等综合要素的同步探测、分析和处理，达到国际先进水平。

休闲渔船是用于从事休闲垂钓、体验式捕捞等非生产性渔业活动的渔业船舶，包括休闲垂钓船、体验式捕捞船等。作为休闲渔业重要载体的休闲渔船，其船型特征、搭载人员和船上设备等都与传统渔船差异较大。目前，休闲渔船在数量上以休闲垂钓船居多，船长尺度多在12～15米范围，船型与游艇接近，船上配备个人钓具。体验式捕捞船以拖网、蟹笼船居多，船型尺度稍大，船上配备远小于正常生产捕捞能力的渔机和渔具，部分休闲渔船还具有简单的加工、餐饮功能。这一类型的船舶目前还处在发展当中。

CHAPTER II   OTHER FISHING VESSELS

With the development of aquaculture industry, culturing vessels emerged, initially used as auxiliary tools for farming production and then mainly for transporting farming seeds, materials, feed and personnel. Basically, culturing vessels are small ships and light boats, with length generally below 20m and mostly around 12m. With the development of the marine aquaculture industry, marine fish farming vessels have attracted greater attention and been launched one after another. Such fish farming vessels, which function as marine production factories with complex equipment and processing facilities, and strict management are equivalent to fishery base vessels and some of them are modified from large ships. China's first large-size fish farming vessel will enter service soon.

Fishery auxiliary vessels refer to the vessels serving fishery production, scientific research and teaching, such as refrigerated vessels, factory vessels, fishery supply vessels, fishery survey vessels, etc. Fishery carriers are productive fishery auxiliary ships used to transport catches, semi-finished products and finished fish. Most of the fishery carriers have the function of supplying fresh water, fuel and necessary production and living materials for fishing vessels. The fishery carriers generally have a refrigeration function, large ones also have sea processing capability, and small ones have chilled storage and transportation capability. The main technical indicators of fishery carriers are rapidity, loading capacity, stability, freshness capacity and freshness quality. At present, the largest and ultra-low temperature refrigerated carrier independently developed by China is more than 100m in length, with refrigerated cabin volume of more than 7,000m^3 and the lowest design temperature of $-55°C$.

Fishery resources survey ships are mainly used to survey and study potential exploitable fishing grounds. They examine the times of the fishing season, species, distribution density and the change in dynamics of fish resources. They further test fishing gear and fishing and processing methods for preserving the freshness of the catch. The ship generally has laboratories for fish, marine, chemistry, plankton and benthos as well as fresh processing for the purpose of scientific research. China's ocean-going fishery resources survey ships are highly sophisticated and are designed to synchronise detection, analysis and processing of fishery resources and share data on hydrology, physics, chemistry, acoustics and remote sensing.

Recreational fishing vessels, including experiential fishing vessels, are for non-productive fishing activities. Recreational fishing boats differ greatly from traditional fishing boats in terms of their characteristics, personnel and equipment. At present, recreational fishing vessels generally have a the length between 12-15m. Their shape is similar to a yachts, and are equipped with personal fishing gear. Experiential fishing vessels are mostly trawlers and crabbers of a slightly larger size, equipped with fishing machinery and fishing gear far smaller than the normal production fishing capacity. Some recreational fishing boats also have simple processing and catering functions. This type of vessel is still under development.

第一节 养殖渔船

SECTION 1　CULTURING VESSEL

辽绥渔养 35027　沿海养殖渔船　1995 年
LIAO SUI YU YANG 35027　Culturing Vessel, Coastal　1995
主尺度 $L×B×D$（m×m×m）：19.1×4.3×1.5

粤遂渔养 79003　沿海养殖渔船　1999 年
YUE SUI YU YANG 79003　Culturing Vessel, Coastal　1999
主尺度 $L×B×D$（m×m×m）：26.7×5.9×1.6

浙椒渔养 85011　沿海养殖渔船　2001 年
ZHE JIAO YU YANG 85011　Culturing Vessel, Coastal　2001
主尺度 $L×B×D$（m×m×m）：23×4.3×1.9

SHIPS OF CHINA

辽水丰渔养 05002　内陆水域养殖渔船　2007 年
LIAO SHUI FENG YU YANG 05002　Culturing Vessel, Inland Waterway　2007
主尺度 $L×B×D$（m×m×m）：32.6×8×1.2

桂峨渔 11465　内陆水域养殖渔船　2008 年
GUI E YU 11465　Culturing Vessel, Inland Waterway　2008
主尺度 $L×B×D$（m×m×m）：12.4×1.7×0.8

苏如渔养 08376　沿海养殖渔船　2010 年
SU RU YU YANG 08376　Culturing Vessel, Coastal　2010
主尺度 $L×B×D$（m×m×m）：28.3×5.4×2

新泰渔养 23151　内陆水域养殖渔船　2012 年
XIN TAI YU YANG 23151　Culturing Vessel, Inland Waterway　2012
主尺度 $L×B×D$（m×m×m）：35×6.4×1.7

苏大渔养 08996 沿海养殖渔船 2013 年
SU DA YU YANG 08996 Culturing Vessel, Coastal 2013
主尺度 $L \times B \times D$ (m×m×m)：29.3×5.8×2.3

闽古渔养 92004 内陆水域养殖渔船 2014 年
MIN GU YU YANG 92004 Culturing Vessel, Inland Waterway 2014
主尺度 $L \times B \times D$ (m×m×m)：12×1.9×0.8

蒙巴渔养 23029 内陆水域养殖渔船 2014 年
MENG BA YU YANG 23029 Culturing Vessel, Inland Waterway 2014
主尺度 $L \times B \times D$ (m×m×m)：14.4×3.5×0.6

粤惠东渔养 90138　沿海养殖渔船　2014 年
YUE HUI DONG YU YANG 90138　Culturing Vessel, Coastal　2014
主尺度 *L×B×D*（m×m×m）：38.6×6.8×3.5

浙淳渔养 11905　内陆水域养殖渔船　2015 年
ZHE CHUN YU YANG 11905　Culturing Vessel, Inland Waterway　2015
主尺度 *L×B×D*（m×m×m）：29.8×6×3.1

赣崇义渔养 90107　内陆水域养殖渔船　2017 年
GAN CHONG YI YU YANG 90107　Culturing Vessel, Inland Waterway　2017
主尺度 *L×B×D*（m×m×m）：19.6×3.8×1.3

鲁牟渔养 61539　沿海木质养殖渔船　2018 年
LU MOU YU YANG 61539　Wooden Culturing Vessel, Coastal　2018
主尺度 *L×B×D*（m×m×m）：13.4×3×1

第二节 渔业辅助船

SECTION 2　　FISHERY AUXILIARY VESSELS

北斗　远洋渔业资源调查船 1984 年
BEI DOU　Fishery Resource Survey Vessel, Ocean-going　1984
主尺度　$L×B×D$ (m×m×m)：79.3×14×5.3

福远渔 F86　远洋渔获冷藏运输船 1988 年
FU YUAN YU F86　Refrigerated Fish Carrier, Ocean-going　1988
主尺度　$L×B×D$ (m×m×m)：84.3×12.2×6.8

闽平渔运 61658　海洋活鱼运输船 2002 年
MIN PING YU YUN 61658　Live Fish Carrier, Marine　2002
主尺度　$L×B×D$ (m×m×m)：72.5×9.8×6.1

南锋　远洋渔业资源调查船　2009 年
NAN FENG　Fishery Resource Survey Vessel, Ocean-going　2009
主尺度　$L×B×D$（m×m×m）：56.2×12.5×7.8

华盛渔加 2　海洋大型渔业加工船　2012 年
HUA SHENG YU JIA 2　Large Fishery Factory Vessel, Marine　2012
主尺度　$L×B×D$（m×m×m）：33.3×6.5×3.5

浙苍渔冷 00888　海洋大型渔业加工船　2013 年
ZHE CANG YU LENG 00888　Large Fishery Factory Vessel, Marine　2013
主尺度　$L×B×D$（m×m×m）：98.5×16×5

辽长渔运 18039　海洋玻璃钢渔业冷海水渔获运输船　2015 年
LIAO CHANG YU YUN 18039　FRP Refrigerated Seawater Fish Carrier, Marine　2015
主尺度　$L×B×D$（m×m×m）：18×4.2×1.6

中巨冷 1 远洋渔获冷藏运输船 2016 年
ZHONG JU LENG 1 Refrigerated Fish Carrier, Ocean-going 2016
主尺度 $L \times B \times D$ (m×m×m)：116×16.6×9.2

中渔科 211 海洋渔业资源调查船 2017 年
ZHONG YU KE 211 Fishery Resource Survey Vessel, Marine 2017
主尺度 $L \times B \times D$ (m×m×m)：48.9×8×5.2

淞航　远洋渔业资源调查船　2017年
SONG HANG　Fishery Resource Survey Vessel, Ocean-going　2017
主尺度 $L×B×D$ (m×m×m)：66.7×12.4×7.6

浙渔科2　海洋渔业资源调查船　2017年
ZHE YU KE 2　Fishery Resource Survey Vessel, Marine　2017
主尺度 $L×B×D$ (m×m×m)：84.5×15×8

苏阜渔运 32002　内河渔业运输船 2018 年
SU FU YU YUN 32002　Fishery Carrier, Inland Waterway 2018
主尺度 $L×B×D$（m×m×m）：41.4×7×3.3

浙苍渔加 08888　海洋渔业加工船 2019 年
ZHE CANG YU JIA 08888　Fishery Factory Vessel, Marine 2019
主尺度 $L×B×D$（m×m×m）：65.6×15×5

蓝海 201　远洋渔业资源调查船 2019 年
LAN HAI 201　Fishery Resource Survey Vessel, Ocean-going 2019
主尺度 $L×B×D$（m×m×m）：85×15×8.7

第三节 休闲渔船

SECTION 3 RECREATIONAL FISHING VESSEL

流水坑渔家乐 006　海洋休闲渔船　2007 年
LIU SHUI KENG YU JIA LE 006　Recreational Fishing Vessel, Marine 2007
主尺度　$L×B×D$（m×m×m）：42.8×8×5.2

粤南沙 19888　海洋玻璃钢休闲渔船　2008 年
YUE NAN SHA 19888　FRP Recreational Fishing Vessel, Marine 2008
主尺度　$L×B×D$（m×m×m）：23.3×5×2.2

浙乐渔休 00122　海洋玻璃钢休闲渔船　2013 年
ZHE LE YU XIU 00122　FRP Recreational Fishing Vessel, Marine 2013
主尺度　$L×B×D$（m×m×m）：16.4×4.5×2.3

浙玉渔休 00013 海洋休闲渔船 2016 年
ZHE YU YU XIU 00013 Recreational Fishing Vessel, Marine 2016
主尺度 $L \times B \times D$（m×m×m）：30×5.8×2.6

浙瑞渔休 00315 海洋休闲渔船 2016 年
ZHE RUI YU XIU 00315 Recreational Fishing Vessel, Marine 2016
主尺度 $L \times B \times D$（m×m×m）：34.8×6.4×3

浙奉渔休 60056 海洋休闲渔船 2017 年
ZHE FENG YU XIU 60056 Recreational Fishing Vessel, Marine 2017
主尺度 $L \times B \times D$（m×m×m）：28.9×9.6×3.5

第四篇
工程和服务船舶

PART IV
ENGINEERING AND SERVICE SHIPS

第一章 工程船

CHAPTER I ENGINEERING SHIPS

第一节 挖泥船

挖泥船是工程船舶的重要船型之一，主要用于港口航道建设与维护、围海造地、水域生态环保治理、筑岛固疆等。随着疏浚业的强劲发展，挖泥船已由早期品种单一、高耗低效的小型疏浚船舶发展为高效绿色智能的适应远海的大挖深、远距离输送的大型现代化疏浚船舶。挖泥船按作业原理可分为机械式和水力式两种类型，其中机械式挖泥船主要分为链斗式、铲斗式和抓斗式等；水力式挖泥船主要分为绞吸式和耙吸式等。绞吸式挖泥船系由钢桩或锚系定位，利用旋转绞刀装置挖掘海底疏浚土，由离心泵经吸排泥管系将疏浚土输送到堆积场的挖泥船。绞吸式挖泥船通常以泥泵的输送能力来判断其规格大小。耙吸式挖泥船系通过置于船体两舷或一舷的耙臂系统嵌入水底破土，由离心泵将疏浚土吸入泥舱，航行至指定地点利用开底泥门抛卸疏浚土或利用排岸系统吹填作业的挖泥船。耙吸式挖泥船通常以泥舱舱容积来判断其规格大小。链斗式挖泥船系利用斗桥系统挖掘疏浚土，通常以链斗的挖掘能力来判断其规格大小。铲斗式挖泥船系运用该挖掘机铲斗破土挖掘，铲斗出水后将疏浚土装入舷外倒运泥驳泥舱内的挖泥船，通常以铲斗的型容积来判断其规格大小。抓斗式挖泥船系利用抓斗自由落体重力作用破土挖掘，再由起重机提拉钢丝绳闭合抓斗将疏浚土提升出水面，斗臂回转至舷侧将疏浚土装入倒运泥驳泥舱内的挖泥船，通常以抓斗的型容积来判断其规格大小。

我国早期的挖泥船，主要依赖国外进口。20世纪90年代以来，我国挖泥船的设计与建造进入了自主创新、做大做强的发展阶段。目前我国自主设计建造的6000立方米/小时重型自航绞吸式挖泥船、21000立方米大型耙吸式挖泥船等，技术装备和作业性能均达到世界先进水平。我国挖泥船总量和疏浚能力位居世界首位。

SECTION 1 DREDGER

A dredger is one of the important ship types of engineering vessels. It is mainly used for port channel construction and maintenance, sea-rounding, environmental protection, management of aquatic ecology, island building and boundary fixing. With the strong development of the dredging industry, the dredger has been developed from small dredging ship of single type, high consumption and low efficiency to a large modern, efficient, green and intelligent dredging ship with large dredging depth and long-distance transportation to adapt to distant sea. A dredger can be divided into mechanical and hydraulic types according to the operation principle, among which the mechanical dredger is mainly divided into bucket type, dipper type and grab type, etc. A hydraulic dredger is mainly divided into cutter suction type, trailing suction type, etc. The cutter suction dredger is positioned by a steel pile or anchor system, using the rotating reamer device to dig the dredged soil on the seabed, and the centrifugal pump conveys the dredged soil to the dumpsite through the suction and discharge pipe system. The size of the cutter suction dredger is usually judged by the capacity of the mud pump. The trailing suction Hopper dredger breaks the soil under water through the rake arm system placed on both sides or one side of the hull, and the dredged soil is sucked into the mud chamber by the centrifugal pump, and then sails to the designated place to throw off the dredged soil by using the open bottom mud door or uses the bank discharge system for blowing and filling. The size of trailing suction dredger is usually judged by the volume of mud chamber. The bucket dredger uses a bucket bridge system to excavate dredged soil, and the size of bucket dredger is usually judged by the digging capacity of chain bucket. A bucket dredger uses the bucket of the excavator to break and excavate the soil, and loads the dredged soil into the mud chamber of the outboard dumping barge after the bucket comes out of the water, and the size of the bucket dredger is usually judged by the volume of the bucket. A grab dredger uses the gravity of the free fall of the grab to break and excavate the soil, and then the crane pulls the wire rope to close the grab to lift the dredged soil out of the water, and the bucket arm rotates to the side to load the dredged soil into the inverted hopper. The size of the grab dredger is usually judged by the volume of the grab.

China's early dredgers mainly rely on foreign imports. Since the 1990s, China's dredger design and construction have experienced independent innovation development and become bigger and stronger. At present, China has independently designed and built 6,000m^3/h heavy-duty self-propelled cutter suction dredgers as well as 21,000m^3 large trailing suction dredgers the technical equipment and operational performance of which reached the world's advanced level. Today China now has the biggest dredger fleet in the world.

闽浚 2　2300 立方米耙吸式挖泥船　1987 年
MIN JUN 2　2,300m³ Trailing Suction Hopper Dredger　1987
主尺度　L×B×D（m×m×m）：80.2×14.8×4.9

津航浚 217　1600 立方米/小时绞吸式挖泥船　1987 年
JIN HANG JUN 217　1,600m³/h Cutter Suction Dredger　1987
主尺度　L×B×D（m×m×m）：96×17×4.7

津航浚 406　25 立方米抓斗式挖泥船　1989 年
JIN HANG JUN 406　25m³ Grab Dredger　1989
主尺度　L×B×D（m×m×m）：56×22×3.8

津航浚 306　750 立方米/小时链斗式挖泥船　1989 年
JIN HANG JUN 306　750m³/h Bucket Dredger　1989
主尺度　L×B×D（m×m×m）：95.4×14.4×5.2

虎门 7　4 立方米抓斗式挖泥船　1991 年
HU MEN 7　4m³ Grab Dredger　1991
主尺度　L×B×D（m×m×m）：65.6×12×5

赤湾 1 2800 立方米耙吸式挖泥船 1991 年
CHI WAN 1 2,800m³ Trailing Suction Hopper Dredger 1991
主尺度 $L \times B \times D$ (m×m×m)：81.7×15.8×5.5

吸盘 1 号 1250 立方米／小时自航吸盘挖泥船 1993 年
我国第一艘自主设计建造的吸盘式挖泥船
XI PAN 1 HAO 1,250m³/h Self-propelled Dustpan Suction Dredger 1993
First dustpan suction dredger designed and built by China
主尺度 $L \times B \times D$ (m×m×m)：90×13.8×4.4

通力 5400 立方米耙吸式挖泥船 1994 年
我国第一艘兼有挖抛和挖吹功能的船舶
主尺度 $L \times B \times D$ (m×m×m)：111.4×21×8.1

TONG LI 5,400m³ Trailing Suction Hopper Dredger 1994
China's first ship with throwing and blowing functions

捷龙　3000 立方米/小时绞吸式挖泥船　1994 年
JIE LONG　3,000m³/h Cutter Suction Dredger　1994
主尺度 $L \times B \times D$ (m×m×m)：96×14.9×4.3

航浚 11　2000 立方米耙吸式挖泥船　1998 年
HANG JUN 11　2,000m³ Trailing Suction Hopper Dredger　1998
主尺度 $L \times B \times D$ (m×m×m)：85×15×5.5

吸扬 12 号　1750 立方米/小时绞吸式挖泥船　1998 年
我国第一艘自主设计建造的大型绞吸式挖泥船
XI YANG SHI ER HAO　1,750m³/h Cutter Suction Dredger　1998
First large cutter suction dredger designed and built by China
主尺度 $L \times B \times D$ (m×m×m)：100.9×16×4.6

虎门 8　1500 立方米耙吸式挖泥船　1999 年
HU MEN 8　1,500m³ Trailing Suction Hopper Dredger　1999
主尺度 $L \times B \times D$ (m×m×m)：69.2×14×5.1

航浚 14 号　700 立方米自航耙吸式挖泥船　1999 年
我国第一艘自主设计建造的自航耙吸式挖泥船
HANG JUN 14 HAO　700m³ Self-propelled Trailing Suction Hopper Dredger　1999
First self-propelled trailing suction dredger designed and built by China
主尺度 $L \times B \times D$ (m×m×m)：72.8×14×5.2

吸扬 15 号　2250 立方米/小时绞吸式挖泥船　1999 年
XI YANG SHI WU HAO　2,250m³/h Cutter Suction Dredger　1999
主尺度 $L \times B \times D$ (m×m×m)：93.8×16×4.6

东祥　200 立方米抓斗式挖泥船　2000 年
DONG XIANG　200m³ Grab Dredger　2000
主尺度 $L \times B \times D$ (m×m×m)：100×36×6

斗轮 1 号　400 立方米/小时内河斗轮挖泥船　2001 年
DOU LUN 1 HAO　400m³/h Cutter Wheel Dredger, Inland Waterway　2001
主尺度 $L \times B \times D$ (m×m×m)：51×10.6×2.8

神华浚 1　5800 立方米自航耙吸式挖泥船　2004 年
SHEN HUA JUN 1　5,800m³ Self-propelled Trailing Suction Hopper Dredger　2004
主尺度 $L \times B \times D$ (m×m×m)：113.8×22×7.7

天狮　3000 立方米 / 小时绞吸式挖泥船 2006 年
TIAN SHI　3,000m³/h Cutter Suction Dredger 2006
主尺度 $L \times B \times D$ (m×m×m)：108×18.2×5.2

云浚 1 号　5000 立方米耙吸式挖泥船 2007 年
YUN JUN 1 HAO　5,000m³ Trailing Suction Hopper Dredger 2007
主尺度 $L \times B \times D$ (m×m×m)：109×18.8×8.1

新海虎　13500 立方米耙吸式挖泥船 2007 年
我国第一艘自主设计建造的大型先进耙吸式挖泥船
XIN HAI HU　13,500m³ Trailing Suction Hopper Dredger 2007
First advanced large trailing suction dredger designed and built by China
主尺度 $L \times B \times D$ (m×m×m)：150.7×27×11

鄂黄冈工程 0007　296 立方米 / 小时链斗式挖泥船 2008 年改建
E HUANG GANG GONG CHENG 0007　296m³/h Bucket Dredger Converted in 2008
主尺度 $L \times B \times D$ (m×m×m)：44×11.4×2

唐绞 2008　2500 立方米 / 小时绞吸式挖泥船 2008 年
TANG JIAO 2008　2,500m³/h Cutter Suction Dredger 2008
主尺度 $L \times B \times D$ (m×m×m)：100×16.8×4.8

长狮 1 号　3580 立方米 / 小时大型绞吸式挖泥船　2008 年
我国设计建造的大型先进绞吸式挖泥船
CHANG SHI YI HAO　3,580m³/h Large Cutter Suction Dredger　2008
Advanced large cutter suction dredger designed and built by China
主尺度　$L \times B \times D$ (m×m×m)：103×19×5.2

长鲸 2　10080 立方米耙吸式挖泥船　2008 年
CHANG JING 2　10,080m³ Trailing Suction Hopper Dredger　2008
主尺度　$L \times B \times D$ (m×m×m)：131.4×24.6×10

新海凤　16888 立方米大型耙吸式挖泥船　2008 年
我国设计建造的大型先进耙吸式挖泥船
主尺度　$L \times B \times D$ (m×m×m)：160.2×27×11.8

XIN HAI FENG　16,888m³ Trailing Suction Hopper Dredger　2008
Advanced large trailing suction dredger designed and built by China

新海蚌 27立方米新型抓斗式挖泥船 2009年
我国设计建造的新型抓斗式挖泥船
XIN HAI BENG 27m³ Novel Grab Dredger 2009
Novel grab dredger designed and built by China
主尺度 $L \times B \times D$ (m×m×m)：65.8×24×4.8

天麒号 4500立方米/小时绞吸式挖泥船 2009年
TIAN QI HAO 4,500m³/h Cutter Suction Dredger 2009
主尺度 $L \times B \times D$ (m×m×m)：120×20.3×6.6

港航浚7 2500立方米/小时斗轮式挖泥船 2009年
GANG HANG JUN 7 2,500m³/h Cutter Wheel Dredger 2009
主尺度 $L \times B \times D$ (m×m×m)：100×15.4×4

港航浚6 2500立方米/小时斗轮挖泥船 2009年
GANG HANG JUN 6 2,500m³/h Cutter Wheel Dredger 2009
主尺度 $L \times B \times D$ (m×m×m)：100×15.4×4

长鲸 6　13280 立方米耙吸式挖泥船　2010 年
长江大型疏浚船舶
CHANG JING 6　13,280m³ Trailing Suction Hopper Dredger　2010
Large dredger in Yangtze River
主尺度 $L×B×D$ (m×m×m)：157.8×27×10.5

通程　18343 立方米耙吸式挖泥船　2010 年
TONG CHENG　18,343m³ Trailing Suction Hopper Dredger　2010
主尺度 $L×B×D$ (m×m×m)：162.3×28.5×15

新海豚　3500 立方米 / 小时绞吸式挖泥船　2010 年
XIN HAI TUN　3,500m³/h Cutter Suction Dredger　2010
主尺度 $L×B×D$ (m×m×m)：104.4×19.6×5.2

华安龙　4500 立方米 / 小时绞吸式挖泥船　2010 年
HUA AN LONG　4,500m³/h Cutter Suction Dredger　2010
主尺度 $L×B×D$ (m×m×m)：116.1×18.2×5.2

天鲸号 4500 立方米 / 小时大型自航绞吸式挖泥船 2010 年
我国设计建造的大型先进自航绞吸式挖泥船
主尺度 $L×B×D$ (m×m×m)：127.5×23×8.3

TIAN JING HAO 4,500m^3/h Large Self-propelled Cutter Suction Dredger 2010
Advanced large self-propelled cutter suction dredger designed and built by China

通途 20281 立方米耙吸式挖泥船 2011 年
TONG TU 20,281m^3 Trailing Suction Hopper Dredger 2011
主尺度 $L×B×D$ (m×m×m)：165.7×30×15

丽天 68　6500 立方米 / 小时斗轮式挖泥船　2011 年
LI TIAN 68　6,500m³/h Cutter Wheel Dredger　2011
主尺度　$L \times B \times D$（m×m×m）：68.3×13.6×3.9

长狮 9　2000 立方米 / 小时自航绞吸式挖泥船　2012 年
我国第一艘自主设计建造的自航式绞吸挖泥船
CHANG SHI 9　2,000m³/h Self-propelled Cutter Suction Dredger　2012
First self-propelled cutter suction dredger designed and built by China
主尺度　$L \times B \times D$（m×m×m）：91×22.4×5.3

长江口 01　12000 立方米自航耙吸式挖泥船　2012 年
CHANG JIANG KOU 01　12,000m³ Self-propelled Trailing Suction Hopper Dredger　2012
主尺度　$L \times B \times D$（m×m×m）：132×27.3×10

长江口 02　12000 立方米耙吸式挖泥船　2013 年
CHANG JIANG KOU 02　12,000 m³ Trailing Suction Hopper Dredger　2013
主尺度　$L \times B \times D$（m×m×m）：132×27.3×10

航驳 3001 3000 立方米自航式开体泥驳 2013 年
HANG BO 3001 3,000m³ Self-propelled Split Hopper Barge 2013
主尺度 $L×B×D$ (m×m×m)：97×18×6.1

浚泽 100 立方米/小时绞吸式挖泥船 2014 年
JUN ZE 100m³/h Cutter Suction Dredger 2014
主尺度 $L×B×D$ (m×m×m)：49.5×7.9×2

长鹰 7 2 立方米自航钢耙抓斗挖泥船 2014 年
CHANG YING 7 2m³ Self-propelled Grab Dredger with Steel Harrow 2014
主尺度 $L×B×D$ (m×m×m)：52.25×14×3.5

第四篇 工程和服务船舶
PART IV ENGINEERING AND SERVICE SHIPS

津泰 30立方米BA1100型反铲式挖泥船 2014年改建
我国先进的反铲式挖泥船
主尺度 $L \times B \times D$ (m×m×m): 66.9×21.6×4

JIN TAI Type BA1100 30m³ Backhoe Dredger Converted in 2014
China's advanced backhoe dredger

川宏68 60立方米抓斗式挖泥船 2014年
多用途工程船，具有打捞、起重和疏浚能力
主尺度 $L \times B \times D$ (m×m×m): 121.9×31.9×6.5

CHUAN HONG 68 60m³ Grab Dredger 2014
Multi-purpose engineering ship with salvage, lifting and dredging capabilities

长江口驳 2　7100 立方米自航泥驳　2015 年
CHANG JIANG KOU BO 2　7,100m³ Self-propelled Dump Barge　2015
主尺度 $L×B×D$ （m×m×m）：101.7×22×9

浚洋 1　21000 立方米耙吸式挖泥船　2016 年
我国大型先进的耙吸式挖泥船
JUN YANG 1　21,000m³ Trailing Suction Hopper Dredger　2016
Advanced large trailing suction dredger in China
主尺度 $L×B×D$ （m×m×m）：167.5×31×12.2

长鲸 7　6000 立方米自航耙吸式挖泥船　2018 年
我国第一艘全电力推进耙吸式挖泥船
CHANG JING 7　6,000m³ Self-propelled Trailing Suction Hopper Dredger　2018
First fully electric trailing suction dredger in China
主尺度 $L×B×D$ （m×m×m）：122×24.8×9.6

天鲲号　6000 立方米 / 小时绞吸式挖泥船　2018 年
我国设计建造的重型自航绞吸式挖泥船
主尺度 $L \times B \times D$（m×m×m）：140×27.8×9

TIAN KUN HAO　6,000m³/h Cutter Suction Dredger　2018
Heavy-duty self-propelled cutter suction dredger designed and built by China

长鹰 8　18 立方米铲斗式挖泥船　2019 年
CHANG YING 8　18m³ Dipper Dredger　2019
主尺度 $L \times B \times D$（m×m×m）：72.4×20.8×4.8

长鲸 9　13800 立方米自航耙吸式挖泥船　2019 年
我国自主开发设计建造的内河最大自航耙吸式挖泥船
主尺度　$L×B×D$（m×m×m）：150×29.2×11

CHANG JING 9　13,800m³ Self-propelled Trailing Suction Hopper Dredger　2019
Largest self-propelled trailing suction dredger operating in inland waterway designed and built by China

长狮 19　3500 立方米 / 小时自航绞吸式挖泥船　2020 年
长江中下游维护疏浚全电力驱动自航绞吸式挖泥船
主尺度　$L×B×D$（m×m×m）：117.12×25.8×7.8

CHANG SHI 19　3,500m³/h Self-propelled Cutter Suction Dredger　2020
Self-propelled electric cutter suction dredger for maintenance and dredging in the middle and lower reaches of the Yangtze River

第二节　起重船

起重船又称浮吊，主要用于水上货物过驳和大件物体、结构物、工程结构件的吊装。起重能力一般从数百吨至数千吨不等，多为非自航式。起重船上配备有起重设备，其吊臂分为固定式和旋转式。由于起重船移动灵活、作业方式多样，被广泛应用于海上构筑物的建设、桥梁建设、海洋资源开发和沉船打捞等领域。

除起重方式与起重能力大型化和专业化外，新技术也在起重船上得到了广泛应用。我国自主设计建造的新型自航起重船，具备12000吨固定吊重能力和7000吨360度全回转吊重能力，并配有动力定位系统(DP-2)。

SECTION 2　CRANE SHIP

A crane ship, also known as floating crane, is mainly used for the barging of water cargo, and lifting of large objects and engineering structures. Their lifting capacity generally ranges from hundreds of tons to thousands of tons, and most of them are non-self-propelled. The crane ship is equipped with lifting equipment, and its jib is divided into fixed and rotary types. Due to the flexibility of movement and various operation methods, crane ships are widely used in offshore structure construction, bridge construction, marine resources development, wreck salvage, etc.

In addition to the trend of larger and specialized lifting methods and capacity, new technologies have also been widely used in crane ships. China has independently designed and constructed a new self-propelled crane ship, which has a 12,000 ton fixed lifting capacity and a 7,000 ton 360-degree rotary lifting capacity, and is equipped with a dynamic positioning system (DP-2).

勇士　1000吨打捞起重船　1984年购进
参与《瘗鹤铭》打捞工程项目
YONG SHI　1,000T Salvage Heavy Lift Ship　Purchased in 1984
Involved in the *YI HE MING* salvage project
主尺度 $L×B×D$ (m×m×m)：80.4×25.4×7.8

救捞6号　200吨起重船　1994年
长江先进救捞起重船
JIU LAO 6 HAO　200T Heavy Lift Ship　1994
Advanced salvage ship in the Yangtze River
主尺度　$L×B×D$ （m×m×m）：50.3×20×4

天威　700吨全回转起重船　1996年
TIAN WEI　700T Full Slewing Crane Ship　1996
主尺度　$L×B×D$ （m×m×m）：83.7×32×6

德瀛　1700吨全回转打捞起重船　1996年
DE YING　1,700T Fully Revolving Salvage Crane Ship　1996
主尺度　$L×B×D$ （m×m×m）：115×45×9

华天龙　4000 吨全回转打捞起重船　2007 年
HUA TIAN LONG　4,000T Fully Revolving Salvage Crane Ship　2007
主尺度 $L×B×D$ (m×m×m)：174.9×48×16.5

龙海号　500 吨黑龙江起重船　2008 年
LONG HAI HAO　500T Heavy Lift Ship, Heilongjiang River　2008
主尺度 $L×B×D$ (m×m×m)：93×26×3.4

蓝鲸　7500 吨全回转起重船　2008 年
我国设计建造的大型先进起重船
LAN JING　7,500T Fully Revolving Crane Ship　2008
Advanced large crane ship designed and built by China
主尺度　$L×B×D$（m×m×m）：239×50×20.4

三航风范　2400 吨双臂架重船　2009 年
SAN HANG FENG FAN　2,400T Double-Derrick Heavy Lift Ship　2009
主尺度　$L×B×D$（m×m×m）：96×40.5×7.8

威力　3000 吨全回转打捞起重船　2010 年
WEI LI　3,000T Fully Revolving Salvage Crane Ship　2010
主尺度　$L×B×D$（m×m×m）：141×40×12.8

起重29　1200吨全回转起重船　2011年
QI ZHONG 29　1,200T Full Revolving Crane Ship　2011
主尺度　$L×B×D$（m×m×m）：102×36×10

长大海升　3200吨双臂架起重船　2012年
CHANG DA HAI SHENG　3,200T Double-Derrick Heavy Lift Ship　2012
主尺度　$L×B×D$（m×m×m）：110×48×8.4

德浮 3600　3600 吨双臂架打捞起重船　2013 年
DE FU 3600　3,600T Double-Derrick Salvage Heavy Lift Ship　2013
主尺度　$L×B×D$（m×m×m）：118.9×48×8.8

长天龙　1000 吨起重船　2016 年　　　　　　　　　　**CHANG TIAN LONG**　1,000T Crane Ship　2016
三峡库区电力驱动全回转起重船　　　　　　　　　　　　Three Gorges reservoir electric drive full revolving crane ship
主尺度　$L×B×D$（m×m×m）：108.3×31.2×7

振华 30 12000 吨全回转大型起重船 2016 年改建
由油轮改建为大型起重船
ZHEN HUA 30 12,000T Large Full Slewing Crane Ship Converted in 2016
Large crane ship coverted from oil tanker
主尺度 $L×B×D$ (m×m×m)：297.6×58×28.8

创力 4500 吨全回转打捞起重船 2018 年
CHUANG LI 4,500T Fully Revolving Salvage Crane Ship 2018
主尺度 $L×B×D$ (m×m×m)：198.8×46.6×14.2

德合 5000 吨打捞起重船 2018 年
DE HE 5,000T Salvage Heavy Lift Ship 2018
主尺度 $L×B×D$ (m×m×m)：199×47.6×15

柯力　800 吨全回转打捞起重船 2019 年改建
CALI　800T Fully Revolving Salvage Crane Ship Converted in 2019
主尺度　$L×B×D$（m×m×m）：125.9×32×12

华祥龙　1200 吨插桩式打捞起重船 2020 年
HUA XIANG LONG　1,200T Piling Salvage Crane Ship 2020
主尺度　$L×B×D$（m×m×m）：130×42×9

第三节　其他工程作业船

铺管船是指用于铺设海底管道专用的工程船，多用于海底输油管道、海底输气管道、海底输水管道的铺设。我国建造的世界上第一艘深水铺管起重船，具备3000米级深水铺管能力和4000吨级重型起重能力，并配有动力定位系统(DP-3)，能在除北极外的全球无限航区作业。

布缆船是指专门用于敷设海底电缆的工程船。海底电缆敷设使人们能远隔重洋进行有线通信。目前世界上已建成百万多公里海底光缆线路。我国首制电力推进配有动力定位系统(DP-2)的专用布缆船，布缆速度最大可达18米/分。

混凝土搅拌船，即具有船载混凝土搅拌站的工程船，主要用于跨海大桥、岛礁开发、岸线整备、人工岛建造和港口码头等水上工程建设。混凝土搅拌船配备有抓斗起重机、生产物料输送系统、称量系统、搅拌系统和浇注系统。

打桩船是指用于水上打桩作业的船舶，船体为钢箱型结构，在甲板的端部装有打桩架，可前俯后仰以适应施打斜桩的需要，广泛应用于桥梁、码头、水利工程施工。

浮船坞是一种用于修、造船的工程船舶，尺度面积大，具有较大举力。它不仅用于修、造船舶，还可用于打捞沉船、运送深水船舶通过浅水航道等。目前我国自主建造的大型浮船坞总长410米，型宽82米，最大沉深20米，举力85000吨，实现中央控制室遥控操作，自动化程度高，可承修10000标准箱以上的集装箱船和世界上大部分的油轮和散货船。

沉管安放船是一种具有海底隧道管节定位、沉放和安装等功能的施工专用船舶。目前我国新建造的自航式沉管安放船，是世界上第一艘集沉管浮运、定位、沉放和安装等功能于一体的、配有动力定位系统(DP)和循迹功能的专用船。

整平船是在世界航运业船舶大型化和港口深水化发展的大趋势下，得到快速发展的船型。我国新建造的自升平台式碎石铺设整平船，集定位测量、水下抛石、深水整平、质量检测功能于一体，是深水整平领域的第五代核心装备。

SECTION 3 OTHER ENGINEERING SHIPS

A Pipe-laying ship refers to a specialized engineering vessel dedicated to laying submarine pipelines, mostly oil, gas and water pipelines. China built the world's first deep-water pipe-laying crane ship, with a 3,000-metre deep-water pipe-laying capacity and 4,000-ton heavy lifting capacity equipped with a power positioning system (DP-3). It can operate in the unrestricted navigation area globally except in the Arctic.

A cable laying ship refers to an engineering ship specially used for laying submarine cables. Submarine cable laying enables people to communicate by wire across the ocean. At present, more than one million kilometers of submarine optical cable lines have been built in the world. China's first electric propulsion cable laying ship is equipped with a dynamic positioning system (DP-2) and has a maximum cable laying speed of 18 m/min.

A floating concrete mixer is an engineering ship with on-board concrete mixing plant. This vessel is mainly used for water engineering construction such as cross-sea bridges, island development, shoreline preparation, artificial island construction, port terminals, etc. A floating concrete mixer is equipped with a grab crane, a production material handling system, as well as weighing, mixing and pouring systems. A floating pile driver is a vessel used for piling operations on water. The hull is of steel box structure, equipped with a piling frame at the end of the deck, which can be tilted forward and back depending on the angle of the batter piling. It is widely used in the construction of bridges, wharves and water conservancy projects.

A floating dock is used for repairing and building ships, with large area and large lifting force, and it can also be deployed to salvage wrecks and transport deep water ships through shallow water. At present, China has independently built large oating dock with an overall length of 410 metres, a moulded width of 82 metres, a maximum sinking depth of 20 metres, and a lifting capacity of 85,000 tons. It can be operated remotely from the central control room with a high degree of automation and can repair container ships of more than 10,000 TEU as well as most oil tankers and bulk carriers in the world.

The immersed tube placement vessel is a kind of specialised engineering ship with the functions of positioning, sinking and installation of joints in submarine tunnels. China's first ship of this kind has recently been built and is the first specialized ship in the world that integrates the functions of floating, positioning, sinking and installation of immersed tubes. It is further equipped with a dynamic positioning system (DP) and tracing function.

A leveling ship is a rapidly developing ship type under the general trend of large-size shipping and deep-water port development. China's newly built gravel laying and leveling vessel, integrates position measurement, underwater riprap, deep water leveling and quality inspection functions. The vessel is self-elevating and is the fifth generation of core equipment in the field of deep water leveling.

三航砂 2　60 米砂桩船　1987 年
SAN HANG SHA 2　60m Sand Pile Driving Barge　1987
主尺度　$L×B×D$ (m×m×m)：55×25×4

天砼　240 立方米 / 小时混凝土搅拌船　1989 年
TIAN TONG　240m^3/h Floating Concrete Mixer　1989
主尺度　$L×B×D$ (m×m×m)：55×25×6

三航砼 15　100 立方米 / 小时混凝土搅拌船　1989 年
SAN HANG TONG 15　100m³/h Floating Concrete Mixer　1989
主尺度 $L \times B \times D$ (m×m×m)：82.5×19.5×4.5

宁波海力 802　60 米打桩船　1991 年
NING BO HAI LI 802　60m Pile Driving Ship　1991
主尺度 $L \times B \times D$ (m×m×m)：60×24×4

南通 150000 吨级浮船坞 1991 年
我国建造的 15 万吨级大型浮船坞，举力 36000 吨
主尺度 $L×B×D$（m×m×m）：269.8×58×18.5

NAN TONG 150,000DWT Floating Dock 1991
150,000DWT floating dock built by China, with a lifting capacity of 36,000 tons

砂桩 3 号 58 米挤密砂桩船 1992 年
SHA ZHUANG 3 HAO 58m Sand Compaction Ship 1992
主尺度 $L×B×D$（m×m×m）：58×26×4

递缆 1 号 长江递缆船 1998 年
DI LAN 1 HAO Hawser Handling Barge, Yangtze River 1998
主尺度 $L×B×D$（m×m×m）：38×7×2

宝马号　10000 米海缆施工船　2001 年
BAO MA HAO　10,000m Submarine Cable Laying Vessel　2001
主尺度 $L×B×D$（m×m×m）：105.8×20×12

蓝疆　300 米起重铺管船　2001 年
LAN JIANG　300m Pipe-laying Crane Ship　2001
主尺度 $L×B×D$（m×m×m）：157.5×48×12.5

青平 2 号　45 米 ×22 米基床抛石整平船　2002 年
QING PING 2 HAO　45m×22m Rubble Bed Leveling Barge　2002
主尺度 $L×B×D$（m×m×m）：60.8×34×16

宁波海力 801　95 米全回转打桩船　2003 年
NING BO HAI LI 801　95m Full Slewing Pile Driving Ship　2003
主尺度 $L×B×D$（m×m×m）：80×30×6

航工砼 1601　160 立方米 / 小时搅拌船　2004 年
HANG GONG TONG 1601　160m³/h Floating Mixer　2004
主尺度 $L×B×D$（m×m×m）：85.8×23.4×5.5

天铺 1 号 40 米铺排船 2007 年
TIAN PU 1 HAO 40m Geotextiles-laying Ship 2007
主尺度 $L×B×D$ (m×m×m)：62.4×18×4

粤工桩 8 93.5 米打桩船 2005 年
YUE GONG ZHUANG 8 93.5m Pile Driving Ship 2005
主尺度 $L×B×D$ (m×m×m)：70.5×28×5.2

海洋石油 229 35000 吨导管架下水驳 2008 年
我国建造的大型导管架下水驳船
主尺度 $L×B×D$ (m×m×m)：234.7×65×14.3

HAI YANG SHI YOU 229 35,000T Jacket Launching Barge 2008
Large-size jacket launching barge built by China

中远海运峨眉山　300000 吨级浮船坞　2009 年
我国建造的 30 万吨级大型浮船坞，举力 85000 吨
主尺度 $L×B×D$（m×m×m）：410×82×28

ZHONG YUAN HAI YUN E MEI SHAN　300,000DWT Floating Dock　2009
300,000DWT floating dock built by China, with a lifting capacity of 85,000tons

长鹭 2 号　长江钻爆船　2009 年
CHANG LU 2 HAO　Rock Drill Barge, Yangtze River　2009
主尺度 $L×B×D$（m×m×m）：52.4×17×3.8

三航砼 21　200 立方米/小时混凝土搅拌船　2009 年
SAN HANG TONG 21　200m³/h Floating Concrete Mixer　2009
主尺度 $L×B×D$（m×m×m）：72×21.7×4.8

汉工排 6 号　长江航道铺排船　2010 年改建
HAN GONG PAI 6 HAO　Yangtze River Waterway Geotextiles-laying Ship　Converted in 2010
主尺度 $L×B×D$（m×m×m）：73×18×3

长雁 22　大型航道铺排船　2010 年
CHANG YAN 22　Large Waterway Geotextiles-laying Ship　2010
主尺度 $L×B×D$（m×m×m）：72.5×20×3.7

华翔 238　珠江采砂船　2010 年
HUA XIANG 238　Pearl River Sand Dredger　2010
主尺度 $L×B×D$（m×m×m）：75×21×6

海洋石油 201 3000 米深水铺管船 2012 年
我国第一艘自主设计建造的自航深水铺管起重船
HAI YANG SHI YOU 201 3,000m Deep-water Pipe-laying Ship 2012
First self-propelled deep-water pipe-laying crane ship designed and built independently by China
主尺度 $L \times B \times D$ (m×m×m)：204.7×39.2×14

津安 2 80000 吨沉管安装船 2012 年
与津安 3 配合作业，参加港珠澳大桥工程建设项目
JIN AN 2 80,000T Immersed Tube Placement Ship 2012
In cooperation with JIN AN 3 to participate in the construction project of Hong Kong-Zhuhai-Macao Bridge
主尺度 $L \times B \times D$ (m×m×m)：42.4×56.4×9

津平 1 51.2 米 ×25.2 米自升式抛石整平船 2012 年
我国第一艘自主设计建造的深水抛石整平船，参与港珠澳大桥工程建设项目
JIN PING 1 51.2m×25.2m Self-elevating Rubble Bed Leveling Barge 2012
China's first self-designed deep-water rubble bed leveling barge involved in the construction project of Hong Kong-Zhuhai-Macao Bridge
主尺度 $L \times B \times D$ (m×m×m)：88.8×46×5.5

中油管道 601 6 米铺管船 2013 年
CPP601 6m Pipe-laying Ship 2013
主尺度 $L×B×D$ (m×m×m)：121.2×36×9.6

铺沙 1 箱形工程作业船 2013 年
PU SHA 1 Box Type Engineering Operation Ship 2013
主尺度 $L×B×D$ (m×m×m)：39×13.6×2.3

华东　100000吨级浮船坞　2014年改建
举力 38500 吨
HUA DONG　100,000DWT Floating Dock　Converted in 2014
With a lifting capacity of 38,500tons
主尺度 $L×B×D$（m×m×m）：314×63×18.5

皖工桩 7　60米长江打桩船　2014年
WAN GONG ZHUANG 7　60m Yangtze River Floating Pile Driver　2014
主尺度 $L×B×D$（m×m×m）：42×16.8×3.2

海洋石油 285　深水多功能水下工程船　2016年
HAI YANG SHI YOU 285　Multi-functional Deep-water Engineering Ship　2016
主尺度 $L×B×D$（m×m×m）：125.8×25×10.8

DCOC-1　深层水泥搅拌船 2017 年
DCOC-1　Deep Concrete Mixer　2017
主尺度 $L×B×D$ (m×m×m)：74×32×5

东方海工 01　500 米布缆船 2017 年
DONG FANG HAI GONG 01　500m Cable Layer　2017
主尺度 $L×B×D$ (m×m×m)：86.6×28×5.5

海洋石油 295 海上管道挖沟动力定位工程船 2017 年
HAI YANG SHI YOU 295 Dynamic Positioning Ship for Pipeline Trenching at Sea 2017
主尺度 $L×B×D$（m×m×m）：95×22.6×8.6

海洋石油 286 3000 米深水工程船 2017 年改建　　HAI YANG SHI YOU 286 3,000m Deep-water Engineering Ship Converted in 2017
我国第一艘深水多功能水下工程船　　China's first multifunctional deep-water engineering ship
主尺度 $L×B×D$（m×m×m）：140.8×29×12.8

建基 5002 60 米布缆船 2018 年
JIAN JI 5002 60m Cable Layer 2018
主尺度 $L \times B \times D$ (m×m×m)：82.3×27.4×4.9

启帆 9 100 米海底电缆施工船 2018 年
QI FAN 9 100m Submarine Cable Construction Ship 2018
主尺度 $L \times B \times D$ (m×m×m)：110×32×6.5

海洋石油 791 海底管道巡检专用船 2018 年
我国第一艘电力推进海底管道巡检专用船
主尺度 $L \times B \times D$ (m×m×m)：65.2×14×7.6

HAI YANG SHI YOU 791 Specialized Ship for Submarine Pipeline Inspection 2018
China's first electrically propelled ship for submarine pipeline inspection

SHIPS OF CHINA

一航津安 1　80000 吨沉管安装船 2019 年
我国自主设计建造的集沉管隧道浮运、安装于一体的船舶，用于深中通道建设工程
主尺度 $L×B×D$ (m×m×m)：195×75×14.7

YI HANG JIN AN 1　80,000DWT Immersed Tube Placement Ship 2019
China's self-designed and built ship which integrates the floating transportation and installation of immersed tube tunnel and is used in the construction of Shenzhen-Zhongshan Channel

一航津平 2　57 米×44 米自升式碎石铺设整平船 2019 年
YI HANG JIN PING 2　57m×44m Self-elevating Gravel Laying and Leveling Barge 2019
主尺度 $L×B×D$ (m×m×m)：96.4×63.3×6.5

三航桩 20　133 米打桩船 2020 年
SAN HANG ZHUANG 20　133m Pile Driving Ship 2020
主尺度 $L×B×D$ (m×m×m)：118.5×38×7.2

第二章 海洋平台
CHAPTER II OFFSHORE UNITS

第一节 海洋钻井平台

海洋钻井平台是在海洋油气等资源勘探开发活动中主要用于钻井和修井作业的海上结构物。海洋钻井平台按照结构形式分为自升式平台、坐底式平台、半潜式平台和钻井船等。

自升式钻井平台主要由桩腿、浮体和升降机构构成。作业时，通过升降机构下放桩腿，桩腿站立在海床后，由桩腿支撑提升浮体离开海面一定高度（气隙）；拖航时，桩腿收回，浮体处于漂浮状态；作业水深在60米以下的平台桩腿一般采用圆柱形桩腿，60米以上的一般采用桁架式桩腿。该类平台的作业水深从20世纪80年代的90米以下发展到现在的130米以上。

坐底式钻井平台由甲板、沉垫和中间的连接支撑构件组成。甲板上配置有钻井设备和上部设施，下部沉垫内为压载水舱；作业时，向压载水舱内注水，使其沉坐到海底形成支撑，平台则露出海面成为钻井场地；

作业完成后，排出压载水舱内的水，使沉垫升起脱离海底，可实施平台转移。坐底式钻井平台仅适合在浅水或滩海区域作业。

半潜式钻井平台为用立柱将上部主甲板结构与水下船体或柱靴连接的浮式平台，适用于深水和超深水。作业时，采用锚泊系统和/或动力定位系统定位，漂浮于海面进行钻井勘探作业，由于其水线面小，运动性能优良，能够适应恶劣的海况。

我国从20世纪70年代开始在渤海使用自升式和坐底式钻井平台进行钻井勘探作业，并逐步在东海和南海进行勘探开发，自主建造了一些圆柱形桩腿的自升式平台及坐底式钻井平台。1984年建造第一座半潜式钻井平台，2003年我国开始建造400英尺桁架式自升式钻井平台，开始了海洋钻井装备的大发展。目前，我国自升式钻井平台设计建造技术已达国际先进水平，已成为半潜式钻井平台建造大国，自主研发的第六代半潜式钻井平台最大作业水深可达3658米，钻井深度可达15250米，配备动力定位系统（DP-3），达到世界先进水平。

SECTION 1   OFFSHORE DRILLING UNITS

An offshore drilling unit is an offshore structure mainly used for drilling and well repair operations in the exploration and development of offshore oil and gas resources. According to the structure type, offshore drilling units are divided into self-elevating drilling units, bottom supported and semi-submersible platforms, and drilling ships.

The self-elevating drilling unit is mainly composed of legs, a buoyant hull and lifting mechanisms. During operations, the legs are lowered by the lifting mechanisms, and after standing on the seabed, the buoyant hull is supported by the legs to lift a certain height away from the sea surface. During towing, the legs are retracted and the buoyant hull is in a floating state. The legs of the platforms which have an operating water depth below 60m are generally cylindrical legs, while truss legs are generally used for platforms with operating water depth above 60m. The operating water depth of this type of platform has developed from below 90m in the 1980s to more than 130m today.

The bottom supported drilling unit consists of a deck, a mat and a connecting support member in the middle. The deck is equipped with drilling equipment and upper facilities, and ballast water tanks are arranged in the lower mat. During operation, water is injected into the ballast water tank to make it sit on the sea floor to form a support, and the platform is exposed to the surface to become a drilling site. After the operation is completed, the water in the ballast water tank is drained, and the mat is lifted off the sea floor, so that the platform can be moved. The bottom supported drilling unit is only suitable for operation in shallow water or beach areas.

The semi-submersible drilling unit is a floating platform that connects the upper main deck structure with the submerged hull or column boot with columns, and is suitable for deep water and ultra-deep water. During operations, it adopts a mooring system and/or a dynamic positioning system for positioning and floats on the sea surface for drilling and exploration operation. Due to its small waterline surface and highly adaptable motion performance, the platform can withstand harsh sea conditions.

China started to use self-elevating and bottom supported drilling unit for exploration in the Bohai Sea in the 1970s, gradually carrying out exploration and development in the East China Sea and the South China Sea, and built some self-elevating drilling units with cylindrical legs and bottom supported drilling unit independently. In 1984, the first semi-submersible drilling unit was built and in 2003, China started to build 400ft truss self-elevating drilling unit, which heralds a great development in offshore drilling equipment. At present, the design and construction technology of self-elevating drilling units in China has reached international advanced level, and China has become a prime destination for the construction of semi-submersible drilling units. The independently developed sixth-generation semi-submersible drilling unit has a maximum operating water depth of 3,658m and a drilling depth of 15,250m, and is equipped with the dynamic positioning system (DP-3), reaching the world advanced level.

南海九号　1524 米 GVA4500 半潜式钻井平台　1988 年
NAN HAI JIU HAO　1,524m GVA4500 Semi-submersible Drilling Unit　1988
主尺度 $L \times B \times D$ （m×m×m）：99.4×70.7×35.9

胜利二号　6.8 米极浅海步行坐底式钻井平台 1988 年
SHENG LI NO. 2　6.8m Walking Type Bottom Supported Drilling Unit in Neritic Area　1988
主尺度 $L \times B \times D$ （m×m×m）：72×42.5×2.5

中油海1号　7.8米极浅海自升式气垫组合钻井平台 1998年
ZHONG YOU HAI 1 HAO　7.8m Self-elevating/Hovercraft Drilling Unit in Neritic Area　1998
主尺度　L×B×D（m×m×m）：66×36×4

海洋石油931　100米自升式钻井平台 2004年购进
HAI YANG SHI YOU 931　100m Self-elevating Drilling Unit Purchased in 2004
主尺度　L×B×D（m×m×m）：88×33.6×9.7

海洋石油941　400英尺JU2000E自升式钻井平台 2006年 我国第一座400英尺自升式钻井平台，最大钻井深度9150米
主尺度　L×B×D（m×m×m）：100.1×76×9.5

HAI YANG SHI YOU 941　400ft JU2000E Self-elevating Drilling Unit　2006 China's first 400ft self-elevating drilling unit, with a maximum drilling depth of 9,150m

中油海 5　40 米自升式钻井平台　2007 年
ZHONG YOU HAI 5　40m Self-elevating Drilling Unit　2007
主尺度 $L \times B \times D$ (m×m×m)：75×49.2×5.2

中油海 3　10 米坐底式钻井平台　2007 年　　**ZHONG YOU HAI 3　10m Bottom Supported Drilling Unit　2007**
我国自主设计建造的新型坐底式钻井平台　　Novel type of bottom supported drilling unit designed and built by China
主尺度 $L \times B \times D$ (m×m×m)：78.4×41×5.2

中油海 9 300 英尺 L780 自升式钻井平台 2008 年
ZHONG YOU HAI 9 300ft L780 Self-elevating Drilling Unit 2008
主尺度 $L×B×D$ (m×m×m)：81.4×53.3×7.6

海洋石油 936 300 英尺 CJ46 自升式钻井平台 2009 年
HAI YANG SHI YOU 936 300ft CJ46 Self-elevating Drilling Unit 2009
主尺度 $L×B×D$ (m×m×m)：92.7×62×7.8

胜利十号 50米自升式钻井平台 2010年
SHENG LI NO. 10 50m Self-elevating Drilling Unit 2010
主尺度 $L×B×D$ (m×m×m)：75×52×5.5

海洋石油 921 200英尺 L780 自升式钻井平台 2010年
HAI YANG SHI YOU 921 200ft L780 Self-elevating Drilling Unit 2010
主尺度 $L×B×D$ (m×m×m)：81.4×53.3×7.6

勘探六号 375英尺 BMPC375 自升式钻井平台 2010年
KAN TAN LIU HAO 375ft BMPC375 Self-elevating Drilling Unit 2010
主尺度 $L×B×D$ (m×m×m)：72.1×68.4×8.5

海洋石油 981　3000 米深水半潜式钻井平台　2011 年
我国建造的第六代深水半潜式钻井平台，获国家科学技术进步奖特等奖
HAI YANG SHI YOU 981　3,000m Deep-water Semi-submersible Drilling Unit　2011
Sixth-generation deep-water semi-submersible drilling unit built by China and awarded the special national prize for progress in science and technology
主尺度　$L \times B \times D$ (m×m×m)：114.1×78.7×38.6

新胜利一号　50 米自升式钻井平台　2014 年
XIN SHENG LI YI HAO　50m Self-elevating Drilling Unit　2014
主尺度　$L \times B \times D$ (m×m×m)：78.5×54×5.6

凯旋一号　400 英尺 Workhorse 自升式钻井平台　2014 年
KAI XUAN YI HAO　400ft Workhorse Self-elevating Drilling Unit　2014
主尺度 $L×B×D$ (m×m×m)：98.6×67.1×7.9

中油海 16　400 英尺 JU2000E 自升式钻井平台　2014 年
ZHONG YOU HAI 16　400ft JU2000E Self-elevating Drilling Unit　2014
主尺度 $L×B×D$ (m×m×m)：98.7×78.4×9.5

HARMONI VICTORY
400 英尺 R-550D 自升式钻井平台　2016 年
HARMONI VICTORY
400ft R-550D Self-elevating Drilling Unit　2016
主尺度 $L×B×D$ (m×m×m)：79.2×79.6×8.2

蓝鲸 1　3658 米 D90 双井架超深水半潜式钻井平台　2016 年南海可燃冰试采平台
主尺度 $L×B×D$（m×m×m）：117×89×36.3

BLUE WHALE I　3,658m Ultra Deep-water D90 Double-derrick Semi-submersible Drilling Unit　2016
South China Sea combustible ice test mining unit

ENERGY EMERGER　375 英尺 CJ50 自升式钻井平台　2017 年
ENERGY EMERGER　375ft CJ50 Self-elevating Drilling Unit　2017
主尺度 $L×B×D$（m×m×m）：69.1×62×7.8

海洋石油 982 1500 米 A5000 深水半潜式钻井平台 2018 年 我国建造的第六代深水半潜式钻井平台
主尺度 $L×B×D$（m×m×m）：114.5×70.5×29.6

HAI YANG SHI YOU 982 1,500m Deep-water A5000 Semi-submersible Drilling Unit 2018
Sixth-generation deep-water semi-submersible drilling unit built by China

大连开拓者 3050 米深水钻井船 2018 年
DALIAN DEVELOPER 3,050m Deep-water Drilling Ship 2018
主尺度 $L×B×D$（m×m×m）：291.3×50×27

中油海 19 300 英尺 DSJ300 自升式钻井平台 2019 年
ZHONG YOU HAI 19 300ft DSJ300 Self-elevating Drilling Unit 2019
主尺度 $L×B×D$（m×m×m）：92.7×66.5×8

第二节　风电安装平台

海上风电安装平台是用于海上风电机组施工、安装和维护的海上工程装备，平台配备专门用于风机安装的大型起重机和打桩设备，主要有自升式、坐底式、坐底箱形式等几种类型，一般具有较大的主甲板面积。自升式风电安装平台可在站立状态进行风电安装作业，安装效率高，部分平台配置了动力定位系统或首尾推进器，可实现动力定位作业或在风场内短距离迁移，部分平台甚至可以完全自航。

随着新型海洋经济的发展，我国海上风电安装平台在数量上逐步攀升。目前国内先后建造了数十座风电安装平台，其中起重能力最大已达2500吨，作业水深最大可达70米，是中国海上风机安装作业从浅海走向近海的关键利器。

SECTION 2　WIND POWER INSTALLATION UNITS

An offshore wind power installation unit is used for offshore wind turbine construction and the installation and maintenance of offshore engineering equipment. The unit mainly includes a self-elevating, bottom supported, and bottom supported box types and is equipped with large cranes and piling equipment specifically for the installation of wind turbines, generally with a large main deck area. Self-elevating wind power installation units can perform wind power installation operation in standing state, with high efficiency. Some units are equipped with a dynamic positioning system or bow and stern thrusters and are able to achieve dynamic positioning operations or short distance migration in the wind farm, while others can be completely self-propelled.

With the development of the new marine economy, the number of China's offshore wind power installation units is gradually increasing. At present, China has built dozens of wind power installation units, of which the maximum lifting capacity has reached 2,500 tons with an operating water depth of up to 70 metres. They are the key tool for moving China's offshore wind turbine installation from shallow sea to offshore.

海洋风电38　250吨自升式风电安装平台　2013年我国建造的第一代自升式海上风电安装平台
HAI YANG FENG DIAN 38　250T Self-elevating Wind Power Installation Unit　2013
First-generation self-elevating offshore wind power installation unit built by China
主尺度 $L \times B \times D$ (m×m×m)：89.6×36×5

华电 1001　700 吨自升式风电安装平台　2013 年
HUA DIAN 1001　700T Self-elevating Wind Power Installation Unit　2013
主尺度 $L×B×D$（m×m×m）：140×39×6.6

龙源振华贰号　800 吨自升式风电安装平台　2014 年
LONG YUAN ZHEN HUA ER HAO　800T Self-elevating Wind Power Installation Unit　2014
主尺度 $L×B×D$（m×m×m）：80.8×42×6

三航风华　1000吨自升式风电安装平台　2016年
SAN HANG FENG HUA　1,000T Self-elevating Wind Power Installation Unit　2016
主尺度　$L×B×D$（m×m×m）：81.6×40.8×7.2

福船三峡　1000吨自升式风电安装平台　2017年
FU CHUAN SAN XIA　1,000T Self-elevating Wind Power Installation Unit　2017
主尺度　$L×B×D$（m×m×m）：119.2×40.8×7.8

精锐01 800吨自升式风电安装平台 2017年
JING YIN 01 800T Self-elevating Wind Power Installation Unit 2017
主尺度 $L \times B \times D$ (m×m×m)：125×40×7

海洋风电36 350吨自升式风电安装平台 2018年改建
由坐底式改建为自升式风电安装平台
HAI YANG FENG DIAN 36 350T Self-elevating Wind Power Installation Unit Converted in 2018
Wind power installation unit converted from a bottom-supported type to a self-elevating type
主尺度 $L \times B \times D$ (m×m×m)：89.6×36×5

中天7 600吨自升式风电安装平台 2018年
ZHONG TIAN 7 600T Self-elevating Wind Power Installation Unit 2018
主尺度 $L \times B \times D$ (m×m×m)：106×38.4×6.6

港航平 9　1200 吨自升式风电安装平台　2018 年
GANG HANG PING 9　1,200T Self-elevating Wind Power Installation Unit　2018
主尺度　$L×B×D$（m×m×m）：118.8×42×6.8

顺一 1600　1800 吨坐底式风电安装平台　2018 年
SHUN YI 1600　1,800T Bottom Supported Wind Power Installation Unit　2018
主尺度　$L×B×D$（m×m×m）：123.6×58×6.6

龙源振华三号　2000 吨自升式风电安装平台　2018 年
LONG YUAN ZHEN HUA SAN HAO　2,000T Self-elevating Wind Power Installation Unit　2018
主尺度 $L×B×D$（m×m×m）：128.5×43.2×8.4

铁建风电 01　1300 吨自升式风电安装平台　2019 年
TIE JIAN FENG DIAN 01　1,300T Self-elevating Wind Power Installation Unit　2019
主尺度 $L×B×D$（m×m×m）：108.6×42×8.5

三航风和　1200 吨自升式风电安装平台　2019 年
SAN HANG FENG HE　1,200T Self-elevating Wind Power Installation Unit　2019
主尺度 $L×B×D$（m×m×m）：127.6×40.8×7.2

第三节　其他海洋平台

SECTION 3　OTHER OFFSHORE UNITS

海洋石油281　40米自升式多功能支持平台　2009年
HAI YANG SHI YOU 281　40m Self-elevating Multi-functional Support Unit 2009
主尺度 $L×B×D$（m×m×m）：76×49×5.2

海洋石油901　115英尺自升助航式作业平台　2010年
HAI YANG SHI YOU 901　115ft Liftboat 2010
主尺度 $L×B×D$（m×m×m）：59.1×42.7×6.3

永乐科考　40米半潜式科学试验平台　2019年　　YONG LE KE KAO　40m Semi-submersible Scientific Test Platform 2019
由两个半潜浮式模块柔性拼接组成　　　　　　　　Flexibly spliced by two semi-submersible floating modules
主尺度 $L×B×D$（m×m×m）：63×25×11

第三章　服务船

服务船船型比较繁杂，总体上可分为拖船、近海供应船、救助船等，以及兼有溢油回收、消防、守护、抛锚等多种功能的服务船舶等。

拖船特征为在船长中点后方设有拖钩、拖缆机等拖曳设备，专用于在水上拖曳船舶或其他浮体；拖船又分为港作拖船、近海拖船和远洋拖船。港作拖船主要是用于操纵停靠港口的大型船舶离靠码头、进出港口和港内调头移位等；远洋拖船主要用于海上救助人员和遇难船，有一定的排水量以确保有较好的适航性；近海拖船则用于近海拖带，其性能介于港作拖船和远洋拖船之间。近海供应船主要用于向移动式或固定式的近海工程设施运送燃料、淡水、备品与物资，并可作为平台人员的交通工具。船型特征为起居处所及驾驶室设于船首部，并具有尾部货物甲板。有的船舶还具备为钻井平台提供抛锚服务、拖带钻井平台或其他近海装置，以及为近海装置提供守护补给等多种辅助功能。

较大型服务船往往集拖船和近海供应功能于一体，有的还兼有消防、抛锚、守护、浮油回收等功能。

CHAPTER III　SERVICE SHIPS

The different types of service ship are complicated, and can be generally divided into tugs, offshore supply vessels, rescue ships, and vessels with multiple functions such as oil spill recovery, firefighting, stand-by and anchoring.

Tugs, characterized by towing equipment such as a towing hook and towing winch behind midship, are used for towing ships or other floating objects on the water. They can be further divided into harbour tugs, offshore tugs and ocean-going tugs. Harbour tugs are mainly used to manoeuvre large ships docked in ports to leave and enter Ocean-going tugs are mainly used to rescue crew and ships in distress at sea, and have a certain displacement to ensure good seaworthiness. Offshore tugs are used for offshore towing, and their performance is between harbour tugs and ocean-going tugs. Offshore supply vessels are mainly used to deliver fuel, fresh water, spare parts and materials to mobile or fixed offshore engineering facilities, and can be used as transportation for platform personnel. This type of ship is featured with the accommodation and bridge at the bow and a cargo deck at the stern. Some ships also have various auxiliary functions such as providing anchoring services for drilling unit, towing drilling unit or other offshore installations, and providing guards and supplies for offshore installations.

Larger service ships often combine towing and offshore supplying functions, and some also have functions such as firefighting, anchoring, guarding, oil recovery, etc.

第一节 拖船/供应船

SECTION 1   TUG/SUPPLY VESSELS

胜利 221　1600 千瓦拖船 / 近海供应船 1987 年
SHENG LI 221　1,600kW Tug/Offshore Supply Vessel 1987
主尺度　$L×B×D$（m×m×m）：56×12.2×3.7

海河拖 9　2352 千瓦拖船 1988 年
HAI HE TUO 9　2,352kW Tug 1988
主尺度　$L×B×D$（m×m×m）：32.8×9.5×4.3

云港十号　2352 千瓦拖船 1988 年
YUN GANG SHI HAO　2,352kW Tug 1988
主尺度　$L×B×D$（m×m×m）：35.6×9.5×4.4

宜港拖 1001　1060 千瓦内河拖船　1989 年
YI GANG TUO 1001　1,060kW Tug, Inland Waterway　1989
主尺度　$L×B×D$（m×m×m）：41×9×3

港鑫 7　2208 千瓦内河拖船　1990 年
GANG XIN 7　2,208kW Tug, Inland Waterway　1990
主尺度　$L×B×D$（m×m×m）：33.2×8.8×3.8

德顺　5300 千瓦拖船 / 近海供应船　1990 年
DE SHUN　5,300kW Tug/Offshore Supply Vessel　1990
主尺度　$L×B×D$（m×m×m）：81.4×16×7.2

德意　7820 千瓦拖船　1990 年
将"基辅"号退役航母从俄罗斯拖航到中国天津港
DE YI　7,820kW Tug　1990
Towed the retired aircraft carrier *KIEV* from Russia to Tianjin Port, China
主尺度　$L×B×D$（m×m×m）：95×15.2×7.5

滨海 284　5880 千瓦拖船 / 近海供应船　1992 年
BIN HAI 284　5,880kW Tug/Offshore Supply Vessel　1992
主尺度　$L×B×D$（m×m×m）：68.3×14×5.8

华诚　4000 千瓦近海供应船 1995 年
HUA CHENG　4,000kW Offshore Supply Vessel　1995
主尺度　$L×B×D$（m×m×m）：71.5×15.8×7

久盛拖 1　2132 千瓦内河拖船 1993 年
JIU SHENG TUO 1　2,132kW Tug, Inland Waterway　1993
主尺度　$L×B×D$（m×m×m）：32.8×8.8×3.9

津港轮 14 号　2942 千瓦拖船 1996 年
JIN GANG LUN 14 HAO　2,942kW Tug　1996
主尺度　$L×B×D$（m×m×m）：38×10×4.5

华祥　5734 千瓦远洋拖船 1996 年
20 世纪 90 年代从国外引进的具有破冰功能的大马力远洋救助拖轮
HUA XIANG　5,734kW Tug, Ocean-going　1996
Large horsepower ocean-going rescue tug with ice-breaking function imported from abroad in the 1990s
主尺度　$L×B×D$（m×m×m）：72.7×18×9

德翔 10560 千瓦拖船 1998 年
我国自主设计建造的大功率多功能海洋救助拖轮
DE XIANG 10,560kW Tug 1998
High-power multi-functional marine rescue tug designed and built by China
主尺度 $L×B×D$ (m×m×m)：93.9×15.6×8.4

德鲲 5920 千瓦拖船 / 近海供应船 / 救助船 2001 年
DE KUN 5,920kW Tug/Offshore Supply Vessel/Rescue Ship 2001
主尺度 $L×B×D$ (m×m×m)：65.6×14×6.9

滨海 253 3900 千瓦近海供应船 2001 年
BIN HAI 253 3,900kW Offshore Supply Vessel 2001
主尺度 $L×B×D$ (m×m×m)：70.3×16×7

华源 3008 2700 千瓦内河拖船 2004 年
HUA YUAN 3008 2,700kW Tug, Inland Waterway 2004
主尺度 $L×B×D$ (m×m×m)：36×9.7×4.5

南海 222 10400 千瓦拖船/近海供应船 2004 年
NAN HAI 222 10,400kW Tug/Offshore Supply Vessel 2004
主尺度 $L \times B \times D$ (m×m×m)：69.2×16.8×7.6

胜海 9 1324 千瓦近海供应船 2006 年
SHENG HAI 9 1,324kW Offshore Supply Vessel 2006
主尺度 $L \times B \times D$ (m×m×m)：69.4×13.8×4

三航拖 3002 2600 千瓦拖船 2007 年
SAN HANG TUO 3002 2,600kW Tug 2007
主尺度 $L \times B \times D$ (m×m×m)：50×12.5×5.2

东方兴 2942 千瓦近海供应船 2008 年
DONG FANG XING 2,942kW Offshore Supply Vessel 2008
主尺度 $L \times B \times D$ (m×m×m)：54.5×12×5.7

德涓　3676 千瓦拖船 / 近海供应船　2010 年
DE JUAN　3,676kW Tug/Offshore Supply Vessel　2010
主尺度 $L×B×D$（m×m×m）：59.2×14×6

海洋石油 252　近海供应船 / 溢油回收船　2010 年
HAI YANG SHI YOU 252　Offshore Supply Vessel/Oil Spill Recovery Ship　2010
主尺度 $L×B×D$（m×m×m）：68.1×16×6.8

勘探 311　5440 千瓦近海供应船　2011 年
KAN TAN 311　5,440kW Offshore Supply Vessel　2011
主尺度 $L×B×D$（m×m×m）：76×17.6×7.5

泛洋108　5884千瓦拖船/近海供应船　2011年
FAN YANG 108　5,884kW Tug/Offshore Supply Vessel　2011
主尺度　$L \times B \times D$ (m×m×m)：77×18×7.5

德涛　6600千瓦拖船/近海供应船　2012年
DE TAO　6,600kW Tug/Offshore Supply Vessel　2012
主尺度　$L \times B \times D$ (m×m×m)：73.9×17.2×7.6

勘探225　12000千瓦拖船/近海供应船　2012年
KAN TAN 225　12,000kW Tug/Offshore Supply Vessel　2012
主尺度　$L \times B \times D$ (m×m×m)：81×19.5×8.5

海洋石油681　16000千瓦拖船/近海供应船　2012年
HAI YANG SHI YOU 681　16,000kW Tug/Offshore Supply Vessel　2012
主尺度　$L \times B \times D$ (m×m×m)：93.4×22×9.5

龙工拖3701　368千瓦拖船　2014年
LONG GONG TUO 3701　368kW Tug　2014
主尺度　$L \times B \times D$（m×m×m）：28×7×2.4

德深　16000千瓦拖船/近海供应船　2014年
DE SHEN　16,000kW Tug/Offshore Supply Vessel　2014
主尺度　$L \times B \times D$（m×m×m）：90×20×8.8

德恒　7060千瓦近海供应船　2014年
DE HENG　7,060kW Offshore Supply Vessel　2014
主尺度　$L \times B \times D$（m×m×m）：93.8×20×8

海洋石油 525 4860 千瓦近海拖船 2015 年
采用 LNG 燃料动力系统
主尺度 $L \times B \times D$ (m×m×m): 40.8×11.6×5.5

HAI YANG SHI YOU 525 4,860kW Offshore Tug 2015
With LNG fuel power system

南油国援 1 2660 千瓦内河拖船 2015 年
NAN YOU GUO YUAN 1 2,660kW Tug, Inland Waterway 2015
主尺度 $L \times B \times D$ (m×m×m): 36.8×10.2×4.6

华虎 16000 千瓦拖船 / 近海供应船 2015 年
HUA HU 16,000kW Tug/Offshore Supply Vessel 2015
主尺度 $L \times B \times D$ (m×m×m): 89.2×22×9

海洋石油691　16000千瓦拖船/近海供应船 2015年
HAI YANG SHI YOU 691　16,000kW Tug/Offshore Supply Vessel 2015
主尺度 L×B×D（m×m×m）：102×22×9.5

海洋石油630　5110千瓦拖船/近海供应船 2017年
HAI YANG SHI YOU 630　5,110kW Tug/Offshore Supply Vessel 2017
主尺度 L×B×D（m×m×m）：68.8×14.8×6.9

华吉 5440千瓦近海供应船 2017年
HUA JI 5,440kW Offshore Supply Vessel 2017
主尺度 L×B×D（m×m×m）：81.8×17.2×7.8

益拖202 2660千瓦拖船 2019年
YICK TUG 202 2,660kW Tug 2019
主尺度 L×B×D（m×m×m）：37×14.4×5.1

海洋石油550 双燃料5000马力LNG动力供应船 2020年
具有绿色船舶标志
HAI YANG SHI YOU 550 5,000hp LNG Duel-fuelled Supply Ship 2020
With green ship notation
主尺度 L×B×D（m×m×m）：70.6×15.8×6.8

第二节 其他服务船
SECTION 2 OTHER SERVICE SHIPS

环卫1　垃圾回收船　1986年
HUAN WEI 1　Sewage Recovery Ship　1986
主尺度 $L×B×D$ (m×m×m)：46×12×5.5

海特3102　长江引航船　1987年
HAI TE 3102　Pilot Ship, Yangtze River　1987
主尺度 $L×B×D$ (m×m×m)：33.8×6.8×3.3

连汇清8　浮油回收船　1989年
LIAN HUI QING 8　Oil Recovery Vessel　1989
主尺度 $L×B×D$ (m×m×m)：32×6.8×2.8

龙消501　248千瓦黑龙江消防船　1994年
LONG XIAO 501　248kW Fire Fighting Ship, Heilongjiang River　1994
主尺度 $L×B×D$ (m×m×m)：26×8.5×2

琼引 2 号　海南港引航船 1995 年
QIONG YIN NO. 2　Pilot Ship,
Hainan Port 1995
主尺度　$L×B×D$（m×m×m）：36×9.8×4.4

利海油 29　珠江溢油（污油）回收船 1995 年
LI HAI YOU 29　Spilled (Effluent) Oil
Recovery Vessel, Pearl River 1995
主尺度　$L×B×D$（m×m×m）：38.9×7.8×2.5

胜利 617　油污水处理船 1995 年
SHENG LI 617　Oily Water Treatment Vessel 1995
主尺度　$L×B×D$（m×m×m）：73.1×16×4

长引 001　长江引航船 2000 年
CHANG YIN 001　Pilot Ship, Yangtze River 2000
主尺度　$L×B×D$（m×m×m）：21×3.4×1.7

SHIPS OF CHINA

沪港引1　上海引航船 2004年改建
大型先进引航船
HU GANG YIN 1　Pilot Ship, Shanghai　Converted in 2004
Advanced large pilot ship
主尺度　$L×B×D$（m×m×m）：108.2×15.8×7.7

永洁99号　珠江溢油（污油）回收船 2005年改建
YONG JIE 99 HAO　Spilled (Effluent) Oil Recovery Vessel, Pearl River Converted in 2005
主尺度　$L×B×D$（m×m×m）：57×13×4

长公消1202　880千瓦长江消防船 2007年改建
CHANG GONG XIAO 1202　880kW Fire Fighting Ship, Yangtze River　Converted in 2007
主尺度　$L×B×D$（m×m×m）：36×6.5×3

三峡清漂1　300立方米长江多功能清漂船 2007年
SAN XIA QING PIAO 1　300m^3 Multi-functional Floating Garbage Ship, Yangtze River　2007
主尺度　$L×B×D$（m×m×m）：49×15×3.5

珠江号　3280 千瓦珠江消防船 2008 年
ZHU JIANG HAO　3,280kW Fire Fighting Ship, Pearl River 2008
主尺度　$L×B×D$ (m×m×m)：39×9×4

安和　青岛引航船 2008 年
AN HE　Pilot Ship, Qingdao 2008
主尺度　$L×B×D$ (m×m×m)：15.4×4.9×2.3

海洋石油 251　溢油（污油）回收 / 消防船 2008 年
HAI YANG SHI YOU 251　Spilled (Effluent) Oil Recovery/Fire Fighting Ship 2008
主尺度　$L×B×D$ (m×m×m)：47.5×9.4×4.2

SHIPS OF CHINA

水上环卫 03　珠江垃圾回收船　2009 年
SHUI SHANG HUAN WEI 03　　Sewage Recovery Ship, Pearl River　2009
主尺度 *L*×*B*×*D*（m×m×m）：29×6.8×2

浙嘉兴工 8　748 千瓦内河抛锚船　2009 年
ZHE JIA XING GONG 8　　748kW Anchor Vessel, Inland Waterway　2009
主尺度 *L*×*B*×*D*（m×m×m）：41.4×12×2.8

沪环运货 5002　上海垃圾集装箱船　2010 年
HU HUAN YUN HUO 5002　　Garbage Container Ship, Shanghai　2010
主尺度 *L*×*B*×*D*（m×m×m）：48.9×9.5×2.9

三峡浮吊 1 号　长江溢油（污油）回收驳　2010 年
SAN XIA FU DIAO 1 HAO　Spilled (Effluent) Oil Recovery Barge, Yangtze River　2010
主尺度　$L \times B \times D$ (m×m×m)：40×10.8×2

沪消 2　1268 千瓦上海消防船　2011 年
HU XIAO 2　1,268kW Fire Fighting Ship, Shanghai　2011
主尺度　$L \times B \times D$ (m×m×m)：40×8×3.4

广州港引航 2 号　广州引航船　2012 年
GUANG ZHOU GANG YIN HANG 2 HAO　Pilot Ship, Pearl River　2012
主尺度　$L \times B \times D$ (m×m×m)：26×5.8×3

海巡 12002　长江溢油（污油）回收船 2012 年
HAI XUN 12002　Spilled (Effluent) Oil Recovery Vessel, Yangtze River 2012
主尺度 *L*×*B*×*D*（m×m×m）：32.8×9.6×2.8

长引 007　长江引航船 2015 年
CHANG YIN 007　Pilot Ship, Yangtze River 2015
主尺度 *L*×*B*×*D*（m×m×m）：34.7×8.5×4

德濠　3000 立方米溢油回收船 / 近海供应船 2015 年
DE JING　3,000m³ Spilled (Effluent) Oil Recovery Ship/Offshore Supply Vessel 2015
主尺度 *L*×*B*×*D*（m×m×m）：90.9×20×8.2

宇航 2　2648 千瓦抛锚船 2016 年
YU HANG 2　2,648kW Anchor Vessel 2016
主尺度 *L*×*B*×*D*（m×m×m）：41.7×12×4.4

浦消 1 号 4480 千瓦消防船 2017 年
PU XIAO 1 HAO 4,480kW Fire Fighting Ship 2017
主尺度 L×B×D (m×m×m): 53.2×12.8×6

金鑫 116 2940 千瓦抛锚船 2018 年
JIN XIN 116 2,940kW Anchor Vessel 2018
主尺度 L×B×D (m×m×m): 39×11.6×3.5

沪港引 6 上海引航船 2019 年
HU GANG YIN 6 Pilot Ship, Shanghai 2019
主尺度 L×B×D (m×m×m): 118×19×7.8

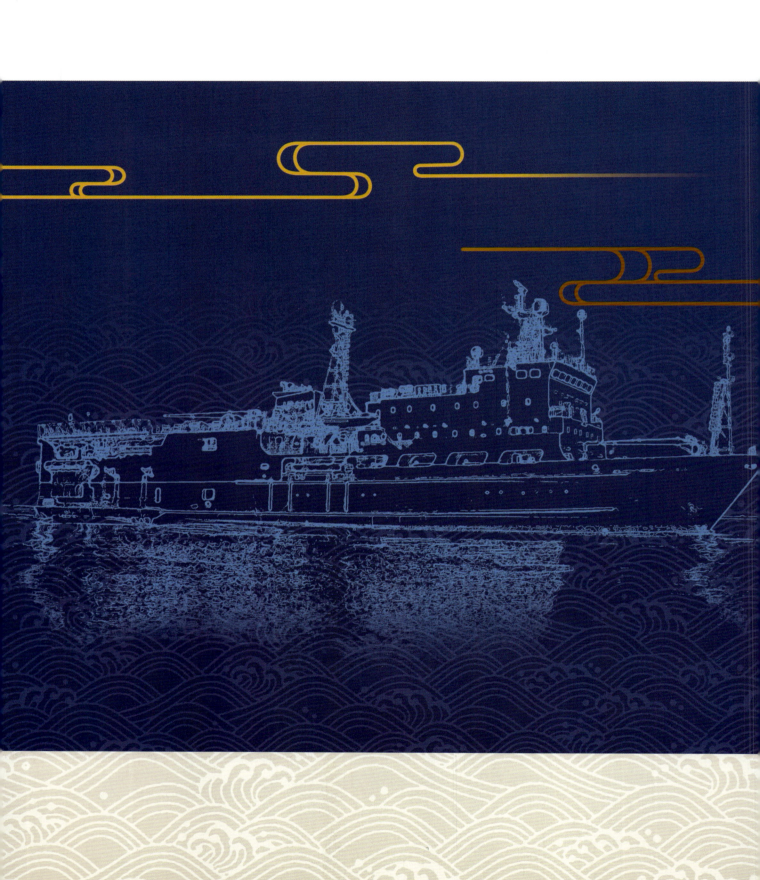

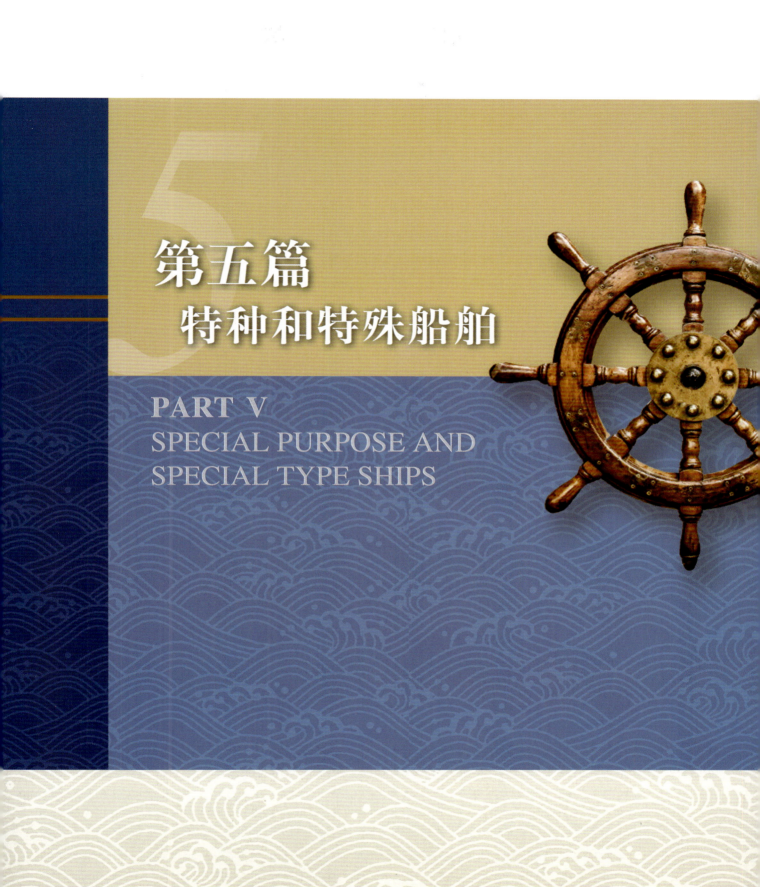

第五篇
特种和特殊船舶

PART V
SPECIAL PURPOSE AND
SPECIAL TYPE SHIPS

第一章　特种用途船

科考/调查船、勘探船、测量船按国际公约的分类归类于特种用途船，船上除配有必要的船员外，还载有一定数量的特殊专业人员和工作人员，称为特殊人员。

我国海洋科考调查船在20世纪80年代中期开始进入深远海及极地进行调查。21世纪以来，海洋科考调查船发展很快，从百吨级发展到万吨级，涵盖物探船、天然气水合物综合调查船、综合测量船、海洋极地科考船、远望系列航天测量船、5000～10000米载人深潜器等。船上配备有先进的海洋调查仪器以及卫星通信和导航系统，可进行地质、地球物理、气象、化学、生物和环境保护等多项综合调查。目前，我国自主设计建造的典型海洋科考船已经处于国际先进水平。例如：大型综合科考船，具备深海钻探能力、破冰能力和深潜调查综合能力；大型极地科考船，采用船艏、船艉双向破冰技术，能够在1.5米厚冰环境中连续破冰航行；大型综合地质调查船，以举升式岩心钻探功能为主、同时兼顾地球物理调查和海洋水文环境调查等功能；大型远洋综合测量船，具备水深测量、底质探测和海流测量等海道测量多项功能；我国研制的7000米级作业型载人潜水器，在马里亚纳海沟最大下潜深度达7062米，具备深海探矿、海底高精度地形测量、可疑物探测与捕获、深海生物考察等功能，达到国际先进水平。

教学实习船是专门为航海类专业学生教学实习而进行设计的，布置有各类教学实习和科研场所、配套的生活设施，还设有航海教学训练室、轮机功能测试室、现代化教室等。大型现代教学实习船还可通过装备先进的探测与实验分析等系统，进行多学科、多种海洋要素的综合观测，是集教学、科研、生产于一体的教学实习船舶。

CHAPTER I   SPECIAL PURPOSE SHIPS

Research ships, exploration and survey ships are classified as special purpose ships according to international conventions. These vessels are provided with necessary crew members as well as a certain number of professionals called special personnel.

China's marine research and survey ships began to enter deep sea and the polar regions for investigation in the mid-1980s. Since the beginning of the 21st century, marine research and survey ships have developed rapidly from 100 DWT to 10,000 DWT, covering seismic survey vessel, comprehensive survey ships for natural gas hydrate, comprehensive survey ships, marine polar research ships, space survey ships of the YUAN WANG series, 5,000-10,000m manned deep sea submersibles. The ships are equipped with advanced marine survey instruments as well as satellite communication and navigation systems, and can conduct a number of comprehensive investigations in geology, geophysics, meteorology, chemistry, biology and environmental protection. China's independent design and construction of typical marine research ships is now well established at international level. For examples, a large-size comprehensive scientific research ship with deep sea drilling, ice-breaking and deep diving investigation ability, a large-size polar scientific research ship, which adopts the bow and stern two-way icebreaking technology and is capable of continuous ice-breaking in a 1.5m thick ice environment. Another vessel is a large-size comprehensive geological survey ship, mainly featuring the function of lifting core drilling, as well as geophysical survey and marine hydrological environment survey. The examples also extend to a large-size ocean-going comprehensive survey ship, which has multiple functions such as water depth measurement, sediment detection and current measurement; the 7,000m manned submersible, which has a maximum diving depth of 7,062m in the Mariana Trench and is used for deep-sea prospecting, the high-precision topographic survey of seabeds, the detection and capture of suspicious objects and deep-sea biological investigation, reaching the international advanced level.

The training ship, specially designed for teaching and training the students majoring in navigation, has various teaching, practice and scientific research spaces, supporting living facilities, a navigation teaching and training room, engine function test room, as well as modern classrooms. Large-size modern training ship can also carry out multi-disciplinary and comprehensive observation of various marine elements by equipping advanced detection and experimental analysis systems, which makes it a ship integrating teaching, scientific research and production.

第一节　科考／调查船

SECTION 1　RESEARCH/SURVEY SHIPS

雪龙　极地科考船　1993年购进改建
我国第一艘极地科考船
主尺度 $L×B×D$（m×m×m）：167×22.6×13.5

XUE LONG　Polar Research Ship Purchased and Converted in 1993
China's first polar research ship

科学三号 海洋地质生态环境综合考察船 2006 年
KE XUE SAN HAO Comprehensive Marine Geology and Ecological Environment Research Ship 2006
主尺度 $L×B×D$ (m×m×m): 73.9×10.2×4.6

实验 1 综合科学考察船 2009 年
SHI YAN 1 Comprehensive Scientific Research Ship 2009
主尺度 $L×B×D$ (m×m×m): 60.9×26×10.5

第五篇 特种和特殊船舶
PART V SPECIAL PURPOSE AND SPECIAL TYPE SHIPS

海洋六号 海洋天然气水合物调查船 2010 年
我国第一艘海洋天然气水合物调查船
HAI YANG LIU HAO Marine Gas Hydrate Survey Ship 2010
China's first marine gas hydrate survey ship
主尺度 $L \times B \times D$ (m×m×m)：106×17.4×8.3

深潜号 300 米饱和潜水支持母船 2012 年
我国第一艘自主设计建造的 300 米饱和潜水支持母船
主尺度 $L \times B \times D$ (m×m×m)：125.7×25×10.6

SHEN QIAN HAO 300m Saturation Dive Support Ship 2012
First 300m saturation dive support ship designed and built by China

465

科学 深远海综合科学考察船 2012 年
KE XUE Abyssopelagic Comprehensive Research Ship 2012
主尺度 $L \times B \times D$ (m×m×m)：99.8×17.8×8.9

中国考古 01 水上考古工作船 2014 年
我国第一艘水上考古工作船
ZHONG GUO KAO GU 01 Aquatic Archaeological Work Ship 2014
China's first aquatic archaeological work ship
主尺度 $L \times B \times D$ (m×m×m)：57.9×10.8×4.8

创新一 近海资源生态环境综合考察船 2016 年
CHUANG XIN YI Comprehensive Research Ship for Offshore Resources, Ecology and Environment 2016
主尺度 $L×B×D$ (m×m×m)：48.7×9×4

瑞利 10 号 双体监测船 2016 年
具有较强的水下探测和信息搜集能力
RUI LI 10 HAO Monitoring Catamaran 2016
With strong underwater detection and information collection capabilities
主尺度 $L×B×D$ (m×m×m)：82×32×11.6

电科 1 号 海洋信息设备综合试验船 2016 年
我国第一艘海洋信息设备综合试验船
DIAN KE 1 HAO Comprehensive Test Ship with Marine Information Devices 2016
China's first comprehensive test ship with marine information devices
主尺度 $L×B×D$ (m×m×m)：89.2×18×5.5

SHIPS OF CHINA

探索一号　深潜作业支持船　2016 年改建
"深海勇士" 4500 米深潜海试作业支持船
主尺度　$L×B×D$ （m×m×m）：94.5×17.9×8

TAN SUO YI HAO　Deep Diving Support Ship　Converted in 2016
Support ship for 4,500m deep diving operation of *SHEN HAI YONG SHI*

张謇　多学科多功能综合考察船　2016 年
ZHANG JIAN　Multi-disciplinary and Multi-functional Comprehensive Research Ship　2016
主尺度　$L×B×D$ （m×m×m）：97.6×17.8×8.4

向阳红 03　海洋环境综合科考船 2016 年
XIANG YANG HONG 03　Comprehensive Marine Environment Research Ship 2016
主尺度 $L\times B\times D$ (m×m×m)：99.8×17.8×8.9

海洋地质十号　海洋地质科考船 2017 年
HAI YANG DI ZHI SHI HAO　Marine Geology Research Ship 2017
主尺度 $L\times B\times D$ (m×m×m)：75.8×15.4×7.6

嘉庚　水文化学生物地质综合科考船 2017 年
JIA GENG　Comprehensive Research Ship for Hydrology, Chemistry, Biology and Geology 2017
主尺度 $L\times B\times D$ (m×m×m)：77.7×16.2×8

海洋地质九号 海洋地质综合调查船 2017 年
HAI YANG DI ZHI JIU HAO Comprehensive Survey Ship for Marine Geology 2017
主尺度 $L×B×D$ (m×m×m)：87.1×17×7.8

沈括 多学科深海科学考察船 2018 年
SHEN KUO Multi-disciplinary Deep-Sea Research Ship 2018
主尺度 $L×B×D$ (m×m×m)：63×23×9.4

深海一号 潜水器支持母船 2019 年
SHEN HAI YI HAO Submersible Support Vessel 2019
主尺度 $L×B×D$ (m×m×m)：90.2×16.8×8.3

东方红 3 海洋综合科学考察船 2019 年
DONG FANG HONG 3 Comprehensive Marine Research Ship 2019
主尺度 $L×B×D$ (m×m×m)：103.8×18×8.7

SHIPS OF CHINA

雪龙2　极地科考破冰船　2019年
我国第一艘自主建造的极地科考破冰船
主尺度 $L \times B \times D$ (m×m×m)：122.5×22.3×11.8

XUE LONG 2　Polar Research Icebreaker　2019
First polar research icebreaker built by China

海龙号　饱和潜水支持船　2019年
我国设计建造新型先进的饱和潜水支持船，最大作业水深300米
主尺度 $L \times B \times D$ (m×m×m)：124×24×10.2

ORIENTAL DRAGON　Saturation Dive Support Vessel　2019
Advanced saturation dive support ship designed and built by China, with a maximum working depth of 300m

探索二号 载人潜水器支持保障母船 2020年
我国第一艘万米深潜器（奋斗者号）海试支持保障船
主尺度 $L \times B \times D$ (m×m×m)：87.3×18.8×7.4

TAN SUO ER HAO Manned Diving Vehicle Support Vessel 2020
China's first support vessel for the the sea trial of 10,000m deep-sea submersible (*FEN DOU ZHE*)

实验6 地球物理综合科学考察船 2020年
新一代3500吨级综合考察船
主尺度 $L \times B \times D$ (m×m×m)：90.6×17×8

SHI YAN 6 Comprehensive Research Ship for Geophysics 2020
A new generation of 3,500DWT comprehensive research ship

第二节 地质勘探／测量船

SECTION 2   GEOLOGICAL EXPLORATION/SURVEY SHIPS

龙测 3005   41 米黑龙江航道测量船 1986 年
LONG CE 3005   41m Hydrographical Survey Ship, Heilongjiang River 1986
主尺度 $L×B×D$（m×m×m）：41×8×2

龙测 3008   37 米黑龙江航道测量船 1990 年
LONG CE 3008   37m Hydrographical Survey Ship, Heilongjiang River 1990
主尺度 $L×B×D$（m×m×m）：37×7×2

东方明珠   4 缆海洋物探船 1994 年
DONG FANG MING ZHU   4-Cable Seismic Survey Vessel, Marine 1994
主尺度 $L×B×D$（m×m×m）：78.7×16×7

远望3 远洋航天测量船 1995 年
承担卫星等航天器飞行试验的海上测量和控制任务
主尺度 $L\times B\times D$（m×m×m）：179.9×22.2×11.6

YUAN WANG 3 Space Tracking Ship, Ocean-going 1995
Undertaking the maritime tracking and monitoring tasks of spacecraft flight tests such as satellites, etc.

豫三昆仑号 水文测量船 1998 年
YU SAN KUN LUN HAO Hydrological Survey Ship 1998
主尺度 $L\times B\times D$（m×m×m）：28×5.4×1.8

海洋石油 719　8 缆海洋物探船　2001 年
HAI YANG SHI YOU 719　8-Cable Seismic Survey Vessel, Marine　2001
主尺度 $L \times B \times D$ (m×m×m)：79.8×18×7.4

海巡 1668　航道港口综合测量船　2006 年
HAI XUN 1668　Comprehensive Hydrographical and Port Survey Ship　2006
主尺度 $L \times B \times D$ (m×m×m)：43.2×7.8×3.6

东方勘探一号　6 缆海洋物探船　2007 年
DONG FANG KAN TAN NO. 1　6-Cable Seismic Survey Vessel, Marine　2007
主尺度 $L \times B \times D$ (m×m×m)：65.8×13.8×5.1

远望 5 远洋航天测量船 2007 年
承担卫星等航天器飞行试验的海上测量和控制任务
主尺度 $L×B×D$ (m×m×m)：222×25.2×11.7

YUAN WANG 5　Space Tracking Ship, Ocean-going　2007
Undertaking the maritime tracking and monitoring tasks of spacecraft flight tests such as satellites, etc.

航勘 201　内河钻探船 2010 年
HANG KAN 201　River Drill Vessel　2010
主尺度 $L×B×D$ (m×m×m)：37×8×2

海豹六号　海洋物探震源船 2010 年
HAI BAO LIU HAO　Seismic Survey Vessel, Marine　2010
主尺度 $L×B×D$ (m×m×m)：47.9×8.8×3.7

航道 1 号　长江航道综合测量船兼战枯水指挥船　2010 年
HANG DAO 1 HAO　Comprehensive Channel Survey and Low-water Command Ship, Yangtze River　2010
主尺度 $L×B×D$（m×m×m）：50×9×3

海洋石油 720　12 缆海洋物探船　2011 年
HAI YANG SHI YOU 720　12-Cable Seismic Survey Vessel, Marine　2011
主尺度 $L×B×D$（m×m×m）：107.4×24×9.6

发现 6　14 缆海洋物探船　2013 年
FA XIAN 6　14-Cable Seismic Survey Vessel, Marine　2013
主尺度 $L×B×D$（m×m×m）：100.1×24×9

宁道测 901　40 米级长江 A 型测量船 2014 年
NING DAO CE 901　40m Type A Survey Vessel, Yangtze River　2014
主尺度 $L\times B\times D$ (m×m×m)：44.9×8.2×3.6

海洋石油 707　海洋工程勘察船 2015 年
HAI YANG SHI YOU 707　Engineering Exploration Vessel, Marine　2015
主尺度 $L\times B\times D$ (m×m×m)：80.3×17.8×7.6

海洋石油 771　物探采集作业支持船 2016 年
HAI YANG SHI YOU 771　Support Ship for Geophysical Survey and Acquisition Operation　2016
主尺度 $L\times B\times D$ (m×m×m)：65×16×7.5

远望 7　远洋航天测量船　2016 年
承担卫星等航天器飞行试验的海上测量和控制任务
主尺度　$L×B×D$（m×m×m）：224.9×27.2×12

YUAN WANG 7　Space Tracking Ship, Ocean-going　2016
Undertaking the maritime tracking and monitoring tasks of spacecraft flight tests such as satellites, etc.

海巡 16601　航道港口综合测量船　2019 年
HAI XUN 16601　Comprehensive Hydrographical and Port Survey Ship　2019
主尺度　$L×B×D$（m×m×m）：25.1×5.2×1.8

向阳红 22　浮标作业船　2019 年
我国第一艘大型浮标作业船
XIANG YANG HONG 22　Buoy Laying Ship　2019
China's first large-size buoy laying ship
主尺度　$L×B×D$（m×m×m）：89.7×18×7.2

蛟龙　7000 米深海载人潜水器　2009 年
我国第一艘自主设计与集成的深海载人潜水器
JIAO LONG　7,000m Deep-sea Manned Submersible　2009
China's first self-designed and integrated deep-sea manned submersible
主尺度　$L×B×D$（m×m×m）：8×3.5×3

深海勇士　4500 米深海载人潜水器　2017 年
我国自主研发制造的深海载人潜水器
SHEN HAI YONG SHI　4,500m Deep-sea Manned Submersible　2017
Deep-sea manned submersible developed and built by China
主尺度　$L×B×D$（m×m×m）：8×3×3.5

奋斗者号　11000 米深海载人潜水器　2020 年
我国自主研发制造的全海深载人潜水器
FEN DOU ZHE HAO　11,000m Deep-sea Manned Submersible　2020
Deep-sea manned submersible developed and built by China
主尺度　$L×B×D$（m×m×m）：10.2×3.2×4.48

第三节　教学实习船
SECTION 3　TRAINING VESSEL

育龙　大连海事大学远洋教学实习船　1989 年
我国第一艘万吨级海洋教学实习船，可供 126 名学生海上实习
主尺度 $L×B×D$ (m×m×m)：139.8×20.8×11.4

YU LONG　Dalian Maritime University Training Vessel, Ocean-going　1989
China's first 10,000DWT marine training vessel for training of 126 students at sea

育锋　上海海事大学远洋教学实习船　1992 年
可供 103 名学生海上实习
YU FENG　Shanghai Maritime University Training Vessel, Ocean-going　1992
For training of 103 students at sea
主尺度 $L×B×D$ (m×m×m)：139.8×20.8×11.4

长航福海　武汉理工大学远洋教学实习船　2012 年
46000 吨散货船兼教学实习船，可供 40 名学生海上实习
CHANG HANG FU HAI　Wuhan University of Technology Training Vessel, Ocean-going　2012
46,000DWT bulk carrier and training vessel for training of 40 students at sea
主尺度 $L×B×D$ (m×m×m)：190×32.3×15.8

育明 上海海事大学远洋教学实习船 2012 年
可供 160 名学生海上实习
YU MING Shanghai Maritime University Training Vessel, Ocean-going 2012
For training of 160 students at sea
主尺度 $L×B×D$ (m×m×m)：189.9×32.3×15.7

育德 集美大学远洋教学实习船 2015 年
可供 143 名学生海上实习
YU DE Jimei University Training Vessel, Ocean-going 2015
For training of 143 students at sea
主尺度 $L×B×D$ (m×m×m)：199.9×32.3×18

育鹏 大连海事大学远洋教学实习船 2016 年
可供 90 名学生海上实习
主尺度 $L×B×D$ (m×m×m)：199.8×27.8×15.5

YU PENG Dalian Maritime University Training Vessel, Ocean-going 2016
For training of 90 students at sea

第二章 特殊船
CHAPTER II SPECIAL SHIPS

第一节 海巡/救助船

　　海巡船是中国海事监管部门行使海上管理职责的工作平台，负责外国籍船舶入出境及在我国港口、水域的监督管理，以及船舶载运危险货物及其他货物的安全监督，在和平开发和利用海洋资源、履行国际公约中发挥着重要作用。我国先进的海巡船配备有目前世界上最先进的导航雷达，与电子海图和综合航行信息显示组成综合航行系统，实现了导航的数字化，船上还有直升机起降平台、直升机库和飞行指挥塔等全套船载系统。

　　救助船是指专用于对发生碰撞、触礁、搁浅和火灾等海难事故的船进行施救的船舶，是国家专业救助机构执行海上与内陆水域人命救助、船舶和财产救助、海上消防、清除溢油污染等任务的工作平台。我国沿岸各海区部署有70余艘救助船，大型先进的救助船配备有完备的消防系统、大功率拖带系统、先进的溢油回收装置、潜水作业平台、直升机起降平台和深海搜寻扫测设备等，而且航速快、抗风能力强、具有破冰能力，可实现全天候水上专业救助。

SECTION 1   SEA PATROL/RESCUE SHIPS

Sea patrol ships are the working platform for China Maritime Safety Administration (MSA), mainly used for the supervision and management of foreign ships entering and leaving China's ports and waters, as well as the safety supervision of ships carrying dangerous goods and other cargoes. They play an important role in the peaceful development and utilization of marine resources and the implementation of international conventions. China's advanced sea patrol ships are equipped with the world's most advanced navigation radar, and comprehensive navigation systems combining electronic charts and integrated navigation information display; they are also equipped with a full set of shipboard systems, including helicopter landing platform, helicopter hangar, flight command tower, etc.

Rescue ships are dedicated to rescue ships which have been in a collision or which have struck a rock or experienced a grounding, fire or other marine accident. They are the working platform for national rescue bodies to carry out rescue at sea and inland waters, salvage of ship and property, firefighting at sea, oil spill pollution removal and other tasks. There are more than 70 rescue ships deployed in various sea areas along the coast of China. Large advanced rescue ships are equipped with complete firefighting systems, high-power towing systems, advanced oil spill recovery devices, diving operation platforms, helicopter landing platforms, deep-sea search and survey equipment, etc. They have fast speeds combined with strong wind resistance and ice-breaking capability to enable all-weather rescue.

海巡 01015   40 米海事巡逻船 1988 年
HAI XUN 01015   40m Maritime Patrol Vessel 1988
主尺度 $L \times B \times D$ (m×m×m)：40×8.4×4.5

海巡 0103   56 米海事巡逻船 1990 年
HAI XUN 0103   56m Maritime Patrol Vessel 1990
主尺度 $L \times B \times D$ (m×m×m)：55.5×10×4.6

海巡 21　93 米大型海事巡视船　2002 年
海事系统第一艘千吨级海上巡视船
HAI XUN 21　93m Large Maritime Patrol Vessel 2002
First 1,000DWT maritime patrol vessel in China MSA system
主尺度 $L \times B \times D$ (m×m×m)：93.2×11.2×5.4

海巡 31　113 米大型远洋海事巡逻船　2005 年
大型先进海事巡逻船
HAI XUN 31　113m Large Maritime Patrol Vessel, Ocean-going 2005
Advanced large maritime patrol vessel
主尺度 $L \times B \times D$ (m×m×m)：112.8×13.8×6.5

海巡 1468　60 米 B 型海事巡逻船　2009 年
HAI XUN 1468　60m Type B Maritime Patrol Vessel 2009
主尺度 $L \times B \times D$ (m×m×m)：64×10.2×5

海巡 11　114 米大型远洋海事巡逻船　2009 年
大型高性能海事巡逻船
主尺度　$L \times B \times D$ (m×m×m)：114.4×13.8×6.5

HAI XUN 11　114m Large Maritime Patrol Vessel, Ocean-going　2009
Large high-performance maritime patrol vessel

海巡 1203　46 米长江海事巡逻船　2010 年
HAI XUN 1203　46m Maritime Patrol Vessel, Yangtze River　2010
主尺度　$L \times B \times D$ (m×m×m)：46×8×3

海巡 01 129 米大型海事巡逻船 2013 年
兼具海事巡航监管和救助功能先进的大型综合执法船
主尺度 $L×B×D$ (m×m×m)：128.6×16×7.9

HAI XUN 01 129m Large Maritime Patrol Vessel 2013
Large comprehensive law enforcement vessel with advanced maritime patrol, supervision and rescue functions

云航政 6 23 米澜沧江海事巡逻船 2018 年
YUN HANG ZHENG 6 23m Maritime Patrol Vessel, Lantsang River 2018
主尺度 $L×B×D$ (m×m×m)：23×4.2×1.7

海巡 09　165 米大型海事巡逻船　2020 年
我国第一艘万吨级海事巡逻船，具有智能船舶标志
主尺度 $L×B×D$ (m×m×m)：165×20.6×9.5

HAI XUN 09　165 m Large Maritime Patrol Vessel　2020
China's first 10,000T maritime patrol vessel, with intelligent ship notation

北海救 199　1940 千瓦救助船　1981 年
BEI HAI JIU 199　1,940kW Rescue Vessel　1981
主尺度 $L×B×D$ (m×m×m)：60.2×11.6×5.7

南海救 209　高速救助船 1990 年
NAN HAI JIU 209　High-speed Rescue Vessel 1990
主尺度　$L×B×D$ (m×m×m)：49.9×8×4.6

东海救 131　6720 千瓦救助船 2005 年
DONG HAI JIU 131　6,720kW Rescue Vessel 2005
主尺度　$L×B×D$ (m×m×m)：77×14×6.8

北海救 111　9000 千瓦远洋救助船 2005 年
系列救助船中的首制船
主尺度　$L×B×D$ (m×m×m)：98×15.2×7.6

BEI HAI JIU 111　9,000kW Rescue Vessel 2005
First ship in rescue vessel series

北海救 201　高速双体救助船 2006 年
BEI HAI JIU 201　High-speed Rescue Catamaran　2006
主尺度 $L×B×D$ (m×m×m)：49.9×13.1×4.5

南海救 111　9000 千瓦救助船 2006 年
NAN HAI JIU 111　9,000kW Rescue Vessel　2006
主尺度 $L×B×D$ (m×m×m)：98×15.2×7.6

南海救 101　14000 千瓦远洋救助船 2007 年
先进多功能远洋救助船
主尺度 $L×B×D$ （m×m×m）：109.7×16.2×7.6

NAN HAI JIU 101　14,000kW Rescue Vessel, Ocean-going　2007
Advanced multi-functional ocean-going rescue vessel

东海救 101　14400 千瓦远洋救助船 2012 年
DONG HAI JIU 101　14,400kW Rescue Vessel, Ocean-going　2012
主尺度 $L×B×D$ （m×m×m）：117×16.2×7.8

第五篇　特种和特殊船舶
PART V　SPECIAL PURPOSE AND SPECIAL TYPE SHIPS

东海救 117　9000 千瓦救助船　2013 年
具备溢油回收功能
主尺度 $L×B×D$ (m×m×m)：99.4×15.2×7.6

DONG HAI JIU 117　9,000kW Rescue Vessel　2013
With oil spill recovery function

北海救 117　9000 千瓦救助船　2014 年
具备破冰功能
主尺度 $L×B×D$ (m×m×m)：98.6×15.2×7.6

BEI HAI JIU 117　9,000kW Rescue Vessel　2014
With ice-breaking function

493

东海救 203　5120 千瓦高速双体救助船　2015 年
DONG HAI JIU 203　5,120kW High-speed Rescue Catamaran　2015
主尺度　$L×B×D$ (m×m×m)：49.9×13.1×4.5

北海救 119　9000 千瓦救助船　2015 年
具备破冰功能
BEI HAI JIU 119　9,000kW Rescue Vessel　2015
With ice-breaking function
主尺度　$L×B×D$ (m×m×m)：99×15.2×7.6

东海救 102　12000 千瓦救助船　2015 年
DONG HAI JIU 102　12,000kW Rescue Vessel　2015
主尺度　$L×B×D$ (m×m×m)：127.7×16×8.1

南海救 102 12000 千瓦救助船 2016 年
我国第一艘搭载 6000 米深海搜寻设备的工作母船
主尺度 $L×B×D$ (m×m×m)：127.7×16×8.1

NAN HAI JIU 102 12,000kW Rescue Vessel 2016
China's first support ship equipped with 6,000m deep-sea search devices

南海救 321 2058 千瓦救助船 2018 年
NAN HAI JIU 321 2,058kW Rescue Vessel 2018
主尺度 $L×B×D$ (m×m×m)：21.4×6.1×3.2

龙救 1501 1102 千瓦黑龙江救助拖船 2018 年
LONG JIU 1501 1,102kW Rescue Tug, Heilongjiang River 2018
主尺度 $L×B×D$ (m×m×m)：43.8×9.5×3

北海救气垫 01　全垫升气垫救助艇 2019 年
BEI HAI JIU QI DIAN 01　Fully Cushioned Rescue Hovercraft 2019
主尺度 $L×B×D$（m×m×m）：7.4×2.3×0.7

东海救 151　4000 千瓦救助船 2019 年
DONG HAI JIU 151　4,000kW Rescue Vessel 2019
主尺度 $L×B×D$（m×m×m）：69.5×14.6×6.8

第二节　海警／海监／渔政船

海警船是中国海警部门开展海上维权和执法，维护国家海洋主权和打击海上违法犯罪活动的执法船舶。近年来，我国建造的大型海警船配备了先进的光电取证系统、无线图像接收系统、北斗定位系统等装备，设有船载直升机平台，装备有舰载摩托艇和舰炮、机枪、水炮等武器系统。

海监船用于政府机关依照有关法律和规定，对国家管辖海域（包括海岸带）实施巡航监视，查处侵犯海洋权益、违法使用海域、损害海洋环境与资源、破坏海上设施、扰乱海上秩序等违法违规行为，还可满足海洋执法监察和海洋环境调查等应用需求。我国建造的大型海监船配备了世界上最先进的自动控位和定向系统、直升机升降平台、国内最先进的卫星通信与计算机网络系统。

渔政船是执行渔政执法任务的船舶，主要有渔政监督船、渔港监督船和渔业救助船等。主要承担渔场巡视并监督、检查渔船（含外国渔船）执行国家法律法规和相关国际条约协定的情况，维护国家渔业权益，保护渔业资源和水域生态环境，维护渔场生产秩序，处理海上渔业纠纷和涉外渔业案件，以及配合海上救助等任务。我国新建造的大型渔政船吨位大、航速快、通导设备先进，并配有船载直升机，具有专业执法、全天候巡航、快速灵活应对周边紧急事态的能力。

SECTION 2　COAST GUARD / MARINE SURVEILLANCE / FISHERY ADMINISTRATION SHIPS

Coast Guard ships are the law enforcement vessels of Chinese marine police department to carry out maritime rights maintenance and law enforcement, safeguard national maritime sovereignty and combat maritime criminal activities. In recent years, the large Coast Guard ships built in China are equipped with advanced photoelectric forensic systems, wireless image receiving systems, Beidou positioning systems, helicopter platform, motorboat, artillery, machine gun and water cannon.

Marine surveillance ships are used by Government bodies to carry out patrol in sea areas under national jurisdiction, including coastal zones, in accordance with relevant laws and regulations. They investigate and deal with violations of maritime rights and interests including the illegal use of sea areas, damage to the marine environment and resources, destruction to offshore facilities and the disturbance of marine order. They can apply maritime law enforcement supervision and marine environment investigation. The large marine surveillance ships built in China are equipped with the world's most advanced automatic position control and orientation systems, helicopter landing platform, and the most advanced satellite communication and computer network system in China.

Fishery administration ships are vessels that perform fishery law enforcement tasks, mainly including fishery supervision ships, fishing port supervision ships and fishery rescue ships. They mainly undertake fishing patrol, supervise and inspect the implementation of national laws and regulations and relevant international treaties and agreements by fishing vessels, including foreign fishing vessels. They further safeguard national fishery rights and interests, protect fishery resources and aquatic ecology, maintain the production order of fishing grounds, handle maritime fishery disputes and foreign-related fishery cases and cooperate with maritime rescue and other tasks. China's newly built fishery administration ships have large tonnage, fast speed, advanced navigation equipment and are equipped with shipboard helicopters. They are capable of professional law enforcement, all-weather cruising, and quick and flexible response to emergencies.

中国海警 1212　95 米海警船　1988 年
ZHONG GUO HAI JING 1212　95m Coast Guard Ship　1988
主尺度 $L \times B \times D$ (m×m×m)：94.9×14×5.7

中国海警 31101　93 米海警船　2007 年
ZHONG GUO HAI JING 31101　93m Coast Guard Ship　2007
主尺度 $L \times B \times D$ (m×m×m)：92.6×12×5.5

中国海警 3401　99 米海警船　2013 年
ZHONG GUO HAI JING 3401　99m Coast Guard Ship　2013
主尺度 $L×B×D$ (m×m×m)：99×15.2×7.6

中国海警 3306　98 米海警船　2014 年
ZHONG GUO HAI JING 3306　98m Coast Guard Ship　2014
主尺度 $L×B×D$ (m×m×m)：98×15.2×7.8

中国海警 2306　98 米海警船　2014 年
ZHONG GUO HAI JING 2306　98m Coast Guard Ship　2014
主尺度 $L×B×D$ (m×m×m)：98×15.2×7.8

中国海警 2401　99 米海警船　2014 年
ZHONG GUO HAI JING 2401　99m Coast Guard Ship　2014
主尺度　$L \times B \times D$ (m×m×m)：99×15.2×7.6

中国海警 1301　111 米海警船　2014 年
ZHONG GUO HAI JING 1301　111m Coast Guard Ship　2014
主尺度　$L \times B \times D$ (m×m×m)：110.8×14×8.4

中国海警 2501　129 米海警船　2015 年
ZHONG GUO HAI JING 2501　129m Coast Guard Ship　2015
主尺度　$L \times B \times D$ (m×m×m)：128.6×16×7.9

中国海警 3901 165 米海警船 2015 年
ZHONG GUO HAI JING 3901 165m Coast Guard Ship 2015
主尺度 $L×B×D$ (m×m×m)：165×21.8×9.7

中国海警 44014 55 米海警船 2017 年
ZHONG GUO HAI JING 44014 55m Coast Guard Ship 2017
主尺度 $L×B×D$ (m×m×m)：54.9×7.6×4.2

中国海警 31301 134 米海警船 2018 年
ZHONG GUO HAI JING 31301 134m Coast Guard Ship 2018
主尺度 $L×B×D$ (m×m×m)：133.9×15.4×6.2

中国海监 36　26 米海监船　2009 年
ZHONG GUO HAI JIAN 36　26m Marine Surveillance Ship　2009
主尺度 $L×B×D$（m×m×m）：26.4×5.4×2.6

中国海监 3011　65 米海监船　2013 年
ZHONG GUO HAI JIAN 3011　65m Marine Surveillance Ship　2013
主尺度 $L×B×D$（m×m×m）：65×9×4.6

中国海监 9020　80 米海监船　2013 年
ZHONG GUO HAI JIAN 9020　80m Marine Surveillance Ship　2013
主尺度 $L×B×D$（m×m×m）：79.9×10.6×5.1

中国海监 3015 89 米海监船 2014 年
ZHONG GUO HAI JIAN 3015 89m Marine Surveillance Ship 2014
主尺度 $L \times B \times D$ (m×m×m)：88.9×12.2×6.3

中国海监 2166 89 米海监船 2017 年
ZHONG GUO HAI JIAN 2166 89m Marine Surveillance Ship 2017
主尺度 $L \times B \times D$ (m×m×m)：88.9×12.2×6.3

SHIPS OF CHINA

中国渔政 45001　55 米渔政船 2001 年
ZHONG GUO YU ZHENG 45001　55m Fishery Administration Ship 2001
主尺度　$L×B×D$ （m×m×m）：55×7.8×4

中国渔政 13001　55 米渔政船 2002 年
ZHONG GUO YU ZHENG 13001　55m Fishery Administration Ship 2002
主尺度　$L×B×D$ （m×m×m）：55×7.8×3.9

第五篇　特种和特殊船舶
PART V　SPECIAL PURPOSE AND SPECIAL TYPE SHIPS

中国渔政 32544　40 米渔政船　2003 年
ZHONG GUO YU ZHENG 32544　40m Fishery Administration Ship　2003
主尺度　$L×B×D$（m×m×m）：40.1×6.4×3.2

中国渔政 32518　28 米渔政船　2005 年
ZHONG GUO YU ZHENG 32518　28m Fishery Administration Ship　2005
主尺度　$L×B×D$（m×m×m）：28.4×5.6×2.7

中国渔政 44183　61 米渔政船 2005 年
ZHONG GUO YU ZHENG 44183　61m Fishery Administration Ship 2005
主尺度　$L×B×D$（m×m×m）：61×8.4×4.5

中国渔政 35306　41 米渔政船 2006 年
ZHONG GUO YU ZHENG 35306　41m Fishery Administration Ship 2006
主尺度　$L×B×D$（m×m×m）：40.8×6.2×3.1

中国渔政 21201　49 米渔政船 2006 年
ZHONG GUO YU ZHENG 21201　49m Fishery Administration Ship 2006
主尺度　$L×B×D$（m×m×m）：49×7.4×3.5

中国渔政 31001　67 米渔政船 2008 年
ZHONG GUO YU ZHENG 31001　67m Fishery Administration Ship 2008
主尺度　$L×B×D$（m×m×m）：66.5×8.5×4.3

第五篇 特种和特殊船舶
PART V SPECIAL PURPOSE AND SPECIAL TYPE SHIPS

中国渔政 310　108 米大型渔政船　2010 年
我国第一艘配载直升机的先进渔政执法船
主尺度 $L×B×D$ (m×m×m)：108×14×8.4

ZHONG GUO YU ZHENG 310　108m Large Fishery Administration Ship　2010
China's first advanced fishery law enforcement ship equipped with helicopters

中国渔政 21103　57 米渔政船　2012 年
ZHONG GUO YU ZHENG 21103　57m Fishery Administration Ship　2012
主尺度 $L×B×D$ (m×m×m)：57.3×8.2×4.2

中国渔政 206　129 米大型渔政船　2012 年
大型先进渔政船
ZHONG GUO YU ZHENG 206　129m Large Fishery Administration Ship　2012
Advanced large-size fishery administration ship
主尺度 $L×B×D$ (m×m×m)：129.3×17×8.1

中国渔政 23528　42 米渔政船　2013 年
ZHONG GUO YU ZHENG 23528　42m Fishery Administration Ship　2013
主尺度 $L \times B \times D$（m×m×m）：42×7.6×2.3

中国渔政 45005　83 米渔政船　2014 年
系列船中的首制船
主尺度 $L \times B \times D$（m×m×m）：83.3×11.6×5

ZHONG GUO YU ZHENG 45005　83m Fishery Administration Ship　2014
First ship in series

中国渔政 34027　32 米渔政船　2015 年
ZHONG GUO YU ZHENG 34027　32m Fishery Administration Ship　2015
主尺度 $L \times B \times D$（m×m×m）：32×6.6×2

第三节 缉私/公安船

缉私/公安船是依照国家相关法律法规,在国家的领海、内水、界河和界湖内,主要从事缉私、执法等公务活动的船艇。根据这类船舶的设计需求特殊性,其布置、构造、配备和安全要求与常规商用运输船舶有较大区别,船舶尺度小,但配备的马力较大,航速较高,操纵性好。高速公务船的船体材料主要有钢质、全铝合金、钢铝混合、玻璃钢、钢玻混合等。部分船舶因维权或紧急顶靠或拖带被执法船需求,要求船体结构具有较高的抗撞耐挤压能力。根据执行任务的需要,部分船舶还配有轻型武器(如机枪、手枪、弹药等)或火炮等装备。

SECTION 3   REVENUE CUTTER/PUBLIC SECURITY SHIPS

The revenue cutter or public security ship is mainly used to engage in official activities such as anti-smuggling and law enforcement in the territorial sea, internal waters, boundary rivers and lakes of the country in accordance with relevant national laws and regulations. According to the special design needs of these ships, their arrangement, structure, equipment and safety requirements are different to conventional commercial transportation ships, which are small in size but with larger horsepower, higher speed and good manoeuvrability. The hull materials of high-speed Government ships mainly include steel, full aluminum alloy, steel-aluminum mixed, reinforced fiber glass and steel-glass mixed. Some of the ships, requested by law enforcement ships for rights maintenance or emergency pushing or towing, should have the hull structure with high anti-collision and extrusion resistance. Depending on requirements, some ships are also equipped with light weapons, such as machine guns, pistols, ammunition, or artillery, etc.

海关 902　58米缉私艇　1989年
系列船型中的代表船
主尺度 $L×B×D$ (m×m×m):58×7.6×4.3

HAI GUAN 902　58m Revenue Cutter 1989
A representative ship in ship type series

SHIPS OF CHINA

海关 826　44 米缉私艇　1996 年
HAI GUAN 826　44m Revenue Cutter　1996
主尺度 $L \times B \times D$ (m×m×m): 44.2×6.4×3.5

中国海关 1001　51 米缉私艇　2001 年
系列船型中的代表船
主尺度 $L \times B \times D$ (m×m×m): 51.4×7.5×4.1

ZHONG GUO HAI GUAN 1001　51m Revenue Cutter　2001
A representative ship in ship type series

中国海关 2011　26 米缉私艇　2014 年
ZHONG GUO HAI GUAN 2011　26m Revenue Cutter　2014
主尺度 $L \times B \times D$ (m×m×m): 26×5.5×2.7

中国海关 751 31 米海关监管艇 2015 年
ZHONG GUO HAI GUAN 751 31m Customs Control Boat 2015
主尺度 $L×B×D$（m×m×m）：30.7×7.2×3.3

水警南沙 27 米巡逻船 2010 年
SHUI JING NAN SHA 27m Patrol Ship 2010
主尺度 $L×B×D$（m×m×m）：27×4.8×2

水警羊城 48 米巡逻船 2010 年
SHUI JING YANG CHENG 48m Patrol Ship 2010
主尺度 $L×B×D$（m×m×m）：47.7×7.8×3.2

长江公安 3003　35 米巡逻船 2011 年
CHANG JIANG GONG AN 3003　35m Patrol Ship　2011
主尺度 $L×B×D$ (m×m×m)：34.6×5.2×2.3

边检 3166　53 米巡逻船 2016 年
BIAN JIAN 3166　53m Patrol Ship　2016
主尺度 $L×B×D$ (m×m×m)：53×8.5×4.3

赣昌公安 1302　26 米巡逻船 2019 年
GAN CHANG GONG AN 1302　26m Patrol Ship　2019
主尺度 $L×B×D$ (m×m×m)：26.3×4.8×2.1

第四节 其他特殊船

SECTION 4　OTHER SPECIAL TYPE SHIPS

黑龙江　37 米黑龙江工作艇　1987 年
HEI LONG JIANG　37m Work Boat, Heilongjiang River　1987
主尺度 $L×B×D$（m×m×m）：37×9.6×2.4

龙标 111　27 米黑龙江航标船　1988 年
LONG BIAO 111　27m Buoy Tender, Heilongjiang River　1988
主尺度 $L×B×D$（m×m×m）：27×5×1.5

渝道标 2403　29 米长江航标船　1988 年
YU DAO BIAO 2403　29m Buoy Tender, Yangtze River　1988
主尺度 $L×B×D$（m×m×m）：29×5×2

海巡 1701　60 米航标船　1989 年
HAI XUN 1701　60m Buoy Tender　1989
主尺度　$L×B×D$（m×m×m）：59.5×9.6×4.2

海巡 1502　56 米航标船　1990 年
HAI XUN 1502　56m Buoy Tender　1990
主尺度　$L×B×D$（m×m×m）：55.5×10×4.6

海巡 1501　59 米航标船　1990 年
HAI XUN 1501　59m Buoy Tender　1990
主尺度 $L \times B \times D$ (m×m×m)：58.4×9.8×4.4

航道管理 01　34 米黑龙江巡逻船　1992 年
HANG DAO GUAN LI 01　34m Patrol Ship, Heilongjiang River　1992
主尺度 $L \times B \times D$ (m×m×m)：34×6×1.9

 SHIPS OF CHINA

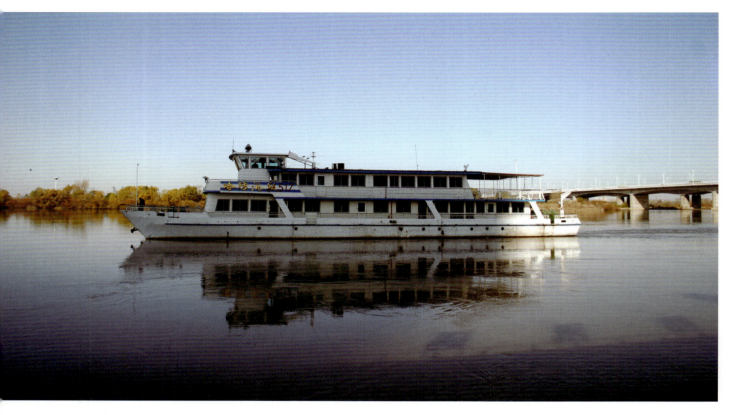

哈防汛艇 517　41 米黑龙江指挥艇　1995 年
HA FANG XUN TING 517　41m Command Boat, Heilongjiang River 1995
主尺度 $L \times B \times D$ (m×m×m)：41×9×2.5

航荣　40 米长江双体航标船　1997 年
HANG RONG　40m Buoy Cataraman, Yangtze River 1997
主尺度 $L \times B \times D$ (m×m×m)：40×10.6×2.8

海巡 17041　32 米航标船　1998 年
HAI XUN 17041　32m Buoy Tender 1998
主尺度 $L \times B \times D$ (m×m×m)：32.1×5.6×2.7

海巡 172 42 米航标船 1998 年
HAI XUN 172 42m Buoy Tender 1998
主尺度 $L \times B \times D$ (m×m×m)：72.2×12×6

海巡 15016 34 米航标船 2000 年
HAI XUN 15016 34m Buoy Tender 2000
主尺度 $L \times B \times D$ (m×m×m)：33.7×5.8×2.9

北方号　50米黑龙江巡逻船　2004年
BEI FANG HAO　50m Patrol Ship, Heilongjiang River　2004
主尺度 $L \times B \times D$ (m×m×m)：49.6×8.1×2.2

宁道标001　76米长江大型航标船　2007年
NING DAO BIAO 001　76m Large Buoy Tender, Yangtze River　2007
主尺度 $L \times B \times D$ (m×m×m)：76×12×6

宁道标402　40米级长江A型航标船　2010年
NING DAO BIAO 402　40m Type A Buoy Tender, Yangtze River　2010
主尺度 $L \times B \times D$ (m×m×m)：36×7.5×2.6

海巡 1640　62 米航标船　2010 年
HAI XUN 1640　62m Buoy Tender　2010
主尺度　$L×B×D$（m×m×m）：61.8×12×5.1

海巡 153　73 米航标船　2011 年
HAI XUN 153　73m Buoy Tender　2011
主尺度　$L×B×D$（m×m×m）：73.3×14×6.2

宁道标 002　75 米长江大型航标船　2011 年
NING DAO BIAO 002　75m Large Buoy Tender, Yangtze River　2011
主尺度　$L×B×D$（m×m×m）：74.8×13×6.2

盛中 2　26 米快艇　2012 年
SHENG ZHONG 2　26m Speed Boat　2012
主尺度　$L×B×D$（m×m×m）：26×4.8×2.2

航政管理 001　42 米黑龙江巡逻船　2014 年
HANG ZHENG GUAN LI 001　42m Patrol Ship, Heilongjiang River　2014
主尺度　$L×B×D$（m×m×m）：42×7.8×2.4

晋卿　47 米特殊用途船　2016 年
JIN QING　47m Special Purpose Ship　2016
主尺度　$L×B×D$（m×m×m）：47.1×7×3.3

海安 0982　29 米快艇　2017 年
HAI AN 0982　29m Speed Boat　2017
主尺度　$L×B×D$（m×m×m）：28.9×5.2×2.2

蒙工 010006　30 米内河航标船　2018 年改建
MENG GONG 010006　30m Buoy Tender, Inland Waterway converted in 2018
主尺度　$L×B×D$（m×m×m）：30×6.2×1.4

海巡 160 73 米大型航标船 2019 年
HAI XUN 160 73m Large Buoy Tender 2019
主尺度 $L×B×D$ (m×m×m)：73.3×14×6.2

深海 01 78 米海上危险品应急指挥船 2020 年
SHEN HAI 01 78m Dangerous-goods Emergency Command Ship 2020
主尺度 $L×B×D$ (m×m×m)：78.1×12.8×5.5

南海一号 迄今发现年代最早、最大的南宋时代木质古沉船
（图片为仿制品）
NAN HAI YI HAO The earliest and largest wooden ancient shipwreck in the Southern Song Dynasty discovered so far (the picture is a replica)
主尺度 $L×B×D$ (m×m×m)：41.8×11×4

第三章　游艇

　　游艇是指船舶所有人自身用于游览观光、休闲娱乐等活动的船舶。我国游艇业从20世纪80至90年代进入起步阶段，随着社会消费水平的提高，需求人群增多，2002年至2012年游艇进入较快发展期，其种类也越来越多，主要包括商务艇、休闲游艇、钓鱼游艇、运动帆艇和赛艇等。

　　2012年后，我国游艇行业在层次和结构上都发生了转变，大众化中小船艇数量增长较快，目前游艇建造企业超过120家，注册的游艇数量超过5000艘，主要分布在三亚、厦门、深圳等沿海城市。游艇娱乐向大众化发展，根据不同客户需求呈现多元化和个性化，产品细分将成为发展趋势。此外，随着船舶绿色技术、信息技术的发展和人工智能的加速应用，智能舒适型、体验型游艇将是未来游艇发展的主要方向。

CHAPTER III   YACHTS

　　Yacht refers to a vessel commonly used for sightseeing, recreation, racing and pleasure. China's yacht industry emerged in 1980s and 1990s. However, from 2002 to 2012, demand increased and the yachting sector expanded, mainly including commercial yachts, leisure yachts, fishing yachts, sailing yachts, rowing boats, etc.

　　After 2012, China's yacht industry has undergone major changes and the number of small-to-medium-size yachts for the mass market has grown faster. There are more than 120 yacht builders and more than 5,000 registered yachts, mainly in Sanya, Xiamen, Shenzhen and other coastal cities. As yachting becomes more popular, the sector is diversifying and the bespoke tailoring of yachts to the owner's different design needs and requirements is becoming a growing trend. In addition, with the development of green and information technology of ships as well as the accelerated AI application, intelligent, comfortable and experience-oriented yachts are becoming the prime areas of future development.

九肚山　温州33米游艇　1986年
JIU DU SHAN　33m Yacht, Wenzhou　1986
主尺度　$L×B×D$（m×m×m）：33×6.4×3.4

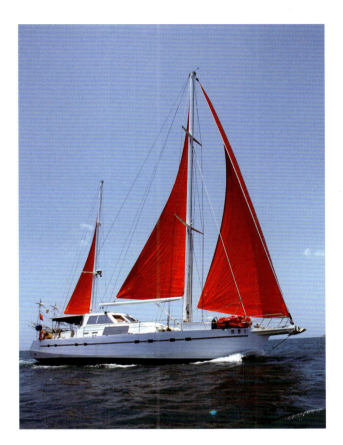

翟墨1　三亚24米游艇 1994年
ZHAI MO 1　24m Yacht, Sanya 1994
主尺度 $L\times B\times D$ (m×m×m)：24×5.5×1.9

时代海岸鸿洲1　三亚22米游艇 2007年
SHI DAI HAI AN HONG ZHOU 1　22m Yacht, Sanya 2007
主尺度 $L\times B\times D$ (m×m×m)：21.7×5.5×2.9

阿尔滨号　大连29米游艇 2008年
A ER BIN HAO　29m Yacht, Dalian 2008
主尺度 $L\times B\times D$ (m×m×m)：28.5×6.8×3.6

半岛城邦1号　深圳34米游艇 2008年
BAN DAO CHENG BANG 1 HAO　34m Yacht, Shenzhen 2008
主尺度 $L\times B\times D$ (m×m×m)：34.5×7.6×3.5

万达 3 号　三亚 31 米游艇　2010 年
WAN DA 3 HAO　31m Yacht, Sanya　2010
主尺度 $L \times B \times D$ (m×m×m)：31.4×6.8×3.7

半山半岛 3　三亚 20 米游艇　2011 年
BAN SHAN BAN DAO 3　20m Yacht, Sanya　2011
主尺度 $L \times B \times D$ (m×m×m)：19.7×9.5×2.6

佳豪一号　上海 21 米游艇　2011 年
JIA HAO YI HAO　21m Yacht, Shanghai　2011
主尺度 $L \times B \times D$ (m×m×m)：21.4×5.6×2.8

宏力企业　三亚 24 米游艇　2011 年
HONG LI QI YE　24m Yacht, Sanya　2011
主尺度 $L \times B \times D$ (m×m×m)：23.7×6.4×3.4

中骏集团壹号 厦门 24 米游艇 2011 年
ZHONG JUN JI TUAN YI HAO 24m Yacht, Xiamen 2011
主尺度 $L×B×D$ (m×m×m)：23.7×6.4×3.7

蓝龙号 大连 25 米游艇 2011 年
LAN LONG HAO 25m Yacht, Dalian 2011
主尺度 $L×B×D$ (m×m×m)：24.9×5.7×3.1

鸿洲 23 深圳 20 米游艇 2013 年
HONG ZHOU 23 20m Yacht, Shenzhen 2013
主尺度 $L×B×D$ (m×m×m)：19.9×5.4×3

利米特 三亚 28 米游艇 2014 年
LI MI TE 28m Yacht, Sanya 2014
主尺度 $L×B×D$ (m×m×m)：27.5×6.6×3.3

黄海集团　青岛 24 米游艇　2015 年
HUANGHAI GROUP　24m Yacht, Qingdao 2015
主尺度 $L \times B \times D\,(m \times m \times m)$：24×6.4×3.2

华润石梅湾　清澜 38 米游艇　2015 年
HUA RUN SHI MEI WAN　38m Yacht, Qinglan 2015
主尺度 $L \times B \times D\,(m \times m \times m)$：37.8×7.4×3.6

百艇汇 78　上海 23 米游艇　2018 年
BAI TING HUI 78　23m Yacht, Shanghai　2018
主尺度 $L×B×D$（m×m×m）：23.5×10.4×2.9

智腾　青岛 21 米游艇　2019 年
ZHI TENG　21m Yacht, Qingdao　2019
主尺度 $L×B×D$（m×m×m）：21.1×5.4×2.3

游龙 88　威海 24 米游艇　2019 年
YOU LONG 88　24m Yacht, Weihai　2019
主尺度 $L×B×D$（m×m×m）：23.8×5.1×2.3

御风者 1　深圳 43 米游艇　2019 年
YU FENG ZHE 1　43m Yacht, Shenzhen　2019
主尺度 $L×B×D$（m×m×m）：43.1×12.2×5.2

索引 INDEXES

船舶名称	船舶所有人	Name of Vessel	Owner	页码
A				
阿尔滨号	大连博阳建设工程有限公司	A ER BIN HAO	Dalian Boyang Construction Engineering Co., Ltd.	523
安达1号	泸州市安达港口有限公司	AN DA 1 HAO	Luzhou Anda Port Co., Ltd.	307
安和	青岛引航站	AN HE	Qingdao Pilot Station	455
安华勇士	华光海运控股	ANTWERPEN VENTURE	Wah Kwong Maritime Transport Holdings Ltd.	82
安吉2	上海安盛汽车船务有限公司	AN JI 2	Shanghai Ansheng Automotive Shipping Co., Ltd.	101
安吉201	上汽安吉物流股份有限公司	AN JI 201	SAIC Anji Logistics Co., Ltd.	232
安吉204	上海安盛汽车船务有限公司	AN JI 204	Shanghai Ansheng Automotive Shipping Co., Ltd.	233
安吉23	安吉航运有限公司	AN JI 23	Anji Shipping Co., Ltd.	104
安吉26	安吉航运有限公司	AN JI 26	Anji Shipping Co., Ltd.	104
安吉27	上海安盛汽车船务有限公司	AN JI 27	Shanghai Ansheng Automotive Shipping Co., Ltd.	105
安强76	舟山安嘉海运有限公司	AN QIANG 76	Zhoushan Anjia Shipping Co.,Ltd.	30
安信货9号	九江市安信航运有限公司	AN XIN HUO 9 HAO	Jiujiang Anxin Shipping Co., Ltd.	188
B				
BRIGHT VENTURE	华光海运控股	BRIGHT VENTURE	Wah Kwong Maritime Transport Holdings Ltd.	22
巴都	重庆市巴都游轮有限公司	BA DU	Chongqing Badu Cruise Co., Ltd.	292
白鹭洲	招商局南京油运股份有限公司	BAI LU ZHOU	Nanjing Tanker Corporation	53
白羊座	天津西南海运有限公司	GAS ARIES	Tianjin Southwest Maritime Limited	84
百合源	深圳中远龙鹏液化气运输有限公司	BAI HE YUAN	Shenzhen COSCO LPG Shipping Co., Ltd.	80
百花源	深圳中远龙鹏液化气运输有限公司	BAI HUA YUAN	Shenzhen COSCO LPG Shipping Co., Ltd.	82
百艇汇78	上海恰尔思游艇有限公司	BAI TING HUI 78	Shanghai Choisi Yacht Co., Ltd.	527
板新贰号	南京市板桥汽渡管理处	BAN XIN ER HAO	Nanjing Banqiao Car Ferry Management Division	315
半岛城邦1号	深圳国际游艇俱乐部有限公司	BAN DAO CHENG BANG 1 HAO	Shenzhen International Marine Club Co., Ltd.	523
半潜驳9号	中交一航局第五工程有限公司	BAN QIAN BO 9 HAO	No.5 Engineering Co., Ltd. of CCCC First Harbor Engineering Co., Ltd.	117
半山半岛3	三亚半山半岛帆船港有限责任公司	BAN SHAN BAN DAO 3	Sanya Serenity Marina Co., Ltd.	524
棒棰岛	中远海运客运有限公司	BANG CHUI DAO	COSCO SHIPPING Ferry Co., Ltd.	142
宝航11	上海宝钢航运有限公司	BAO HANG 11	Shanghai Baosteel Shipping Co., Ltd.	251
宝华	渤海轮渡集团股份有限公司	BAO HUA	Bohai Ferry Group Co., Ltd.	142
宝马号	中英海底系统有限公司	BAO MA HAO	S.B. Submarine Systems Co., Ltd.	409
宝泽	深圳市海鸿船务有限公司	BAO ZE	Shenzhen Haihong Shipping Co., Ltd.	83
北斗	中国水产科学研究院黄海水产研究所	BEI DOU	Yellow Sea Fisheries Research Institute, Chinese Academy of Fishery Sciences	371
北方号	黑龙江省航道局	BEI FANG HAO	Heilongjiang Waterway Bureau	518
北海凤凰	上海北海船务股份有限公司	BEI HAI FENG HUANG	Shanghai Northsea Shipping Co., Ltd.	59
北海救111	交通运输部北海救助局	BEI HAI JIU 111	Beihai Rescue Bureau of the Ministry of Transport	490
北海救117	交通运输部北海救助局	BEI HAI JIU 117	Beihai Rescue Bureau of the Ministry of Transport	493
北海救119	交通运输部北海救助局	BEI HAI JIU 119	Beihai Rescue Bureau of the Ministry of Transport	494
北海救199	交通运输部北海救助局	BEI HAI JIU 199	Beihai Rescue Bureau of the Ministry of Transport	489
北海救201	交通运输部北海救助局	BEI HAI JIU 201	Beihai Rescue Bureau of the Ministry of Transport	491
北海救气垫01	交通运输部北海救助局	BEI HAI JIU QI DIAN 01	Beihai Rescue Bureau of the Ministry of Transport	496
北海之星	上海北海船务股份有限公司	BEI HAI ZHI XING	Shanghai Northsea Shipping Co., Ltd.	50
北湖	上海崇明客运轮船有限公司	BEI HU	Shanghai Chongming Passenger Ship Co., Ltd.	316

中文名	公司（中文）	英文名	Company (English)	页码
北极星	上海时代航运有限公司	BEI JI XING	Shanghai Time Shipping Co., Ltd.	6
北京号	新长铁路有限责任公司	BEI JING HAO	Xinchang Railway Co., Ltd.	311
北琴海	黑龙江省兴凯湖风景名胜区管理委员会	BEI QIN HAI	Heilongjiang Xingkai Lake Scenic Spot Administration Committee	279
北游15	北海新绎游船有限公司	BEI YOU 15	Beihai Ennova Cruise Co., Ltd.	137
北游16	北海新绎游船有限公司	BEI YOU 16	Beihai Ennova Cruise Co., Ltd.	161
北游18	北海新绎游船有限公司	BEI YOU 18	Beihai Ennova Cruise Co., Ltd.	159
北游19	北海新绎游船有限公司	BEI YOU 19	Beihai Ennova Cruise Co., Ltd.	157
北游26	北海新绎游船有限公司	BEI YOU 26	Beihai Ennova Cruise Co., Ltd.	165
边检3166	上海出入境边防检查总站	BIAN JIAN 3166	Shanghai Entry-Exit Frontier Inspection Station	512
滨海253	中海油田服务股份有限公司	BIN HAI 253	China Oilfield Services Limited	444
滨海284	中海油田服务股份有限公司	BIN HAI 284	China Oilfield Services Limited	442
滨海606	中海油田服务股份有限公司	BIN HAI 606	China Oilfield Services Limited	60
博丰油供16	天津博丰顺通燃料销售有限公司	BO FENG YOU GONG 16	Tianjin Bofeng Shuntong Fuel Sales Co., Ltd.	66
渤海宝珠	渤海轮渡集团股份有限公司	BO HAI BAO ZHU	Bohai Ferry Group Co., Ltd.	146
渤海翠珠	渤海轮渡集团股份有限公司	BO HAI CUI ZHU	Bohai Ferry Group Co., Ltd.	148
渤海恒通	天津渤海轮渡融资租赁有限公司	BO HAI HENG TONG	Tianjin Bohai Ferry Financial Leasing Co., Ltd.	105
渤海金珠	渤海轮渡集团股份有限公司	BO HAI JIN ZHU	Bohai Ferry Group Co., Ltd.	145
渤海钻珠	天津渤海轮渡融资租赁有限公司	BO HAI ZUAN ZHU	Tianjin Bohai Ferry Financial Leasing Co., Ltd.	149
不肯去观音	舟山市旅游客运服务有限公司	BU KEN QU GUAN YIN	Zhoushan Tourist Passenger Service Co., Ltd	136

C

中文名	公司（中文）	英文名	Company (English)	页码
昌荣1号	中水集团远洋股份有限公司	CHANG RONG NO.1	CNFC Overseas Fisheries Co., Ltd.	351
"长航洋山3001"船组	上海新洋山集装箱运输有限公司	CHANG HANG YANG SHAN 3001 COMBINATION	Shanghai Xinyangshan Container Lines Co., Ltd.	249
"长江2048"船队	武汉长江轮船公司	CHANG JIANG 2048 COMBINATION	Wuhan Yangtze Shipping Company	238
"长江22040"船队	武汉长江轮船公司	CHANG JIANG 22040 COMBINATION	Wuhan Yangtze Shipping Company	238
"长江24001"船队	武汉长江轮船公司	CHANG JIANG 24001 COMBINATION	Wuhan Yangtze Shipping Company	237
"长江26004"船队	武汉长江轮船公司	CHANG JIANG 26004 COMBINATION	Wuhan Yangtze Shipping Company	236
"长江2809"船队	南京长江油运物流有限公司	CHANG JIANG 2809 COMBINATION	Nanjing Changjiang Tanker Logistics Co., Ltd.	237
"长江62034"船队	南京长江油运公司	YANGTZE 62034 COMBINATION	CSC Nanjing Tanker Corporation	239
"长江63002"船队	南京长江油运公司	CHANG JIANG 63002 COMBINATION	CSC Nanjing Tanker Corporation	238
"长江63003"船队	南京长江油运公司	CHANG JIANG 63003 COMBINATION	CSC Nanjing Tanker Corporation	238
长城	香港联成轮船公司	REGENT TAMPOPO	Regent Shipping Limited	5
长大海升	保利长大工程有限公司	CHANG DA HAI SHENG	Poly Changda Engineering Co., Ltd.	401
长发海	长航货运有限公司	CHANG FA HAI	CSC Bulk Shipping Co., Ltd.	14
长公消1202	长江航运公安局宜昌分局	CHANG GONG XIAO 1202	Yichang Branch of Yangtze River Shipping Public Security Bureau	454
长航朝天皓月	重庆长江轮船有限公司	CHANG HANG CHAO TIAN HAO YUE	Chongqing Changjiang Shipping Co., Ltd.	299
长航朝天门	重庆长江轮船有限公司	CHANG HANG CHAO TIAN MEN	Chongqing Changjiang Shipping Company	287
长航飞翔4	重庆长江轮船有限公司	CHANG HANG FEI XIANG 4	Chongqing Changjiang Shipping Company	320
长航福海	香港明华船务有限公司	CHANG HANG FU HAI	Hong Kong Ming Wah Shipping Co., Ltd.	482
长航和海	交银金融租赁有限责任公司	CHANG HANG HE HAI	Bank of Communications Financial Leasing Co., Ltd.	18
长航集运0325	交银金融租赁有限责任公司	CHANG HANG JI YUN 0325	Bank of Communications Financial Leasing Co., Ltd.	202
长航江浩	深圳招商滚装运输有限公司	CHANG HANG JIANG HAO	China Merchants Shenzhen RO-RO Shipping Co., Ltd.	229
长航江平	深圳招商滚装运输有限公司	CHANG HANG JIANG PING	China Merchants Shenzhen RO-RO Shipping Co., Ltd.	230
长航江荣	深圳招商滚装运输有限公司	CHANG HANG JIANG RONG	China Merchants Shenzhen RO-RO Shipping Co., Ltd.	234
长航江泰	深圳招商滚装运输有限公司	CHANG HANG JIANG TAI	China Merchants Shenzhen RO-RO Shipping Co., Ltd.	233
长航江旺	深圳招商滚装运输有限公司	CHANG HANG JIANG WANG	China Merchants Shenzhen RO-RO Shipping Co., Ltd.	232
长航江兴	深圳招商滚装运输有限公司	CHANG HANG JIANG XING	China Merchants Shenzhen RO-RO Shipping Co., Ltd.	230

中文船名	公司（中文）	English Name	Company (English)	Page
长航江渝112	武汉长江轮船公司	CHANG HANG JIANG YU 112	Wuhan Yangtze Shipping Company	257
长航洋山1	上海新洋山集装箱运输有限公司	CHANG HANG YANG SHAN 1	Shanghai Xinyangshan Container Lines Co., Ltd.	39
长航油188	南京金源船务实业有限公司	CHANG HANG YOU 188	Jinyuan Nanjing Shipping Industry Co., Ltd.	68
长和	上海长江轮船有限公司	SCSC FORTUNE	Shanghai Changjiang Shipping Co., Ltd.	92
长和	香港明华船务有限公司	YANGTZE HARMONY	Hong Kong Ming Wah Shipping Co., Ltd.	96
长吉	深圳招商滚装运输有限公司	CHANG JI	China Merchants Shenzhen RO-RO Shipping Co., Ltd.	98
长吉隆	深圳招商滚装运输有限公司	CHANG JI LONG	China Merchants Shenzhen RO-RO Shipping Co., Ltd.	102
长江02034	重庆长江轮船公司	CHANG JIANG 02034	Chongqing Changjiang Shipping Company	241
长江1号	宜昌长江高速客轮有限责任公司	CHANG JIANG 1 HAO	Yichang Yangtze River High-Speed Passenger Liner Co., Ltd.	320
长江63001	南京长江油运公司	CHANG JIANG 63001	CSC Nanjing Tanker Corporation	240
长江64001	南京长江油运公司	CHANG JIANG 64001	CSC Nanjing Tanker Corporation	243
长江82017	上海长江轮船公司	CHANG JIANG 82017	Shanghai Changjiang Shipping Company	243
长江9号	宜昌长江高速客轮有限责任公司	CHANG JIANG 9 HAO	Yichang Yangtze River High-Speed Passenger Liner Co., Ltd.	321
长江公安3003	长江航运公安局南京分局	CHANG JIANG GONG AN 3003	Nanjing Branch of Yangtze River Shipping Public Security Bureau	512
长江公主	长江轮船海外旅游总公司	CHANG JIANG GONG ZHU	Changjiang Cruise Overseas Travel Company	267
长江黄金1号	重庆交通旅投投资集团有限公司	YANGTZE GOLD 1	Chongqing Tourism Investment Group Co., Ltd.	272
长江黄金2号	重庆交通旅投投资集团有限公司	YANGTZE GOLD 2	Chongqing Tourism Investment Group Co., Ltd.	272
长江口01	长江口航道管理局	CHANG JIANG KOU 01	Yangtze Estuary Waterway Management Bureau	391
长江口02	长江口航道管理局	CHANG JIANG KOU 02	Yangtze Estuary Waterway Management Bureau	391
长江口驳2	长江口航道管理局	CHANG JIANG KOU BO 2	Yangtze Estuary Waterway Management Bureau	394
长江明珠	长江轮船海外旅游总公司	CHANG JIANG MING ZHU	Changjiang Cruise Overseas Travel Company	266
长江三峡10	宜昌交运三峡游轮有限公司	CHANG JIANG SAN XIA 10	Yichang Transportation Three Gorges Cruises Co., Ltd.	299
长江三峡6	宜昌交运长江游轮有限公司	CHANG JIANG SAN XIA 6	Yichang Transportation Changjiang Tourist Ship Co., Ltd.	288
长江探索	湖北东方皇家旅游船有限公司	CHANG JIANG TAN SUO	Hubei Eastern Royal Cruises Co., Ltd.	268
长江天使	长江轮船海外旅游总公司	CHANG JIANG TIAN SHI	Changjiang Cruise Overseas Travel Company	269
长江壹号	长江海外游轮旅游有限公司	CHANG JIANG YI HAO	Changjiang Cruise Overseas Travel Co., Ltd.	271
长江之星	长江轮船海外旅游总公司	CHANG JIANG ZHI XING	Changjiang Cruise Overseas Travel Company	266
长江之珠	招商局南京油运股份有限公司	YANGTZE PEARL	Nanjing Tanker Corporation	55
长鲸2	长江南京航道工程局	CHANG JING 2	Changjiang Nanjing Waterway Engineering Bureau	387
长鲸6	长江武汉航道工程局	CHANG JING 6	Changjiang Wuhan Waterway Engineering Bureau	389
长鲸7	长江南京航道工程局	CHANG JING 7	Changjiang Nanjing Waterway Engineering Bureau	394
长鲸9	长江南京航道工程局	CHANG JING 9	Changjiang Nanjing Waterway Engineering Bureau	396
长鹭2号	长江重庆航道工程局	CHANG LU 2 HAO	Changjiang Chongqing Waterway Engineering Bureau	412
长隆	长荣海运股份有限公司	EVER GLORY	Evergreen Marine Corporation	47
长茂1	南京长江油运物流有限公司	CHANG MAO YI	Nanjing Tanker Corporation Logistics Co., Ltd.	226
长燃41号	中石化长江燃料有限公司	CHANG RAN 41 HAO	China Changjinag Bunker (SINOPEC) Co., Ltd.	215
长燃51	武汉长燃运输公司	CHANG RAN 51	Wuhan Branch Company of China Changjinag Bunker (SINOPEC) Co., Ltd.	216
长燃油2001	中石化长江燃料有限公司	CHANG RAN YOU 2001	China Changjinag Bunker (SINOPEC) Co., Ltd.	246
长山岛	中远海运客运有限公司	CHANG SHAN DAO	COSCO SHIPPING Ferry Co., Ltd.	148
长神2号	巴东神农溪旅游发展有限公司	CHANG SHEN 2 HAO	Badong Shennong Stream Tourism Development Co., Ltd.	262
长盛鸿	深圳招商滚装运输有限公司	CHANG SHENG HONG	China Merchants Shenzhen RO-RO Shipping Co., Ltd.	101
长狮19	长江武汉航道工程局	CHANG SHI 19	Changjiang Wuhan Waterway Engineering Bureau	396
长狮1号	长江武汉航道局	CHANG SHI YI HAO	Changjiang Wuhan Waterway Bureau	387
长狮9	长江重庆航道工程局	CHANG SHI 9	Changjiang Chongqing Waterway Engineering Bureau	391
长顺	香港明华船务有限公司	YANGTZE FORTUNE	Hong Kong Ming Wah Shipping Co., Ltd.	96
长泰鸿	深圳招商滚装运输有限公司	CHANG TAI HONG	China Merchants Shenzhen RO-RO Shipping Co., Ltd.	102
长天龙	武汉长江航道救助打捞局	CHANG TIAN LONG	Wuhan Changjiang Waterway Rescue and Salvage Bureau	402
长通海	长航凤凰股份有限公司	CHANG TONG HAI	Chang Jiang Shipping Group Phoenix Co., Ltd.	249
长喜	长荣海运股份有限公司	EVER BLISS	Evergreen Marine Corporation	45
长兴1009	石首市长兴船务有限公司	CHANG XING 1009	Shishou Changxing Shipping Co., Ltd.	192
长亚一号	武汉长亚航运有限公司	CHANG YA YI HAO	Wuhan Changya Shipping Co., Ltd.	187
长雁22	长江重庆航道工程局	CHANG YAN 22	Changjiang Chongqing Waterway Engineering Bureau	413
长引001	长江引航中心	CHANG YIN 001	Yangtze River Pilotage Center	453
长引007	长江引航中心	CHANG YIN 007	Yangtze River Pilotage Center	458

长鹰7	长江重庆航道工程局	CHANG YING 7	Changjiang Chongqing Waterway Engineering Bureau	392
长鹰8	长江宜昌航道工程局	CHANG YING 8	Changjiang Yichang Waterway Engineering Bureau	395
长跃海	长航凤凰股份有限公司	CHANG YUE HAI	Chang Jiang Shipping Group Phoenix Co., Ltd.	249
长运大件	四川长江水运有限责任公司	CHANG YUN DA JIAN	Sichuan Yangtze River Water Transportation Co., Ltd.	176
长航珊瑚	招商局南京油运股份有限公司	CSC CORAL	Nanjing Tanker Corporation	54
长航鑫海	香港明华船务有限公司	CSC XIN HAI	Hong Kong Ming Wah Shipping Co., Ltd.	93
长航勇士	招商局南京油运股份有限公司	CSC BRAVE	Nanjing Tanker Corporation	62
常安口	中远海运特种运输股份有限公司	CHANG AN KOU	COSCO SHIPPING Specialized Carriers Co., Ltd.	100
常发口	广州远洋运输有限公司	CHANG FA KOU	Guangzhou Ocean Shipping Co., Ltd.	98
畅明6号	天津东疆航运有限公司	CHANG MING 6 HAO	Tianjin Dongjiang Shipping Co., Ltd.	6
畅明胜	天津畅明航运集团有限公司	CHANG MING SHENG	Tianjin Changming Shipping Group Co., Ltd.	10
畅明洋	天津畅明航运集团有限公司	CHANG MING YANG	Tianjin Changming Shipping Group Co., Ltd.	17
城中湖07	浙江千岛湖旅游股份有限公司	CHENG ZHONG HU 07	Zhejiang Qiandao Lake Tourism Co., Ltd.	295
赤峰口	广州远洋运输有限公司	CHI FENG KOU	Guangzhou Ocean Shipping Co., Ltd.	98
赤湾1	深圳大铲岛集团有限公司	CHI WAN 1	Shenzhen Dachandao Group Co.,Ltd.	383
重轮J3001	重庆轮船（集团）有限公司	CHONG LUN J3001	Chongqing Shipping (Group) Co., Ltd.	198
重轮J3007	重庆轮船（集团）有限公司	CHONG LUN J3007	Chongqing Shipping (Group) Co., Ltd.	200
重轮货5008	重庆轮船（集团）有限公司	CHONG LUN HUO 5008	Chongqing Shipping (Group) Co., Ltd.	180
重轮集3012	重庆太平洋国际物流有限公司	CHONG LUN JI 3012	Chongqing Pacific International Logistics Co., Ltd.	203
重轮集3021	重庆轮船（集团）有限公司	CHONG LUN JI 3021	Chongqing Shipping (Group) Co., Ltd.	210
崇明	中波轮船股份公司	CHONG MING	Chinese-Polish Joint Stock Shipping Company	87
崇明1	上海市崇明客运轮船有限公司	CHONG MING 1	Shanghai Chongming Passenger Ship Co., Ltd.	312
川宏68	上海崇和船舶融资租赁有限公司	CHUAN HONG 68	Shanghai Chonghe Marine Financial Leasing Co., Ltd.	393
船长3	上海快乐船长游船有限公司	CHUAN ZHANG 3	Shanghai Happy Captain Cruise Co., Ltd.	282
船长8	上海长江轮渡公司	CHUAN ZHANG 8	Shanghai Changjiang Ferry Company	283
串通918	重庆市万州区串通滚装运输（集团）有限公司	CHUAN TONG 918	Chongqing Wanzhou District Chuan Tong RO-RO Transportation (Group) Co., Ltd.	300
创力	交通运输部上海打捞局	CHUANG LI	Shanghai Salvage Bureau, Ministry of Transport	403
创新一	中国科学院烟台海岸带研究所	CHUANG XIN YI	Yantai Institute of Coastal Zone Research, Chinese Academy of Sciences	467
创新之路	中交国际航运有限公司	INNOVATION WAY	CCCC International Shipping Corp.	112
春江海	上海新海天航运有限公司	CHUN JIANG HAI	Shanghai Xinhaitian Shipping Co., Ltd.	249
春秋	无锡市外事旅游游船公司	CHUN QIU	Wuxi Foreign Affairs & Tourism Company	274

D

DCOC-1	香港海洋投资发展有限公司	DCOC-1	Hong Kong Ocean Investment Development Co., Ltd.	417
大德	中远海运特种运输股份有限公司	DA DE	COSCO SHIPPING Specialized Carriers Co., Ltd.	94
大丰港和顺号	江苏大丰港畅明海运有限公司	DA FENG GANG HE SHUN HAO	Jiangsu Dafeng Harbour Changming Ocean Carrier Co., Ltd.	100
大华	渤海轮渡集团股份有限公司	DA HUA	Bohai Ferry Group Co., Ltd.	142
大建	中外运航运有限公司	GREAT CREATION	Sinotrans Shipping Limited	13
大连开拓者	大连开发钻探有限公司	DALIAN DEVELOPER	Dalian Developer Drilling Co., Ltd.	431
大连勇士	华光海运控股	DALIAN VENTURE	Wah Kwong Maritime Transport Holdings Ltd.	56
大明湖	中远海运能源运输股份有限公司	DA MING HU	COSCO SHIPPING Energy Transportation Co., Ltd.	52
大明山	天津西南海运有限公司	DA MING SHAN	Tianjin Southwest Maritime Limited	74
大鹏昊	中国液化天然气运输（控股）有限公司	DAPENG SUN	China LNG Shipping (Holdings) Limited	77
大庆73	中远海运能源运输股份有限公司	DA QING 73	COSCO SHIPPING Energy Transportation Co., Ltd.	50
大欣	香港明华船务有限公司	GREAT CHEER	Hong Kong Ming Wah Shipping Co., Ltd.	17
大洋	重庆涪陵港江水运有限公司	DA YANG	Chongqing Fuling River Transportation Co., Ltd.	214
大洋98	重庆涪陵港江水运有限公司	DA YANG 98	Chongqing Fuling River Transportation Co., Ltd.	225
大源湖	中远海运能源运输股份有限公司	DA YUAN HU	COSCO SHIPPING Energy Transportation Co., Ltd.	53
大智	中外运航运有限公司	GREAT INTELLIGENCE	Sinotrans Shipping Limited	22
大洲1006	温州市大洲远洋渔业有限公司	DA ZHOU 1006	Wenzhou Ocean Fishing Co., Ltd.	338
岱山9	岱山县蓬莱客运轮船有限公司	DAI SHAN 9	Daishan Penglai Passenger Shipping Co., Ltd.	145
德渤	交通运输部烟台打捞局	DE BO	Yantai Salvage Bureau, Ministry of Transport	114
德渤2	交通运输部烟台打捞局	DE BO 2	Yantai Salvage Bureau, Ministry of Transport	114
德浮15001	交通运输部烟台打捞局	DE FU 15001	Yantai Salvage Bureau, Ministry of Transport	118

中文名	公司	Name	Company	Page
德浮2号	交通运输部烟台打捞局	DE FU ER HAO	Yantai Salvage Bureau, Ministry of Transport	117
德浮3600	交通运输部烟台打捞局	DE FU 3600	Yantai Salvage Bureau, Ministry of Transport	402
德合	交通运输部烟台打捞局	DE HE	Yantai Salvage Bureau, Ministry of Transport	403
德恒	交通运输部广州打捞局	DE HENG	Guangzhou Salvage Bureau, Ministry of Transport	448
德凛	交通运输部上海打捞局	DE JING	Shanghai Salvage Bureau, Ministry of Transport	458
德涓	交通运输部烟台打捞局	DE JUAN	Yantai Salvage Bureau, Ministry of Transport	446
德鲲	交通运输部广州打捞局	DE KUN	Guangzhou Salvage Bureau, Ministry of Transport	444
德深	交通运输部上海打捞局	DE SHEN	Shanghai Salvage Bureau, Ministry of Transport	448
德顺	交通运输部广州救捞局	DE SHUN	Guangzhou Salvage Bureau, Ministry of Transport	442
德涛	交通运输部上海打捞局	DE TAO	Shanghai Salvage Bureau, Ministry of Transport	447
德翔	交通运输部烟台打捞局	DE XIANG	Yantai Salvage Bureau, Ministry of Transport	444
德新海	中远海运散货运输有限公司	DE XIN HAI	COSCO SHIPPING Bulk Co., Ltd.	16
德意	交通运输部上海打捞局	DE YI	Shanghai Salvage Bureau, Ministry of Transport	442
德瀛	交通运输部烟台打捞局	DE YING	Yantai Salvage Bureau, Ministry of Transport	398
递缆1号	长江航道局	DI LAN 1 HAO	Changjiang Waterway Bureau	408
滇游1号	昆明格兰特游艇有限公司	DIAN YOU 1 HAO	Kunming Gelante Yacht Co., Ltd.	282
电科1号	中电科海洋信息技术研究院有限公司	DIAN KE 1 HAO	CETC Ocean Co., Ltd.	467
鼎达集86	嘉兴市鼎达航运有限公司	DING DA JI 86	Jiaxing Dingda Shipping Co., Ltd.	208
鼎达集96	嘉兴市鼎达航运有限公司	DING DA JI 96	Jiaxing Dingda Shipping Co., Ltd.	207
鼎衡1	上海鼎衡船务有限责任公司	DING HENG 1	Shanghai Dingheng Shipping Co., Ltd.	71
鼎衡5	上海鼎衡船务有限责任公司	DING HENG 5	Shanghai Dingheng Shipping Co., Ltd.	71
东电号	四川长江水运有限公司	DONG DIAN HAO	Sichuan Yangtze River Water Transportation Co., Ltd.	175
东方春	深圳市鹏星船务有限公司	DONG FANG CHUN	Shenzhen Pengxing Shipping Co., Ltd.	156
东方海工01	宁波东方电缆股份有限公司	DONG FANG HAI GONG 01	Ningbo Orient Wires & Cables Co., Ltd.	417
东方海泰	天津永续航运集团有限公司	DONG FANG HAI TAI	Tianjin Younysun Shipping Group Co., Ltd.	14
东方红3	中国海洋大学	DONG FANG HONG 3	Ocean University of China	471
东方华晨2	广东东方华晨海运有限公司	DONG FANG HUA CHEN 2	Guangdong Dongfang Huachen Shipping Co., Ltd	129
东方勘探一号	天津海龙石油地球物理勘探有限公司	DONG FANG KAN TAN NO. 1	Hilong Geophysical Co., Ltd.	476
东方明珠	中海油田服务股份有限公司	DONG FANG MING ZHU	China Oilfield Services Limited	474
东方兴	天津东方近海船务有限公司	DONG FANG XING	Tianjin East Offshore Marine Services Co,.Ltd.	445
东桂11	广西梧州同舟船务运输有限公司	DONG GUI 11	Guangxi Wuzhou Tongzhou Shipping and Transport Co., Ltd.	221
东桂16	广西梧州同舟船务运输有限公司	DONG GUI 16	Guangxi Wuzhou Tongzhou Shipping and Transport Co., Ltd.	73
东海210	宁波东海海运有限公司	DONG HAI 210	Ningbo Donghai Shipping Co., Ltd.	61
东海救101	交通运输部东海救助局	DONG HAI JIU 101	Donghai Rescue Bureau of the Ministry of Transport	492
东海救102	交通运输部东海救助局	DONG HAI JIU 102	Donghai Rescue Bureau of the Ministry of Transport	494
东海救117	交通运输部东海救助局	DONG HAI JIU 117	Donghai Rescue Bureau of the Ministry of Transport	493
东海救131	交通运输部东海救助局	DONG HAI JIU 131	Donghai Rescue Bureau of the Ministry of Transport	490
东海救151	交通运输部东海救助局	DONG HAI JIU 151	Donghai Rescue Bureau of the Ministry of Transport	496
东海救203	交通运输部东海救助局	DONG HAI JIU 203	Donghai Rescue Bureau of the Ministry of Transport	494
东海绿洲	上海崇明客运轮船有限公司	DONG HAI LV ZHOU	Shanghai Chongming Passenger Ship Co., Ltd.	317
东湖号	武汉市轮渡公司	DONG HU HAO	Wuhan Ferry Company	288
东极	舟山市普陀区东极海运有限公司	DONG JI	Zhoushan Putuo Dongji Shipping Co., Ltd	124
东江湖1号	湖南东江湖旅游水上客运有限责任公司	DONG JIANG HU 1 HAO	Hunan Dongjiang Lake Aquatic Passenger Transportation Co., Ltd.	319
东茂6	茂名市祥源船舶运输有限公司	DONG MAO 6	Maoming Xiangyuan Shipping Co., Ltd.	70
东琪	重庆安浩船务有限公司	DONG QI	Chongqing Anhao Shipping Co., Ltd.	222
东祥	中交广州航道局有限公司	DONG XIANG	CCCC Guangzhou Dredging Co., Ltd.	385
东渔1518	浙江兴鹏远洋渔业有限公司	DONG YU 1518	Zhejiang Xingpeng Ocean Fishery Co., Ltd.	354
东屿岛5号	中远海运博鳌有限公司	DONG YU DAO 5 HAO	COSCO SHIPPING Boao Co., Ltd.	317
东远3	山东远达船舶股份有限公司	DONG YUAN 3	Shandong Yuanda Shipping Co., Ltd.	126
冬青海	中远散货运输有限公司	DONG QING HAI	COSCO Bulk Carrier Co., Ltd.	9
斗轮1号	长江宜昌航道工程局	DOU LUN 1 HAO	Changjiang Yichang Waterway Engineering Bureau	385
杜鹃号	大理市航运公司	DU JUAN HAO	Dali Shipping Company	276

E

ENERGY EMERGER	山东海洋工程装备有限公司	ENERGY EMERGER	Shandong Offshore Equipment Co., Ltd.	430
峨嵋山	重庆轮船（集团）有限公司	E MEI SHAN	Chongqing Shipping (Group) Co., Ltd.	301
鄂鸿运818	湖北鸿远船务有限公司	E HONG YUN 818	Hubei Hongyuan Shipping Co., Ltd.	196
鄂黄冈工程0007	黄冈市宇洋船务有限公司	E HUANG GANG GONG CHENG 0007	Huanggang Yuyang Shipping Co., Ltd.	386
鄂黄石华新散2号	华新水泥（黄石）散装储运有限公司	E HUANG SHI HUA XIN SAN 2 HAO	Huaxin Cement (Huangshi) Bulk Storage & Transportation Co., Ltd.	186
洱海一号	大理旅游集团公司游船分公司	ER HAI YI HAO	Tourist Ship Branch Company of Dali Tourism Group	280

F

发现6	中石化海洋石油工程有限公司	FA XIAN 6	SINOPEC Offshore Oilfield Services Company	478
发展之路	中交国际航运有限公司	DEVELOPMENT WAY	CCCC International Shipping Corp.	107
泛亚号	泛亚液化天然气运输有限公司	PAN ASIA	PANASIA LNG Transportation Co., Ltd.	79
泛洋108	浙江海油平台船舶有限公司	FAN YANG 108	Zhejiang Offshore-petroluem Shipping Co.,Ltd.	447
泛洲10	江苏泛洲船务有限公司	FAN ZHOU 10	Jiangsu Fanzhou Shipping Co., Ltd.	112
飞鸽	北部湾旅游股份有限公司	FEI GE	Beibu Gulf Tourism Co., Ltd.	156
飞逸1号	北海新绎游船有限公司	FEI YI 1 HAO	Beihai Ennova Cruise Co., Ltd.	157
飞翼11	上海市客运轮船有限公司	FEI YI 11	Shanghai Passenger Ship Co., Ltd.	319
飞鱼01	黑龙江海事局镜泊湖培训中心	FEI YU 01	Jingpo Lake Training Center of Heilongjiang Maritime Safety Administration	320
飞舟9	舟山海峡轮渡集团有限公司	FEI ZHOU 9	Zhoushan Strait Ferry Group Co., Ltd.	160
分节油63001	南京长江油运公司	FEN JIE YOU 63001	CSC Nanjing Tanker Corporation	244
分节油65011	南京长江油运公司	FEN JIE YOU 65011	CSC Nanjing Tanker Corporation	245
奋斗者号	中国科学院深海与工程研究院	FEN DOU ZHE HAO	Institute of Deep-Sea Science and Engineering, Chinese Academy of Sciences	481
枫林湾	中海油轮运输有限公司	FENG LIN WAN	China Shipping Tanker Co., Ltd.	49
凤凰岭	海南海峡航运股份有限公司	FENG HUANG LING	Hainan Strait Shipping Co., Ltd.	149
凤凰松	中远海运特种运输股份有限公司	FENG HUANG SONG	COSCO SHIPPING Specialized Carriers Co., Ltd.	92
凤山烟雨	杭州市水上公共观光巴士有限公司	FENG SHAN YAN YU	Hangzhou Sightseeing Water Bus Co., Ltd.	296
芙蓉源	中远海运能源运输股份有限公司	FU RONG YUAN	COSCO SHIPPING Energy Transportation Co., Ltd.	81
福船三峡	中铁福船海洋工程有限公司	FU CHUAN SAN XIA	China Railway Fuchuan Marine Engineering Co.,Ltd.	434
福宁湾	中远海运特种运输股份有限公司	FU NING WAN	COSCO SHIPPING Specialized Carriers Co., Ltd.	63
福荣海	辽宁远洋渔业股份有限公司	FU RONG HAI	Liaoning Deep Sea Fisheries Co., Ltd.	331
福远渔098	宏东渔业股份有限公司	FU YUAN YU 098	Hongdong Fisheries Co., Ltd.	346
福远渔163	中渔（福建）渔业有限公司	FU YUAN YU 163	Zhongyu (Fujian) Fisheries Co., Ltd.	361
福远渔7869	福建省平潭县远洋渔业集团有限公司	FU YUAN YU 7869	Fujian Pingtan Ocean Fishery Group Co., Ltd.	356
福远渔8679	福建省平潭县远洋渔业集团有限公司	FU YUAN YU 8679	Fujian Pingtan Ocean Fishery Group Co., Ltd.	362
福远渔961	宏东渔业股份有限公司	FU YUAN YU 961	Hongdong Fisheries Co., Ltd.	345
福远渔9613	福州宏龙海洋水产有限公司	FU YUAN YU 9613	Fuzhou Honglong Ocean Fishing Co., Ltd.	347
福远渔976	宏东渔业股份有限公司	FU YUAN YU 976	Hongdong Fisheries Co., Ltd.	360
福远渔9801	福建世海渔业有限公司	FU YUAN YU 9801	Fujian Shihai Fisheries Co., Ltd.	336
福远渔F86	福建省长福渔业有限公司	FU YUAN YU F86	Fujian Changfu Fishery Co., Ltd.	371
抚远东方一号	抚远县外事办公室	FU YUAN DONG FANG YI HAO	Foreign Affairs Office of Fuyuan County	282
抚远长城1701	抚远县人民政府外事办	FU YUAN CHANG CHENG 1701	Foreign Affairs Office of the People's Government of Fuyuan County	259
富安283	广西贵港市富安运输公司	FU AN 283	Guangxi Guigang Fuan Transportation Co., Ltd.	201
富瀚口	广州远洋运输有限公司	FU HAN KOU	Guangzhou Ocean Shipping Co., Ltd.	102
富顺399	扬州万兴船务有限公司	FU SHUN 399	Yangzhou Wanxing Shipping Co., Ltd.	31

G

赣昌公安1302	南昌市公安局新建分局	GAN CHANG GONG AN 1302	Xinjian Branch of Nanchang Bureau of Public Security	512
赣崇义渔养90107	崇义章源投资控股有限公司阳明湖渔业分公司	GAN CHONG YI YU YANG 90107	Yangming Lake Fishery Branch of Chongyi Zhangyuan Investment Holding Co., Ltd.	370
赣丰城货8199	江西明远物流贸易有限公司	GAN FENG CHENG HUO 8199	Jiangxi Mingyuan Logistics and Trading Co., Ltd.	192
赣恒顺1号	抚州市长江实业集团有限公司	GAN HENG SHUN 1 HAO	Fuzhou Yangtze River Industry Group Co., Ltd.	217

中文名	公司（中文）	英文名	公司（英文）	页码
赣恒顺2号	抚州市长江实业集团有限公司	GAN HENG SHUN 2 HAO	Fuzhou Yangtze River Industry Group Co., Ltd.	182
赣吉安货3169	江西朋腾水陆联运有限公司	GAN JI AN HUO 3169	Jiangxi Pengteng Water & Land Multimodal Transportation Co., Ltd.	197
赣九江货1139	瑞昌市亚力船务有限公司	GAN JIU JIANG HUO 1139	Ruichang Yali Shipping Co., Ltd.	187
港航浚6	天津港航工程有限公司	GANG HANG JUN 6	Tianjin Port & Channel Engineering Co., Ltd.	388
港航浚7	天津港航工程有限公司	GANG HANG JUN 7	Tianjin Port & Channel Engineering Co., Ltd.	388
港航平9	天津港航工程有限公司	GANG HANG PING 9	Tianjin Port & Channel Engineering Co., Ltd.	436
港联油6	湖北省黄石市鄂东海运有限责任公司	GANG LIAN YOU 6	Hubei Huangshi Edong Shipping Co., Ltd.	67
港盛1000	重庆港盛船务有限公司	GANG SHENG 1000	Chongqing Gangsheng Ship Service Co., Ltd.	198
港盛1003	重庆港盛船务有限公司	GANG SHENG 1003	Chongqing Gangsheng Ship Service Co., Ltd.	199
港鑫7	华晟融资租赁股份有限公司	GANG XIN 7	Huasheng Financial Leasing Co., Ltd.	441
工行牡丹号	武汉两江游览轮船旅游有限公司	GONG HANG MU DAN HAO	Wuhan Liangjiang Tour Ship Travel Co., Ltd.	279
工银1	工银金融租赁有限公司	GONG YIN 1	ICBC Financial Leasing Co., Ltd.	18
公主	云南省思茅地区澜沧江航运公司	GONG ZHU	Yunnan Simao Region Lantsang River Shipping Company	275
鼓浪屿	星旅远洋国际邮轮有限公司	PIANO LAND	Astro Ocean International Cruise Co. Ltd.	123
观光26号	桂林五福旅游船运有限公司	GUAN GUANG 26 HAO	Guilin Wufu Travel Shipping Co., Ltd.	296
广东工行	广州蓝海豚游船有限公司	GUANG DONG GONG HANG	Guangzhou Blue Dolphin Cruise Co., Ltd.	291
广州港引航2号	广州港引航站	GUANG ZHOU GANG YIN HANG 2 HAO	Guangzhou Port Pilot Station	457
广州湾	中远海运特种运输股份有限公司	GUANG ZHOU WAN	COSCO SHIPPING Specialized Carriers Co., Ltd.	75
桂北渔65828	个人	GUI BEI YU 65828	Individually owned	360
桂北渔80208	个人	GUI BEI YU 80208	Individually owned	359
桂峨渔11465	个人	GUI E YU 11465	Individually owned	368
桂平滨海2288	桂平市滨海船务有限责任公司	GUI PING BIN HAI 2288	Guiping Binhai Shipping Co., Ltd.	185
桂运3568	广西柳州泰升航运有限责任公司	GUI YUN 3568	Guangxi Liuzhou Taisheng Shipping Co., Ltd.	220
"国裕海拖1号"船组	武汉江裕海运发展有限公司	GUO YU HAI TUO 1 HAO COMBINATION	Wuhan Jiangyu Shipping Development Co., Ltd.	250
国际839	大连国际合作远洋渔业有限公司	GUO JI 839	Dalian International Cooperation Deep Sea Fisheries Co., Ltd.	337
国际902	大连国际合作远洋渔业有限公司	GUO JI 902	Dalian International Cooperation Deep Sea Fisheries Co., Ltd.	353
国粤06	广东国粤水运有限公司	GUO YUE 06	Guangdong Guoyue Water Transportation Co., Ltd.	206

H

中文名	公司（中文）	英文名	公司（英文）	页码
HARMONI VICTORY	TSC集团控股有限公司	HARMONI VICTORY	TSC Group Holdings Limited	429
哈渡客439	哈尔滨交通集团轮渡旅游有限公司	HA DU KE 439	Harbin Traffic and Transportation Group Ferry Travel Co., Ltd.	306
哈防汛艇517	哈尔滨市水务局	HA FANG XUN TING 517	Harbin Water Authority	516
哈客渡008	哈尔滨市顺航江上旅游客运有限公司	HA KE DU 008	Harbin Shun Hang Jiang Shang Tourist Transportation Co., Ltd.	307
海安0982	广东海安水运技术服务有限公司广州分公司	HAI AN 0982	Guangzhou Branch of Guangdong Haian Shuiyun Technology Service Co., Ltd.	520
海豹六号	中国石油集团东方地球物理勘探有限责任公司	HAI BAO LIU HAO	BGP INC., China National Petroleum Corporation	477
海丰广西	海丰广西船务有限公司	SITC GUANGXI	SITC GUANGXI Shipping Company Limited	43
海港特001	上海港复兴船务有限公司	HAI GANG TE 001	Shanghai Port Fuxing Shipping Co., Ltd.	117
海港星01	江苏海企港华燃气股份有限公司	HAI GANG XING 01	Jiangsu Haiqi Ganghua Gas Development Co., Ltd.	227
海港星02	江苏海企港华燃气股份有限公司	HAI GANG XING 02	Jiangsu Haiqi Ganghua Gas Development Co., Ltd.	228
海供油303	上海中燃船舶燃料有限公司	HAI GONG YOU 303	Shanghai Chimbusco Marine Bunker Supply Co., Ltd.	246
海供油31	上海中燃船舶燃料有限公司	HAI GONG YOU 31	Shanghai Chimbusco Marine Bunker Supply Co., Ltd.	220
海供油9	上海中燃船舶燃料有限公司	HAI GONG YOU 9	Shanghai Chimbusco Marine Bunker Supply Co., Ltd.	212
海关826	中华人民共和国上海海关	HAI GUAN 826	Shanghai Customs of the PRC	510
海关902	中华人民共和国拱北海关	HAI GUAN 902	Gongbei Customs of the PRC	509
海关山126	湖北省黄石市鄂东海运有限责任公司	HAI GUAN SHAN 126	Hubei Huangshi Edong Shipping Co., Ltd.	64
海河观光9	天津津旅海河游船股份有限公司	HAI HE GUAN GUANG 9	JTG Haihe Cruises Co., Ltd.	284
海河拖9	东营港海河港务有限公司	HAI HE TUO 9	Dongying Haihe Port Services Co. Ltd.	440
海虹一号	海南海峡航运股份有限公司	HAI HONG YI HAO	Hainan Strait Shipping Co., Ltd.	127
海口九号	海口能运船务有限公司	HAI KOU JIU HAO	Haikou Neng Yun Shipping Co., Ltd.	150
海琨	珠海高速客轮有限公司	HAI KUN	Zhuhai High-Speed Passenger Ferry Co., Ltd.	159

海蓝鲸	渤海国际轮渡（香港）有限公司	OCEAN BLUE WHALE	Bohai International Ferry (Hong Kong) Co., Ltd.	131
海龙号	卓美亚海工公司	ORIENTAL DRAGON	Jumeirah Offshore Pte. Ltd	472
海牛1003	重庆海牛运输有限公司	HAI NIU 1003	Chongqing Hainiu Transportation Co., Ltd.	183
海鸥7号	海南亚龙湾海底世界旅游有限公司	HAI OU 7 HAO	Hainan Yalong Bay Underwater World Tourism Co., Ltd.	135
海鸥	中海客轮有限公司	HAI OU	China Shipping Passenger Liner Co., Ltd.	157
海润3	江门市崖门船业有限公司	HAI RUN 3	Jiangmen Yamen Shipping Co., Ltd.	330
海上巨人	东方海外货柜航运公司	SEAWISE GIANT	Orient Overseas Container Line Limited	49
海神17	长岛渤海映华海上游有限公司	HAI SHEN 17	Changdao Bohaiyinghua Marine Tourism Co., Ltd.	135
海神6号	莆田市忠湄轮渡有限责任公司	HAI SHEN 6 HAO	Putian Zhongmei Ferry Co., Ltd.	133
海盛集002	绍兴海盛航运有限公司	HAI SHENG JI 002	Shaoxing Haisheng Shipping Co., Ltd.	209
海顺安9	厦门海顺安海上旅游有限公司	HAI SHUN AN 9	Xiamen Haishun'An Marine (Tourism) Co., Ltd.	134
海棠之星1号	海南蜈支洲旅游开发股份有限公司	HAI TANG ZHI XING 1 HAO	Hainan Wuzhizhou Tourism Development Corporation	164
海特3102	长江引航中心	HAI TE 3102	Yangtze River Pilotage Center	452
海娃2	大连老虎滩旅游开发有限公司	HAI WA 2	Dalian Laohutan Tourism Development Co., Ltd.	136
海王之星	中远海运特种运输股份有限公司	HAI WANG ZHI XING	COSCO SHIPPING Specialized Carriers Co., Ltd.	91
海峡号	福建海峡高速客滚航运有限公司	HAI XIA HAO	Fujian Cross Strait Ferry Corporation	147
海象	天津（河北）海运有限公司	HAI XIANG	Tianjin (Hebei) Shipping Co., Ltd.	11
海鑫油619	中国航油集团海鑫航运有限公司	HAI XIN YOU 619	China National Aviation Fuel (CNAF) Haixin Shipping Corporation	68
海星	大理西电实业有限责任公司	HAI XING	Dali Xidian Industry Co., Ltd.	295
海巡01	中华人民共和国上海海事局	HAI XUN 01	Shanghai Maritime Safety Administration of the PRC	488
海巡01015	中华人民共和国宝山海事局	HAI XUN 01015	Baoshan Maritime Safety Administration of the PRC	485
海巡0103	中华人民共和国吴淞海事局	HAI XUN 0103	Wusong Maritime Safety Administration of the PRC	485
海巡09	中华人民共和国广东海事局	HAI XUN 09	Guangdong Maritime Safety Administration of the PRC	489
海巡11	中华人民共和国山东海事局	HAI XUN 11	Shandong Maritime Safety Administration of the PRC	487
海巡12002	中华人民共和国武汉海事局	HAI XUN 12002	Wuhan Maritime Safety Administration of the PRC	458
海巡1203	中华人民共和国长江海事局	HAI XUN 1203	Yangtze River Maritime Safety Administration of the PRC	487
海巡13202	中华人民共和国黑河海事局	HAI XUN 13202	Heihe Maritime Safety Administration of the PRC	320
海巡1468	中华人民共和国深圳海事局	HAI XUN 1468	Shenzhen Maritime Safety Administration of the PRC	486
海巡1501	交通运输部北海航海保障中心	HAI XUN 1501	Northern Navigation Service Center, Maritime Safety Administration, P.R.China	515
海巡15016	交通运输部北海航海保障中心	HAI XUN 15016	Northern Navigation Service Center, Maritime Safety Administration, P.R.China	517
海巡1502	交通运输部北海航海保障中心	HAI XUN 1502	Northern Navigation Service Center, Maritime Safety Administration, P.R.China	514
海巡153	中华人民共和国天津海事局	HAI XUN 153	Tianjin Maritime Safety Adminitration of P.R.China	519
海巡160	交通运输部东海航海保障中心	HAI XUN 160	Eastern Navigation Service Center, Maritime Safety Administration, P.R.China	521
海巡1640	交通运输部东海航海保障中心	HAI XUN 1640	Eastern Navigation Service Center, Maritime Safety Administration, P.R.China	519
海巡16601	交通运输部东海航海保障中心	HAI XUN 16601	Eastern Navigation Service Center, Maritime Safety Administration, P.R.China	480
海巡1668	交通运输部东海航海保障中心	HAI XUN 1668	Eastern Navigation Service Center, Maritime Safety Administration, P.R.China	476
海巡1701	交通运输部南海航海保障中心	HAI XUN 1701	Southern Navigation Service Center, Maritime Safety Administration, P.R.China	514
海巡17041	交通运输部南海航海保障中心	HAI XUN 17041	Southern Navigation Service Center, Maritime Safety Administration, P.R.China	516
海巡172	交通运输部南海航海保障中心	HAI XUN 172	Southern Navigation Service Center, Maritime Safety Administration, P.R.China	517
海巡21	中华人民共和国上海海事局	HAI XUN 21	Shanghai Maritime Safety Administration of the PRC	486
海巡31	中华人民共和国广东海事局	HAI XUN 31	Guangdong Maritime Safety Administration of the PRC	486
海洋地质九号	青岛海洋地质研究所	HAI YANG DI ZHI JIU HAO	Qingdao Institute of Marine Geology	470
海洋地质十号	广州海洋地质调查局	HAI YANG DI ZHI SHI HAO	Guangzhou Marine Geological Survey Bureau	469
海洋风电36	南通市海洋水建工程有限公司	HAI YANG FENG DIAN 36	Nantong Ocean Water Conservancy Engineering Co., Ltd.	435
海洋风电38	南通市海洋水建工程有限公司	HAI YANG FENG DIAN 38	Nantong Ocean Water Conservancy Engineering Co.,Ltd.	432
海洋六号	广州海洋地质调查局	HAI YANG LIU HAO	Guangzhou Marine Geological Survey Bureau	465

海洋石油201	海洋石油工程股份有限公司	HAI YANG SHI YOU 201	Offshore Oil Engineering Co., Ltd.	414
海洋石油229	海洋石油工程股份有限公司	HAI YANG SHI YOU 229	Offshore Oil Engineering Co., Ltd.	411
海洋石油251	天津中海油能源发展油田设施管理有限公司	HAI YANG SHI YOU 251	CNOOC Oilfield Facility Manager Co., Ltd.	455
海洋石油252	天津中海油能源发展油田设施管理有限公司	HAI YANG SHI YOU 252	CNOOC Oilfield Facility Manager Co., Ltd.	446
海洋石油278	海洋石油工程股份有限公司	HAI YANG SHI YOU 278	Offshore Oil Engineering Co., Ltd.	110
海洋石油281	中海油能源发展股份有限公司	HAI YANG SHI YOU 281	CNOOC Energy Technology & Services Ltd.	438
海洋石油285	海洋石油工程股份有限公司	HAI YANG SHI YOU 285	Offshore Oil Engineering Co., Ltd.	416
海洋石油286	海洋石油工程股份有限公司	HAI YANG SHI YOU 286	Offshore Oil Engineering Co., Ltd.	418
海洋石油295	海洋石油工程股份有限公司	HAI YANG SHI YOU 295	Offshore Oil Engineering Co., Ltd.	418
海洋石油301	中海油能源发展股份有限公司	HAI YANG SHI YOU 301	CNOOC Energy Technology & Services Ltd.	77
海洋石油525	中海油能源发展股份有限公司	HAI YANG SHI YOU 525	CNOOC Energy Technology & Services Ltd.	449
海洋石油550	中海油田服务股份有限公司	HAI YANG SHI YOU 550	China Oilfield Services Limited	451
海洋石油630	中海油田服务股份有限公司	HAI YANG SHI YOU 630	China Oilfield Services Limited	450
海洋石油681	中海油田服务股份有限公司	HAI YANG SHI YOU 681	China Oilfield Services Limited	447
海洋石油691	中海油田服务股份有限公司	HAI YANG SHI YOU 691	China Oilfield Services Limited	450
海洋石油707	中海油田服务股份有限公司	HAI YANG SHI YOU 707	China Oilfield Services Limited	479
海洋石油719	中海油田服务股份有限公司	HAI YANG SHI YOU 719	China Oilfield Services Limited	476
海洋石油720	中海油田服务股份有限公司	HAI YANG SHI YOU 720	China Oilfield Services Limited	478
海洋石油771	中海油田服务股份有限公司	HAI YANG SHI YOU 771	China Oilfield Services Limited	479
海洋石油791	中海油能源发展装备技术有限公司	HAI YANG SHI YOU 791	CNOOC Enertech Equipment Technology Co., Ltd.	419
海洋石油901	中海油田服务股份有限公司	HAI YANG SHI YOU 901	China Oilfield Services Limited	438
海洋石油921	中海油田服务股份有限公司	HAI YANG SHI YOU 921	China Oilfield Services Limited	427
海洋石油931	中海油田服务股份有限公司	HAI YANG SHI YOU 931	China Oilfield Services Limited	424
海洋石油936	中海油田服务股份有限公司	HAI YANG SHI YOU 936	China Oilfield Services Limited	426
海洋石油941	中海油田服务股份有限公司	HAI YANG SHI YOU 941	China Oilfield Services Limited	424
海洋石油981	中国海洋石油集团有限公司	HAI YANG SHI YOU 981	China National Offshore Oil Corp.	428
海洋石油982	中海油田服务股份有限公司	HAI YANG SHI YOU 982	China Oilfield Services Limited	431
海义伍	江门市崖门船业有限公司	HAI YI WU	Jiangmen Yamen Shipping Co., Ltd.	339
汉工排6号	长江武汉航道工程局	HAN GONG PAI 6 HAO	Changjiang Wuhan Waterway Engineering Bureau	413
汉海1号	安徽大禹航运有限公司	HAN HAI YI HAO	Anhui Dayu Shipping Co., Ltd.	252
汉拿山	江苏韩通赢吉重工有限公司	HAN NA SHAN	Jiangsu Hantong Wing Heavy Industry Co., Ltd.	119
汉水女神号	湖北新神韵汉江旅游有限公司	HAN SHUI NV SHEN HAO	Hubei Xinshenyun Hanjiang Tourism Co., Ltd.	285
汉唐上海	上海汉唐航运有限公司	HAN TANG SHANG HAI	Shanghai Hantang Shipping Co., Ltd.	251
汉唐苏州	上海汉唐航运有限公司	HAN TANG SU ZHOU	Shanghai Hantang Shipping Co., Ltd.	252
航驳3001	招银金融租赁有限公司	HANG BO 3001	CMB Financial Leasing Co., Ltd.	392
航道1号	长江航道局	HANG DAO 1 HAO	Changjiang Waterway Bureau	478
航道管理01	黑龙江省航道局	HANG DAO GUAN LI 01	Heilongjiang Provincial Waterway Bureau	515
航电2号	贵州沿河乌江轮船有限责任公司	HANG DIAN 2 HAO	Guizhou Yanhe Wujiang Shipping Co., Ltd.	184
航工半潜驳2号	中交第二航务工程局有限公司	HANG GONG BAN QIAN BO 2 HAO	CCCC Second Harbour Engineering Co., Ltd.	115
航工半潜驳3号	中交第二航务工程局有限公司	HANG GONG BAN QIAN BO 3 HAO	CCCC Second Harbour Engineering Co., Ltd.	119
航工砼1601	中交第二航务工程局有限公司	HANG GONG TONG 1601	CCCC Second Harbour Engineering Co., Ltd.	410
航供油1003	上海航道物流有限公司	HANG GONG YOU 1003	Shanghai Waterway Logistics Co., Ltd.	67
航供油501	上海航道物流有限公司	HANG GONG YOU 501	Shanghai Waterway Logistics Co., Ltd.	63
航供油驳9	上海航道物流有限公司	HANG GONG YOU BO 9	Shanghai Waterway Logistics Co., Ltd.	67
航浚11	长江南京航道工程局	HANG JUN 11	Changjiang Nanjing Waterway Engineering Bureau	384
航浚14号	长江武汉航道工程局	HANG JUN 14 HAO	Changjiang Wuhan Waterway Engineering Bureau	384
航勘201	武汉长江航道救助打捞局	HANG KAN 201	Wuhan Changjiang Waterway Rescue and Salvage Bureau	477
航荣	长江上海航道处	HANG RONG	Changjiang Shanghai Waterway Department	516
航万933	重庆国发运输有限公司	HANG WAN 933	Chongqing Guofa Transportation Co., Ltd.	185
航政管理001	黑龙江省航道局	HANG ZHENG GUAN LI 001	Heilongjiang Provincial Waterway Bureau	520
濠江明珠	珠海市环珠澳海上观光有限公司	HAO JIANG MING ZHU	Zhuhai-Macao Sea Tours Co., Ltd.	276

中文名	中文公司	英文名	英文公司	页码
合恒	中远海运散货运输有限公司	HE HENG	COSCO SHIPPING Bulk Co., Ltd.	25
和平之星	厦门湾海上旅游客运有限公司	HE PING ZHI XING	Xiamen Bay Tourists & Transportation Co., Ltd.	158
和谐号	青海省青海湖旅游集团有限公司	HE XIE HAO	Qinghai Province Qinghai Lake Tourism Group Co., Ltd.	289
和谐云港	龙江国际船舶租赁有限公司	HARMONY YUNGANG	Longjiang International Ship Lease Co., Ltd.	150
河北创新	河北远洋运输集团股份有限公司	HEBEI INNOVATOR	Hebei Ocean Shipping Co., Ltd.	24
河北领先	河北远洋运输集团股份有限公司	HEBEI NO.1	Hebei Ocean Shipping Co., Ltd.	17
河北伟岸	河北远洋运输集团股份有限公司	HEBEI MOUNTAIN	Hebei Ocean Shipping Co., Ltd.	54
河北张家口	河北远洋运输集团股份有限公司	HEBEI ZHANGJIAKOU	Hebei Ocean Shipping Co., Ltd.	20
河牛136	重庆市河牛滚装船运输有限公司	HE NIU 136	Chongqing Heniu RO-RO Shipping Co., Ltd.	201
河牛58	重庆市河牛滚装船运输有限公司	HE NIU 58	Chongqing Heniu RO-RO Shipping Co., Ltd.	183
河牛796	重庆市河牛滚装船运输有限公司	HE NIU 796	Chongqing Heniu RO-RO Shipping Co., Ltd.	302
河牛81	重庆市河牛滚装船运输有限公司	HE NIU 81	Chongqing Heniu RO-RO Shipping Co., Ltd.	208
鹤山星航311	鹤山市星航船务运输有限公司	HE SHAN XING HANG 311	Heshan Xinghang Shipping and Transport Co., Ltd.	194
鹤油03	中国石化燃料油销售有限公司	HE YOU 03	SINOPEC Fuel Oil Sales Corporation Limited	213
黑龙江	黑龙江省航道局	HEI LONG JIANG	Heilongjiang Waterway Bureau	513
恒达沥青005	武汉海通船舶运输有限公司	HENG DA LI QING 005	Wuhan Haitong Shipping Co., Ltd.	220
恒达沥青058	武汉海通船舶运输有限公司	HENG DA LI QING 058	Wuhan Haitong Shipping Co., Ltd.	222
恒辉2	石狮市恒通船务有限公司	HENG HUI 2	Shishi Hengtong Shipping Co., Ltd.	35
恒晖39	浙江恒晖海运有限公司	HENG HUI 39	Zhejiang Henghui Shipping Co., Ltd.	69
恒顺8	安徽安瑞航运有限公司	HENG SHUN 8	Anhui Anrui Shipping Co., Ltd.	175
恒通海	天津恒通航运有限公司	HENG TONG HAI	Tianjin Hengtong Shipping Co., Ltd.	13
恒通鑫运	安徽奥鑫船务有限公司	HENG TONG XIN YUN	Anhui Aoxin Shipping Co., Ltd.	113
恒信	上海鼎衡船务有限责任公司	HENG XIN	Shanghai Dingheng Shipping Co., Ltd.	72
恒星	深圳市鹏星船务有限公司	HENG XING	Shenzhen Pengxing Shipping Co., Ltd.	160
恒裕	洋浦国信海洋船务有限公司	HENG YU	Yangpu Guoxin Ocean Shipping Co., Ltd.	87
恒运1	北海恒运物流有限公司	HENG YUN 1	Beihai Hengyun Logistics Co., Ltd.	99
红宝石壹号	江门市崖门船业有限公司	HONG BAO SHI YI HAO	Jiangmen Yamen Shipping Co., Ltd.	335
宏力企业	河南省宏力集团有限公司	HONG LI QI YE	Henan Honliv Group Co., Ltd.	524
宏翔518	福建南翔海运有限公司	HONG XIANG 518	Fujian Nanxiang Shipping Co., Ltd.	31
鸿富368	东莞市鸿富运输有限公司	HONG FU 368	Dongguan Hongfu Transportation Co., Ltd.	31
鸿翔	上海崇明县轮船公司	HONG XIANG	Shanghai Chongming Shipping Company	166
鸿运21	平乐县昭洲旅游车船有限公司	HONG YUN 21	Pingle Zhaozhou Travel Vehicles & Ships Co., Ltd.	275
鸿洲23	深圳鸿洲国际游艇会有限公司	HONG ZHOU 23	Shenzhen Visun International Yacht Club Co., Ltd.	525
虎门7	深圳大铲岛集团有限公司	HU MEN 7	Shenzhen Dachandao Group Co.,Ltd.	382
虎门8	深圳大铲岛集团有限公司	HU MEN 8	Shenzhen Dachandao Group Co.,Ltd.	384
沪崇渔1256	个人	HU CHONG YU 1256	Individually owned	330
沪港引1	上海港引航站	HU GANG YIN 1	Shanghai Maritime Pilots' Association, China	454
沪港引6	上海国际港务（集团）股份有限公司	HU GANG YIN 6	Shanghai International Port (Group) Co., Ltd.	459
沪航3	上海市客运轮船有限公司	HU HANG 3	Shanghai Passenger Ship Co., Ltd.	305
沪航货1	上海市航运公司	HU HANG HUO 1	Shanghai Shipping Corporation	194
沪航客22	上海市客运轮船有限公司	HU HANG KE 22	Shanghai Passenger Ship Co., Ltd.	304
沪航客74	上海市轮渡有限公司	HU HANG KE 74	Shanghai Ferry Co., Ltd.	304
沪航客88	上海市轮渡有限公司	HU HANG KE 88	Shanghai Ferry Co., Ltd.	305
沪航客92	上海市轮渡有限公司	HU HANG KE 92	Shanghai Ferry Co., Ltd.	309
沪环运货5002	上海环境物流有限公司	HU HUAN YUN HUO 5002	Shanghai Chengtou Environment Group Co., Ltd.	456
沪消2	上海市消防局	HU XIAO 2	Shanghai Fire Prevention Bureau	457
沪油12	上海强辉海运有限公司	HU YOU 12	Shanghai Qianghui Shipping Co., Ltd.	62
沪渔1205	上海蒂尔远洋渔业有限公司	HU YU 1205	Shanghai Dier Deep Sea Fisheries Co., Ltd	333
沪振华货11	上海兴旺港口货运有限责任公司	HU ZHEN HUA HUO 11	Shanghai Xingwang Port Freight Co., Ltd.	174
沪振华货20	上海兴旺港口货运有限责任公司	HU ZHEN HUA HUO 20	Shanghai Xingwang Port Freight Co., Ltd.	182
华安龙	中交广州航道局有限公司	HUA AN LONG	CCCC Guangzhou Dredging Co., Ltd.	389
华辰56	舟山市华辰海运有限公司等	HUA CHEN 56	Zhoushan Huachen Shipping Co., Ltd.	65
华诚	深圳华威近海船舶运输股份有限公司	HUA CHENG	Shenzhen Huawei Offshore Shipping Transport Co., Ltd.	443
华达609	厦门信华达船运有限公司	HUA DA 609	Xiamen Xinhuada Shipping Co., Ltd.	47

华电1001	华电曹妃甸重工装备有限公司	HUA DIAN 1001	Huadian Caofeidian Heavy Industries Co., Ltd.	433
华东	上海华润大东船务工程有限公司	HUA DONG	Huarun Dadong Dockyard Co., Ltd.	416
华东明珠VI	荣成华东海运有限公司	HUADONG PEARL VI	Rongcheng Huadong Ferry Co., Ltd.	124
华海龙	交通运输部广州打捞局	HUA HAI LONG	Guangzhou Salvage Bureau, Ministry of Transport	109
华航机6168	常州市安顺航运有限公司	HUA HANG JI 6168	Changzhou Anshun Shipping Co., Ltd.	187
华航长运	华中航运集团有限公司	HUA HANG CHANG YUN	Huazhong Shipping Group Co., Ltd.	179
华虎	深圳华威近海船舶运输股份有限公司	HUA HU	Shenzhen Huawei Offshore Shipping Transport Co., Ltd.	449
华吉	深圳华威近海船舶运输股份有限公司	HUA JI	Shenzhen Huawei Offshore Shipping Transport Co., Ltd.	451
华凯	福建外贸中心船务有限公司	HUA KAI	Fujian Foreign Trade Centre Shipping Co., Ltd.	35
华润电力1	天津中海华润航运有限公司	HUA RUN DIAN LI 1	Tianjin CS & CR Shipping Co., Ltd.	12
华润石梅湾	海南华润石梅湾旅游开发有限公司	HUA RUN SHI MEI WAN	China Resources Shimei Bay Tourism Delelopment (Hainan) Ltd.	526
华山号	长阳航运公司	HUA SHAN HAO	Changyang Shipping Company	259
华盛渔加2	瑞安市华盛水产有限公司	HUA SHENG YU JIA 2	Ruian Huasheng Aquatic Products Co., Ltd.	372
华天龙	交通运输部广州打捞局	HUA TIAN LONG	Guangzhou Salvage Bureau, Ministry of Transport	399
华通油78	泰州市华通船务有限公司	HUA TONG YOU 78	Taizhou Huatong Shipping Co., Ltd.	223
华铜海	广州远洋运输有限公司	HUA TONG HAI	Guangzhou Ocean Shipping Co., Ltd.	5
华威8	福建鑫海船务有限公司	HUA WEI 8	Fujian Xinhai Shipping Co., Ltd.	72
华夏神女2	重庆大美长江三峡游轮股份有限公司	HUA XIA SHEN NV 2	Chongqing Damei Three Gorges Cruises Co., Ltd.	273
华祥	交通运输部上海救捞局	HUA XIANG	Shanghai Salvage Bureau, Ministry of Transport	443
华祥8	浙江华祥海运有限公司	HUA XIANG 8	Zhejiang Huaxiang Shipping Co., Ltd.	78
华祥龙	交通运输部广州打捞局	HUA XIANG LONG	Guangzhou Salvage Bureau, Ministry of Transport	404
华翔238	博罗县水上运输总公司石湾公司	HUA XIANG 238	Shiwan Branch of Boluo Water Transportation Corporation	413
华兴龙	交通运输部广州打捞局	HUA XING LONG	Guangzhou Salvage Bureau, Ministry of Transport	112
华洋龙	交通运输部广州打捞局	HUA YANG LONG	Guangzhou Salvage Bureau, Ministry of Transport	110
华源3008	镇江兴电实业有限公司	HUA YUAN 3008	Zhenjiang Xingdian Industry Co., Ltd.	444
环卫1	秦皇岛港务集团有限公司船舶分公司	HUAN WEI 1	Qinhuangdao Harbor Group Co., Ltd. Shipping Branch	452
寰岛019	海南亚龙湾海底世界旅游有限公司	HUAN DAO 019	Hainan Yalong Bay Underwater World Tourism Co., Ltd.	163
黄船023	中船黄埔文冲船舶有限公司	HUANG CHUAN 023	CSSC Huangpu Wenchong Shipbuilding Co., Ltd.	311
黄海集团	青岛黄海制药有限责任公司	HUANGHAI GROUP	Qingdao Huanghai Pharmaceutical Co., Ltd.	526
黄河一代天骄	洛阳市黄河小浪底港航有限公司	HUANG HE YI DAI TIAN JIAO	Luoyang Yellow River Xiaolangdi Port & Shipping Co., Ltd.	277
黄鹤楼号	武汉江汉朝宗轮船旅游有限公司	HUANG HE LOU HAO	Wuhan Jianghan Chaozong Cruise Co., Ltd.	287
黄山12	黄山市新安江游船服务有限公司	HUANG SHAN 12	Huangshan Xin'an River Cruise Service Co., Ltd.	277
惠智海	中远海运散货运输有限公司	HUI ZHI HAI	COSCO SHIPPING Bulk Co., Ltd.	23

J

机场19	粤兴船舶用品有限公司	JI CHANG 19	Yuexing Shipping Products Co., Ltd.	164
吉祥698	宜昌吉祥滚装船运输有限公司	JI XIANG 698	Yichang Jixiang RO-RO Shipping Co., Ltd.	301
吉祥松	中远海运特种运输股份有限公司	JI XIANG SONG	COSCO SHIPPING Specialized Carriers Co., Ltd.	93
集发南海	大连集发船舶管理有限公司	JI FA NAN HAI	Dalian Jifa Ship Management Co., Ltd.	44
集海昌3号	江西物流企业有限公司	JI HAI CHANG 3 HAO	Jiangxi Logistics Enterprise Co., Ltd.	198
集远	长伟国际航运实业有限公司	JI YUAN	Wuhan Associated Marine Transport Inc.	248
佳航88	广州佳航船务货运有限公司	JIA HANG 88	Guangzhou Jiahang Shipping Co., Ltd.	195
佳豪一号	上海佳豪船舶科技发展有限公司	JIA HAO YI HAO	Shanghai Jiahao Shipping Technology Development Co., Ltd.	524
嘉庚	厦门大学	JIA GENG	Xiamen University	469
嘉信1号	宁波大榭开发区嘉信海运有限公司	JIA XIN 1 HAO	Ningbo Daxie Development Area Jiaxin Shipping Co., Ltd.	71
假日	上海万邦邮轮有限公司	JIA RI	Shanghai Wanbang Cruise Co., Ltd.	124
建基5002	上海康益海洋工程有限公司	JIAN JI 5002	Shanghai Kang Yi Marine Engineering Co., Ltd.	419
建民2	大连建民船务有限公司	JIAN MIN 2	Dalian Jianmin Shipping Co., Ltd.	132
建荣268	天津建荣海运有限公司	JIAN RONG 268	Tianjin Jianrong Shipping Co., Ltd.	90
建荣966	天津建荣海运有限公司	JIAN RONG 966	Tianjin Jianrong Shipping Co., Ltd.	86
建业002号	西双版纳建业航运有限公司	JIAN YE 002 HAO	Xishuangbanna Jianye Shipping Co., Ltd.	318
江城1号	武汉市轮渡公司	JIANG CHENG 1 HAO	Wuhan Ferry Company	308
江城5号	武汉市轮渡公司	JIANG CHENG 5 HAO	Wuhan Ferry Company	309

中文名	公司	英文名	英文公司	页码
江城汽渡01号	武汉市汽车轮渡管理所	JIANG CHENG QI DU 01 HAO	Wuhan Car Ferry Management Office	313
江海直达1	浙江新一海海运有限公司	JIANG HAI ZHI DA 1	Zhejiang Xinyihai Shipping Co., Ltd.	253
江汉18	武汉长江轮船公司	JIANG HAN 18	Wuhan Yangtze Shipping Co., Ltd.	257
江汉21号轮	武汉长江轮船公司	JIANG HAN 21 HAO LUN	Wuhan Yangtze Shipping Company	260
江汉59号	武汉长江轮船公司	JIANG HAN 59 HAO	Wuhan Yangtze Shipping Company	258
江和89	扬州江和船务运输有限公司	JIANG HE 89	Yangzhou Jianghe Shipping and Transport Co., Ltd.	184
江华6号	奉节县江华航运有限公司	JIANG HUA 6 HAO	Fengjie County Jianghua Shipping Co., Ltd.	306
江淮货9	蚌埠市江淮航运有限责任公司	JIANG HUAI HUO 9	Bengbu Jianghuai Shipping Co., Ltd.	175
江隆9001	重庆市江隆船务有限公司	JIANG LONG 9001	Chongqing Jianglong Shipping Co., Ltd.	224
江南长兴号	江南造船（集团）有限责任公司	JIANG NAN CHANG XING HAO	Jiangnan Shipyard (Group) Co., Ltd.	138
江申115	上海长江客货轮公司	JIANG SHEN 115	Shanghai Yangtze Passenger & Cargo Shipping Co., Ltd.	258
江苏渡26号	江苏暨阳轮渡有限公司	JIANG SU DU 26 HAO	Jiangsu Jiyang Ferry Co., Ltd.	315
江苏渡7号	江苏长博集团有限公司	JIANG SU DU 7 HAO	Jiangsu Changbo Group Co., Ltd.	310
江苏路渡2007	江苏通沙汽车轮渡管理处	JIANG SU LU DU 2007	Jiangsu Tongsha Car Ferry Management Division	310
江苏路渡3011	江苏镇扬汽渡有限公司	JIANG SU LU DU 3011	Jiangsu Zhenyang Car Ferry Co., Ltd.	314
江夏鸿	上海海一航运有限公司	JIANG XIA HONG	Shanghai Ocean Pioneer Shipping Co., Ltd..	250
江夏文	上海海一航运有限公司	JIANG XIA WEN	Shanghai Ocean Pioneer Shipping Co., Ltd..	250
江渝118号轮	重庆长江轮船公司	JIANG YU 118 HAO LUN	Chongqing Changjiang Shipping Company	260
蛟龙	中国大洋矿产资源勘探开发协会	JIAO LONG	China Ocean Mineral Resources R & D Association	481
捷龙	中交广州航道局有限公司	JIE LONG	CCCC Guangzhou Dredging Co., Ltd.	384
金城一号	兰州水运集团有限公司	JIN CHENG YI HAO	Lanzhou Water Transportation Group Co., Ltd.	281
金汇58	上海远洋渔业公司	JIN HUI 58	Shanghai Deep Sea Fisheries Company	342
金汇8	上海开创远洋渔业有限公司	JIN HUI 8	Shanghai Kaichuang Deep Sea Fisheries Co., Ltd.	340
金吉源	福建省万达海运有限公司	JIN JI YUAN	Fujian Province Wanda Shipping Co., Ltd.	88
金龙江	中俄国境河流航行联合委员会中方办公室	JIN LONG JIANG	China Office of China-Russia Joint Committee on Border River Navigation	261
金泰7	武汉均泰物流有限公司	JIN TAI 7	Wuhan Juntai Logistics Co., Ltd.	15
金鑫116	启东市金鑫船舶劳务有限公司	JIN XIN 116	Qidong Jinxin Shipping Labor Service Co., Ltd.	459
金源518	南京金源船务实业有限公司	JIN YUAN 518	Jinyuan Nanjing Shipping Industry Co., Ltd.	61
金珠湖	中港客运联营有限公司	JIN ZHU HU	Zhongshan-Hong Kong Passenger Shipping Co-Op Co., Ltd.	163
金紫荆	广东徐闻海峡航运有限公司	JIN ZI JING	Guangdong Xuwen Strait Shipping Co., Ltd.	143
津安2	中交第一航务工程局有限公司	JIN AN 2	CCCC First Harbor Engineering Co., Ltd.	414
津港轮14号	天津港轮驳有限公司	JIN GANG LUN 14 HAO	Tianjin Port Tugboat & Lighter Co., Ltd.	443
津航浚217	中交天津航道局有限公司	JIN HANG JUN 217	CCCC Tianjin Dredging Co., Ltd.	382
津航浚306	中交烟台环保疏浚有限公司	JIN HANG JUN 306	CCCC Yantai Environmental Protection Dredging Co, Ltd.	382
津航浚406	中交烟台环保疏浚有限公司	JIN HANG JUN 406	CCCC Yantai Environmental Protection Dredging Co, Ltd.	382
津平1	中交第一航务工程局有限公司	JIN PING 1	CCCC First Harbor Engineering Co., Ltd.	414
津泰	中交天津航道局有限公司	JIN TAI	CCCC Tianjin Dredging Co., Ltd.	393
锦海86	江西锦海航运有限公司	JIN HAI 86	Jiangxi Jinhai Shipping Co., Ltd.	197
锦江之宇	上海锦江航运（集团）有限公司	JJ SKY	Jinjiang Shanghai Shipping (Group) Co., Ltd.	91
锦龙100	黄冈龙达船务有限公司	JIN LONG 100	Huanggang Long Da Shipping Co., Ltd.	219
锦绣中华	湖北扬子江锦绣中华游船有限公司	SPLENDID CHINA	Hubei Yangtze River Splendid China Cruise Co., Ltd.	267
晋卿	三沙市船务管理局	JIN QING	Sansha Shipping Management Bureau	520
京远626	烟台京远渔业有限公司	JING YUAN 626	Yantai Jingyuan Fisheries Co., Ltd.	356
京远906	烟台京远渔业有限公司	JING YUAN 906	Yantai Jingyuan Fisheries Co., Ltd.	351
经纬7188	蚌埠市金海航运有限责任公司	JING WEI 7188	Bengbu Jinhai Shipping Co., Ltd.	178
精铟01	广东精铟海洋工程股份有限公司	JING YIN 01	Keen Offshore Engineering Co., Ltd.	435
景颇河	上海泛亚航运有限公司	JING PO HE	Shanghai PANASIA Shipping Co., Ltd.	36
镜泊湖430	牡丹江镜泊湖观光船旅游有限责任公司	JING PO HU 430	Mudanjiang Jingpo Lake Sightseeing Ship Co., Ltd.	286
镜客游4010	牡丹江镜泊湖观光船旅游有限责任公司	JING KE YOU 4010	Mudanjiang Jingpo Lake Sightseeing Ship Co., Ltd.	281
九肚山	温州威斯康工业有限公司	JIU DU SHAN	Wenzhou Wiscon Industry Co., Ltd.	522
九石化1902	中国石油化工股份有限公司九江分公司	JIU SHI HUA 1902	China Petroleum & Chemical Corporation Jiujiang Branch	243

中文名	公司中文	English Name	Company English	Page
久盛拖1	张家港市久盛企业服务有限公司	JIU SHENG TUO 1	Zhangjiagang Jiusheng Corporation Service Co., Ltd.	443
久鑫011	江苏泰和船务有限公司	JIU XIN 011	Jiangsu Taihe Shipping Co., Ltd.	219
玖龙王子	唐山纳隆达海运有限公司	JIU LONG WANG ZI	Tangshan Nalongda Shipping Co., Ltd.	128
救捞6号	长江航道工程局有限责任公司	JIU LAO 6 HAO	Changjiang Yangtze River Waterway Engineering Bureau Co., Ltd.	398
巨鲸	镇江市华兴船务有限公司	JU JING	Zhenjiang Huaxing Shipping Co., Ltd.	30
君旅号	武汉市轮渡公司	JUN LV HAO	Wuhan Ferry Company	298
浚洋1	中交广州航道局有限公司	JUN YANG 1	CCCC Guangzhou Dredging Co., Ltd.	394
浚泽	中交天航滨海环保浚航工程有限公司	JUN ZE	CCCC-TDC Binhai Environmental Channel Dredging Co., Ltd.	392

K

中文名	公司中文	English Name	Company English	Page
开创	上海远洋渔业公司	KAI CHUANG	Shanghai Deep Sea Fisheries Company	325
开元	北京新城基业资产运营有限公司	KAI YUAN	Beijing Xincheng Jiye Assets Operation Co., Ltd.	286
凯旋一号	工银租赁有限公司	KAI XUAN YI HAO	ICBC Financial Leasing Co., Ltd.	429
凯鸿	海宏轮船（香港）有限公司	NEW CENTURY	Associated Maritime Company (Hong Kong) Limited	52
凯吉	海宏轮船（香港）有限公司	NEW TALISMAN	Associated Maritime Company (Hong Kong) Limited	55
凯力	海宏轮船（香港）有限公司	NEW VITALITY	Associated Maritime Company (Hong Kong) Limited	58
凯勇	海宏轮船（香港）有限公司	NEW VALOR	Associated Maritime Company (Hong Kong) Limited	50
凯浙	海宏轮船（香港）有限公司	NEW ENTERPRISE	Associated Maritime Company (Hong Kong) Limited	55
凯征	海宏轮船（香港）有限公司	NEW JOURNEY	Associated Maritime Company (Hong Kong) Limited	58
勘探225	广东粤新海洋工程装备股份有限公司	KAN TAN 225	Guangdong Yuexin Ocean Engineering Co., Ltd.	447
勘探311	中石化海洋石油工程有限公司	KAN TAN 311	SINOPEC Offshore Oilfield Services Company	446
勘探六号	中石化海洋石油工程有限公司	KAN TAN LIU HAO	SINOPEC Offshore Oilfield Services Company	427
柯力	交通运输部上海打捞局	CALI	Shanghai Salvage Bureau, Ministry of Transport	404
科学	中国科学院海洋研究所	KE XUE	Institute of Oceanology, Chinese Academy of Sciences	466
科学三号	中国科学院海洋研究所	KE XUE SAN HAO	Institute of Oceanology, Chinese Academy of Sciences	464
昆仑油106	中远海运石油运输有限公司	KUN LUN YOU 106	COSCO Petrochina shipping Co., Ltd.	63
昆仑油201	中远海运能源运输股份有限公司	KUN LUN YOU 201	COSCO SHIPPING Energy Transportation Co., Ltd.	65
鲲顺	上海长石海运有限公司	KUN SHUN	Shanghai Changshi Shipping Co., Ltd.	84

L

中文名	公司中文	English Name	Company English	Page
兰春	万海航运股份有限公司	WAN HAI 283	Wan Hai Lines Ltd.	47
蓝鲸	中海油海洋石油工程股份有限公司	LAN JING	CNOOC Offshore Oil Engineering Co., Ltd.	400
蓝海201	中国水产科学研究院东海水产研究所	LAN HAI 201	East China Sea Fishery Research Institute, Chinese Academy of Fishery Sciences	375
蓝疆	海洋石油工程股份有限公司	LAN JIANG	Offshore Oil Engineering Co., Ltd.	409
蓝鲸	长江海外游轮旅游有限公司	BLUE WHALE	Changjiang Cruise Overseas Travel Co., Ltd.	268
蓝鲸1	中集来福士海洋工程有限公司	BLUE WHALE I	CIMC Raffles Offshore Ltd.	430
蓝龙号	大连蓝鲸游艇有限公司	LAN LONG HAO	Dalian Blue Whale Yacht Co., Ltd.	525
澜湄1号	西双版纳凤凰国际航运有限公司	LAN MEI 1 HAO	Xishuangbanna Phoenix International Shipping Co., Ltd.	318
乐从	中远海运特种运输股份有限公司	LE CONG	COSCO SHIPPING Specialized Carriers Co., Ltd.	89
乐辉88	云阳县乐辉船务有限公司	LE HUI 88	Yunyang Lehui Shipping Co., Ltd.	180
乐锦	中远海运特种运输股份有限公司	LE JIN	COSCO SHIPPING Specialized Carriers Co., Ltd.	89
乐亭05	乐亭县佳和捕捞有限公司	LAO TING 05	Laoting Jiahe Fishing Co., Ltd.	341
乐同	中远海运特种运输股份有限公司	LE TONG	COSCO SHIPPING Specialized Carriers Co., Ltd.	89
丽天68	江苏省对外经贸股份有限公司	LI TIAN 68	Jiangsu Provincial Foreign Trade Corporation	391
利海油29	广州市利海船舶防污工程有限公司	LI HAI YOU 29	Guangzhou Lihai Shipping Antifouling Engineering Co., Ltd.	453
利米特	海南圣帝诺游艇会有限公司	LI MI TE	Hainan Sundiro Yacht Club Co., Ltd.	525
连汇清8	大连汇通水域工程有限公司	LIAN HUI QING 8	Dalian Huitong Waterway Engineering Co., Ltd.	452
连松湖	中远海运能源运输股份有限公司	LIAN SONG HU	COSCO SHIPPING Energy Transportation Co., Ltd.	57
连油10	中国船舶燃料有限责任公司	LIAN YOU 10	China Marine Bunker (PetroChina) Co., Ltd.	61
连运湖	中远海运能源运输股份有限公司	LIAN YUN HU	COSCO SHIPPING Energy Transportation Co., Ltd.	53
良河	中国华粮物流集团新良海运有限公司	LIANG HE	CGLC Xinliang Shipping Co., Ltd.	86
辽大高渔25358	个人	LIAO DA GAO YU 25358	Individually owned	326
辽丹渔7716	东港市吉富渔业有限公司	LIAO DAN YU 7716	Donggang Jifu Fishery Co., Ltd.	359
辽东渔537	辽宁大平渔业集团有限公司	LIAO DONG YU 537	Liaoning Daping Fishery Group Co., Ltd.	332

辽水丰渔养05002	丹东英波鸭绿江生态科技股份有限公司	LIAO SHUI FENG YU YANG 05002	Dandong Yingbo Yalu River Ecology Technology Co., Ltd.	368
辽绥渔养35027	个人	LIAO SUI YU YANG 35027	Individually owned	367
辽长渔55112	长海县小长山岛镇吉隆水产养殖场	LIAO CHANG YU 55112	Changhai County Xiaochangshandao Town Jilong Aquatic Products Farm	350
辽长渔运18039	獐子岛集团股份有限公司	LIAO CHANG YU YUN 18039	Zhangzidao Group Co., Ltd.	372
辽庄渔65066	个人	LIAO ZHUANG YU 65066	Individually owned	344
辽庄渔85161	庄河市远大渔业捕捞有限公司	LIAO ZHUANG YU 85161	Zhuanghe Yuanda Fishing Co., Ltd.	336
林都号	嘉荫县船务有限责任公司	LIN DU HAO	Jiayin Shipping Co., Ltd.	284
林园	上海浦海航运有限公司	LIN YUAN	Shanghai Puhai Shipping Co., Ltd.	35
灵秀2号	泰宁县大金湖航运发展有限公司	LING XIU 2 HAO	Taining County Dajin Lake Shipping Development Co., Ltd.	291
流水坑渔家乐006	个人	LIU SHUI KENG YU JIA LE 006	Individually owned	376
"龙推312"船组	黑河港务局有限公司	LONG TUI 312 COMBINATION	Heihe Port Authority Co., Ltd.	310
"龙推317"船队	方正县沙河子港务局有限公司	LONG TUI 317 COMBINATION	Fangzheng Shahezi Port Authority Co., Ltd.	237
"龙推603"船队	同江龙航港务有限公司	LONG TUI 603 COMBINATION	Tongjiang Longhang Port Service Co., Ltd.	236
龙标111	黑龙江省航道局	LONG BIAO 111	Heilongjiang Provincial Waterway Bureau	513
龙测3005	黑龙江省航道局	LONG CE 3005	Heilongjiang Waterway Bureau	474
龙测3008	黑龙江省航道局	LONG CE 3008	Heilongjiang Waterway Bureau	474
龙川9	武汉海通船舶运输有限公司	LONG CHUAN 9	Wuhan Haitong Shipping Co., Ltd.	224
龙达8801	北海龙达渔业捕捞有限责任公司	LONG DA 8801	Beihai Longda Fishery & Fishing Co., Ltd.	334
龙渡004	同江龙航港务有限公司	LONG DU 004	Tongjiang Longhang Port Service Co., Ltd.	312
龙发	中国水产有限公司	LONG FA	China National Fisheries Corp.	331
龙工拖3701	黑龙江省航道局	LONG GONG TUO 3701	Heilongjiang Provincial Waterway Bureau	448
龙工拖8002	黑龙江省航道局	LONG GONG TUO 8002	Heilongjiang Waterway Bureau	242
龙海号	黑龙江省龙航大型设备江海运输有限公司	LONG HAI HAO	Heilongjiang Longhang Heavy Equipment and River-Sea Transport Co., Ltd.	399
龙救1501	黑龙江省航运救捞站	LONG JIU 1501	Heilongjiang Provincial Shipping Salvage Station	495
龙客108	黑河港务局有限公司	LONG KE 108	Heihe Port Authority Co., Ltd.	257
龙客201	黑河港务局有限公司	LONG KE 201	Heihe Port Authority Co., Ltd.	308
龙客203	黑河港务局有限公司	LONG KE 203	Heihe Port Authority Co.,Ltd.	290
龙客208	黑河港务局有限公司	LONG KE 208	Heihe Port Authority Co., Ltd.	258
龙捞驳601	黑龙江省航运救捞站	LONG LAO BO 601	Heilongjiang Shipping Salvage Station	244
龙腾20	黑龙江省三江外轮代理有限公司	LONG TENG 20	Heilongjiang Sanjiang Ocean Shipping Agency Co., Ltd.	321
龙腾星光	宜昌江腾游轮有限公司	LONG TENG XING GUANG	Yichang Jiangteng Cruise Co., Ltd.	270
龙推611	哈尔滨船务公司	LONG TUI 611	Harbin Shipping Co., Ltd.	240
龙消501	黑河港务局有限公司	LONG XIAO 501	Heihe Harbor Authority Co., Ltd.	452
龙源振华贰号	江苏龙源振华海洋工程有限公司	LONG YUAN ZHEN HUA ER HAO	Jiangsu Longyuan Zhenhua Marine Engineering Co., Ltd.	433
龙源振华叁号	江苏龙源振华海洋工程有限公司	LONG YUAN ZHEN HUA SAN HAO	Jiangsu Longyuan Zhenhua Marine Engineering Co., Ltd.	437
隆兴801	大连远洋渔业金枪鱼钓有限公司	LONG XING 801	Dalian Ocean Fishing Company Limited	356
鲁东渔60003	个人	LU DONG YU 60003	Individually owned	349
鲁海渔1482	个人	LU HAI YU 1482	Individually owned	329
鲁河	上海泛亚航运有限公司	LU HE	Shanghai PANASIA Shipping Co., Ltd.	36
鲁黄远渔118	青岛中泰远洋渔业有限公司	LU HUANG YUAN YU 118	Qingdao Zhongtai Deep Sea Fisheries Co., Ltd.	355
鲁岚渔65767	个人	LU LAN YU 65767	Individually owned	361
鲁牟渔养61539	烟台华民源水产养殖有限公司	LU MOU YU YANG 61539	Yantai Huaminyuan Aquatic Products Breeding Co., Ltd.	370
鲁蓬远渔017	民生金融租赁股份有限公司	LU PENG YUAN YU 017	Minsheng Financial Leasing Co., Ltd.	354
鲁青远渔026	青岛福瑞渔业有限公司	LU QING YUAN YU 026	Qingdao Furui Fisheries Co., Ltd.	354
鲁青远渔117	青岛永康顺远洋渔业有限公司	LU QING YUAN YU 117	Qingdao Yongkangshun Ocean Fishery Co., Ltd.	356
鲁青远渔209	青岛远洋渔业有限公司	LU QING YUAN YU 209	Qingdao Deep Sea Fisheries Co., Ltd.	333
鲁青远渔228	青岛浩洋远洋渔业有限公司	LU QING YUAN YU 228	Qingdao Haoyang Deep Sea Fisheries Co., Ltd.	338
鲁青远渔338	青岛红利昂渔业有限公司	LU QING YUAN YU 338	Qingdao Hongli'ang Fisheries Co., Ltd.	335
鲁荣渔58930	荣成市桥北渔业有限公司	LU RONG YU 58930	Rongcheng Qiaobei Fisheries Co., Ltd.	357
鲁荣渔69689	个人	LU RONG YU 69689	Individually owned	334

鲁荣远渔118	山东蓝越远洋渔业有限公司	LU RONG YUAN YU 118	Shandong Blue Ocean Fisheries Co., Ltd.	340
鲁荣远渔938	荣成市远洋渔业有限公司	LU RONG YUAN YU 938	Rongcheng Ocean Fisheries Co., Ltd.	357
鲁荣远渔989	荣成市荣远渔业有限公司	LU RONG YUAN YU 989	Rongcheng Rongyuan Fisheries Co., Ltd.	333
鲁乳渔64919	个人	LU RU YU 64919	Individually owned	337
鲁泰安货0089	泰安市兴龙航运有限公司	LU TAI AN HUO 0089	Taian Xinglong Shipping Co., Ltd.	175
鲁威高渔65007	个人	LU WEI GAO YU 65007	Individually owned	348
鲁威渔0137	个人	LU WEI YU 0137	Individually owned	329
鲁威远渔388	威海昌和渔业有限公司	LU WEI YUAN YU 388	Weihai Changhe Fishery Co., Ltd.	354
鲁文渔53797	个人	LU WEN YU 53797	Individually owned	335
鲁文渔67558	个人	LU WEN YU 67558	Individually owned	329
鲁烟开远渔977	烟台开发区渔港发展有限公司	LU YAN KAI YUAN YU 977	Yantai Development Zone Yugang Development Co., Ltd.	334
伦明	阳明海运股份有限公司	YM WELLNESS	Yang Ming Marine Transport Corporation	44
绿动6005	上海绿色动力水上运输公司	LV DONG 6005	Shanghai Green Power Water Transportation Company	181
绿动8008	上海绿色动力水上运输公司	LV DONG 8008	Shanghai Green Power Water Transportation Company	207

M

马当江洲渡2	马鞍山太平汽车轮渡有限责任公司	MA DANG JIANG ZHOU DU 2	Maanshan Taiping Automobile Ferry Co., Ltd.	311
孖洲交1	友联船厂（蛇口）有限公司	MA ZHOU JIAO 1	Yiu Lian Dockyards (Shekou) Limited	264
满江海	南京鹏飞智慧物流股份有限公司	MAN JIANG HAI	Nanjing Pan-Flying Intelligent Logistics Co., Ltd.	11
茂盛2	嵊泗县同舟客运轮船有限公司	MAO SHENG 2	Shengsi Tongzhou Passenger Shipping Co., Ltd.	160
美维凯娅	四川金石租赁股份有限公司	MVPRINCE	Sichuan Jinshi Leasing Co., Ltd.	268
美维凯珍	重庆市东江实业有限公司	MEI WEI KAI ZHEN	Chongqing Dongjiang Industry Co., Ltd.	271
蒙巴渔养23029	内蒙古乌梁素海水产养殖科技有限公司	MENG BA YU YANG 23029	Inner Mongolia Wuliangsuhai Aquatic Products Breeding Technology Co., Ltd.	369
蒙工010006	呼伦贝尔海事局	MENG GONG 010006	Hulun Buir Maritime Safety Administration	520
蒙工010029	呼伦贝尔呼伦湖生态环境保护与开发投资有限责任公司	MENG GONG 010029	Hulun Buir Hulun Lake Ecological Environment Protection & Development Investment Co., Ltd.	265
蒙游010026	额尔古纳宏凡旅游开发有限公司	MENG YOU 010026	Erguna Hongfan Tourism Development Co., Ltd.	275
梦想02	浙江千岛湖旅游股份有限公司	MENG XIANG 02	Zhejiang Qiandao Lake Tourism Co., Ltd.	293
民发	武汉经纬液化气船务有限公司	MIN FA	Wuhan Jingwei Liquefied Petroleum Gas Shipping Co., Ltd.	226
民福	民生轮船股份有限公司	MIN FU	Minsheng Shipping Co., Ltd.	232
民河	中远集装箱运输有限公司	MIN HE	COSCO Container Lines Co., Ltd.	33
民恒号	上海民生船舶有限公司	MIN HENG HAO	Shanghai Minsheng Shipping Co., Ltd.	233
民货853	民生轮船股份有限公司	MIN HUO 853	Minsheng Shipping Co., Ltd.	245
民觉	民生轮船股份有限公司	MIN JUE	Minsheng Shipping Co., Ltd.	203
民楷	民生轮船股份有限公司	MIN KAI	Minsheng Shipping Co., Ltd.	199
民快	民生轮船股份有限公司	MIN KUAI	Minsheng Shipping Co., Ltd.	234
民生	民生轮船股份有限公司	MIN SHENG	Minsheng Shipping Co., Ltd.	230
民苏	民生轮船股份有限公司	MIN SU	Minsheng Shipping Co., Ltd.	231
民宪	民生轮船股份有限公司	MIN XIAN	Minsheng Shipping Co., Ltd.	231
民治	民生轮船股份有限公司	MIN ZHI	Minsheng Shipping Co., Ltd.	197
闽东渔61226	个人	MIN DONG YU 61226	Individually owned	345
闽福鼎渔01918	个人	MIN FU DING YU 01918	Individually owned	358
闽福鼎渔02333	个人	MIN FU DING YU 02333	Individually owned	347
闽古渔养92004	个人	MIN GU YU YANG 92004	Individually owned	369
闽浚2	福州港航务工程处	MIN JUN 2	Fuzhou Harbor Engineering Department	382
闽闽渔61108	个人	MIN MIN YU 61108	Individually owned	344
闽南平货4599	南平市樟湖水路运输有限公司	MIN NAN PING HUO 4599	Nanping Zhanghu Waterway Transport Co., Ltd.	175
闽平渔运61658	个人	MIN PING YU YUN 61658	Individually owned	371
闽三明渡3005	永安市恒彬船舶运输有限公司	MIN SAN MING DU 3005	Yongan Hengbin Shipping Co., Ltd.	312
闽狮渔03989	个人	MIN SHI YU 03989	Individually owned	336
闽狮渔06868	个人	MIN SHI YU 06868	Individually owned	362
闽狮渔07607	个人	MIN SHI YU 07607	Individually owned	348
闽霞渔01110	个人	MIN XIA YU 01110	Individually owned	348
闽霞渔02287	个人	MIN XIA YU 02287	Individually owned	326

闽漳渔60256	个人	MIN ZHANG YU 60256	Individually owned	355
明锋	香港明华船务有限公司	PACIFIC PIONEER	Hong Kong Ming Wah Shipping Co., Ltd.	9
明祥	永修县航运有限公司	MING XIANG	Yongxiu Shipping Co., Ltd.	64
明兴	香港明华船务有限公司	PACIFIC PROSPECT	Hong Kong Ming Wah Shipping Co., Ltd.	10
明勇	香港明华船务有限公司	PACIFIC VALOR	Hong Kong Ming Wah Shipping Co., Ltd.	21
明远	香港明华船务有限公司	PACIFIC VISION	Hong Kong Ming Wah Shipping Co., Ltd.	28
明志	香港明华船务有限公司	PACIFIC WARRIOR	Hong Kong Ming Wah Shipping Co., Ltd.	26
铭珠湖	粤兴船舶用品有限公司	MING ZHU HU	Yuexing Shipping Products Co., Ltd.	164
木兰	黑龙江海运公司哈尔滨分公司	MU LAN	Heilongjiang Shipping Group Co., Ltd. Harbin Branch	247

N

NEW EMPEROR	钟云（香港）航运有限公司	NEW EMPEROR	Zhongyun (Hong Kong) Shipping Limited	15
南锋	中国水产科学研究院南海水产研究所	NAN FENG	South China Sea Fisheries Research Institute，Chinese Academy of Fishery Sciences	372
南港18	广州市南港船务有限公司	NAN GANG 18	Guangzhou Nangang Shipping Co., Ltd.	204
南海222	中海油田服务股份有限公司	NAN HAI 222	China Oilfield Services Limited	445
南海九号	中海油田服务股份有限公司	NAN HAI JIU HAO	China Oilfield Services Limited	423
南海救101	交通运输部南海救助局	NAN HAI JIU 101	Nanhai Rescue Bureau of the Ministry of Transport	492
南海救102	交通运输部南海救助局	NAN HAI JIU 102	Nanhai Rescue Bureau of the Ministry of Transport	495
南海救111	交通运输部南海救助局	NAN HAI JIU 111	Nanhai Rescue Bureau of the Ministry of Transport	491
南海救209	交通运输部南海救助局	NAN HAI JIU 209	Nanhai Rescue Bureau of the Ministry of Transport	490
南海救321	交通运输部南海救助局	NAN HAI JIU 321	Nanhai Rescue Bureau of the Ministry of Transport	495
南海神广州日报	广州广舶游船有限公司	NAN HAI SHEN GUANG ZHOU RI BAO	Guangzhou Guangbo Cruise Co., Ltd.	280
南海一号		NAN HAI YI HAO		521
南海之梦	三沙南海梦之旅邮轮有限公司	NAN HAI ZHI MENG	Sansha Nanhai Dream Cruises Co., Ltd.	147
南和油26	佛山市南海和油运输有限公司	NAN HE YOU 26	Foshan Nanhai Heyou Transportation Co., Ltd.	224
南宽501号	西双版纳州轮船公司	NAN KUAN 501 HAO	Xishuangbanna Shipping Company	173
南炼5	南京盛航海运股份有限公司	NAN LIAN 5	Nanjing Shenghang Shipping Co., Ltd.	72
南南燃油33	广东省佛山市禅城区陶兴船舶运输有限公司	NAN NAN RAN YOU 33	Guangdong Foshan Chancheng District Taoxing Shipping Co., Ltd.	216
南宁和顺078	广西和顺水运集团股份有限公司	NAN NING HE SHUN 078	Guangxi Heshun Shipping Group Co., Ltd.	210
南宁和顺238	广西和顺水运集团股份有限公司	NAN NING HE SHUN 238	Guangxi Heshun Shipping Group Co., Ltd.	210
南沙叁拾捌号	番禺南沙港客运有限公司	NANSHA NO.38	Panyu Nansha Port Passenger Transport Co., Ltd.	159
南天顺	交通运输部广州打捞局	NAN TIAN SHUN	Guangzhou Salvage Bureau, Ministry of Transport	115
南通	南通中远海运船务工程有限公司	NAN TONG	COSCO Nantong Shipyard Co., Ltd.	408
南星	香港信德集团下属远东水翼船务有限公司	NAN XING	Far East Hydrofoil Co., Ltd. under Shun Tak Holdings	166
南油国援1	南京长江油运公司	NAN YOU GUO YUAN 1	CSC Nanjing Tanker Corporation	449
南运油363	广东海雄油运有限公司	NAN YUN YOU 363	Guangdong Haixiong Tanker Corporation	217
宁安1	中海散货运输（上海）有限公司	NING AN 1	China Shipping Bulk Carrier (Shanghai) Co., Ltd.	8
宁波海力801	中交二航局第三工程有限公司	NING BO HAI LI 801	No.3 Engineering Co., Ltd. of CCCC Second Harbor Engineering Co., Ltd.	410
宁波海力802	中交二航局第一工程有限公司	NING BO HAI LI 802	First Construction Company of CCCC Second Harbor Engineering Co., Ltd.	407
宁道标001	长江南京航道局	NING DAO BIAO 001	Changjiang Nanjing Waterway Bureau	518
宁道标002	长江南京航道局	NING DAO BIAO 002	Changjiang Nanjing Waterway Bureau	519
宁道标402	长江南京航道局	NING DAO BIAO 402	Changjiang Nanjing Waterway Bureau	518
宁道测901	长江南京航道局	NING DAO CE 901	Changjiang Nanjing Waterway Bureau	479
宁化401	招商局南京油运股份有限公司	NING HUA 401	Nanjing Tanker Corporation	248
宁化403	南京长江油运公司	NING HUA 403	CSC Nanjing Tanker Corporation	212
宁化419	招商局南京油运股份有限公司	NING HUA 419	Nanjing Tanker Corporation	71
宁化501	江西东港航运有限公司	NING HUA 501	Jiangxi Donggang Shipping Co., Ltd.	219
宁化运2号	南京中港船业有限公司	NING HUA YUN 2 HAO	Nanjing Zhonggang Shipping Co., Ltd.	227
宁顺	招商局南京油运股份有限公司	NING SHUN	Nanjing Tanker Corporation	80
宁泰16	舟山宁泰远洋渔业有限公司	NING TAI 16	Zhoushan Ningtai Ocean Fisheries Co., Ltd.	353
牛山宿雁	湖南东江湖旅游水上客运有限责任公司	NIU SHAN SU YAN	Hunan Dongjiang Lake Aquatic Passenger Transportation Co., Ltd.	318

O

ORE TIANJIN	香港明华船务有限公司	ORE TIANJIN	Hong Kong Ming Wah Shipping Co., Ltd.	28

P

PACIFIC RIZHAO	太平洋气体船（香港）控股有限公司	PACIFIC RIZHAO	Pacific Gas (Hong Kong) Holdings Limited	84
鹏顺	招商局南京油运股份有限公司	PENG SHUN	Nanjing Tanker Corporation	82
平安源	中远海运能源运输股份有限公司	PING AN YUAN	COSCO SHIPPING Energy Transportation Co., Ltd.	82
平南永佳889	平南县永佳船务有限责任公司	PING NAN YONG JIA 889	Pingnan Yongjia Shipping Co., Ltd.	178
平太荣19	平太荣远洋渔业集团有限公司	PING TAI RONG NO.19	Pingtairong Ocean Fishery Group Co., Ltd.	352
铺沙1	中交广州航道局有限公司	PU SHA 1	CCCC Guangzhou Dredging Co., Ltd.	415
埔油10号	中国船舶燃料广州有限公司	PU YOU 10 HAO	China Marine Bunker Guangzhou Co., Ltd.	61
浦海211	上海浦海航运有限公司	PU HAI 211	Shanghai Puhai Shipping Co., Ltd.	205
浦海215	中国上海外轮代理有限公司	PU HAI 215	China Ocean Shipping Agency Shanghai Co., Ltd.	196
浦消1号	洋浦经济开发区管理委员会	PU XIAO 1 HAO	Yangpu Economic Development Zone Administrative Committee	459
普陀岛	中远海运客运有限公司	PU TUO DAO	COSCO SHIPPING Ferry Co., Ltd.	144
普陀山	舟山海星轮船有限公司	PU TUO SHAN	Zhoushan Haixing Steam Shipping Co., Ltd.	126
普远801	舟山市普陀远洋渔业有限公司	PU YUAN 801	Zhoushan Putuo Deep Sea Fishery Co., Ltd.	352

Q

启帆9	浙江启明海洋电力工程有限公司	QI FAN 9	Zhejiang Qiming Ocean Electric Power Engineering Co., Ltd.	419
启航舰旗	郑州市启航游船有限公司	QI HANG JIAN QI	Zhengzhou Qihang Cruise Co., Ltd.	321
起重29	中交第一航务工程局有限公司	QI ZHONG 29	CCCC First Harbor Engineering Co., Ltd.	401
乾峰826	重庆市乾峰船务有限公司	QIAN FENG 826	Chongqing Qianfeng Shipping Co., Ltd.	218
乾坤	中波轮船股份公司	QIAN KUN	Chinese-Polish Joint Stock Shipping Company	93
黔蕴号	贵州乌江水电开发有限责任公司东风发电厂	QIAN YUN HAO	Dongfeng Power Plant of Guizhou Wujiang Hydropower Development Co., Ltd.	263
强舟88	湖北强舟滚装船运输有限公司	QIANG ZHOU 88	Hubei Qiangzhou RO-RO Shipping Co., Ltd.	303
乔泰15号	重庆市乔泰船务运输有限公司	QIAO TAI 15 HAO	Chongqing Qiaotai Shipping and Transport Co., Ltd.	192
侨乡号	山东侨乡集团股份有限公司	QIAO XIANG HAO	Shandong Qiaoxiang Group Co., Ltd.	136
勤力331	江门市新会区勤力运输有限公司	QIN LI 331	Jiangmen Xinhui District Qinli Transportation Co., Ltd.	195
青海湖11	青海省青海湖旅游集团有限公司	QING HAI HU 11	Qinghai Province Qinghai Lake Tourism Group Co., Ltd.	285
青平2号	中交第一航务工程局有限公司	QING PING 2 HAO	CCCC First Harbor Engineering Co., Ltd.	410
清平山	中远海运散货运输有限公司	QING PING SHAN	COSCO SHIPPING Bulk Co., Ltd.	21
青油9	中国船舶燃料青岛有限公司	QING YOU 9	China Marine Bunker Qingdao Co., Ltd.	60
清江号	南京长江金和油运公司	QING JIANG HAO	Nanjing Changjiang Jinhe Tanker Co., Ltd.	222
清江画廊15号	湖北清江画廊旅游开发有限公司	QING JIANG HUA LANG SHI WU HAO	Hubei Qingjiang Gallery Tourism Development Co., Ltd.	290
晴川阁	武汉市轮渡公司	QING CHUAN GE	Wuhan Ferry Company	309
庆宜210	重庆重轮航运有限公司	QING YI 210	Chongqing Chonglun Shipping Co., Ltd.	301
琼儋渔19327	个人	QIONG DAN YU 19327	Individually owned	357
琼临渔12242	个人	QIONG LIN YU 12242	Individually owned	346
琼陵水12222	个人	QIONG LING SHUI 12222	Individually owned	359
琼沙3号	三沙市船务管理局	QIONG SHA 3 HAO	Sansha Shipping Management Bureau	128
琼引2号	海南港航拖轮有限公司	QIONG YIN NO.2	Hainan Harbor Tugboat Co., Ltd.	453
群明	阳明海运股份有限公司	YM WHOLESOME	Yang Ming Marine Transport Corporation	44

R

任达8号	云南同饮一江水国际旅游航运有限公司	REN DA 8 HAO	Yunnan Tongyinyijiangshui International Tourism Shipping Co., Ltd.	264
日立勇士	华光海运控股	HITACHI VENTURE	Wah Kwong Maritime Transport Holdings Ltd.	24
日月山	青海省青海湖旅游集团有限公司	RI YUE SHAN	Qinghai Province Qinghai Lake Tourism Group Co., Ltd.	298
日照东方	日照港（香港）船务有限公司	RI ZHAO ORIENT	Rizhao Port (Hong Kong) Shipping Co., Ltd.	150
荣安城	中远海运（厦门）有限公司	RONG AN CHENG	COSCO SHIPPING (Xiamen) Co., Ltd.	95
荣华湾	中远海运特种运输股份有限公司	RONG HUA WAN	COSCO SHIPPING Specialized Carriers Co., Ltd.	75
瑞春	岚桥万国有限公司	LANDBRIDGE GLORY	Lanqiao Wanguo Co., Ltd.	59
瑞利10号	中国船舶重工集团公司第七一五研究所	RUI LI 10 HAO	CSSC 715th Research Institute	467
瑞星	深圳市鹏星船务有限公司	RUI XING	Shenzhen Pengxing Shipping Co., Ltd.	161

润航8999	扬州润航船务有限公司	RUN HANG 8999	Yangzhou Runhang Shipping Co., Ltd.	181
润隆928	增城市顺运船务有限公司	RUN LONG 928	Zengcheng Shunyun Shipping Co., Ltd.	194
润通油8	佛山市南海西樵润通达船舶运输有限公司	RUN TONG YOU 8	Foshan Nanhai Xiqiao Runtongda Shipping Co., Ltd.	215
润通518	阜南县润通航运有限公司	RUN TONG 518	Funan County Runtong Shipping Co., Ltd.	180
润泽驳1004	徐州市润泽航运有限公司	RUN ZE BO 1004	Xuzhou Runze Shipping Co., Ltd.	246

S

SEIYO GODDESS	大连新凯船舶管理有限公司	SEIYO GODDESS	Dalian Seacarrier Co., Ltd.	92
三港6号	宜昌三港船务有限公司	SAN GANG 6 HAO	Yichang Sangang Shipping Co., Ltd.	179
三国	宜昌江腾游轮有限公司	SAN GUO	Yichang Jiangteng Cruise Co., Ltd.	269
三航风范	中交第三航务工程局有限公司	SAN HANG FENG FAN	CCCC Third Harbor Engineering Co., Ltd.	400
三航风和	中交第三航务工程局有限公司	SAN HANG FENG HE	CCCC Third Harbor Engineering Co., Ltd.	437
三航风华	中交第三航务工程局有限公司	SAN HANG FENG HUA	CCCC Third Harbor Engineering Co., Ltd.	434
三航砂2	中交第三航务工程局有限公司	SAN HANG SHA 2	CCCC Third Harbor Engineering Co., Ltd.	406
三航砼15	中交三航局第二工程有限公司	SAN HANG TONG 15	No.2 Engineering Co., Ltd. of CCCC Third Harbor Engineering Co., Ltd.	407
三航砼21	中交第三航务工程局有限公司	SAN HANG TONG 21	CCCC Third Harbor Engineering Co., Ltd.	412
三航拖3002	中交第三航务工程局有限公司	SAN HANG TUO 3002	CCCC Third Harbor Engineering Co., Ltd.	445
三航桩20	中交第三航务工程局有限公司	SAN HANG ZHUANG 20	CCCC Third Harbor Engineering Co., Ltd.	420
三沙气垫船01	三沙市船务管理局	SAN SHA QI DIAN CHUAN 01	Sansha Shipping Management Bureau	167
三通5003	宜昌三通航运有限公司	SAN TONG 5003	Yichang Santong Shipping Co., Ltd.	223
三通801	宜昌三通航运有限公司	SAN TONG 801	Yichang Santong Shipping Co., Ltd.	221
三峡浮吊1号	长江三峡通航管理局	SAN XIA FU DIAO 1 HAO	Three Gorges Navigation Authority	457
三峡清漂1	中国长江三峡工程开发总公司	SAN XIA QING PIAO 1	China Three Gorges Corporation	454
砂桩3号	中交一航局第一工程有限公司	SHA ZHUANG 3 HAO	No.1 Engineering Co., Ltd. of CCCC First Harbor Engineering Co., Ltd.	408
山东德祥	山东海运股份有限公司	SHANDONG DE XIANG	Shandong Shipping Corporation	23
山东鹏程	山东海运（香港）有限公司	SHANDONG PENG CHENG	Shandong Shipping (Hong Kong) Co., Ltd.	20
山东政通	山东海运股份有限公司	SHANDONG ZHENG TONG	Shandong Shipping Corporation	27
上海号	上海港引航站	SHANG HAI HAO	Shanghai Maritime Pilots' Association, China	260
上海轮渡3	上海市轮渡有限公司	SHANG HAI LUN DU 3	Shanghai Ferry Co., Ltd.	309
上汽安吉凤凰	安吉航运（香港）有限公司	SAIC ANJI PHOENIX	Anji Shipping (Hong Kong) Co., Ltd.	101
尚德国盛	上海盛融国际游船有限公司	SHANG DE GUO SHENG	Shanghai Shengrong International Cruise Co., Ltd.	283
尚航99	平潭尚航船务有限公司	SHANG HANG 99	Pingtan Shanghang Shipping Co., Ltd.	91
深港游轮1	深圳东航游轮有限公司	SHEN GANG YOU LUN 1	Shenzhen Donghang Cruise Co., Ltd.	130
深海01	中华人民共和国深圳海事局	SHEN HAI 01	Shenzhen Maritime Safety Adminitration of P.R.China	521
深海一号	中国大洋矿产资源研究开发协会	SHEN HAI YI HAO	China Ocean Mineral Resources R&D Association	471
深海勇士	中国科学院深海科学与工程研究所	SHEN HAI YONG SHI	Institute of Deep-Sea Science and Engineering, Chinese Academy of Sciences	481
深蓝	江苏深蓝远洋渔业有限公司	SHEN LAN	Jiangsu Sunline Deep Sea Fisheries Co., Ltd.	339
深潜号	交通运输部上海打捞局	SHEN QIAN HAO	Shanghai Salvage Bureau, Ministry of Transport	465
神华浚1	神华上航疏浚有限责任公司	SHEN HUA JUN 1	Shenhua & CHEC Dredging Co., Ltd.	385
神龙999	云阳县神龙客货运输有限公司	SHEN LONG 999	Yunyang Shenlong Passenger & Cargo Transportation Co., Ltd.	263
神农溪1号	巴东神农溪旅游发展有限公司	SHEN NONG XI 1 HAO	Badong Shennong Stream Tourism Development Co., Ltd.	278
神游	连云港连岛海上游艇俱乐部	SHEN YOU	Lianyungang Liandao Maritime Yacht Club	135
神州3501	重庆新金航国际物流股份有限公司	SHEN ZHOU 3501	Chongqing New Jinhang International Logistics Co., Ltd.	222
神州号	长江轮船海外旅游总公司	SHEN ZHOU HAO	Changjiang Cruise Overseas Travel Company	268
沈括	上海彩虹鱼科考船科技服务有限公司	SHEN KUO	Shanghai Rainbowfish Reseachship Co., Ltd.	470
"生峡"船队	民生轮船股份有限公司	SHENG XIA COMBINATION	Minsheng Shipping Co., Ltd.	239
生生1	威海市海大客运有限公司	SHENG SHENG 1	Weihai Haida Passenger Transport Co., Ltd.	144
生生2	威海市海大客运有限公司	SHENG SHENG 2	Weihai Haida Passenger Transport Co., Ltd.	148
生态岛2	上海市客运轮船有限公司	SHENG TAI DAO 2	Shanghai Passenger Ship Co., Ltd.	314
生振	民生轮船公司	SHENG ZHEN	Minsheng Shipping Company	240
昇航027	佛山市南海昇航船务有限公司	SHENG HANG 027	Foshan Nanhai Shenghang Shipping Co., Ltd.	191

中文名	公司（中文）	英文名	公司（英文）	页码
圣世	深圳市海昌华海运股份有限公司	SHENG SHI	Shenzhen Haifa Shipping Co., Ltd.	60
胜海9	胜利油田龙玺石油工程服务有限责任公司	SHENG HAI 9	Shengli Oilfield Longxi Petroleum Engineering Service Co., Ltd.	445
胜利221	胜利油田浅海钻井工程公司	SHENG LI 221	Shengli Oilfield Offshore Drilling Co.	440
胜利617	中国石油化工股份有限公司	SHENG LI 617	China Petroleum & Chemical Corporation	453
胜利二号	中石化胜利石油工程有限公司	SHENG LI NO. 2	SINOPEC Shengli Petroleum Engineering Co., Ltd.	423
胜利十号	中石化胜利石油工程有限公司	SHENG LI NO. 10	SINOPEC Shengli Petroleum Engineering Co., Ltd.	427
盛发海	海南海盛航运有限公司	SHENG FA HAI	Hainan Haisheng Shipping Co., Ltd.	16
盛飞601	南京盛飞油运有限公司	SHENG FEI 601	Nanjing Shengfei Oil Transportation Co., Ltd.	65
盛源8号	合肥盛源船务有限公司	SHENG YUAN 8 HAO	Hefei Shengyuan Shipping Co., Ltd.	210
盛中2	嵊泗县盛利航道工程有限公司	SHENG ZHONG 2	Shengsi Shengli Watery Engineering Co., Ltd.	519
嵊翔9	嵊泗县同舟客运轮船有限公司	SHENG XIANG 9	Shengsi Tongzhou Passenger Shipping Co., Ltd.	130
石宝1002	重庆市忠县石宝航运有限公司	SHI BAO 1002	Chongqing Zhongxian Shibao Shipping Co., Ltd.	177
石宝997	重庆市忠县石宝航运有限公司	SHI BAO 997	Chongqing Zhongxian Shibao Shipping Co., Ltd.	202
石南6	莆田市秀屿区石南轮渡有限公司	SHI NAN 6	Putian Xiuyu Shinan Ferry Co., Ltd.	132
石油601	广东民生油轮运输有限公司	SHI YOU 601	Guangdong Minsheng Tanker Transportation Co., Ltd.	213
时代海岸鸿洲1	三亚鸿洲国际游艇会有限公司	SHI DAI HAI AN HONG ZHOU 1	Sanya Visun Royal Yacht Club Co., Ltd.	523
视明	阳明海运股份有限公司	YM WITNESS	Yang Ming Marine Transport Corporation	44
实验1	中国科学院南海海洋研究所	SHI YAN 1	South China Sea Institute of Oceanology, Chinese Academy of Sciences	464
实验6	中国科学院南海海洋研究所	SHI YAN 6	South China Sea Institute of Oceanology, Chinese Academy of Sciences	473
世博志愿者号	上海市轮渡有限公司	SHI BO ZHI YUAN ZHE HAO	Shanghai Ferry Co., Ltd.	308
世纪荣耀	重庆冠达世纪游轮有限公司	SHI JI RONG YAO	Chong Qing Grand Century Cruises Co., Ltd.	273
世纪神话	重庆冠达世纪游轮有限公司	SHI JI SHEN HUA	Chong Qing Grand Century Cruises Co., Ltd.	272
世纪天子	重庆冠达世纪游轮有限公司	SHI JI TIAN ZI	Chong Qing Grand Century Cruises Co., Ltd.	270
世江	中甫（上海）航运有限公司	SHI JIANG	Kingfour Marine Co., Ltd.	103
双泰16	广东徐闻海峡航运有限公司	SHUANG TAI 16	Guangdong Xuwen Strait Shipping Co., Ltd.	148
双泰37	广东徐闻海峡航运有限公司	SHUANG TAI 37	Guangdong Xuwen Strait Shipping Co., Ltd.	152
水警南沙	广州市公安局	SHUI JING NAN SHA	Guangzhou Municipal Public Security Bureau	511
水警羊城	广州市公安局	SHUI JING YANG CHENG	Guangzhou Municipal Public Security Bureau	511
水平7	连云港张徐船务工程有限公司	SHUI PING 7	Lianyungang Zhangxu Marine Engineering Co., Ltd.	30
水瓶座	海南中化船务有限公司	SC AQUARIUS	Hainan Sinochem Shipping Co., Ltd.	72
水上环卫03	广州市城市管理委员会	SHUI SHANG HUAN WEI 03	Guangzhou Municipal Administration Committee	456
睡美人6号	昆明迤海水上客运有限公司	SHUI MEI REN 6 HAO	Kunming Yihai Aquatic Passenger Transportation Co., Ltd.	298
顺行268	广州顺行船务有限公司	SHUN XING 268	Guangzhou Shunxing Shipping Co., Ltd.	188
顺宏海83	佛山市顺德区宏海货运有限公司	SHUN HONG HAI 83	Foshan Shunde Honghai Freight Co., Ltd.	190
顺通集001	绍兴市柯桥区顺通航运有限公司	SHUN TONG JI 001	Shaoxing Keqiao District Shuntong Shipping Co., Ltd.	209
顺一1600	正力海洋工程有限公司	SHUN YI 1600	Zhengli Ocean Engineering Co., Ltd.	436
顺逸01	厦门市通顺海上运输有限公司	SHUN YI 01	Xiamen Tongshun Marine Transportation Co., Ltd.	162
顺源108	海南盛和运贸发展有限公司	SHUN YUAN 108	Hainan Shenghe Transportation and Trade Development Co., Ltd.	80
顺德	粤兴船舶用品有限公司	SHUN DE	Yuexing Shipping Products Co., Ltd.	157
淞航	上海海洋大学	SONG HANG	Shanghai Ocean University	374
苏大渔养08996	盐城瑞源水产品有限公司	SU DA YU YANG 08996	Yancheng Ruiyuan Aquatic Products Co., Ltd.	369
苏阜渔运32002	个人	SU FU YU YUN 32002	Individually owned	375
苏赣渔03369	个人	SU GAN YU 03369	Individually owned	346
苏启渔03109	个人	SU QI YU 03109	Individually owned	360
苏启渔03444	启东甬兴渔业有限公司	SU QI YU 03444	Qidong Yongxing Fisheries Co., Ltd.	361
苏如渔养08376	个人	SU RU YU YANG 08376	Individually owned	368
苏瑞139	大连苏瑞船务有限公司	SU RUI 139	Dalian Surui Shipping Co., Ltd.	80
苏瑞169	大连苏瑞船务有限公司	SU RUI 169	Dalian Surui Shipping Co., Ltd.	81
苏鑫海1	江苏鑫海运输有限公司	SU XIN HAI 1	Jiangsu Xinhai Transportation Co., Ltd.	225
苏州号	中远海运集装箱运输有限公司	SU ZHOU HAO	COSCO SHIPPING Lines Co., Ltd.	140

中文名	中文公司	英文名	英文公司	页码
穗港4001	广州港船务有限公司	SUI GANG 4001	Guangzhou Port Shipping Co., Ltd.	205
穗港渡车2	广州港股份有限公司	SUI GANG DU CHE 2	Guangzhou Port Co., Ltd.	311
穗港渡车6	广州港股份有限公司	SUI GANG DU CHE 6	Guangzhou Port Co., Ltd.	313
穗联和318	广州联和物流有限公司	SUI LIAN HE 318	Guangzhou Lianhe Logistics Co., Ltd.	187
穗水巴08	广州公交集团客轮有限公司	SUI SHUI BA 08	Guangzhou Public Transport Group Liner Co., Ltd.	285

T

中文名	中文公司	英文名	英文公司	页码
THE PLAZA	Venetian Marketing Services Ltd.	THE PLAZA	Venetian Marketing Services Ltd.	161
台沙2138（顺景）	个人	TAI SHA 2138 (SHUN JING)	Individually owned	342
太和号	北京市颐和园管理处	TAI HE HAO	Administration Office of Beijing Summer Palace	274
太阳	中波轮船股份公司	CHIPOLBROK SUN	Chinese-Polish Joint Stock Shipping Company	90
太阳岛	哈尔滨市太阳岛风景区水上观光客运有限公司	TAI YANG DAO	Harbin Taiyangdao Scenic Spot Aquatic Sightseeing Passenger Transportation Co., Ltd.	286
泰安口	中远海运特种运输股份有限公司	TAI AN KOU	COSCO SHIPPING Specialized Carriers Co., Ltd.	107
泰华航368	惠州市泰华航运有限公司	TAI HUA HANG 368	Huizhou Taihua Shipping Co., Ltd.	192
泰隆1	山东省中鲁远洋渔业股份有限公司	TAI LONG 1	Shandong Zhonglu Oceanic Fisheries Co., Ltd.	340
坦机119	中山市船务货运有限公司	TAN JI 119	Zhongshan City Shipping & Freight Co., Ltd.	174
坦机16	中山市船务货运有限公司	TAN JI 16	Zhongshan City Shipping & Freight Co., Ltd.	173
探索二号	中国科学院深海科学与工程研究所	TAN SUO ER HAO	Institute of Deep-Sea Science and Engineering, Chinese Academy of Sciences	473
探索一号	中国科学院声学研究所南海研究站	TAN SUO YI HAO	Hainan Acoustics Laboratory, Institute of Acoustics, Chinese Academy of Sciences	468
唐绞2008	唐山曹妃甸疏浚有限公司	TANG JIAO 2008	Tangshan Caofeidian Dredging Co., Ltd.	386
桃花山	锂川航运有限公司	PEACH MOUNTAIN	Li Chuan Shipping S.A.	12
桃林湾	中远海运能源运输股份有限公司	TAO LIN WAN	COSCO SHIPPING Energy Transportation Co., Ltd.	57
特步	广州蓝海豚游船有限公司	TE BU	Guangzhou Blue Dolphin Cruise Co., Ltd.	274
腾龙1号	武汉腾龙油品运输有限责任公司	TENG LONG 1 HAO	Wuhan Tenglong Oil Transportation Co., Ltd.	222
滕王阁号	南昌滕王阁游轮客运有限公司	TENG WANG GE HAO	Nanchang Tengwangge Cruise Co., Ltd.	289
天成2号	阳江市海陵岛天成游船有限公司	TIAN CHENG 2 HAO	Yangjiang City Hailing Island Tiancheng Sight-Seeing Boat Co., Ltd.	131
天鹅	中海客轮有限公司	TIAN E	China Shipping Passenger Liner Co., Ltd.	139
天恩1001	湖北天恩石化气船有限公司	TIAN EN 1001	Hubei Tianen Petroleum Gas Shipping Co., Ltd.	226
天恩102	湖北天恩石化气船有限公司	TIAN EN 102	Hubei Tianen Petroleum Gas Shipping Co., Ltd.	245
天福	中远海运特种运输股份有限公司	TIAN FU	COSCO SHIPPING Specialized Carriers Co., Ltd.	95
天海1号	黄石天海航运有限公司	TIAN HAI 1 HAO	Huangshi Tianhai Shipping Co., Ltd.	200
天鲸号	中交天津航道局有限公司	TIAN JING HAO	CCCC Tianjin Dredging Co., Ltd.	390
天鲲号	中交建融租赁有限公司	TIAN KUN HAO	CCCC Financial Leasing Co., Ltd.	395
天力288	清远市天力运输有限公司	TIAN LI 288	Qingyuan Tianli Transportation Co., Ltd.	190
天丽海	中远散货运输有限公司	TIAN LI HAI	COSCO Bulk Carrier Co., Ltd.	13
天龙轮	湖北皇家长江旅游船有限公司	TIAN LONG LUN	Hubei Royal Yangtze River Cruise Co., Ltd.	259
天龙星	中远海运散货运输有限公司	TIAN LONG XING	COSCO SHIPPING Bulk Co., Ltd.	12
天隆河	中远海运集装箱运输有限公司	TIAN LONG HE	COSCO SHIPPING Lines Co., Ltd.	41
天门山	重庆重轮航运有限公司	TIAN MEN SHAN	Chongqing Chonglun Shipping Co., Ltd.	302
天鹏	中海客轮有限公司	TIAN PENG	China Shipping Passenger Liner Co., Ltd.	140
天铺1号	中交天航港湾建设工程有限公司	TIAN PU 1 HAO	CCCC Tianhang Harbour Engineering Co., Ltd.	411
天麒号	中交天津航道局有限公司	TIAN QI HAO	CCCC Tianjin Dredging Co., Ltd.	388
天盛15	宁波天盛海运有限公司	TIAN SHENG 15	Ningbo Tiansheng Shipping Co., Ltd.	9
天狮	中交烟台环保疏浚有限公司	TIAN SHI	CCCC Yantai Environmental Protection Dredging Co, Ltd.	386
天寿	中远海运特种运输股份有限公司	TIAN SHOU	COSCO SHIPPING Specialized Carriers Co., Ltd.	95
天顺海1	台州天顺海运有限公司	TIAN SHUN HAI 1	Taizhou Tianshun Maritime Transportation Co., Ltd.	70
天砼	中交一航局第一工程有限公司	TIAN TONG	No.1 Engineering Co., Ltd. of CCCC First Harbor Engineering Co., Ltd.	406
天统28	宁波天统航运有限公司	TIAN TONG 28	Ningbo Tiantong Shipping Co., Ltd.	184
天威	中交一航局第一工程有限公司	TIAN WEI	No.1 Engineering Co., Ltd. of CCCC First Harbor Engineering Co., Ltd.	398
天璇星	黄色北极液化天然气运输有限公司	LNG MERAK	Arctic Yellow LNG Shipping Limited	79
铁建风电01	中铁建金融租赁有限公司	TIE JIAN FENG DIAN 01	CRCC Financial Leasing Co., Ltd.	437

中文名	中文公司	英文名	英文公司	页码
铁建潜01	中国铁建港航局集团有限公司	TIE JIAN QIAN 01	CRCC Harbour & Channel Engineering Bureau Group Co., Ltd.	119
通程	中交天津航道局有限公司	TONG CHENG	CCCC Tianjin Dredging Co., Ltd.	389
通力	中交天津航道局有限公司	TONG LI	CCCC Tianjin Dredging Co., Ltd.	383
通途	中交天津航道局有限公司	TONG TU	CCCC Tianjin Dredging Co., Ltd.	390
同心源	深圳中远龙鹏液化气运输有限公司	TONG XIN YUAN	Shenzhen COSCO LPG Shipping Co., Ltd.	82
铜庆3	台山市铜庆废旧物资回收有限公司	TONG QING 3	Taishan Tongqing Waste Materials Recovery Co., Ltd.	213

W

中文名	中文公司	英文名	英文公司	页码
WEALTHY BAY	香港诺斯威国际船舶运输有限公司	WEALTHY BAY	Hong Kong North Wind International Shipping Company Limited	69
皖工桩7	安徽芜湖市源丰港航工程有限公司	WAN GONG ZHUANG 7	Anhui Wuhu Yuanfeng Port and Waterway Engineering Co., Ltd.	416
皖明渔80536	个人	WAN MING YU 80536	Individually owned	363
皖神舟89	蚌埠市神舟机械有限公司	WAN SHEN ZHOU 89	Bengbu Shenzhou Machinery Co., Ltd.	134
皖天渔80646	个人	WAN TIAN YU 80646	Individually owned	364
皖通达588	安徽海拓船务有限责任公司	WAN TONG DA 588	Anhui Haituo Shipping Co., Ltd.	219
皖宣渔80622	个人	WAN XUAN YU 80622	Individually owned	364
皖宣渔82071	个人	WAN XUAN YU 82071	Individually owned	364
万达3号	三亚万达大酒店有限公司	WAN DA 3 HAO	Sanya Wanda Hotel Co., Ltd.	524
万港820	重庆市澜腾运输有限公司	WAN GANG 820	Chongqing Lanteng Transport Co., Ltd.	178
万港拖818	重庆市万州区万港船务有限公司	WAN GANG TUO 818	Chongqing Wanzhou Wangang Shipping Co. Ltd.	242
万里阳光	勐腊县关累港万里阳光水路运输经营户	WAN LI YANG GUANG	Mengla Guanlei Port Wanliyangguang Waterway Transportation Operator	182
万寿舫	北京市颐和园管理处	WAN SHOU FANG	Administration Office of Beijing Summer Palace	296
万祥799	芜湖市万峰航运有限公司	WAN XIANG 799	Wuhu Wanfeng Shipping Co., Ltd.	31
旺顺65	安徽旺顺航运有限公司	WANG SHUN 65	Anhui Wangshun Shipping Co., Ltd.	184
威力	交通运输部上海打捞局	WEI LI	Shanghai Salvage Bureau, Ministry of Transport	400
威游108	威海市旅游码头有限责任公司	WEI YOU 108	Weihai Tourism Terminal Co., Ltd.	132
维多利亚1号	长江轮船海外旅游总公司	WEI DUO LI YA 1 HAO	Changjiang Cruise Overseas Travel Company	267
维多利亚7号	长江海外游轮旅游有限公司	WEI DUO LI YA 7 HAO	Changjiang Cruise Overseas Travel Co., Ltd.	269
潍河	上海远洋运输有限公司	WEI HE	Shanghai Ocean Shipping Co., Ltd.	33
潍营	山东潍营渤海重滚船务有限公司	WEI YING	Shandong Weiying Bohai Heavy RO-RO Shipping Co., Ltd.	98
乌江画廊1	重庆旅投乌江山峡旅游有限公司	WU JIANG HUA LANG 1	Wujiang River Shanxia Travel Co., Ltd. of Chongqing Tourism Investment Group	277
梧州三水司188	梧州市第三水运公司	WU ZHOU SAN SHUI SI 188	Wuzhou 3rd Water Transportation Company	189
五指山	海南海峡航运股份有限公司	WU ZHI SHAN	Hainan Strait Shipping Co., Ltd.	149
武汉东湖号	武汉旅联东湖游船有限公司	WU HAN DONG HU HAO	Wuhan Lvlian Donghu Cruise Co., Ltd.	295
武汉知音号	武汉旅联东湖股份有限公司	WU HAN ZHI YIN HAO	Wuhan Lvlian East Lake Co., Ltd.	294

X

中文名	中文公司	英文名	英文公司	页码
西宝313	珠海西宝物流有限公司	XI BAO 313	Zhuhai Xibao Logistics Co., Ltd.	188
西岛088	三亚西岛大洲旅业有限公司	XI DAO 088	Sanya Xidao Dazhou Tourism Co., Ltd.	165
西岛288	三亚西岛大洲旅业有限公司	XI DAO 288	Sanya Xidao Dazhou Tourism Co., Ltd.	165
西海游0168	九江庐山西海云海轮船有限公司	XI HAI YOU 0168	Jiujiang Lushan Xihai Yunhai Ship Co., Ltd.	293
吸盘1号	长江宜昌航道工程局	XI PAN 1 HAO	Changjiang Yichang Waterway Engineering Bureau	383
吸扬12号	长江武汉航道工程局	XI YANG SHI ER HAO	Changjiang Wuhan Waterway Engineering Bureau	384
吸扬15号	长江南京航道工程局	XI YANG SHI WU HAO	Changjiang Nanjing Waterway Engineering Bureau	385
希望之路	中交国际航运有限公司	WISH WAY	CCCC International Shipping Corp.	108
先行607	广东省珠江货运有限公司	XIAN XING 607	Guangdong Zhujiang Freight Co., Ltd.	241
湘常德客贰号	常德市轮发水上客运有限责任公司	XIANG CHANG DE KE ER HAO	Changde Lunfa Water Passenger Transportation Co., Ltd.	260
湘汉寿货1918	常德文德船务有限公司	XIANG HAN SHOU HUO 1918	Changde Wende Shipping Co., Ltd.	191
湘君	岳阳长鹰运输有限责任公司	XIANG JUN	Yueyang Changying Transportation Co., Ltd.	213
湘水运26	湖南远洋集装箱运输有限公司	XIANG SHUI YUN 26	Hunan Ocean Container Lines Co., Ltd.	253
湘岳阳渔00026	个人	XIANG YUE YANG YU 00026	Individually owned	363

中文名	公司中文	English Name	Company	Page
湘岳阳渔00031	个人	XIANG YUE YANG YU 00031	Individually owned	363
祥瑞	泰昌祥轮船（香港）有限公司	CSK FORTUNE	Tai Chong Cheang Steamship Co. (H.K.) Limited	7
祥云口	中远海运特种运输股份有限公司	XIANG YUN KOU	COSCO SHIPPING Specialized Carriers Co., Ltd.	108
翔富1	深圳市兴航物流发展有限公司	XIANG FU 1	Shenzhen Hopehill Logistics Development Co., Ltd.	201
翔宇98	江苏江淮通集装箱航运有限公司	XIANG YU 98	Jiangsu Jianghuaitong Container Shipping Co., Ltd.	206
翔州1	中船重工（海南）飞船发展有限公司	XIANG ZHOU 1	CSIC (Hainan) WIG Craft Development Co., Ltd.	167
向丹	上海浦海航运有限公司	XIANG DAN	Shanghai Puhai Shipping Co., Ltd.	33
向菊	中海集装箱运输股份有限公司	XIANG JU	China Shipping Container Lines Co., Ltd.	34
向浦	中海集装箱运输股份有限公司	XIANG PU	China Shipping Container Lines Co., Ltd.	33
向阳红03	自然资源部第三海洋研究所	XIANG YANG HONG 03	Third Institute of Oceanography, Ministry of Natural Resources	469
向阳红22	自然资源部东海局	XIANG YANG HONG 22	East China Sea Bureau of Ministry of Natural Resources	481
肖邦	中波轮船股份公司	CHOPIN	Chinese-Polish Joint Stock Shipping Company	86
小三峡6	巫山县小三峡旅游船有限责任（集团）公司	XIAO SAN XIA 6	Wushan Lesser Three Gorges Tourist Ship (Group) Co., Ltd.	278
新安7号	黄山市新安江游船服务有限公司	XIN AN 7 HAO	Huangshan Xin'an River Cruise Service Co., Ltd.	294
新大中	中远海运特种运输股份有限公司	XIN DA ZHONG	COSCO SHIPPING Specialized Carriers Co., Ltd.	88
新高湖	宜昌新高湖滚装客船有限公司	XIN GAO HU	Yichang Xingaohu Ro-Ro Passenger Ship Co., Ltd.	303
新谷301	广州粤港澳国际航运有限公司	XIN GU 301	Guangzhou Yuegangao International Shipping Co., Ltd.	202
新光华	中远海运特种运输股份有限公司	XIN GUANG HUA	COSCO SHIPPING Specialized Carriers Co., Ltd.	111
新海蚌	中交上海航道局有限公司	XIN HAI BENG	CCCC Shanghai Dredging Co., Ltd.	388
新海凤	中港疏浚有限公司	XIN HAI FENG	CHEC Dredging Co., Ltd.	387
新海虎	中港疏浚有限公司	XIN HAI HU	CHEC Dredging Co., Ltd.	386
新海辽	海宏轮船（香港）有限公司	NEW VISION	Associated Maritime Company (Hong Kong) Limited	59
新海天	珠海九洲蓝色干线投资控股有限公司	XIN HAI TIAN	Zhuhai Jiuzhou Blue Seajet Investment Holdings Co., Ltd.	165
新海豚	中交上海航道局有限公司	XIN HAI TUN	CCCC Shanghai Dredging Co., Ltd.	389
新海威	粤兴船舶用品有限公司	XIN HAI WEI	Yuexing Shipping Products Co., Ltd.	163
新鸿基8868	广西贵港市新鸿基船务有限责任公司	XIN HONG JI 8868	Guangxi Guigang Xinhongji Shipping Co., Ltd.	209
新鉴真	中远海运集装箱运输有限公司	XIN JIAN ZHEN	COSCO SHIPPING Lines Co., Ltd.	141
新金桥II	威海威东航运有限公司	NEW GOLDEN BRIDGE II	Weidong Ferry Co., Ltd.	125
新金洋	中远海运能源运输股份有限公司	XIN JIN YANG	COSCO SHIPPING Energy Transportation Co., Ltd.	52
新锦源	锦州锦润海运有限公司	XIN JIN YUAN	Jinzhou Jinrun Shipping Co., Ltd.	86
新浏	江苏省南通市轮船运输公司	XIN LIU	Jiangsu Nantong Shipping Co., Ltd.	258
新洛杉矶	中远海运集装箱运输有限公司	XIN LOS ANGELES	COSCO SHIPPING Lines Co., Ltd.	39
新平江1013	南京长江油运公司	XIN PING JIANG 1013	CSC Nanjing Tanker Corporation	216
新平江3003	南京长江油运公司	XIN PING JIANG 3003	CSC Nanjing Tanker Corporation	220
新浦东	中远海运集装箱运输有限公司	XIN PU DONG	COSCO SHIPPING Lines Co., Ltd.	38
新润18	浙江新润海运有限公司	XIN RUN 18	Zhejiang Xinrun Shipping Co., Ltd.	64
新三峡号	重庆市水利局机关后勤服务中心	XIN SAN XIA HAO	Logistics Service Center of Chongqing Water Conservancy Bureau	265
新盛海	中远散货运输有限公司	XIN SHENG HAI	COSCO Bulk Carrier Co., Ltd.	7
新胜利一号	中石化胜利石油工程有限公司	XIN SHENG LI YI HAO	SINOPEC Shengli Petroleum Engineering Co., Ltd.	428
新世纪112	浙江大洋世家股份有限公司	XIN SHI JI 112	Zhejiang Ocean Family Co., Ltd.	341
新世纪128	中远海运散货运输有限公司	XIN SHI JI 128	COSCO SHIPPING Bulk Co., Ltd.	16
新世纪三十七号	浙江大洋世家股份有限公司	XIN SHI JI NO.37	Zhejiang Ocean Family Co., Ltd.	350
新世纪一号	中海油田服务股份有限公司	XIN SHI JI NO.1	China Oilfield Services Limited	138
新泰渔养23151	新疆阿尔泰冰川鱼股份有限公司	XIN TAI YU YANG 23151	Xinjiang Altai Glacier Fish Co., Ltd.	368
新天恒	舟山市普陀华星航运有限公司	XIN TIAN HENG	Zhoushan Putuo Huaxing Shipping Co., Ltd.	132
新五缘	中远海运（厦门）有限公司	XIN WU YUAN	COSCO SHIPPING (Xiamen) Co., Ltd.	163
新武夷	厦门三联船务企业有限公司	XIN WU YI	Xiamen United Shipping & Enterprises Co., Ltd.	162
新旺海	海南海盛航运有限公司	XIN WANG HAI	Hainan Haisheng Shipping Co., Ltd.	14
新香雪兰	中远海运（青岛）有限公司	XIN XIANG XUE LAN	COSCO SHIPPING (Qingdao) Co., Ltd.	152
新亚洲	中远海运集装箱运输有限公司	XIN YA ZHOU	COSCO SHIPPING Lines Co., Ltd.	40
新永安	威海胶东国际集装箱海运有限公司	NEW GRAND PEACE	Weihai Jiaodong International Container Shipping Co., Ltd.	151

新甬洋	中远海运能源运输股份有限公司	XIN YONG YANG	COSCO SHIPPING Energy Transportation Co., Ltd.	56
新郁金香	秦皇岛经济技术开发区创元海运有限公司	XIN YU JIN XIANG	Qinhuangdao Economic and Technological Development Zone Chuangyuan Shipping Co., Ltd.	127
新长号	新长铁路有限责任公司	XIN CHANG HAO	Xinchang Railway Co., Ltd.	313
新长江06010	长航货运有限公司	XIN CHANG JIANG 06010	CSC Bulk Shipping Co., Ltd.	180
新长江25010	长航货运有限公司	XIN CHANG JIANG 25010	CSC Bulk Shipping Co., Ltd.	179
新重庆	中远海运发展股份有限公司	XIN CHONG QING	COSCO SHIPPING Development Co., Ltd.	38
鑫灿9	昆明鑫灿旅游客运有限公司	XIN CAN 9	Kunming Xincan Tourist Transportation Co., Ltd.	296
鑫河369	凤阳县鑫河航运有限公司	XIN HE 369	Fengyang Xinhe Shipping Co., Ltd.	177
鑫辉66	江西鑫辉船务有限公司	XIN HUI 66	Jiangxi Xinhui Shipping Co., Ltd.	218
鑫盛6号	巴东县鑫盛船舶运输有限公司	XIN SHENG 6 HAO	Badong Xinsheng Shipping Co., Ltd.	178
信风福州	洋浦营信物流有限公司	XIN FENG FU ZHOU	Yangpu Yingxin Logistics Co., Ltd.	88
信风扬子江	中航国际租赁有限公司	XIN FENG YANG ZI JIANG	AVIC International Leasing Co., Ltd.	37
信海12号	海南港航控股有限公司	XIN HAI 12 HAO	Hainan Harbor & Shipping Holding Co., Ltd.	143
信海6号	海南海峡航运有限公司	XIN HAI 6 HAO	Hainan Strait Shipping Co., Ltd.	143
兴桂1062	广西兴桂船运有限公司	XING GUI 1062	Guangxi Xinggui Shipping Co., Ltd.	207
兴运1号	张家港保税区兴运船务有限公司	XING YUN 1 HAO	Zhangjiagang Bonded Area Xingyun Shipping Co., Ltd.	213
"徐联航拖666"船队	徐州联航航运有限公司	XU LIAN HANG TUO 666 COMBINATION	Xuzhou United Shipping Co., Ltd.	239
"徐兴航推669"船队	徐州兴航航运有限公司	XU XING HANG TUI 669 COMBINATION	Xuzhou Xinghang Shipping Co., Ltd.	239
玄武湖	大连远洋运输公司	XUAN WU HU	Dalian Ocean Shipping Company	51
雪龙	中国极地研究中心	XUE LONG	Polar Research Institute of China	463
雪龙2	中国极地研究中心	XUE LONG 2	Polar Research Institute of China	472
寻仙1	秦皇岛新绎旅游有限公司	XUN XIAN 1	Qinhuangdao Ennova Tourism Co., Ltd.	130
寻仙70	长岛渤海长通旅运有限公司	XUN XIAN 70	Changdao Bohai Changtong Travel Transport Co., Ltd.	163
迅隆壹号	深圳招商迅隆船务有限公司	XUN LONG YI HAO	Shenzhen China Merchants Xunlong Shipping Co., Ltd.	158
Y				
雅河	中远集装箱运输有限公司	YA HE	COSCO Container Lines Co., Ltd.	34
亚龙湾	中远海运特种运输股份有限公司	YA LONG WAN	COSCO SHIPPING Specialized Carriers Co., Ltd.	74
雁水湖	大连远洋运输公司	YAN SHUI HU	Dalian Ocean Shipping Company	51
雁顺	招商局南京油运股份有限公司	YAN SHUN	Nanjing Tanker Corporation	83
燕京	天津津神客货轮船有限公司	YAN JING	Tianjin Jinshen Ferry Co., Ltd.	125
扬帆之星1	三亚扬帆游艇俱乐部有限公司	YANG FAN ZHI XING 1	Sanya Yangfan Yacht Club Co., Ltd.	162
扬子江二号	武汉扬子江游船有限公司	YANGTZE NO.2	Wuhan Yangze River Cruise Co., Ltd.	266
羊城8号	广州市羊城散装水泥航运公司	YANG CHENG 8 HAO	Guangzhou Yangcheng Bulk Cement Shipping Company	186
阳航30	阳朔航运总公司	YANG HANG 30	Yangshuo Shipping Corporation	294
椰香公主	海南海峡航运有限公司	YE XIANG GONG ZHU	Hainan Strait Shipping Co., Ltd.	124
一航津安1	中交第一航务工程局有限公司	YI HANG JIN AN 1	CCCC First Harbor Engineering Co., Ltd.	420
一航津平2	中交第一航务工程局有限公司	YI HANG JIN PING 2	CCCC First Harbor Engineering Co., Ltd.	420
宜港拖1001	宜昌港瑞船舶运输有限公司	YI GANG TUO 1001	Yichang Gangrui Shipping Co., Ltd.	441
易水湖12号	易县易水湖水上客运有限公司	YI SHUI HU 12 HAO	Yixian County Yishui Lake Aquatic Passenger Transportation Co., Ltd.	319
益拖202	益丰船务企业有限公司	YICK TUG 202	Yick Fung Shipping & Enterprise Co.	451
逸舟玉桂	浙江外事旅游股份有限公司	YI ZHOU YU GUI	Zhejiang Foreign Affairs Travel Co., Ltd.	297
银河王子	烟台银河轮渡有限公司	YIN HE WANG ZI	Yantai Silver River Ferry Co., Ltd.	143
银平	中远海运散货运输有限公司	YIN PING	COSCO SHIPPING Bulk Co., Ltd.	19
银珠号	上海久和大隆液化气运输有限公司	YIN ZHU HAO	Shanghai JHDL LPG Shipping Co., Ltd.	82
银紫荆	广东徐闻海峡航运有限公司	YIN ZI JING	Guangdong Xuwen Strait Shipping Co., Ltd.	146
印象澜沧江1号	西双版纳印象澜沧江旅游航运有限公司	YIN XIANG LAN CANG JIANG 1 HAO	Xishuangbanna Impression Lantsang River Tourism & Shipping Co., Ltd.	291
瀛洲2	上海崇明客运轮船有限公司	YING ZHOU 2	Shanghai Chongming Passenger Ship Co., Ltd.	317
瀛洲7	上海崇明客运轮船有限公司	YING ZHOU 7	Shanghai Chongming Passenger Ship Co., Ltd.	318
邕航988	南宁邕航船务有限责任公司	YONG HANG 988	Nanning Yihang Shipping Co., Ltd.	205
永安城	厦门远洋运输公司	YONG AN CHENG	Xiamen Ocean Shipping Company	87

永安号1	福建省永安市吉山九龙湾旅游发展有限公司	YONG AN HAO 1	Fujian Yong'an Jishan Jiulong Bay Tourism Development Co., Ltd.	262
永和	招商局南京油运股份有限公司	FOREVER HARMONY	Nanjing Tanker Corporation	73
永洁99号	东莞市永洁船舶清洁服务有限公司	YONG JIE 99 HAO	Dongguan Yongjie Ship Cleaning Services Ltd.	454
永乐01	海南航程旅游发展股份有限公司	YONG LE 01	Hainan Voyage Tourism Development Co., Ltd.	137
永乐科考	中国船舶重工集团公司第七〇二研究所	YONG LE KE KAO	CSIC No.702 Research Institute	438
永明号	京通大运河（北京）文化旅游管理有限公司	YONG MING HAO	Jingtong Grand Canal (Beijing) Culture Tourism Management Co., Ltd.	296
永荣	招商局南京油运股份有限公司	FOREVER GLORY	Nanjing Tanker Corporation	73
永盛	中远海运特种运输股份有限公司	YONG SHENG	COSCO SHIPPING Specialized Carriers Co., Ltd.	90
永顺23	肇庆恒运船舶运输有限公司	YONG SHUN 23	Zhaoqing Hengyun Shipping Co., Ltd.	212
勇士	交通运输部上海打捞局	YONG SHI	Shanghai Salvage Bureau, Ministry of Transport	397
游龙88	威海新云洲海洋科技有限公司	YOU LONG 88	Weihai Xinyunzhou Marine Technology Co., Ltd.	527
游神1	东展船运股份公司	YOU SHEN 1	Dongzhan Shipping Co., Ltd.	71
于家堡1	天津融湾水路运输有限公司	YU JIA PU 1	Tianjin Rongwan Waterway Transportation Co., Ltd.	291
渝道标2403	长江重庆航道局	YU DAO BIAO 2403	Changjiang Chongqing Waterway Bureau	513
渝丰21号	重庆丰都农花航运有限公司	YU FENG 21 HAO	Chongqing Fengdu Nonghua Shipping Co., Ltd.	309
宇航2	连云港宇航海陆运输有限公司	YU HANG 2	Lianyungang Yuhang Sea & Land Transport Co., Ltd.	458
玉池	中海油轮运输有限公司	YU CHI	China Shipping Tanker Co., Ltd.	50
玉衡先锋	中远海运特种运输股份有限公司	YU HENG XIAN FENG	COSCO SHIPPING Specialized Carriers Co., Ltd.	99
玉霄峰	中远海运散货运输有限公司	YU XIAO FENG	COSCO SHIPPING Bulk Co., Ltd.	21
育德	集美大学	YU DE	Jimei University	483
育锋	上海育海航运公司	YU FENG	Shanghai Yuhai Shipping Company	482
育龙	大连海事大学	YU LONG	Dalian Maritime University	482
育明	上海海事大学	YU MING	Shanghai Maritime University	483
育鹏	大连海事大学	YU PENG	Dalian Maritime University	483
御风者1	深圳市纵横四海航海赛事管理有限公司	YU FENG ZHE 1	Shenzhen Across Four Oceans Sailing Event Management Co., Ltd.	527
裕东	裕东海运有限公司	YU DONG	Yu Dong Maritime Limited	68
豫三昆仑号	黄河水利委员会黄河水文水资源局	YU SAN KUN LUN HAO	Yellow River Hydrology and Water Resources Bureau of Yellow River Water Conservancy Commission	475
源明	阳明海运股份有限公司	YM FOUNTAIN	Yang Ming Marine Transport Corporation	39
远达301	肇庆远达船务有限公司	YUAN DA 301	Zhaoqing Yuanda Shipping Co., Ltd.	223
远大湖	中远海运能源运输股份有限公司	COSGREAT LAKE	COSCO SHIPPING Energy Transportation Co., Ltd.	51
远鉴	中远海运物流有限公司	YUAN JIAN	COSCO SHIPPING Logistics Co., Ltd.	113
远江城	上海远江集装箱船务有限公司	YUAN JIANG CHENG	Shanghai Yuanjiang Container Shipping Co., Ltd.	196
远津海	中远海运散货运输有限公司	YUAN JIN HAI	COSCO SHIPPING Bulk Co., Ltd.	29
远景	中远海运物流有限公司	YUAN JING	COSCO SHIPPING Logistics Co., Ltd.	113
远兰湾	海南中远海运能源运输有限公司	YUAN LAN WAN	COSCO SHIPPING Energy Transportation (Hainan) Co., Ltd.	59
远望21	中国卫星海上测控部	YUAN WANG 21	China Satellite Maritime Tracking and Control Department	94
远望3	中国卫星海上测控部	YUAN WANG 3	China Satellite Maritime Tracking and Control Department	475
远望5	中国卫星海上测控部	YUAN WANG 5	China Satellite Maritime Tracking and Control Department	477
远望7	中国卫星海上测控部	YUAN WANG 7	China Satellite Maritime Tracking and Control Department	480
远洋1007	重庆市泽胜船务（集团）有限公司	YUAN YANG 1007	Chongqing Zesheng Shipping (Group) Co., Ltd.	218
远洋3号	重庆市泽胜船务（集团）有限公司	YUAN YANG 3 HAO	Chongqing Zesheng Shipping (Group) Co., Ltd.	214
远洋7606	重庆市泽胜船务（集团）有限公司	YUAN YANG 7606	Chongqing Zesheng Shipping (Group) Co., Ltd.	219
远渔908	中国水产有限公司	YUAN YU 908	China National Fisheries Corp.	329
远真海	中远海运散货运输有限公司	YUAN ZHEN HAI	COSCO SHIPPING Bulk Co., Ltd.	27
远舟8	江西省远舟物流有限公司	YUAN ZHOU 8	Jiangxi Yuanzhou Logistics Co., Ltd.	192
月亮河16号	赤水市月亮河水上公交旅游开发有限责任公司	YUE LIANG HE 16 HAO	Chishui Yuelianghe Water Bus and Tourism Development Co., Ltd.	292
月亮湾	中远海运特种运输股份有限公司	YUE LIANG WAN	COSCO SHIPPING Specialized Carriers Co., Ltd.	74

中文名	公司（中文）	English Name	Company (English)	Page
岳化一号	岳阳安顺船务有限公司	YUE HUA YI HAO	Yueyang Anshun Shipping Co., Ltd.	227
越州舫	绍兴市松陵造船有限责任公司	YUE ZHOU FANG	Shaoxing Songling Shipbuilding Co., Ltd.	297
粤德庆货3868	德庆县回龙水运有限公司	YUE DE QING HUO 3868	Deqing Huilong Water Transportation Co., Ltd.	174
粤电55	广东粤电航运有限公司	YUE DIAN 55	Guangdong Yudean Shipping Co., Ltd.	19
粤鼎湖货0878	肇庆鼎湖汇港水运有限公司	YUE DING HU HUO 0878	Zhaoqing Dinghu Huigang Water Transportation Co., Ltd.	190
粤东源渔10302	个人	YUE DONG YUAN YU 10302	Individually owned	364
粤番禺渡8501	广州市横沥旅游度假农庄开发有限公司	YUE PAN YU DU 8501	Guangzhou Hengli Travel Vacation Farm Development Co., Ltd.	306
粤工桩8	中交第四航务工程局有限公司	YUE GONG ZHUANG 8	CCCC Fourth Harbor Engineering Co., Ltd.	411
粤广宁货2828	广宁县宁港运输有限公司	YUE GUANG NING HUO	Guangning Ninggang Transportation Co., Ltd.	177
粤广州货2888	广州市朗现船务有限公司	YUE GUANG ZHOU HUO 2888	Guangzhou Langxian Shipping Co., Ltd.	191
粤海328	广东省佛山航运公司	YUE HAI 328	Guangdong Foshan Shipping Co., Ltd.	194
粤海518	广东省佛山航运公司	YUE HAI 518	Guangdong Foshan Shipping Co., Ltd.	194
粤海铁1号	海南铁路有限公司	YUE HAI TIE 1 HAO	Hainan Railway Co., Ltd.	153
粤海铁3号	海南铁路有限公司	YUE HAI TIE 3 HAO	Hainan Railway Co., Ltd.	154
粤惠东渔养90138	惠东县海森渔业发展有限公司	YUE HUI DONG YU YANG 90138	Huidong Haisen Fishery Development Co., Ltd.	370
粤惠州货9226	博罗县交通航运公司石湾船务公司	YUE HUI ZHOU HUO 9226	Shiwan Shipping Co., Ltd. of Boluo Shipping Corporation	190
粤惠州货9306	博罗县水上运输总公司港澳运输公司	YUE HUI ZHOU HUO 9306	Hong Kong & Macao Transportation Branch of Boluo Water Transportation Corporation	190
粤惠州油168	惠州市鸿海运输有限公司	YUE HUI ZHOU YOU 168	Huizhou Honghai Transportation Co., Ltd.	212
粤蓝海633	清远市蓝海船务有限公司	YUE LAN HAI 633	Qingyuan Lanhai Shipping Co., Ltd.	177
粤雷渔11071	个人	YUE LEI YU 11071	Individually owned	343
粤廉渔21133	廉江盛创渔业有限公司	YUE LIAN YU 21133	Lianjiang Shengchuang Fisheries Co., Ltd.	349
粤廉渔28288	个人	YUE LIAN YU 28288	Individually owned	328
粤南沙19888	个人	YUE NAN SHA 19888	Individually owned	376
粤清远客6372	清远市清城区白庙水运公司	YUE QING YUAN KE 6372	Qingyuan Qingcheng Baimiao Water Transport Company	261
粤汕城渔16118	广东银鹏动力设备有限公司	YUE SHAN CHENG YU 16118	Guangdong Yinpeng Power Equipment Co., Ltd.	338
粤汕尾渔16117	广东银鹏动力设备有限公司	YUE SHAN WEI YU 16117	Guangdong Yinpeng Power Equipment Co., Ltd.	362
粤遂渔养79003	个人	YUE SUI YU YANG 79003	Individually owned	367
粤霞渔90023	湛江市昊海远洋渔业有限公司	YUE XIA YU 90023	Zhanjiang Haohai Deep Sea Fisheries Co., Ltd.	326
粤新会货1033	江门市新会区兴源船务有限公司	YUE XIN HUI HUO 1033	Jiangmen Xinhui District Xingyuan Shipping Co., Ltd.	177
粤洋18	广州南沙经济技术开发区粤洋船务有限公司	YUE YANG 18	Guangzhou Nansha Economic and Technological Development Zone Yueyang Shipping Co., Ltd.	195
粤英德货8901	英德市华涛汇通船务有限公司	YUE YING DE HUO 8901	Yingde Huatao Huitong Shipping Co., Ltd.	189
粤湛渔01261	个人	YUE ZHAN YU 01261	Individually owned	343
粤湛渔07138	个人	YUE ZHAN YU 07138	Individually owned	343
粤肇庆槽333	肇庆市远达船务有限公司	YUE ZHAO QING CAO 333	Zhaoqing Yuanda Shipping Co. Ltd	214
云港十号	连云港港口集团有限公司	YUN GANG SHI HAO	Lianyungang Port Group Co., Ltd.	440
云航政6	中华人民共和国思茅海事局	YUN HANG ZHENG 6	Simao Maritime Safety Administration of the PRC	488
云宏787	湖北云宏船务物流有限公司	YUN HONG 787	Hubei Yunhong Shipping and Logistics Co., Ltd.	191
云锦	重庆渝鸿船务有限公司	YUN JIN	Chongqing Yuhong Shipping Co., Ltd.	259
云浚1号	江苏筑港建设集团有限公司	YUN JUN 1 HAO	Jiangsu Port Construction Group Co., Ltd.	386
云长号	重庆赤甲旅游客运有限公司	YUN CHANG HAO	Chongqing Chijia Tourist Transportation Co., Ltd.	262
运发号	巴东县运发客运有限责任公司	YUN FA HAO	Badong Yunfa Passenger Transportation Co., Ltd.	306

Z

中文名	公司（中文）	English Name	Company (English)	Page
翟墨1	太平洋杯国际帆船赛管理有限公司	ZHAI MO 1	Pacific Cup International Regatta Management Co., Ltd.	523
张謇	上海彩虹鱼科考船科技服务有限公司	ZHANG JIAN	Shanghai Rainbowfish Researchship Co., Ltd.	468
招商重工1号	招商局重工（深圳）有限公司	ZHAO SHANG ZHONG GONG 1 HAO	China Merchants Heavy Industry (Shenzhen) Co., Ltd.	118
招商重工3	招商局重工（江苏）有限公司	ZHAO SHANG ZHONG GONG 3	China Merchants Heavy Industry(Jiangsu) Co., Ltd.	119
昭君号	包头市九原区奶业公司亿盛渔业养殖厂	ZHAO JUN HAO	Yisheng Fishery Breeding Factory of Baotou Jiuyuan District Dairy Company	288

肇港发0102	肇庆市凯翔船务有限公司	ZHAO GANG FA 0102	Zhaoqing Kai Cheung Shipping Co., Ltd.	176
浙苍渔加08888	个人	ZHE CANG YU JIA 08888	Individually owned	375
浙苍渔冷00888	温州嘉润水产有限公司	ZHE CANG YU LENG 00888	Wenzhou Jiarun Aquatic Products Co., Ltd.	372
浙淳渔养11905	杭州千岛湖发展集团有限公司	ZHE CHUN YU YANG 11905	Hangzhou Qiandao Lake Development Group Co., Ltd.	370
浙岱渔10279	个人	ZHE DAI YU 10279	Individually owned	332
浙奉渔休60056	奉化市翡翠湾海洋渔业发展有限公司	ZHE FENG YU XIU 60056	Fenghua Emerald Bay Ocean Fishery Development Co., Ltd.	377
浙海521	招银金融租赁有限公司	ZHE HAI 521	CMB Financial Leasing Co., Ltd.	15
浙嘉善货03199	嘉善县华跃新型建材有限公司	ZHE JIA SHAN HUO 03199	Jiashan Huayue New-type Building Materials Co., Ltd.	173
浙嘉兴工8	平湖市东芹海洋工程服务有限公司	ZHE JIA XING GONG 8	Pinghu City Dongqin Ocean Engineering Service Co., Ltd.	456
浙椒渔72016	台州市椒江东风海洋渔业公司	ZHE JIAO YU 72016	Taizhou Jiaojiang Dongfeng Deep Sea Fisheries Company	327
浙椒渔76045	台州市椒江海鸥海洋渔业公司	ZHE JIAO YU 76045	Taizhou Jiaojiang Seagull Deep Sea Fisheries Company	326
浙椒渔养85011	台州市恒胜水产养殖专业合作社	ZHE JIAO YU YANG 85011	Taizhou Hengsheng Specialized Cooperative for Aquatic Products Breeding	367
浙乐渔休00122	乐清市东海休闲渔业有限公司	ZHE LE YU XIU 00122	Yueqing Donghai Recreational Fishery Co., Ltd.	376
浙临渔12698	个人	ZHE LIN YU 12698	Individually owned	345
浙临渔12809	个人	ZHE LIN YU 12809	Individually owned	344
浙临渔21696	个人	ZHE LIN YU 21696	Individually owned	328
浙普01858	舟山市正凯船务有限责任公司	ZHE PU 01858	Zhoushan Zhengkai Shipping Co., Ltd.	29
浙普01868	舟山市正凯船务有限责任公司	ZHE PU 01868	Zhoushan Zhengkai Shipping Co., Ltd.	29
浙普渔68318	个人	ZHE PU YU 68318	Individually owned	327
浙瑞渔休00315	瑞安市中瑞休闲渔业有限公司	ZHE RUI YU XIU 00315	Ruian Zhongrui Recreational Fishery Co., Ltd.	377
浙上虞货0529	绍兴益盛航运有限公司	ZHE SHANG YU HUO 0529	Shaoxing Yisheng Shipping Co., Ltd.	181
浙桐乡槽01818	绍兴益盛航运有限公司	ZHE TONG XIANG CAO 01818	Shaoxing Yisheng Shipping Co., Ltd.	189
浙兴169	浙江华胜海运有限公司	ZHE XING 169	Zhejiang Huasheng Shipping Co.,Ltd.	65
浙萧山货25177	绍兴萧山亚娟航运有限公司	ZHE XIAO SHAN HUO 25177	Shaoxing Xiaoshan Yajuan Shipping Co., Ltd.	185
浙鄞渔81266	个人	ZHE YIN YU 81266	Individually owned	358
浙渔科2	浙江海洋大学	ZHE YU KE 2	Zhejiang Ocean University	374
浙玉渔休00013	玉环海都旅游开发有限公司	ZHE YU YU XIU 00013	Yuhuan Yudu Tourism Development Co., Ltd.	377
珍河	中远集装箱运输有限公司	ZHEN HE	COSCO Container Lines Co., Ltd.	34
振奋13	上海友好航运有限公司	ZHEN FEN 13	Shanghai Youhao Shipping Co., Ltd.	8
振奋2	上海嘉禾航运有限公司	ZHEN FEN 2	Shanghai Jiahe Shipping Co., Ltd.	6
振华28	上海振华重工集团股份有限公司	ZHEN HUA 28	Shanghai Zhenhua Heavy Industries Co., Ltd.	107
振华29	上海振华重工集团股份有限公司	ZHEN HUA 29	Shanghai Zhenhua Heavy Industries Co., Ltd.	108
振华30	上海振华船运有限公司	ZHEN HUA 30	Shanghai Zhenhua Shipping Co., Ltd.	403
振华34	上海振华重工集团股份有限公司	ZHEN HUA 34	Shanghai Zhenhua Heavy Industries Co., Ltd.	111
振华35	上海振华重工集团股份有限公司	ZHEN HUA 35	Shanghai Zhenhua Heavy Industries Co., Ltd.	114
振华4	上海振华重工集团股份有限公司	ZHEN HUA 4	Shanghai Zhenhua Heavy Industries Co., Ltd.	113
振华7	上海振华重工集团股份有限公司	ZHEN HUA 7	Shanghai Zhenhua Heavy Industries Co., Ltd.	110
正丰之星	舟山市普陀海源港口服务有限公司	ZHENG FENG ZHI XING	Zhoushan Putuo Haiyuan Port Service Co., Ltd.	138
志航118	广州志航船务有限公司	ZHI HANG 118	Guangzhou Zhihang Shipping Co., Ltd.	206
志航128	广州志航船务有限公司	ZHI HANG 128	Guangzhou Zhihang Shipping Co., Ltd.	204
志航638	广州志航船务有限公司	ZHI HANG 638	Guangzhou Zhihang Shipping Co., Ltd.	196
志航688	广州志航船务有限公司	ZHI HANG 688	Guangzhou Zhihang Shipping Co., Ltd.	186
志航803	广州志航船务有限公司	ZHI HANG 803	Guangzhou Zhihang Shipping Co., Ltd.	174
致远口	中远海运特种运输股份有限公司	ZHI YUAN KOU	COSCO SHIPPING Specialized Carriers Co., Ltd.	109
智腾	智慧航海（青岛）船舶测试有限公司	ZHI TENG	Navigation Brilliance (Qingdao) Ship Test Co., Ltd.	527
中港永和	南京中港船业有限公司	ZHONG GANG YONG HE	Nanjing Zhonggang Shipping Co., Ltd.	61
中谷上海	厦门国达海运有限公司	ZHONG GU SHANG HAI	Xiamen Guoda Shipping Co., Ltd.	44
中国海关1001	中华人民共和国广州海关	ZHONG GUO HAI GUAN 1001	Guangzhou Customs of the PRC	510
中国海关2011	中华人民共和国江门海关	ZHONG GUO HAI GUAN 2011	Jiangmen Customs of the PRC	510
中国海关751	中华人民共和国上海海关	ZHONG GUO HAI GUAN 751	Shanghai Customs of the PRC	511

中文名	所属单位	英文名	英文所属单位	页码
中国海监2166	海南省海洋监察总队	ZHONG GUO HAI JIAN 2166	Hainan Marine Surveillance Corps	503
中国海监3011	中国海监天津市总队	ZHONG GUO HAI JIAN 3011	China Marine Surveillance Tianjin Corps	502
中国海监3015	中国海监天津市总队	ZHONG GUO HAI JIAN 3015	China Marine Surveillance Tianjin Corps	503
中国海监36	青岛市海洋与渔业局	ZHONG GUO HAI JIAN 36	Qingdao Marine and Fisheries Bureau	502
中国海监9020	广东省渔政总队直属一支队	ZHONG GUO HAI JIAN 9020	China Coast Guard	502
中国海警1212	中国海监第一支队	ZHONG GUO HAI JING 1212	The 1st Detachment of China Marine Surveillance	498
中国海警1301	中国海警局	ZHONG GUO HAI JING 1301	China Coast Guard	500
中国海警2306	中国海警局	ZHONG GUO HAI JING 2306	China Coast Guard	499
中国海警2401	中国海警局	ZHONG GUO HAI JING 2401	China Coast Guard	500
中国海警2501	中国海警局	ZHONG GUO HAI JING 2501	China Coast Guard	500
中国海警31101	中国人民武装警察边防部队	ZHONG GUO HAI JING 31101	Frontier Defense Forces of Chinese People's Armed Police	498
中国海警31301	中国海警局	ZHONG GUO HAI JING 31301	China Coast Guard	501
中国海警3306	中国海警局	ZHONG GUO HAI JING 3306	China Coast Guard	499
中国海警3401	中国海警局	ZHONG GUO HAI JING 3401	China Coast Guard	499
中国海警3901	中国海警局	ZHONG GUO HAI JING 3901	China Coast Guard	501
中国海警44014	中国海警局	ZHONG GUO HAI JING 44014	China Coast Guard	501
中国考古01	国家文物局	ZHONG GUO KAO GU 01	National Cultural Heritage Administration	466
中国渔政13001	河北省渔政处	ZHONG GUO YU ZHENG 13001	Hebei Fishery Administration Department	504
中国渔政206	中国渔政东海总队	ZHONG GUO YU ZHENG 206	China Fishery Administration Donghai Corps	507
中国渔政21103	大连渔政局	ZHONG GUO YU ZHENG 21103	Dalian Fishery Administration Bureau	507
中国渔政21201	辽宁省丹东市渔政管理处	ZHONG GUO YU ZHENG 21201	Liaoning Dandong Fishery Administration Department	506
中国渔政23528	抚远市渔政渔港监督管理站	ZHONG GUO YU ZHENG 23528	Fuyuan Fishery Administration and Fishing Port Supervision Station	508
中国渔政310	农业部南海区渔政局	ZHONG GUO YU ZHENG 310	Nanhai District Fishery Administration Bureau, Ministry of Agriculture	507
中国渔政31001	上海市农业农村委员会执法总队	ZHONG GUO YU ZHENG 31001	Shanghai Agricultural and Village Committee Law Enforcement Corps	506
中国渔政32518	江苏省赣榆县渔政站	ZHONG GUO YU ZHENG 32518	Jiangsu Ganyu Fishery Administration Station	505
中国渔政32544	江苏省启东市渔政执法大队	ZHONG GUO YU ZHENG 32544	Jiangsu Qidong Fishery Administration Law Enforcement Corps	505
中国渔政34027	巢湖管理局渔政管理总站	ZHONG GUO YU ZHENG 34027	Fishery Administration Management Main Station, Chaohu Management Bureau	508
中国渔政35306	福建省泉州市海洋与渔业执法支队	ZHONG GUO YU ZHENG 35306	Fujian Quanzhou Marine and Fishery Law Enforcement Detachment	506
中国渔政44183	广东省珠海渔政支队	ZHONG GUO YU ZHENG 44183	Guangdong Zhuhai Fishery Administration Detachment	506
中国渔政45001	中国渔政广西壮族自治区检查大队	ZHONG GUO YU ZHENG 45001	Guangxi Zhuangzu Autonomous Region Inspection Corps, China Fishery Administration	504
中国渔政45005	中国渔政广西支队	ZHONG GUO YU ZHENG 45005	China Fishery Administration Guangxi Detachment	508
中海环球	中远海运集装箱运输有限公司	CSCL GLOBE	COSCO SHIPPING Lines Co., Ltd.	43
中海荣华	中远海运散货运输有限公司	CSB GLORY	COSCO SHIPPING Bulk Co., Ltd.	26
中海兴旺	中远海运散货运输有限公司	CSB FORTUNE	COSCO SHIPPING Bulk Co., Ltd.	25
中海亚洲	中远海运集装箱运输有限公司	CSCL ASIA	COSCO SHIPPING Lines Co., Ltd.	39
中海之春	中远海运集装箱运输有限公司	CSCL SPRING	COSCO SHIPPING Lines Co., Ltd.	42
中海之星	中远海运集装箱运输有限公司	CSCL STAR	COSCO SHIPPING Lines Co., Ltd.	41
中航903	中山港航集团股份有限公司	ZHONG HANG 903	Zhongshan Port & Shipping Group Co., Ltd.	194
中华复兴	渤海轮渡集团股份有限公司	ZHONG HUA FU XING	Bohai Ferry Group Co., Ltd.	151
中华和平	中国航运股份有限公司	CHINA PEACE	Chinese Maritime Transport Ltd.	14
中华泰山	渤海邮轮有限公司	CHINESE TAISHAN	Bohai Cruise Co., Ltd.	123
中巨18	舟山中巨远洋渔业有限公司	ZHONG JU 18	Zhoushan Zhongju Ocean Fisheries Co., Ltd.	356

中文名	公司中文	English Name	Company English	Page
中巨冷1	舟山中巨远洋渔业有限公司	ZHONG JU LENG 1	Zhoushan Zhongju Ocean Fisheries Co., Ltd.	373
中骏集团壹号	厦门冠骏航空仓储服务有限公司	ZHONG JUN JI TUAN YI HAO	Xiamen Guanjun Aviation Storage Service Co., Ltd.	525
中能福石	中远海运能源运输股份有限公司	CESI GLADSTONE	COSCO SHIPPING Energy Transportation Co., Ltd.	78
中燃21	中国船舶燃料湛江有限公司	ZHONG RAN 21	China Marine Bunker Zhanjiang Co., Ltd.	62
中燃33	中国船舶燃料青岛有限公司	ZHONG RAN 33	China Marine Bunker Qingdao Co., Ltd.	66
中燃37	中国船舶燃料广州有限公司	ZHONG RAN 37	China Marine Bunker Guangzhou Co., Ltd.	66
中水706	中水集团远洋股份有限公司	ZHONG SHUI 706	CNFC Overseas Fisheries Co., Ltd.	352
中天7	中天科技集团海洋工程有限公司	ZHONG TIAN 7	Zhongtian Technology Marine Engineering Co., Ltd.	435
中铁渤海1号	中铁渤海铁路轮渡有限责任公司	ZHONG TIE BO HAI 1 HAO	Sinorail Bohai Train Ferry Co., Ltd.	153
中铁渤海3号	中铁渤海铁路轮渡有限责任公司	ZHONG TIE BO HAI 3 HAO	Sinorail Bohai Train Ferry Co., Ltd.	154
中外运渤海	中外运集装箱运输有限公司	ZHONG WAI YUN BO HAI	Sinotrans Container Lines Co., Ltd.	45
中外运青岛	中外运集装箱运输有限公司	SINOTRANS QINGDAO	Sinotrans Container Lines Co., Ltd.	42
中油管道601	中国管道海洋工程有限公司	CPP601	China Pipeline Marine Engineering Co., Ltd.	415
中油海1号	中国石油集团海洋工程有限公司	ZHONG YOU HAI YI HAO	CNPC Offshore Engineering Co., Ltd.	424
中油海19	凯思租赁（天津）有限公司	ZHONG YOU HAI 19	Kaisi Leasing (Tianjin) Co., Ltd.	431
中油海16	中国石油集团海洋工程有限公司	ZHONG YOU HAI 16	CNPC Offshore Engineering Co., Ltd.	429
中油海3	中国石油集团海洋工程有限公司	ZHONG YOU HAI 3	CNPC Offshore Engineering Co., Ltd.	425
中油海5	中国石油集团海洋工程有限公司	ZHONG YOU HAI 5	CNPC Offshore Engineering Co., Ltd.	425
中油海9	中国石油集团海洋工程有限公司	ZHONG YOU HAI 9	CNPC Offshore Engineering Co., Ltd.	426
中渔科211	中国水产科学研究院东海水产研究所	ZHONG YU KE 211	East China Sea Fishery Research Institute, Chinese Academy of Fishery Sciences	373
中远安特卫普	中远海运集装箱运输有限公司	COSCO ANTWERP	COSCO SHIPPING Lines Co., Ltd.	37
中远大洋洲	中远海运集装箱运输有限公司	COSCO OCEANIA	COSCO SHIPPING Lines Co., Ltd.	40
中远海运巴拿马	中远海运集装箱运输有限公司	COSCO SHIPPING PANAMA	COSCO SHIPPING Lines Co., Ltd.	45
中远海运白羊座	中远海运集装箱运输有限公司	COSCO SHIPPING ARIES	COSCO SHIPPING Lines Co., Ltd.	46
中远海运多瑙河	中远海运集装箱运输有限公司	COSCO SHIPPING DANUBE	COSCO SHIPPING Lines Co., Ltd.	45
中远海运峨眉山	中远海运重工有限公司	ZHONG YUAN HAI YUN E MEI SHAN	COSCO SHIPPING Heavy Industry Co., Ltd.	412
中远海运金牛座	中远海运集装箱运输有限公司	COSCO SHIPPING TAURUS	COSCO SHIPPING Lines Co., Ltd.	46
中远海运开拓	中远海运特种运输股份有限公司	ZHONG YUAN HAI YUN KAI TUO	COSCO SHIPPING Specialized Carriers Co., Ltd.	96
中远海运宇宙	中远海运集装箱运输有限公司	COSCO SHIPPING UNIVERSE	COSCO SHIPPING Lines Co., Ltd.	47
中远盛世	中远海运特种运输股份有限公司	COSCO SHENG SHI	COSCO SHIPPING Specialized Carriers Co., Ltd.	103
中远腾飞	中远海运特种运输股份有限公司	COSCO TENG FEI	COSCO SHIPPING Specialized Carriers Co., Ltd.	103
中远之星	厦门闽台轮渡有限公司	COSCO STAR	Xiamen Mintai Ferry Co., Ltd.	146
重任1500	交通运输部广州打捞局	ZHONG REN 1500	Guangzhou Salvage Bureau, Ministry of Transport	116
重任3	交通运输部上海打捞局	ZHONG REN 3	Shanghai Salvage Bureau, Ministry of Transport	116
舟桥3	嵊泗县同舟客运轮船有限公司	ZHOU QIAO 3	Shengsi Tongzhou Passenger Shipping Co., Ltd.	133
舟山群岛东极	舟山市普陀区东极海运有限公司	ZHOU SHAN QUN DAO DONG JI	Zhoushan Putuo Dongji Shipping Co., Ltd.	129
舟渔9	中国水产舟山海洋渔业有限公司	ZHOU YU NO.9	China Aquatic Zhoushan Marine Fisheries Co. Ltd.	355
珠港西江能源01	广东省云浮珠港新能源公司	ZHU GANG XI JIANG NENG YUAN 01	Guangdong Yunfu Zhugang New Energy Company	228
珠江号	中国人民武装警察部队广东省广州市消防支队	ZHU JIANG HAO	CAPF Guangzhou Fire Brigade Branch, Guangdong Province	455
珠江红船	广州珠控文化发展有限公司	ZHU JIANG HONG CHUAN	Guangzhou Zhukong Culture Development Co., Ltd.	293
珠江水晶	广州金航游轮股份有限公司	ZHU JIANG SHUI JING	Guangzhou Jinhang Cruise Co., Ltd.	291
竹源	深圳中远龙鹏液化气运输有限公司	ZHU YUAN	Shenzhen COSCO LPG Shipping Co., Ltd.	80
紫荆八号	广东徐闻港航控股有限公司	ZI JING BA HAO	Guangdong Xuwen Harbor & Shipping Co., Ltd.	141
紫荆一号	广东徐闻港航控股有限公司	ZI JING YI HAO	Guangdong Xuwen Harbor & Shipping Co., Ltd.	140
紫阳商舫	紫阳县文化旅游投资发展有限公司	ZI YANG SHANG FANG	Ziyang County Culture Tour Investment Development Co., Ltd.	297
紫玉兰	连云港中韩轮渡有限公司	ZI YU LAN	Lianyungang C-K Ferry Co., Ltd.	128
总统七号	武汉扬子江游船有限公司	ZONG TONG QI HAO	Wuhan Yangze River Cruise Co., Ltd.	273
总统一号	武汉扬子江游船有限公司	ZONG TONG YI HAO	Wuhan Yangze River Cruise Co., Ltd.	269

后记

《中国船谱·第二卷》编纂工作由交通运输部主持，中国船级社承担，人民交通出版社股份有限公司出版发行。

本卷编写过程中，组织召开的重要会议有：2020年3月30日第一次专家委员会会议，审议通过了编纂大纲和技术要求；2020年4月13日编审委员会专题会议，审议批准了《中国船谱·第二卷》编纂大纲；2020年4月24日编纂工作委员会第一次会议，审议通过了编纂工作实施方案；2020年8月20日第二次专家委员会会议，审议通过了初步筛选船舶和版面设计初步方案；2021年1月22日第三次专家委员会暨初稿评审会，审议通过大纲修订方案和《中国船谱·第二卷》初稿；2021年3月2日编纂工作委员会第二次会议，审议通过了《中国船谱·第二卷》第二稿；2021年5月21日编审工作委员会第二次会议，审议通过了《中国船谱·第二卷》送审稿。

本卷编写过程中，坚持尊重历史、传承文化、保证质量、实事求是。查阅了相关史料，力求保持史谱的一致性，包括《水运史》《中国航海史》《中国船舶检验史》《新中国船舶工业七十年大事记》《中国船型汇编》《中国海洋渔船图集》《中国渔业年鉴》等，参考了全国内河简统选优船型，京杭运河、川江及三峡库区和珠江水系标准船型等资料。为达到广泛覆盖面，在全国范围内开展了面向社会的船舶信息网上申报活动，社会征集船舶4000余艘；选择重点船公司开展集中征集工作，包括中国远洋海运集团、招商局集团、中国交通建设集团、中国农业发展集团和交通运输部救捞局等，集中征集船舶2500余艘；充分利用交通运输部海事局、中国船级社和农业农村部渔业渔政管理局所管理的现有船舶数据库，对约20万艘船舶数据进行分析和筛选。

本卷编写过程中，中国船级社组织编写人员和各分社全力以赴开展工作。专家委员会给予了技术把关和指导，交通运输部办公厅、政研室、科技司、水运局、海事局、救捞局以及农业农村部渔业渔政管理局、中国海警局、海关总署缉私局等相关主管部门给予了支持和指导，协调提供资源和信息，开放数据库等。人民交通出版社股份有限公司认真校审，确保出版质量。

本卷编写过程中，得到了中国远洋海运集团、招商局集团、中国交通建设集团、中国农业发展集团、中国航海学会、中国船东协会、中国造船工程学会、中国船舶工业行业协会、交通运输部水运科学研究院、中国水产科学研究院渔业机械仪器研究所、相关地方船检和渔检部门、北京宝锐亿韬科技发展有限公司以及相关企事业单位和社会同行的支持和帮助，在此一并表示感谢。

《中国船谱·第二卷》所选用的图片和数据信息来源于船东、相关管理部门、船检部门、渔船研究机构等，图片和数据信息仅限于《中国船谱·第二卷》编纂出版和宣介使用。

POSTSCRIPT

The compilation work of the *Ships of China - Volume II* is presided over by the Ministry of Transport and undertaken by China Classification Society (CCS). The book is published by China Communications Press Co., Ltd.

For compilation of this volume, a number of important meetings were convened. The first Expert Panel meeting was held on March 30, 2020, during which the compilation outline and the technical requirements were considered and adopted. On April 13, a special meeting of the Editorial Board was held, with the outline of the *Ships of China - Volume II* deliberated and approved. On April 24, the Compilation Working Committee held the first meeting, reviewed and approved the implementation plan for the compilation work. On August 20, the Expert Panel held the second meeting, reviewed and approved the preliminary plan for ship information screening and layout design. On January 22, 2021, the Expert Panel held the third meeting, reviewed, considered and adopted the outline revision plan together with the first draft of the *Ships of China - Volume II*. On March 2, 2021, the second meeting of the Compilation Working Committee was convened, with the second draft of the *Ships of China - Volume II* reviewed and approved. On May 21, 2021, the Editorial Board held the second meeting, reviewed and approved the final draft of the *Ships of China - Volume II*.

During the writing of the book, the principles of respecting history, inheriting culture, ensuring quality and seeking truth from the facts were followed. By resourcing the relevant historical data, efforts were made to maintain the consistency with the previous books, including the *History of Water Transport*, the *History of Chinese Navigation*, the *History of Chinese Ship Survey*, the *Chronicle of Seventy Years of New China Shipbuilding Industry*, the *Compilation of Chinese Ship Types*, the *Atlas of Chinese Marine Fishing Vessels* and the *China Fisheries Yearbook*, and reference was made to the data such as the Simplified Selection of Superior Ship Types for Nationwide Inland Rivers in China and the standard ship types for the Waterway Systems of Beijing-Hangzhou Grand Canal, the Chuanjiang River, the Three Gorges Reservoir and the Pearl River. In order to achieve wide coverage of ships, a nationwide online public collection of ship information has been carried out, with information of over 4,000 ships collected, and the key shipping companies have been selected for centralized ship collection, including China COSCO SHIPPING Corporation Limited, China Merchants Group, China Communications Construction Company Limited, China National Agricultural Development Group Co., Ltd. and China Rescue and Salvage under the Ministry of Transport, etc., with information of over 2,500 ships collected. In addition, the data of about 200,000 ships were analyzed and screened with the full utilization of the existing ship database managed by Maritime Safety Administration of the Ministry of Transport, China Classification Society, and Fishery Administration of the Ministry of Agriculture and Rural Affairs.

CCS organized the editors and its branches to make every effort to assist the work. The Expert Panel reviewed technical details and provided guidance. The General Office, Policy Research Office, Department of Science and Technology, Department of Water Transport, Maritime Safety Administration and China Rescue and Salvage of the Ministry of Transport, Fishery Administration of the Ministry of Agriculture and Rural Affairs, China Coast Guard, Anti-

Smuggling Bureau of General Administration of Customs and other competent authorities provided strong support and guidance by coordinating the provision of resources and information and allowing the access to the database. Moreover, the China Communications Press Co., Ltd. earnestly proofread and reviewed the book to ensure the quality of publication.

Here, sincere appreciation is also given to China COSCO SHIPPING Corporation Limited, China Merchants Group, China Communications Construction Company Limited, China National Agricultural Development Group Co., Ltd., China Institute of Navigation, China Shipowners' Association, Chinese Society of Naval Architects and Marine Engineers, China Association of the National Shipbuilding Industry, China Waterborne Transport Research Institute, Fishery Machinery and Instrument Research Institute under the Chinese Academy of Fishery Sciences, relevant local ship survey and fishing vessel inspection departments, Beijing Baorui Yitao Technology Development Co., Ltd. and other relevant enterprises, public institutions and social peers for their support and help.

The pictures and data information used in the book are from ship owners, relevant management departments, ship survey departments, fishing vessel research institutes, etc., and they are used only for the purpose of the compilation, publication, publicity and presentation of the *Ships of China - Volume II*.